Multiethnic Education

Third Edition

Multiethnic Education

Theory and Practice

James A. Banks
University of Washington, Seattle

Allyn and Bacon
Boston • London • Toronto • Sydney • Tokyo • Singapore

Series Editor: Virginia Lanigan
Editorial Assistant: Nicole DePalma
Production Administrator: Marjorie Payne
Editorial-Production Service: Grace Sheldrick, Wordsworth Associates
Cover Administrator: Linda Dickinson
Cover Designer: Suzanne Harbison
Composition Buyer: Linda Cox
Manufacturing Buyer: Louise Richardson

Copyright © 1994, 1988, 1981 by Allyn and Bacon
A Division of Simon & Schuster, Inc.
160 Gould Street
Needham Heights, MA 02194

Library of Congress Cataloging-in-Publication Data

Banks, James A.
    Multiethnic education : theory and practice / James A. Banks. —
3rd ed.
        p. cm.
    Includes bibliographical references and index.
    ISBN 0–205–14745–3
    1. Minorities—Education—United States. 2. Intercultural
education—United States. I. Title.
LC3731.B365 1994
371.97'0973—dc20   93–15713
                                                                                              CIP

Printed in the United States of America

10 9 8 7 6 5 4   98 97 96

To Lula, Cherry Ann, Rosie Mae, and Tessie Mae,
important women in my life,
and to Angela and Patricia,
with the hope that this book
will help to make their adult world
better than ours

Brief Contents

Contents

PART II   *Conceptual and Philosophical Issues*   65

Preface

In response to the ethnic revival movements that emerged in the 1960s, educators and policy makers in many parts of the world have implemented programs and practices designed to respond more adequately to the needs of ethnic and immigrant groups and to help these groups become more structurally integrated into their societies. These various programs and practices are characterized by many different goals and strategies and are supported by diverse and often conflicting philosophical positions. Programs related to ethnic education are often conceptualized differently and known by a variety of names, including *multiracial education, multiethnic education, multicultural education,* and *antiracist education. Multicultural education* is the term used most widely in the United States, the United Kingdom, Canada, and Australia. *Intercultural education* is a term used frequently in European nations, including France, Germany, the Netherlands, and Switzerland.

Despite educators' attempts to implement sound programs in multicultural education, there are, as in any emerging field, conceptual inconsistencies, philosophical conflicts, and widespread disagreement about what should be the proper role of public and state schools, colleges, and universities in the ethnic education of students. Educators and social scientists with diverse and conflicting ideological positions are proposing a wide range of educational reforms and programs related to ethnic and cultural diversity.

The debate about multicultural education has intensified since the second edition of *Multiethnic Education: Theory and Practice* was published. Since that time a bitter debate over the curriculum canon has developed, and several books that defend the existing Western traditional curriculum have become national bestsellers. The canon debate has taken place primarily in popular magazines and books rather than in scholarly publications.

The debate over multiculturalism has given rise to several organizations that defend the existing curriculum, such as the National Association of Scholars and the Madison Center, and at least two national organizations that promote multicultural education in the schools and colleges. Teachers for a Democratic Culture promotes multiculturalism at the college and university levels. The National Association for Multicultural Education promotes diversity in the nation's elementary and high schools and in teacher education.

As the canon debate continues, several important factors are contributing to the expansion and growth of courses, conferences, and workshops in multicultural education. Demographic changes in the United States are important factors contributing to the growth of multicultural education in the United States. Demographers project that by the turn of the century one of every three U.S. residents will be a person of color. Nearly half of the nation's school-age youths will be students of color by 2020. Students of color now constitute the majority of the school enrollment in about one-fourth of the nation's largest school districts.

Multiethnic Education: Theory and Practice, Third Edition, is designed to help preservice and inservice educators clarify the philosophical and definitional issues related to pluralistic education, derive a clarified philosophical position, design and implement effective teaching strategies that reflect ethnic and cultural diversity, and prepare sound guidelines for multicultural programs and practices. *Multiethnic Education* describes actions that educators can take to institutionalize educational programs and practices related to ethnic and cultural diversity.

Readers acquainted with the second edition of *Multiethnic Education* will notice that this third edition has been substantially revised and reorganized. Much of the text has been rewritten to make it more consistent with current theory, research, and terminology and to make it possible to include two new chapters. Chapters 1 and 8 are new to this edition. I have also incorporated into this edition information and references on multiculturalism and the canon debate. The bibliographies have been thoroughly revised and updated; they also have a new face. The bibliographies have been changed from a footnote style to a modified APA style.

Multiethnic Education: Theory and Practice, Third Edition, is divided into five parts. Part I discusses the dimensions, history, and goals of multicultural education. Multicultural education is conceptualized as a process that has the potential for spearheading substantial curriculum reform.

Conceptual and philosophical issues and problems related to education, ethnicity, and cultural diversity are the focus of Part II. Such major concepts as ethnic group and culture are discussed and defined. The major research and programmatic paradigms related to ethnicity and education are described. The philosophical and ideological issues related to ethnicity and education are also described in this part.

Part III focuses on effective teaching strategies in multicultural education. The teaching strategies described in this section focus on helping students learn how to construct knowledge, make reflective decisions, and participate in meaningful personal, social, and civic action. The first two chapters in Part III include teaching units that illustrate how teachers can help students to acquire the knowledge, values, and skills needed to become effective participants in a pluralistic democratic society.

Part IV focuses on the curriculum. Major topics include the efforts made to reform the curriculum in the last three decades, the limited extent to which curriculum reform has occurred, the nature and goals of the multicultural curriculum, and how the curriculum can be reformed to reflect the ethnic characteristics of students.

Reducing prejudice in students, language diversity, and curriculum guidelines are discussed in Part V. The final chapter, which describes curriculum guidelines, also summarizes some of the major issues, problems, and recommendations presented in *Multiethnic Education: Theory and Practice.* The Appendix consists of a checklist, based on the Guidelines described in Chapter 15, that will help educators determine the extent to which their institutions reflect the ethnic diversity within their societies.

Acknowledgments

I would like to thank several colleagues who helped with the preparation of this edition. Ricardo L. Garcia contributed Chapter 14. Geneva Gay co-authored Chapter 4. I wrote Chapter 15 with the following colleagues: Carlos E. Cortés, Geneva Gay, Ricardo L. Garcia, and Anna S. Ochoa. I would like to thank the following individuals for preparing prepublication reviews of the manuscript: Professor Carlos F. Diaz, Florida Atlantic University; Professor H. Prentice Baptiste, Jr., University of Houston; and Professor Douglas Warring, University of St. Thomas, St. Paul, Minnesota. Even though all of the comments on the manuscript were helpful and informative, I assume total responsibility for the contents of this book.

I am grateful to the National Academy of Education for a Spencer Fellowship that supported my research for three years. Many of the concepts I formulated during these years are incorporated into this and the previous editions. My present and former graduate students at the University of Washington listened to and reacted to many of the ideas in this book as they were formulated and refined.

Grace Sheldrick of Wordsworth Associates has provided editorial/production assistance on my books for at least a decade. I wish to thank her again for her keen insights and professionalism.

I wish to thank Cherry A. McGee Banks, a professor at the University of Washington, Bothell, for stimulating and supporting my intellectual growth for more than two decades and for thoughtful and helpful reactions to the ideas in this book. My daughters, Angela and Patricia, have taught me a great deal about the essence of life and have given me renewed faith that humankind can create a better world.

I would like to thank the following organizations, publishers, and individuals for permitting me to draw freely from the publications noted that I authored:

Academic Press Inc. and Geneva Gay, for (with Geneva Gay) "Ethnicity in Contemporary American Society: Toward the Development of a Typology" *Ethnicity* Vol. 5 (September 1978), pp. 238–252.

The Association for Supervision and Curriculum Development, for "Curricular Models for an Open Society," in Delmo Della-Dora and James E. House, eds., *Education for an Open Society* (Washington, D.C.: Association for Supervision and Curriculum Development, 1974), pp. 43–63; and "The Emerging Stages of Ethnicity: Implications for Staff Development," *Educational Leadership* Vol. 34 (December 1976), pp. 190–193.

Cassell, for a section from one of my chapters in James A. Banks and James Lynch, eds., *Multicultural Education in Western Societies* (London: Holt, Rinehart and Winston, 1986), pp. 10–25.

The Centre for the Study of Curriculum and Instruction, The University of British Columbia, for "Reducing Prejudice in Students: Theory, Research and Strategies," in Kogila Moodley, ed., *Race Relations and Multicultural Education* (Vancouver: Centre for the Study of Curriculum and Instruction, the University of British Columbia, 1985), pp. 65–87.

The Faculty of Education, University of Birmingham (England), for "Ethnic Revitalization Movements and Education," *Educational Review*, Vol. 37, No. 2 (1985), pp. 131–139. Heldref Publications, for "Pluralism, Ideology and Curriculum Reform," *The Social Studies*, Vol. 67 (May–June 1967), pp. 99–106.

Howard University Press, for "Shaping the Future of Multicultural Education," *The Journal of Negro Education*, Vol. 48 (Summer 1979), pp. 237–252.

Longman, Inc., for a figure from my book (with contributions by Ambrose A. Clegg, Jr.), *Teaching Strategies for the Social Studies*, 4th ed. (New York: Longman, Inc., 1990), p. 445.

The National Council for the Social Studies, for "Cultural Democracy, Citizenship Education, and the American Dream," (Presidential Address), *Social Education*, Vol. 47 (March 1983), pp. 231–232; "Should Integration Be a Societal Goal in a Pluralistic Nation?" in Raymond Muessig, ed., *Controversial Issues in the Social Studies* (Washington, D.C.: National Council for the Social Studies, 1975), pp. 197–228; "Ethnic Studies As a Process of Curriculum Reform," *Social Education*, Vol. 40 (February 1976), pp. 76–80; with Carlos E. Cortés, Geneva Gay, Ricardo L. Garcia, and Anna S. Ochoa, *Curriculum Guidelines for Multicultural Education*, revised edition (Washington, D.C.: National Council for the Social Studies, 1992).

The State University of New York Press, for "A Curriculum for Empowerment, Action, and Change," in Christine E. Sleeter, ed., *Empowerment through Multicultural Education* (pp. 125–141, ff. 311–313). Albany: State University of New York Press, 1991.

The University of Chicago Press, for "The Social Studies, Ethnic Diversity and Social Change," *The Elementary School Journal*, Vol. 87 (May 1987), pp. 531–543.

J. A. B.

Multiethnic Education

Part *I*

Dimensions, History, and Goals

Chapter 1
The Dimensions of Multicultural Education

Chapter 2
Multicultural Education: History and Revitalization Movements

Chapter 3
Multicultural Education: Nature, Goals, and Practices

Chapter 1 describes five dimensions of multicultural education conceptualized by the author: (1) content integration, (2) the knowledge construction process, (3) prejudice reduction, (4) an equity pedagogy, and (5) an empowering school culture and social structure. The need for each of these dimensions to be implemented to create comprehensive multicultural education is described and illustrated.

Chapter 2 describes the development of educational reform movements related to ethnic pluralism within an historical context. Historical developments related to ethnicity since the turn of the century, the intergroup education movement of the 1940s and 1950s, new immigrants in the United States, and the ethnic revival movements that have emerged in various Western societies since the 1960s are discussed. A typology that classifies the major phases of ethnic revitalization movements, particularly as they have developed in the United States and the United Kingdom, is also presented in this chapter.

In Chapter 3 the historical development of multicultural education is described. The nature of multicultural education, its goals, problems, and current practices are discussed, as are it promises. Multicultural education is viewed as a process of curriculum reform that has the potential for spearheading change in the total educational environment.

Chapter 1

The Dimensions of Multicultural Education

The Aims and Goals of Multicultural Education

The heated discourse on multicultural education, especially in the popular press and among nonspecialists (Asante, 1991; Asante & Ravitch, 1991; Gray, 1991; Leo, 1990; Schlesinger, 1991), often obscures the theory, research, and developing consensus among multicultural education specialists about the nature, aims, and scope of the field. A major goal of multicultural education—as stated by specialists in the field—is to reform the school and other educational institutions so that students from diverse racial, ethnic, and social-class groups will experience educational equality.

Another important goal of multicultural education—revealed in this literature—is to give both male and female students an equal chance to experience educational success and mobility (Klein, 1985; Sadker & Sadker, 1982). Multicultural education theorists are increasingly interested in how the interaction of race, class, and gender influences education (Banks, 1993; Grant & Sleeter, 1986; Sleeter, 1991). However, the emphasis that different theorists give to each of these variables varies considerably.

Although there is an emerging consensus about the aims and scope of multicultural education (Banks, 1992), the variety of typologies, conceptual schemes, and perspectives within the field reflects its emergent status and the fact that complete agreement about its aims and boundaries has not been attained (Baker, 1983; Banks, 1992; Bennett, 1990; Garcia, 1991: Gollnick & Chinn, 1990). The current bitter debate about the extent to which the histories and cultures of women and people of color should be incorporated into the study of Western civilization in U.S. schools, colleges, and universities has complicated the quest for sound definitions and clear disciplinary boundaries within the field because of the polarized nature of this debate (Asante, 1991; Asante & Ravitch, 1991; Ravitch, 1990; Schlesinger, 1990).

There is general agreement among most scholars and researchers in multicultural education that for it to be implemented successfully, institutional changes must be made, including changes in the curriculum; the teaching materials; teaching and learning styles; the attitudes, perceptions, and behaviors of teachers and administrators; and in the goals, norms, and culture of the school (Banks, 1992; Bennett, 1990; Sleeter & Grant, 1988). However, many school and university practitioners have a limited conception of multicultural education and view it primarily as curriculum reform that involves changing or restructuring the curriculum to include content about ethnic groups, women, and other cultural groups. This conception of multicultural education is widespread because curriculum reform was the main focus when the movement first emerged in the 1960s and 1970s (Blassingame, 1972; Ford, 1973) and because the multiculturalism discourse in the popular media has focused on curriculum reform and largely ignored other dimensions and components of multicultural education (Gray, 1991; Leo, 1990; Schlesinger, 1990, 1991).

The Dimensions and Their Importance

If multicultural education is to become better understood and implemented in ways more consistent with theory, its various dimensions must be more clearly described, conceptualized, and researched. Multicultural education is conceptualized in this chapter as a field that consists of the five dimensions I formulated (1992; 1993): (1) *content integration,* (2) *the knowledge construction process,* (3) *prejudice reduction,* (4) *an equity pedagogy,* and (5) *an empowering school culture and social structure.* The dimensions are based on research, observations, and work in the field from the late 1960s (Banks, 1970) through 1991 (Banks, 1992) (see Figure 1.1). Later in this chapter each of the five dimensions is defined and illustrated.

Educators need to be able to identify, to differentiate, and to understand the meanings of each dimension of multicultural education. *They also need to understand that multicultural education includes but is much more than content integration.* Part of the controversy in multicultural education results from the fact that many writers in the popular press see it only as content integration and as an educational movement that only benefits people of color. When multicultural education is conceptualized broadly, it becomes clear that it is for all students, and not just for low-income students and students of color (Grant & Sleeter, 1989; Parekh, 1986). Research and practice will also improve if we more clearly delineate the boundaries and dimensions of multicultural education.

This chapter defines and describes each of the five dimensions of multicultural education. I discuss the *knowledge construction process* more extensively than the other four dimensions. I believe that the kind of knowledge that teachers examine and master will have a powerful influence on the teaching methods they create, their interpretations of school knowledge, and how they use student

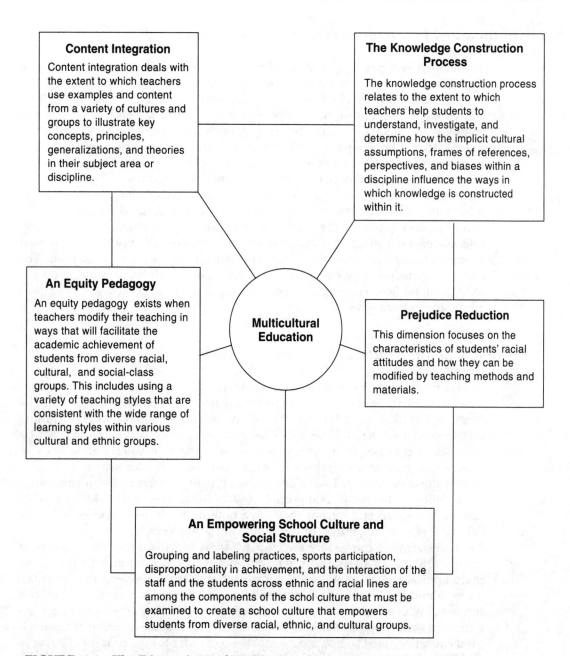

Content Integration

Content integration deals with the extent to which teachers use examples and content from a variety of cultures and groups to illustrate key concepts, principles, generalizations, and theories in their subject area or discipline.

The Knowledge Construction Process

The knowledge construction process relates to the extent to which teachers help students to understand, investigate, and determine how the implicit cultural assumptions, frames of references, perspectives, and biases within a discipline influence the ways in which knowledge is constructed within it.

An Equity Pedagogy

An equity pedagogy exists when teachers modify their teaching in ways that will facilitate the academic achievement of students from diverse racial, cultural, and social-class groups. This includes using a variety of teaching styles that are consistent with the wide range of learning styles within various cultural and ethnic groups.

Multicultural Education

Prejudice Reduction

This dimension focuses on the characteristics of students' racial attitudes and how they can be modified by teaching methods and materials.

An Empowering School Culture and Social Structure

Grouping and labeling practices, sports participation, disproportionality in achievement, and the interaction of the staff and the students across ethnic and racial lines are among the components of the schol culture that must be examined to create a school culture that empowers students from diverse racial, ethnic, and cultural groups.

FIGURE 1.1   The Dimensions of Multicultural Education

cultural knowledge. I view the knowledge construction process as fundamental in the implementation of multicultural education. It has implications for each of the other four dimensions, for example, for the construction of knowledge about pedagogy.

Limitations and Interrelationship of the Dimensions

The dimensions typology is an ideal-type conception in the Weberian sense. It approximates but does not describe reality in its total complexity. Like all classification schema, it has both strengths and limitations. Typologies are helpful conceptual tools because they provide a way to organize and make sense of complex and disparate data and observations. However, their categories are interrelated and overlapping, not mutually exclusive. Typologies are rarely able to encompass the total universe of existing or future cases. Consequently, some cases can be described only by using several of the categories.

The dimensions typology provides a useful framework for categorizing and interpreting the extensive and disparate literature on cultural diversity, ethnicity, and education. However, the five dimensions are conceptually distinct but highly interrelated. *Content intergration*, for example, describes any approach that is used to integrate content about racial and cultural groups into the curriculum. The *knowledge construction process* describes a method in which teachers help students to understand how knowledge is created and reflects the experiences of various ethnic and cultural groups.

The Meaning of Multicultural Education to Teachers

A widely held and discussed idea among theorists is that in order for multicultural education to be effectively implemented within a school, changes must be made in the total school culture as well as within all subject areas, including mathematics and science. Despite the wide acceptance of this basic tenet by theorists, it confuses many teachers, especially those in subject areas such as science and mathematics. This confusion often takes the form of resistance to multicultural education. I have been told by many teachers after a conference presentation on the nature and goals of multicultural education: "These ideas are fine for the social studies but they have nothing to do with science or math. Science is science, regardless of the culture of the students."

This statement can be interpreted in a variety of ways. However, one way of interpreting it is as a genuine belief by a teacher who is unaware of higher-level philosophical and epistemological knowledge and issues in science or mathematics or who does not believe that these issues are related to schoolteaching. The frequency with which I have encountered this belief in staff development conferences and workshops for teachers has convinced me that the meaning of multicultural education must be better contextualized in order for the concept to be more widely understood and accepted by teachers and other practitioners, especially in such subject areas as mathematics and the sciences.

We need to better clarify the different dimensions of multicultural education and help teachers to see more clearly the implications of multicultural education for their own subject areas and teaching situations. The development of active, cooperative, and motivating teaching strategies that makes physics more interesting for students of color might be a more important goal for a physics teacher of a course in which few African American students are enrolling or successfully completing than a search for ways to infuse African contributions to physics into the course. Of course, in the best possible world both goals would be attained. However, given the real world of the schools, we might experience more success in multicultural teaching if we set limited but essential goals for teachers, especially in the early phases of multicultural educational reform.

The development of a phase conceptualization for the implementation of multicultural educational reform would be useful. During the first or early phases, all teachers would be encouraged to determine ways in which they could adapt or modify their *pedagogy* or teaching to a multicultural population with diverse abilities, learning characteristics, and motivational styles. A second or later phase would focus on curriculum *content integration*. One phase would not end when another began. Rather, the goal would be to reach a phase in which all aspects of multicultural educational reform would be implemented simultaneously. Often in multicultural educational reform, the first focus is on content integration rather than on knowledge construction or pedagogy. A content integration focus often results in many mathematics and science teachers believing that multicultural education has little or no meaning for them. The remainder of this chapter describes the dimensions of multicultural education with the hope that it will help teachers and other practitioners determine how they can implement it comprehensively.

Contextualizing Multicultural Education

We need to do a better job of contextualizing the concept of multicultural education. When we tell practitioners that multicultural education implies reform in a discipline or subject area without specifying in detail the nature of that reform, we risk frustrating motivated and committed teachers because they do not have the knowledge and skills to act on their beliefs. Educators who reject multicultural education will use the "irrelevance of multicultural education" argument as a convenient and publicly sanctioned form of resistance and as a justification for inaction.

Many of us who are active in multicultural education have backgrounds in the social sciences and humanities. We consequently understand the content and process implications of multicultural education in these disciplines. A variety of programs, units, and lessons have been developed illustrating how the curriculum can be reformed and infused with multicultural perspectives, issues, and points of view from the social sciences and the humanities (Banks, 1991b; Grant & Sleeter, 1989). As students of society and the sociology of knowledge, we also understand, in general ways, how mathematics and science are cultural systems that developed within social and political contexts (Gould, 1981).

Most mathematics and science teachers do not have the kind of knowledge and understanding of their disciplines that enables them to construct and formulate lessons, units, and examples that deal with the cultural assumptions, frames of references, and perspectives within their disciplines. Few teachers seem able to identify and describe the assumptions and paradigms that underlie science and mathematics. They often make statements such as, "Math and science have no cultural contexts and assumptions. These disciplines are universal across cultures." Knowledge about the philosophical and epistemological issues and problems in science and mathematics, and the philosophy of science, is often limited to graduate seminars and academic specialists in these disciplines (Kuhn, 1970).

Specialists and leaders in multicultural education, because of their academic backgrounds, have been able to identify the basic issues and problems in mathematics and science but have not, in my view, provided the field with the clarity, curriculum work, and examples of lessons that mathematics and science teachers need in order to view the content within their disciplines from multicultural perspectives. Some promising attempts have been made to develop multicultural materials for mathematics and science teachers (Portland Public Schools, 1987). However, more work must be done in this area before most mathematics and science teachers can develop and implement a curriculum content approach to multicultural education.

Multicultural education is largely a way of viewing reality and a way of thinking, and not just content about various ethnic and cultural groups. Much more important work needs to be done in order to provide teachers with the examples and specifics they need. In the meantime, we can help all teachers, including mathematics and science teachers, to conceptualize and develop an *equity pedagogy*, a way of teaching that is not discipline-specific but that has implications for all subject areas and for teaching in general.

The Dimensions of Multicultural Education

Teachers can examine five dimensions of the school when trying to implement multicultural education. These dimensions, identified above, are summarized in Figure 1.1. They are defined and illustrated below.

Content Integration

Content integration deals with the extent to which teachers use examples and content from a variety of cultures and groups to illustrate key concepts, principles, generalizations, and theories in their subject area or discipline. The infusion of ethnic and cultural content into the subject area should be logical and not contrived. The widespread belief that content integration constitutes the whole of multicultural education might be an important factor that causes many teachers of subjects such as mathematics and science to view multicultural education as an endeavor primarily for social studies and language arts teachers.

More opportunities exist for the integration of ethnic and cultural content in some subject areas than in others. In the social studies, the language arts, music, and home economics, there are frequent and ample opportunities for teachers to use ethnic and cultural content to illustrate concepts, themes, and principles. There are also opportunities to integrate the math and science curriculum with ethnic and cultural content (Addison-Wesley, 1992). However, they are not as apparent or as easy to identify as they are in subject areas such as the social studies and the language arts.

In the language arts, for example, the students can examine the ways in which Ebonics (Black English) is similar to and different from mainstream U.S. English. The students can also study how African American oratory is used to engage the audience with the speaker. They can read and listen to speeches by such African Americans as Jesse Jackson, Barbara Jordan, and Martin Luther King, Jr., when studying Ebonics and African American oratory. The importance of oral traditions in Native American cultures could also be examined. Speeches and selections by Native American leaders such as Chief Seattle and Black Elk can be studied and read aloud (McLuhan, 1971).

The scientific explanation of skin color differences, the biological kinship of the human species, and the frequency of certain diseases among specific human groups are also content issues that can be investigated in science. The contributions to science made by cultures such as the Aztecs, the Egyptians, and the Native Americans are other possibilities for content integration in science (Bernal, 1987, 1991; Weatherford, 1988).

The Knowledge Construction Process

The knowledge construction process consists of the methods, activities, and questions teachers use to help students to understand, investigate, and determine how implicit cultural assumptions, frames of reference, perspectives, and biases within a discipline influence the ways in which knowledge is constructed. When the knowledge construction process is implemented in the classroom, teachers help students to understand how knowledge is created and how it is influenced by the racial, ethnic, and the social-class positions of individuals and groups (Code, 1991; Farganis, 1986).

In the Western empirical tradition, the ideal within each academic discipline is the formulation of knowledge without the influence of the researchers' personal or cultural characteristics (Greer, 1969; Kaplan, 1964). However, as critical and postmodern theorists have pointed out, personal, cultural, and social factors influence the formulation of knowledge even when objective knowledge is the ideal within a discipline (Code, 1991; Farganis, 1986; Giroux, 1983; Habermas, 1971; Harding, 1991; Ladner, 1973). Often the researchers themselves are unaware of how their personal experiences and positions within society influence the knowledge they produce. Most mainstream U.S. historians were unaware of how their regional and cultural biases influenced their interpretation of the Reconstruction period until W. E. B. DuBois (1935) published a study that challenged the accepted and established interpretations of that period.

It is important for teachers as well as elementary and high school students to understand how knowledge is constructed within all disciplines, including mathematics and science. Social scientists, as well as physical and biological scientists on the cutting edges of their disciplines, understand the nature and limitations of their fields. However, the disciplines are often taught to students as a body of truth not to be questioned or critically analyzed. Students need to understand, even in the sciences, how cultural assumptions, perspectives, and frames of references influence the questions that researchers ask and the conclusions, generalizations, and principles they formulate.

Students can analyze the knowledge construction process in science by studying how racism has been perpetuated in science by genetic theories of intelligence, Darwinism, and eugenics. Scientists developed theories such as polygeny and crainiometry that supported and reinforced racist assumptions and beliefs in the eighteenth and nineteenth centuries (Gould, 1981). Although science has supported and reinforced institutionalized racism at various times and places, it has also contributed to the eradication of racist beliefs and practices. Biological theories and data that revealed the characteristics that different racial and ethnic groups share, and anthropological theory and research about the universals in human cultures, have contributed greatly to the erosion of racist beliefs and practices (Benedict, 1940; Boas, 1940).

Knowledge Construction and the Transformative Curriculum

The curriculum in the schools must be transformed in order to help students develop the skills needed to participate in the knowledge construction process. The transformative curriculum changes the basic assumptions of the curriculum and enables students to view concepts, issues, themes, and problems from diverse ethnic and cultural perspectives (Banks, 1993).

The transformative curriculum can teach students to think by encouraging them, when they are reading or listening to resources, to consider the author's purposes for writing or speaking, his or her basic assumptions, and how the author's perspective or point of view compares with that of other authors and resources. Students can develop the skills to analyze critically historical and contemporary resources by being given two accounts of the same event or situation that present different perspectives and points of view.

Teaching about Knowledge as a Construction Process

Teachers can use two important concepts in U.S. history to help students to better understand the ways in which knowledge is constructed and to participate in rethinking, reconceptualizing, and constructing knowledge. *The New World* and *The European Discovery of America* are two central ideas that are pervasive in the school and university curriculum as well as within the popular culture. The teacher can begin a unit focused on these concepts with readings, discussions, and visual presentations that describe the archaeological theories about the peopling of the Americas nearly 40,000 years ago by groups that crossed the Bering Strait while hunting for animals and plants to eat. The students can then study about the Aztecs and other highly developed civilizations that developed in the Americas prior to the arrival of the Europeans in the fifteenth century.

After the study of the Native American cultures and civilizations, the teacher can provide the students with brief accounts of some of the earliest Europeans, such as Columbus and Cortes, who came to America. The teacher can then ask the students what they think the term *The New World* means, whose point of view it reflects, and to list other and more neutral words to describe the Americas (Banks with Sebesta, 1982). The students could then be asked to describe *The European Discovery of America* from two different perspectives: (1) from the point of view of an Arawak Indian (Olsen, 1974) (The Arawaks were living in the Caribbean when Columbus arrived there in 1492); and (2) from the point of view of an objective or neutral historian who has no particular attachment to either American Indian or European society.

The major objective of this lesson is to help students to understand knowledge as a social construction and to understand how concepts such as *The New World* and *The European Discovery of America* are not only ethnocentric and Eurocentric terms, but are also normative concepts that serve latent but important political purposes, such as to justify the destruction of Native American peoples and civilizations by Europeans such as Columbus and those who came after him (Golden et al, 1991; Zinn, 1992). *The New World* is a concept that subtly denies the political existence of the Indians and their nations prior to the coming of the Europeans.

The goal of teaching knowledge as a social construction is not to make students cynics or to encourage them to desecrate European heroes such as Columbus and Cortes. Rather, the aim is to help students to understand the nature of knowledge and the complexity of the development of U.S. society and to understand how the history that becomes institutionalized within a society primarily reflects the perspectives and points of views of the victors rather than the vanquished. When viewed within a global context, the students will be able to understand how the creation of historical knowledge in the United States parallels the creation of knowledge in other democratic societies and is a much more open and democratic process than in totalitarian nation-states.

Another important goal of teaching knowledge as a construction process is to help students to develop higher-level thinking skills and empathy for the peoples who have been victimized by the expansion and growth of the United States. When diverse and conflicting perspectives are juxtaposed, students are required to compare, contrast, weigh evidence, and make reflective decisions. They are also able to develop an empathy and an understanding of each group's perspective and point of view. The creation of their own versions of events and situations, and new concepts and terms, also requires students to reason at high levels and to think critically about data and information.

Prejudice Reduction

The prejudice reduction dimension of multicultural education describes the characteristics of students' racial attitudes and strategies that can be used to help them develop more democratic attitudes and values. Researchers have been investigating the characteristics of children's racial attitudes since the 1920s (Lasker, 1929). This research indicates that most young children enter school with negative racial attitudes that mirror those of adults. Research also indicates that effective curricular interventions can help students develop more positive racial and gender attitudes. Since the intergroup education movement of the 1940s and 1950s (Miel with Kiester, 1967; Trager & Yarrow, 1952), a number of investigators have designed interventions to help students to develop more positive racial attitudes and values.

The Modification of Children's Racial Attitudes

In a comprehensive review of the research (Banks, in press), I identify four types of intervention studies that have been conducted to help children develop more democratic racial attitudes and behaviors. These types are *reinforcement* studies, *perceptual differentiation* studies, *curricular intervention* studies, and studies that use *cooperative learning* activities and contact situations. This research indicates that teachers can help students develop more positive racial attitudes by designing and implementing well-planned and well-conceptualized curricular interventions.

In a series of laboratory studies conducted by Williams and Morland (1976) and their colleagues, researchers have been able to reduce white bias in both African American and White children by using reinforcement procedures. In one study (Williams & Edwards, 1969), for example, the investigators showed the children a white horse and a black horse, and a white figure and a brown figure. The researchers were able to reduce white bias in the students by giving them positive reinforcement when they chose positive—rather than negative—adjectives to describe the black horse and the brown figure. Researchers using reinforcement techniques have found that when white bias is reduced using black and white animals and boxes, the changed attitudes are generalized to human figures and photographs. *It is important to point out that these interventions reduce but do not eliminate white bias in young children.*

Katz and Zalk (1978) examined the effects of four different interventions on the racial attitudes of second- and fifth-grade children high in prejudice. They were perceptual differentiation of minority group faces, increased positive interracial contact, vicarious interracial contact, and reinforcement of the color black. The perceptual differentiation treatment was based on the hypothesis that people find it more difficult to differentiate the faces of members of outgroups than to differentiate the faces of members of their own groups. It is not uncommon to hear a member of one racial group say they he or she has trouble telling members of another group apart. Katz and Zalk hypothesized that if they could teach children to better differentiate the faces of outgroups, prejudice would be reduced. Each of the four interventions was effective in reducing prejudice. However, the *vicarious contact* and *perceptual differentiation* treatments had the most long-term effects.

A number of curriculum intervention studies that use multiethnic materials have been conducted. Trager and Yarrow (1952) found that first- and second-grade children who experienced a democratic, multicultural curriculum developed more positive racial attitudes than did students who experienced a traditional, mainstream curriculum. Litcher and Johnson (1969) found that multiethnic readers helped White second-grade children develop more positive racial attitudes. However, when they replicated the study using photographs (Litcher, Johnson, & Ryan, 1973), the children's attitudes were not significantly changed. The Litcher, Johnson, and Ryan study highlights an important trend in the prejudice-reduction literature. Although curricular materials can help students develop more positive racial attitudes, successful intervention is a complicated process that is influenced by a number of factors, including the teacher's racial attitudes and skills, the length of the intervention, the classroom atmosphere, the ethnic and racial composition of the school and classroom, and the racial atmosphere and composition of the community.

Since 1970, a number of researchers have studied the effects of cooperative learning on the academic achievement and racial attitudes of students from different racial and ethnic groups (Aronson & Gonzalez, 1988; Slavin, 1979; 1983). This research has been heavily influenced by the theory developed by Allport (1954). Allport hypothesized that prejudice would be reduced if interracial contact situations have the following characteristics:

1. They are cooperative rather than competitive.
2. The individuals experience equal-status.
3. The individuals have shared goals.
4. The contact is sanctioned by authorities such as parents, the principal, and the teacher.

The research on cooperative learning activities indicates that African American, Mexican American, and White students develop more positive racial attitudes and choose more friends from outside racial groups when they participate in group activities that have the conditions identified by Allport. Cooperative learning activities also have a positive effect on the academic achievement of students of color (Slavin, 1979).

Equity Pedagogy

An equity pedagogy exists when teachers modify their teaching in ways that will facilitate the academic achievement of students from diverse racial, cultural, ethnic, and gender groups. Research indicates, for example, that low-income students, as a group, tend to differ from middle-class students in some important characteristics related to motivation (Lefcourt, 1976). Low-income students tend to be external in their motivational orientations, which means that they tend to attribute their success or failure to outside forces or individuals and not to their own efforts. Middle-income students tend to be more internal in their orientations.

These characteristics of low-income and middle-class students have implications for teaching. Internality is correlated with academic success (Lefcourt, 1976). Thus, in order to increase the academic achievement of low-income students, strategies need to be developed that will enable them to experience success and consequently to learn the relationship between effort and success.

The motivational characteristics of low-income and middle-class students is just one example of how teachers can modify their teaching techniques to increase the academic achievement of students from diverse social-class, cultural, and gender groups. The use of cooperative teaching strategies and techniques can also help teachers to make their instruction more multicultural (Slavin, 1983; Cohen, 1972; 1986). Research indicates that cooperative—rather than competitive—teaching strategies help African American and Mexican American students to increase their academic achievement as well as help all students, including White mainstream students, to develop more positive racial attitudes and values (Aronson & Gonzalez, 1988).

An Empowering School Culture and Social Structure

This dimension of multicultural education involves restructuring the culture and organization of the school so that students from diverse racial, ethnic, and gender groups will experience equality. This variable must be examined and addressed by the entire school staff, including the principal and support staff. It involves an examination of the latent and manifest culture and organization of the school to determine the extent to which it fosters or hinders educational equity.

The four dimensions of multicultural education discussed above, *content integration, the knowledge construction process, prejudice reduction,* and an *equity pedagogy,* each deal with an aspect of a cultural or social system—the school. However, the school can also be conceptualized as one social system, which is larger than its interrelated parts, such as its formal and informal curriculum, teaching materials, counseling programs, and teaching strategies. When conceptualized as a social system, the school is viewed as an institution that "includes a social structure of interrelated statuses and roles and the functioning of that structure in terms of patterns of actions and interactions" (Theodorson & Theodorson, 1969, p. 395). The school can also be conceptualized as a cultural system (Bullivant, 1987) with a specific set of values, norms, ethos, and shared meanings.

Among the variables that need to be examined in order to create a school culture that empowers students from diverse cultural groups are grouping practices (Oakes, 1985), labeling practices, sports participation, and whether there are ethnic turfs that exists in the cafeteria or in other parts of the school. The behavior of the school staff must also be examined in order to determine the subtle messages it gives the students about racial, ethnic, and cultural diversity. Testing practices, grouping practices, tracking, and gifted programs often contribute to ethnic and racial inequality within the school.

A number of school reformers have used a systems approach to reform the school in order to increase the academic achievement of low-income students and students of color. There are a number of advantages to approaching school reform from a holistic perspective. To implement any reform in a school effectively, such as effective prejudice reduction teaching, changes are required in a number of other school variables. Teachers, for example, need more knowledge and need to examine their racial and ethnic attitudes; consequently, they need more time as well as a variety of instructional materials. Many school reform efforts fail because the roles, norms, and ethos of the school do not change in ways that will make the institutionalization of the reforms possible.

The *effective* school reformers is one group of change agents that has approached school reform from a systems perspective. Brookover and Erickson (1975) developed a social-psychological theory of learning, which states that students internalize the conceptions of themselves that are institutionalized within the ethos and structures of the school. Related to Merton's (1968) self-fulfilling prophecy, this theory states that student academic achievement will increase if the adults within the school have high expectations for students, clearly identify the skills they wish them to learn, and teach those skills to them.

Research by Brookover and his colleagues (Brookover et al., 1979; Brookover & Lezotte, 1979) indicates that schools populated by low-income students within the same school district vary greatly in student achievement levels. Consequently, Brookover attributes the differences to variations in the school's social structure. He calls the schools in low-income areas that have high academic achievement *improving* schools. Other researchers, such as Edmonds (1986) and Lezotte (1993), call them *effective* schools.

Comer (1988) has developed a structural intervention model that involves changes in the social-psychological climate of the school. The teachers, principal, and other school professionals make collaborative decisions about the school. The parents also participate in the decision-making process. Comer's data indicate that this approach has been successful in increasing the academic achievement of low-income, inner-city students.

Summary

This chaper describes the goals of multicultural education and its five dimensions. The dimensions are designed to help practicing educators to understand the different aspects of multicultural education and to enable them to implement it comprehensively. The dimensions help educators understand, for example, that content integration is only one important part of comprehensive multicultural education.

The dimensions discussed in this chapter are (1) *content integration,* (2) *the knowledge construction process,* (3) *prejudice reduction,* (4) *an equity pedagogy,* and

(5) *an empowering school culture and social structure.* Content integration deals with the extent to which teachers use examples and content from a variety of cultures and groups to illustrate key concepts, principles, generalizations, and theories in their subject area or discipline. The knowledge construction process relates to the extent to which teachers help students to understand, investigate, and determine how the implicit cultural assumptions, frames of references, perspectives, and biases within a discipline influence the ways in which knowledge is constructed within it.

In the prejudice reduction dimension, teachers help students develop more positive attitudes toward different racial and ethnic groups. Research indicates that most young children come to school with negative racial attitudes that mirror those of adults. It also indicates that the school can help students develop more positive intergroup attitudes and beliefs. An equity pedagogy exists when teachers modify their teaching in ways that will facilitate the academic achievement of students from diverse racial, cultural, gender, and social-class groups. This includes using a variety of teaching styles and approaches that are consistent with the wide range of learning styles within various cultural and ethnic groups.

Another important dimension of multicultural education is a school culture and social structure that promotes gender, racial, and social-class equality. To implement this dimension, the culture and organization of the school must be restructured in a collaborative process that involves all members of the school staff.

References

Addison-Wesley Publishing Company. (1992). *Multiculturalism in Mathematics, Science, and Technology: Readings and Activities.* Menlo Park, CA: Author.

Allport, G. W. (1954). *The Nature of Prejudice.* Cambridge, MA: Addison-Wesley.

Aronson, E., & Gonzalez, A. (1988). Desegregation, Jigsaw, and the Mexican-American Experience. In P. A. Katz & D. A. Taylor (Eds.), *Eliminating Racism: Profiles in Controversy* (pp. 301–314). New York: Plenum Press.

Asante, M. K. (1991). The Afrocentric Idea in Education. *Journal of Negro Education, 60,* 170–180.

Asante, M. K., & Ravitch, D. (1991). Multiculturalism: An Exchange. *The American Scholar, 60,* 267–276.

Baker, G. (1983). *Planning and Organizing for Multicultural Instruction.* Menlo Park, CA: Addison-Wesley.

Banks, J. A. (1970). *Teaching the Black Experience: Methods and Materials.* Belmont, CA: Fearon.

Banks, J. A. (1991a). Multicultural Education: Its Effects on Students' Ethnic and Gender Role Attitudes. In J. P. Shaver (Ed.), *Handbook of Research on Social Studies Teaching and Learning* (pp. 459–469). New York: Macmillan.

Banks, J. A. (1991b). *Teaching Strategies for Ethnic Studies.* (5th ed.). Boston: Allyn and Bacon.

Banks, J. A. (1992). Multicultural Education: Approaches, Developments, and Dimensions. In J. Lynch, C. Modgil, and S. Modgil (Eds.), *Education for Cultural Diversity: Convergence and Divergence* (pp. 83–94). London: Falmer Press.

Banks, J. A. (1993). Multicultural Education: Characteristics and Goals. In J. A. Banks & C. A. M. Banks (Eds.), *Multicultural Education: Issues and Perspectives.* (2nd ed.) (pp. 3–28). Boston: Allyn and Bacon.

Banks, J. A. (in press). Multicultural Education for Young Children: Racial and Ethnic Attitudes and Their Modification. In B. Spodek (Ed.), *Handbook of Research on the Education of Young Children.* New York: Macmillan.

Banks, J. A., with Sebesta, S. L. (1982). *We Americans: Our History and People,* Vols. 1–2. Boston: Allyn and Bacon.

Benedict. R. (1940). *Race, Science and Politics.* New York: Modern Age Publishers.

Bennett, C. I. (1990). *Comprehensive Multicultural Education* (2nd ed.). Boston: Allyn and Bacon.

Bernal, M. (1987, 1991). *Black Athena: The Afroasiatic Roots of Classical Civilization,* Vols. 1–2. New Brunswick, NJ: Rutgers University Press.

Boas, F. (1940). *Race, Language, and Culture.* New York: Macmillan.

Brookover, W. B., Beady, C., Flood, P., Schweitzer, J., & Wisenbaker, J. (1979). *School Social Systems and Student Achievement: Schools Can Make a Difference.* New York: Praeger.

Brookover, W. B., & Erickson, E. (1975). *Sociology of Education.* Homewood, IL: Dorsey.

Brookover, W. B., & Lezotte, L. W. (1979). *Changes in School Characteristics Coincident with Changes in Student Achievement.* East Lansing: Institute for Research on Teaching, College of Education, Michigan State University.

Bullivant, B. M. (1987). *The Ethnic Encounter in the Secondary School.* New York: Falmer Press.

Code, L. (1991). *What Can She Know? Feminist Theory and the Construction of Knowledge.* Ithaca, NY: Cornell University Press.

Cohen, E. G. (1972). Interracial Interaction Disability. *Human Relations, 25,* 9–24.

Cohen, E. G. (1986). *Designing Groupwork: Strategies for the Heterogeneous Classroom.* New York: Teachers College Press.

Comer, J. P. (1988). Educating Poor Minority Children. *Scientific American, 259,* 42–48.

DuBois, W. E. B. (1935). *Black Reconstruction.* New York: Harcourt, Brace.

Edmonds, R. (1986). Characteristics of Effective Schools. In U. Neisser (Ed.), *The School Achievement of Minority Children.* Hillsdale, NJ: Lawrence Erlbaum.

Farganis, S. (1986). *The Social Construction of the Feminine Character.* Totowa, NJ: Rowman & Littlefield.

Ford, N. A. (1973). Black Studies: Threat-or-Challenge. Port Washington, NY: Kennikat Press.

Garcia, R. L. (1991). *Teaching in a Pluralistic Society: Concepts, Models, Strategies* (2nd ed.). New York: Harper/Collins.

Giroux, H. A. (1983). *Theory and Resistance in Education.* South Hadley, MA: Bergin & Garvey.

Golden, R., McConnell, M., Mueller, P., Poppen, C., & Turkovich, M. (1991). *Dangerous Memories: Invasion and Resistance since 1492.* Chicago: Chicago Religious Task Force on Central America.

Gollnick, D. M., & Chinn, P. C. (1990). *Multicultural Education in a Pluralistic Society* (3rd ed). Columbus, OH: Merrill.

Gould, S. J. (1981). *The Mismeasure of Man.* New York: Norton.

Grant, C. A., & Sleeter, C. E. (1986). Race, Class, and Gender in Education Research: An Argument for Integrative Analysis. *Review of Educational Research, 56,* 195–211.

Grant, C. A., & Sleeter, C. E. (1989). *Turning on Learning: Five Approaches for Multicultural Teaching Plans for Race, Class, Gender and Disability.* Columbus, OH: Merrill.

Gray, P. (1991). Whose America? *Time, 138,* 12–17.

Habermas, J. (1971). *Knowledge and Human Interests.* Boston: Beacon Press.

Harding, S. (1991). *Whose Science? Whose Knowledge? Thinking from Women's Lives.* Ithaca, NY: Cornell University Press.

Katz, P. A., & Zalk, S. R. (1978). Modification of Children's Racial Attitudes. *Developmental Psychology, 14,* 447–461.

Klein, S. S. (1985) (Ed.) *Handbook for Achieving Sex Equity through Education.* Baltimore: The John Hopkins University Press.

Kuhn, T. S. (1970). *The Structure of Scientific Revolutions.* (2nd ed., enlarged). Chicago: The University of Chicago Press.

Ladner, J. A. (Ed.). (1973). *The Death of White Sociology.* New York: Vintage Books.

Lasker, B. (1929). *Race Attitudes in Children.* New York: Holt, Rhinehart & Winston.

Lefcourt, H.M. (1976). *Locus of Control: Current Trends in Theory and Research.* Hillsdale, NJ: Lawrence Erlbaum.

Leo, L. (1990). A Fringe History of the World. *U.S. News & World Report, 109,* 25–26.

Lezotte, L. W. (1993). Effective Schools: A Framework for Increasing Student Achievement. In J. A. Banks & C. A. M. Banks (Eds.), *Multicultural Education: Issues and Perspectives* (2nd ed.). Boston: Allyn and Bacon.

Litcher, J. H., & Johnson, D. W. (1969). Changes in Attitudes toward Negroes of White Elementary School Students after use of Multiethnic Readers. *Journal of Educational Psychology, 60,* 148–152.

Litcher, J. H., Johnson, D. W., & Ryan, F. L. (1973). Use of Pictures of Multiethnic Interaction to Change Attitudes of White Elementary School Students toward Blacks. *Psychological Reports, 33,* 367–372.

McLuhan, T. C. (Compiler). (1971). *Touch the Earth: A Self-Portrait of Indian Existence.* New York: Promontory Press.

Merton, R. K. (1968). *Social Theory and Social Structure.* (1968 enlarged ed.) New York: The Free Press.

Miel, A., with Kiester, E., Jr. (1967). *The Shortchanged Children of Suburbia: What Schools Don't Teach about Human Differences and What Can Be Done about It.* New York: The American Jewish Committee.

Oakes, J. (1985). *Keeping Track: How Schools Structure Inequality.* New Haven: Yale University Press.

Olsen, F. (1974). *On the Trail of the Arawaks.* Norman: University of Oklahoma Press.

Parekh, B. (1986). The Concept of Multicultural Education. In S. Modgil, G. K. Verma, K. Mallick, & C. Modgil (Eds.), *Multicultural Education: The Interminable Debate* (pp. 19–31). Philadelphia: Falmer Press.

Portland Public Schools. (1987). *African-American Baseline Essays.* Portland, OR: Multnomah School District 1J.

Ravitch, D. (1990). Diversity and Democracy: Multicultural Education in America. *American Educator, 14,* 16–20, 46–48.

Sadker, M. P., & Sadker, D. M. (1982). *Sex Equity Handbook for Schools.* New York: Longman.

Schlesinger, A., Jr. (1990). When Ethnic Studies are un-American. *Social Studies Review,* 11–13.

Schlesinger, A., Jr. (1991). *The Disuniting of America: Reflections on a Multicultural Society.* Knoxville, TN: Whittle Direct Books.

Slavin, R. E. (1979). Effects of Biracial Learning Teams on Cross-Racial Friendships. *Journal of Educational Psychology, 71,* 381–387.

Slavin, R. E. (1983). *Cooperative Learning.* New York: Longman.

Sleeter, C. E. (Ed.). (1991). *Empowerment through Multicultural Education.* Albany: State University of New York Press.

Sleeter, C. E., & Grant, C. A. (1988). *Making Choices for Multicultural Education: Five Approaches to Race, Class, and Gender.* Columbus, OH: Merrill.

Theodorson, G. A., & Theodorson, A. G. (1969). *A Modern Dictionary of Sociology.* New York: Barnes & Noble.

Trager, H.G., & Yarrow, M. R. (1952). *They Learn What They Live: Prejudice in Young Children.* New York: Harper & Brothers.

Weatherford, J. (1988). *Indian Givers: How the Indians of the Americas Transformed the World.* New York: Fawcett Columbine.

Williams, J. E., & Edwards, C. D. (1969). An Exploratory Study of the Modification of Color and Racial Concept Attitudes in Preschool Children. *Child Development, 40,* 737–750.

Williams, J. E., & Morland, J. K. (1976). *Race, Color, and the Young Child.* Chapel Hill: The University of North Carolina Press.

Zinn, H. (1992). *Columbus, the Indians, & Human Progress.* Westfield, NJ: Open Magazine Pamphlet Series, Pamphlet #19.

Chapter 2

Multicultural Education: History and Revitalization Movements

The Rise of Nativism

Most of the European immigrants who came to North America before 1890 were from nations in Northern and Western Europe, such as the United Kingdom, Germany, Sweden, and Switzerland. Although conflicts developed between these various immigrant groups, the English were dominating the social, economic, and political life in North America by the 1700s. As the twentieth century approached and new waves of immigrants began to arrive in the United States from Southern, Central, and Eastern Europe, the immigrants from Northern and Western Europe began to perceive themselves as the old immigrants and rightful inhabitants of the country. They saw the new immigrants as a threat to U.S. civilization and to its democratic tradition. Sharp and often inaccurate distinctions were made between the new and old immigrants. A movement called *nativism* arose to stop the flood of the new immigrants from arriving in the United States (Higham, 1972). The nativists pointed out that the new immigrants were primarily Catholics, whereas the old immigrants were mainly Protestants. A strong element of anti-Catholicism became an integral part of the nativistic movement.

Because of their Catholicism, cultural differences, and competition for jobs with the old immigrants and native-born Americans, the new immigrants became the victims of blatant nativism. A suspicion and distrust of all foreigners became widespread near the turn of the century. The outbreak of the Great War in Europe in 1914 greatly increased the suspicion and distrust of immigrant groups in the

United States and further stimulated nativistic feelings and groups. Nativism swept through the United States during World War I. Nativists argued for 100 percent Americanism and said that America should be for "Americans." The new immigrant groups tried desperately but unsuccessfully to prove their national loyalty.

Nativism and Education

The public schools, colleges, and universities usually perpetuate the dominant ideologies and values that are promoted and embraced by the powerful groups within society (Katz, 1975). Reflecting the prevailing goals of the nation as articulated by its powerful and economic leaders, the schools and colleges promoted and embraced Americanization and blind loyalty to the nation and also showed a distrust of foreigners and immigrant groups during the turn of the century and World War I periods.

The teaching of German and other foreign languages was prohibited in many schools. German books in school libraries were sometimes burned. Some schools prohibited the playing of music by German composers in music classes and in school assemblies (Moquin, 1971). In this atmosphere of virulent nativism, government-sponsored propaganda, and emphasis on blind patriotism and Americanization, the idea of cultural pluralism in education would have been alien and perhaps viewed as seditious and un-American.

The Melting Pot

The assimilationist ideology that was pervasive near the turn of the century and during World War I was embodied and expressed in the play *The Melting Pot*. This play, written by the English Jewish author Israel Zangwill, opened in New York City in 1908. It became a tremendous success. The great ambition of the play's composer-protagonist, David Quixano, was to create an American symphony that would personify his deep conviction that his adopted land was a nation in which all ethnic differences would mix and from which a new person, superior to all, would emerge. What in fact happened, however, was that most of the immigrant and ethnic cultures stuck to the bottom of the mythical melting pot. Anglo-Saxon culture remained dominant; other ethnic groups had to give up many of their cultural characteristics in order to participate fully in the nation's social, economic, and political institutions (Jones, 1960).

However, as I point out in Chapter 7, cultural influence was not in one direction only. Although the Anglo-Saxon Protestant culture became and remained dominant in the United States, other ethnic groups, such as the Germans, the Irish, Indians, and African Americans, influenced the Anglo-Saxon culture as the Anglo-Saxon culture influenced the culture of these groups. However, the Anglo-Saxon Protestant culture has had the most cogent influence on U.S. culture

(Stewart, 1972). This influence has been in many cases positive. The American ideals of human rights, participatory democracy, and separation of church and state are largely Anglo-Saxon contributions to U.S. civilization.

The American school, like other American institutions, embraced Anglo-conformity goals. Two major goals were to rid ethnic groups of their ethnic traits and to force them to acquire Anglo-Saxon values and behavior. In 1909 Ellwood Patterson Cubberley (1909, pp. 15–16), the famed educational leader, clearly stated a major goal of the common schools:

> *Everywhere these people [immigrants] tend to settle in groups or settlements, and to set up here their national manners, customs, and observances. Our task is to break up these groups or settlements, to assimilate and amalgamate these people as part of our American race, and to implant in their children, as far as can be done, the Anglo-Saxon conception of righteousness, law and order, and popular government, and to awaken in them a reverence for our democratic institutions and for those things in our national life which we as a people hold to be of abiding worth.*

The Call for Cultural Pluralism

In the early years of the twentieth century, a few philosophers and writers, such as Horace Kallen (1924), Randolph Bourne (1916), and Julius Drachsler (1920), strongly defended the rights of the immigrants living in the United States. They rejected the assimilationist argument made by leaders such as Cubberley. They argued that a political democracy must also be a cultural democracy and that the thousands of Southern, Eastern, and Central European immigrant groups had a right to maintain their ethnic cultures and institutions in U.S. society. They used a "salad bowl" argument, maintaining that each ethnic culture would play a unique role in U.S. society but would also contribute to the total society. They argued that ethnic cultures would enrich U.S. civilization. They called their position *cultural pluralism* and said it should be used to guide public and educational policies.

The arguments of the cultural pluralists were a cry in the wilderness. They fell largely on deaf ears. Most of the country's political, business, and educational leaders continued to push for the assimilation of the immigrant and indigenous racial and ethnic groups. They felt that only in this way could a unified nation be made out of so many different ethnic groups with histories of wars and hostilities in Europe. The triumph of the assimilationist forces in U.S. life was symbolized by the Immigration Acts of 1917 and 1924.

The Immigration Act of 1917, designed to halt the immigration of Southern, Central, and Eastern European groups, such as Poles, Greeks, and Italians, required immigrants to pass a reading test to enter the United States. When this act passed but failed to reduce the number of immigrants from these nations enough to please the nativists, they pushed for and succeeded in getting another act passed, the Immigration Act of 1924. This act drastically limited the number of immigrants that could enter the United States from all European nations except those in Northern and Western Europe. It ended the era of massive European immigration to the United States and closed a significant chapter in U.S. history.

Ethnic Education between the Two World Wars

Mainstream U.S. leaders and educators generally ignored the voices advocating pluralistic policies in the early years of the twentieth century. However, because of the tremendous value and cultural diversity within the United States, rarely is there consensus within our society on any important social or educational issue. Consequently, while those who dominated educational policy usually embraced the assimilationist ideology and devoted little time and energy to the education of the nation's ethnic minority groups, other U.S. leaders, researchers, and educators engaged in important discussions about the education of the nation's ethnic minorities, formulated educational policy related to ethnic groups, and did important research on American ethnic communities (Weinberg, 1977). Ironically, however, often the policy formulated by those deeply concerned about the education of ethnic minorities was assimilationist oriented. This indicated the extent to which the assimilationist ideology had permeated U.S. life and thought. However, there were always a few educational leaders who advocated pluralism.

Policies and programs in ethnic education did not suddenly arise during the ethnic revitalization movements of the 1960s and 1970s. These developments gradually evolved over a long period. It is true, however, that they became more intense during various historical periods, usually because of heightened racial consciousness and concern stimulated by events such as racial conflicts and tensions. The evolutionary character of ethnic education in the United States can be illustrated by a brief discussion of the educational policies related to Native Americans, African Americans, and Mexican Americans between the two great world wars. The education of other ethnic groups, such as Jewish Americans, Italian Americans, and Puerto Rican Americans, could also be used to illustrate the evolutionary nature of ethnic education (Krug, 1976). However, the choice of these first three ethnic groups can in part be justified by the fact that educational policy and programs related to them have stimulated enduring and controversial discussions and programs for most of the present century.

Native American Education

How Native Americans should be educated has evoked a continuing debate since the late 1800s (Fuchs & Havighurst, 1973; Szasz, 1974; 1988; Tippeconnic & Swisher, 1992). Since the 1920s, educational policy for Native Americans has vacillated between strong assimilationism to self-determination and cultural pluralism. The landmark Meriam Report, issued in 1928, recommended massive reforms in Native American education (Meriam, 1928). The Report recommended that Indian education be tied more closely to the community, the building of day schools in the community, and the reformation of boarding schools. It also recommended that the curriculum in Indian schools be changed to reflect Indian cultures and the needs of local Indian communities (Szasz, 1974). The 1969 U.S. Senate Report on Indian Education (1969), called the Kennedy Report, stated that many of the reforms recommended by the Meriam Report had not been attained.

African American Education

Developments in the education of African Americans were both active and controversial in the decades between the war years. Carter G. Woodson, an African American historian who received a doctorate from Harvard in 1912, did seminal research and work on Black history and Black education. Woodson founded, with others, the Association for the Study of Negro Life and History in 1915 (Now the Association for the Study of Afro-American Life and History, Inc.) (Woodson, 1933; Woodson & Wesley, 1922). This organization was founded to sponsor and encourage research in African American history and to disseminate this research to scholars and teachers in predominantly African American schools and colleges. The Association started two important publications that are still published: *The Journal of Negro History* and *The Negro History Bulletin*. Woodson began Negro History Week in 1926 to commemorate milestones in African American history. In 1976, this annual commemoration was changed to National Afro-American History Month, which is observed during February.

African American educational policy became very controversial within the Black community. Booker T. Washington and W. E. B. DuBois set forth sharply contrasting views about directions for African American education. Washington, a former slave and the most influential African American leader of his time, believed that African American students needed a practical, industrial education (Harlan, 1972; Washington, 1901). He implemented his ideas at Tuskegee Institute in Tuskegee, Alabama. DuBois, the noted African American scholar and educational philosopher, received his Ph.D. from Harvard in 1895. He believed that a "talented tenth" should be educated for leadership in the African American community. The "talented tenth," he argued, should study the classics, political philosophy, and other academic subject (DuBois, 1961).

Mexican American Education

During the 1930s and 1940s, considerable attention was focused on the education of Mexican Americans by scholars and educators concerned with their educational plight. Most educators during this period, according to Carter and Segura (1979), saw the school as an agency for the acculturation of Mexican American students. Betty Gould (1932), for example, recommended what she considered effective methods for the acculturation of Mexican American students in her 1932 thesis, "Methods of Teaching Mexicans." Carter and Segura (1979, p. 17) described Mexican American education during the 1930s:

> *School programs for Chicano children during the 1930s emphasized vocational training and manual-arts training; learning of English; health and hygiene; and adoption of American core values such as cleanliness, thrift and punctuality. Segregation, especially in the early grades, was regularly recommended and commonly established. It was inexplicably argued that Americanization could best be accomplished by keeping foreigners out of contact with Americans.*

The voices speaking for the education of Mexican Americans during the 1930s and 1940s, however, were not unanimous. George I. Sanchez (1940; 1946), a pioneer Mexican American educator and scholar, urged educators to consider the unique cultural and linguistic characteristics of Mexican American students when planning and implementing educational programs for them.

The Intergroup-Education Movement

Social, political, and economic changes caused by World War II stimulated a curriculum movement related to cultural and ethnic diversity that became known as *intercultural education* or *intergroup education*. World War II created many job opportunities in northern cities. Many African Americans and Whites left the South during the war years in search of jobs. More than 150,000 African Americans left the South each year in the decade between 1940 and 1950 and settled in northern cities (Lemann, 1991). In such northern cities as Chicago and Detroit conflict developed between African Americans and Whites as they competed for jobs and housing. Racial conflict also occurred in the Far West. Mexican Americans and Anglos clashed in serious "zoot-suit" riots in Los Angeles during the summer of 1943. These racial conflicts and tensions severely strained race relations in the nation.

Racial tension and conflict were pervasive in northern cities during the war years. In 1943, race riots took place in Los Angeles, Detroit, and in the Harlem district of New York City. The most destructive riot during the war broke out in Detroit on a Sunday morning in June 1943. More southern migrants had settled in Detroit during this period than in any other city in the United States. The Detroit riot raged for more than thirty hours. When it finally ended, thirty-four persons were dead and property worth millions of dollars had been destroyed (Banks & Banks, 1978). The Detroit riot stunned the nation and stimulated national action by concerned African American and White citizens.

A major goal of intergroup education was to reduce racial and ethnic prejudice and misunderstandings (Taba, Brady, & Robinson, 1952). Activities designed to reduce prejudice and to increase interracial understanding included the teaching of isolated instructional units on various ethnic groups, exhortations against prejudice, organizing assemblies and cultural get-togethers, disseminating information on racial, ethnic, and religious backgrounds, and banning books considered stereotypic and demeaning to ethnic groups. A major assumption of the intergroup-education movement was that factual knowledge would develop respect and acceptance of various ethnic and racial groups (Taba & Wilson, 1946). Unlike the ethnic-studies movement of the late 1960s, however, the emphasis in the intercultural-education movement of the 1940s and 1950s was neither on strong cultural pluralism nor on maintaining or perpetuating strong ethnic loyalties.

Two important national projects were implemented to actualize the goals of intercultural education. The Intergroup Education in Cooperating Schools project, directed by Hilda Taba, was designed to effect changes in elementary and secondary schools (Taba, Brady, & Robinson, 1952). The other project, the College Study in Intergroup Relations, was sponsored by the American Council on Education and directed by Lloyd Allen Cook (1950). The College Study project was the first cooperative effort in the United States to improve the intercultural component of teacher education. Twenty-four colleges with teacher-education programs participated in this project from 1945 to 1949.

The Intergroup-Education Movement Ends

The intergroup-education movement and its related reforms failed to become institutionalized within most U.S. schools, colleges, and teacher-training institutions. This statement should not be interpreted to mean that the movement did not benefit our society and educational institutions. Cook (1947) has noted the tremendous influence the College Study projects had on the individuals who participated in them. The action and research projects undertaken in the College Study contributed to our practical and theoretical knowledge about race relations and about intervention efforts designed to influence attitudes and behavior. The basic idea of the College Study was a sound one that merits replication: teacher-training institutions formed a consortium to develop action and research projects to effect change.

It is also true that many individual teachers and professors, and probably many individual school and teacher-training institutions, continued some elements of the reforms related to intergroup education after the national movement faded. By the 1960s, however, when racial tension intensified in the nation and race riots again sprang up, few U.S. schools and teacher-education institutions had programs and curricula that dealt adequately with the study of racial and ethnic relations. However, most predominantly African American schools and colleges were teaching Black studies and were responding in other ways to many of the unique cultural characteristics of African American students.

As we consider ways to institutionalize reforms related to multicultural education, it is instructive to consider why the reforms related to intergroup education failed to become institutionalized in most U.S. schools and colleges. The reforms related to the movement failed to become institutionalized, in part, for the following six reasons:

1. Mainstream U.S. educators never internalized the ideology and major assumptions on which intergroup education was based.

2. Mainstream U.S. society never understood how the intergroup education movement contributed to the major goals of the U.S. common schools.

3. Most U.S. educators saw intergroup education as a reform project for schools that had open racial conflict and tension and not for what they considered their smoothly functioning and nonproblematic schools.

4. Racial tension in the cities took more subtle forms in the 1950s. Consequently, most U.S. educators no longer saw the need for action designed to reduce racial conflict and problems.

5. Intergroup education remained on the periphery of mainstream educational thought and developments and was financed primarily by special funds. Consequently, when the special funds and projects ended, the movement largely faded.

6. The leaders of the intergroup-education movement never developed a well-articulated and coherent philosophical position that revealed how the intergroup-education movement was consistent with the major goals of the U.S. common schools and with American creed values such as equality, justice, and human rights.

Assimilation Continues and Helps to Shape a Nation

Despite the intergroup-education reforms of the 1940s and 1950s, assimilationist forces and policies dominated U.S. life from about the turn of the century to the beginning of the 1960s. The assimilationist ideology was not seriously challenged during this long period, even though there were a few individuals, such as Marcus Garvey in the 1920s, who championed separatism and ethnic pluralism (Clarke, 1974). These lone voices were successfully ignored or silenced.

Most minority as well as dominant group leaders saw the assimilation of U.S. ethnic groups as the proper societal goal. Social scientists and reformers during this period were heavily influenced by the writings of Robert E. Park, the eminent U.S. sociologist who had once worked as an informal secretary for Booker T. Washington (Cosner, 1977). Park believed that race relations proceeded through four inevitable stages: *contact, conflict, accommodation,* and *assimilation* (Lyman, 1972). The most reform-oriented social scientists and social activists embraced assimilation as both desirable and inevitable within a democratic pluralistic nation such as the United States.

The assimilationist policy shaped a nation from millions of immigrants and from diverse Native American groups. The United States did not become an ethnically Balkanized nation; this could have happened. The assimilationist idea also worked reasonably well for ethnic peoples who were White. However, it did force many of them to become marginal individuals and to deny family and heritage (Klein, 1980; Novak, 1976). This should not be taken lightly, for denying one's basic group identity is a very painful and psychologically unsettling process (Novak, 1971; Tomasi, 1985). However, most, but not all, White ethnic groups in the United States have been able, in time, to climb up the economic and social ladders (Alba, 1990).

The New Pluralism

The assimilationist idea has not worked nearly as well for people of color. This is what African Americans realized by the early 1960s. The unfulfilled promises and dreams of the assimilationist idea were major causes of the Black civil rights movement of the 1960s. By the late 1950s and early 1960s, discrimination in such areas as employment, housing, and education, combined with rising expectations, caused African Americans to lead an unprecedented fight for their rights, which became known as the Black civil rights movement.

Many African Americans who had become highly assimilated were still unable to participate fully in many mainstream U.S. institutions. African Americans were still denied many opportunities because of their skin color (Edwards & Polite, 1992; Landry, 1987). They searched for a new ideal. Many endorsed some form of cultural pluralism. An idea born during the turn of the century was refashioned to fit the hopes, aspirations, and dreams of disillusioned people of color in the 1960s.

African Americans demanded more control over the institutions in their communities and also demanded that all institutions, including the schools, more accurately reflect their ethnic cultures. They demanded more African American teachers and administrators for their youths, textbooks that reflected African American history and culture, and that schools become more sensitive to African American culture (Carmichael & Hamilton, 1967).

Educational institutions, at all levels, began to respond to the Black civil rights movement. The apparent success of the Black civil rights movement caused other ethnic groups of color on the margins of society, such as Mexican Americans, Asian Americans, and Puerto Ricans, to make similar demands for political, economic, and educational changes.

Mexican American studies and Asian American studies courses that paralleled Black studies courses emerged (Burma, 1970; Gee et al., 1976). The reform movements initiated by the groups of color caused many White ethnic groups that had denied their ethnic cultures to proclaim ethnic pride and to push for the insertion of more content about White ethnic groups into the curriculum (Novak, 1971). This movement became known as the *new pluralism*. In a sense, the African American civil rights movement legitimized ethnicity, and other ethnic groups that felt victimized began to search for their ethnic roots and to demand more group and human rights.

The New Immigrants

Since the Immigration Reform Act of 1965 became effective in 1968, the United States has experienced its largest wave of immigrants since the turn of the century. Nearly 80 percent (78.6 percent) more immigrants entered the United States in the decade between 1971 and 1980 than had entered in the years between 1951 and 1960. Immigration to the United States continued at a rapid pace between 1981 and 1988. Nearly 5 million (4,710,700) immigrants settled in the United States during this period (U.S. Bureau of the Census, 1991).

Not only has the number of immigrants entering the United States increased by leaps and bounds since 1968, but the characteristics of the immigrants have also changed dramatically. In the decade between 1951 and 1960, most of the immigrants to the United States came from Europe (about 59.3 percent). However, between 1971 and 1980, Europeans made up only 18 percent of the legal immigrants who settled in the United States. The European percentage of the immigrants to the United States continued to decline during the 1980s. Between 1981 and 1988, they made up 10.8 percent of U.S. legal immigrants (U.S. Bureau of the Census, 1991). Most immigrants during these years came from Asian and Latin American nations, such as the Philippines, Korea, China, Mexico, and Cuba. A significant number of people from the war-torn nations of Indochina sought refuge in the United States when communists gained control of their homelands. By 1990 almost 1 million Vietnamese were living in the United States.

The wave of new immigrants to the United States from non-European nations, and the relatively low birthrate among Whites compared to that of most groups of color, are having a significant impact on U.S. society, particularly on its demographic characteristics. The new wave of immigrants to the United States has hastened the decline in the relative proportion of the White population in the United States. This decline began as early as 1900. Between 1900 and 1980 the White proportion of the U.S. population declined from 87.7 percent to 83.1 percent. During the same time, the proportion of non-Whites in the United States increased from 12.3 percent of the population in 1900 to 16.9 percent in 1980 (Momeni, 1984). These demographic changes would be even more dramatic if the percentage for non-Whites included the 8.1 million Hispanics classified as White in 1980.

The new immigrants, along with the diversity of indigenous U.S. ethnic groups, are having a tremendous influence on the nation's schools. Students of color made up the majority of the school enrollments in 23 of 25 of the nation's largest cities in 1984 (American Council on Education, 1984). Demographers project that students of color will make up about 46 percent of the nation's school-age youths by the year 2020 (Pallas, Natriello, & McDill, 1989). In some urban school districts, more than fifty different languages are spoken.

Even though the characteristics of the students in U.S. schools are changing substantially, conflict often develops between the home and the school and between teachers and students (Delpit, 1988; Heath, 1983). The schools have been reluctant to adapt their curricular and teaching styles to make them more consistent with the needs of students of color and low-income students. In many schools that have multiethnic populations, the curriculum, teaching, and motivational techniques remain Anglocentric.

Racial and ethnic problems are major sources of conflict in many U.S. schools, particularly in urban areas. Disproportionality in achievement, discipline, and dropout rates between mainstream students and students of color is a significant source of tension in most urban school districts. The parents blame teachers and administrators; the school blames the home and the student's culture.

As long as the achievement gap between African Americans and Whites and Anglos and Hispanics is wide, ethnic conflicts and tension in schools will continue. Improving the academic achievement of students of color and low-income students, and developing and implementing a multicultural curriculum that reflects the cultures, experiences, and perspectives of diverse groups, will help reduce the racial conflict and tension in U.S. schools and increase the academic achievement of all students.

Ethnic Revitalization Movements: A Phase Typology

The ethnic revival movements in the United States echoed throughout the world as groups such as the Jamaicans in the United Kingdom, the Australian Aborigines, and the Moluccans and Surinamese in the Netherlands demanded more social, political, and educational equality in their societies (Cropley, 1983; Eldering & Kloprogge, 1989). In both the United States and the United Kingdom, multicultural education has created tremendous debate over goals (Banks & Lynch, 1986; Modgil et al., 1986). However, the two nations appear to be in different phases of ethnic revitalization and consequently in different stages of debate.

This section describes a typology that attempts to outline the major phases of the development of ethnic revitalization movements in Western societies. The typology is a preliminary ideal-type construct in the Weberian sense and constitutes a set of hypotheses based on the existing and emerging theory and research and on my study of ethnic behavior in several Western nations. Because it is drawn primarily from ethnic events in the United States, it might be less generalizable in other nations. Observers in other nations must determine the extent to which the typology is valid in their societies. This typology is presented to stimulate discussion and analysis and to help educators better interpret ethnic events in Western nations.

I am conceptualizing ethnic revitalization as consisting of four major phases: *a precondition phase; a first or early phase; a later phase;* and *a final phase* (see Table 2.1). The typology is an ideal-type construct and should be considered as dynamic and multifaceted rather than as static and one-dimensional. The divisions between the phases are blurred rather than sharp. One phase does not end abruptly and another begins; rather, the phases blend and overlap. As with any ideal-type typology, the phases approximate reality rather than directly describe it. No actual ethnic movement exemplifies each characteristic of the four phases.

Ethnic Revitalization: The Precondition Phase

Ethnic revitalization movements usually arise within societies that have a history of imperialism, colonialism, and institutionalized racism. Groups with particular ethnic, racial, and cultural characteristics are denied equality and structural inclu-

TABLE 2.1   Phases in the Development of Ethnic Revitalization Movements

The Precondition Phase

This phase is characterized by the existence of a history of colonialism, imperialism, racism, an institutionalized democratic ideology, and efforts by the nation-state to close the gap between democratic ideals and societal realities. These events create rising expectations among victimized ethnic groups that pave the way for ethnic protest and a revitalization movement.

The First Phase

This phase is characterized by ethnic polarization, an intense identity quest by victimized ethnic groups, and single-causal explanations. An effort is made by ethnic groups to get racism legitimized as a primary explanation of their problems. Both radical reformers and staunch conservatives set forth single-causal explanations to explain the problems of victimized ethnic groups.

The Later Phase

This phase is characterized by meaningful dialogue between victimized and dominant ethnic groups, multiethnic coalitions, reduced ethnic polarization, and the search for multiple-causal explanations for the problems of victimized ethnic groups.

The Final Phase

Some elements of the reforms formulated in the earlier phases become institutionalized during this phase. Other victimized cultural groups echo their grievances, thereby expanding and dispersing the focus of the ethnic reform movement. Conservative ideologies and policies become institutionalized during this phase, thus paving the way for the development of a new ethnic revitalization movement.

sion into the nation-state. These societies also have a national democratic ideology stating that equality and justice should exist for all individuals and groups within the nation-state. The first phase of revitalization begins when the nation-state takes steps to close the gap between its democratic ideals and the inequality institutionalized within it.

The attempt to improve the conditions of marginalized groups—usually stimulated by action taken by these groups—creates rising expectations and hope and causes these groups to perceive their condition as intolerable. The ethnic revitalization movement is born out of the hope and rising expectations created by the nation-state when it attempts to eliminate some of its most blatant forms of institutionalized racism and discrimination. The desegregation of the armed forces and state universities after World War II and the *Brown* v. *Board of Education* Supreme Court decision (1954), which made *de jure* school segregation illegal, were key events in the United States that stimulated the birth of the civil rights movement.

Ethnic Revitalization: The First Phase

In the first phase of ethnic revitalization, positions are sharply drawn and ardent, single-causal explanations tend to predominate, controversy is bitter, and the debate tends to take the form of "us and them"—you are either for us or with them. Racism is usually the major issue in the debate during the early stages of ethnic revitalization because it has usually not been previously acknowledged as an important component of the society. It is during the early stages of ethnic revitalization that groups that perceive themselves as oppressed or as victims of racism force the dominant society to acknowledge that racism is institutionalized within it.

The debate between radical reforms and conservative defenders of the status quo remains stalemated and single-focused until the existence of racism is acknowledged by the dominant group and meaningful steps are taken to eliminate it. Until this acknowledgment occurs in official statements, policies, and actions, radical reformers continue to perceive racism as the single cause of the social, economic, and educational problems of excluded ethnic groups. Radical reformers will not search for or find more complex variables that explain the problems of victimized ethnic groups until mainstream leaders acknowledge the existence of institutionalized racism. In other words, institutionalized racism must become legitimized as an explanation, and serious steps must be taken to eliminate it, before an ethnic revitalization movement can reach a phase in which other explanations will be accepted by radical reformers who articulate the interests of groups that are victims of institutionalized racism.

During the early phase of ethnic revitalization, ethnic groups, in their efforts to shape new identities and to legitimize their histories and cultures, often glorify those histories and cultures and emphasize the ways their people have been oppressed by the dominant group and mainstream society. This early combination of protest and ethnic polarization must be understood within a broad social and political context. Groups that perceive themselves as oppressed and that internalize the dominant society's negative stereotypes and myths about themselves are likely to express strong group feelings during the early stages of ethnic revitalization. They also attempt to shape a new identity. During this phase the group is also likely to reject outside ethnic and racial groups, to romanticize its past, and to view contemporary social and political conditions quite subjectively.

An ethnic group in the early stage of revitalization is also likely to demand that the school curriculum portray a romanticized version of its history (to compensate for past omissions and errors) and to emphasize how the group has been victimized by other ethnic and racial groups. Extremely negative sanctions are directed against members of the ethnic group who do not endorse a strong "ethnic" position. Consequently, little fruitful dialogue is likely to take place either within or between different ethnic groups. Members of both the "oppressed" and the "oppressive" groups remain ardent in their positions during the first phase of revitalization.

Educational institutions tend to respond to the first phases of ethnic revitalization with quickly conceptualized and hurriedly formulated programs designed primarily to silence ethnic protest rather than to contribute to equality and to the structural inclusion of ethnic groups into society. In both the United States and the United Kingdom, many early programs related to ethnic groups were poorly conceptualized and implemented without careful and thoughtful planning. Such programs are usually attacked and eliminated during the later phases of ethnic revitalization, when the institutionalization of ethnic programs and reforms begins. Their weakness becomes the primary justification for the elimination. When such programs were attacked and eliminated in the United States, many careful and sensitive observers noted that they had been designed to fail.

The Rise of Antiegalitarian Ideology and Research

The ideology and research that radical reformers develop during the early stage of ethnic revitalization do not go unchallenged. An ideological war takes place between radical reformers and conservatives who defend the status quo. While radical and liberal reformers develop ideology and research to show how the ethnic groups' major problems are caused by institutionalized racism and the wider society, antiegalitarian advocates and researchers develop an ideology and research stating that the failure of ethnic groups in school and society is due to their own inherited and socialized characteristics (Herrnstein, 1971; Jensen, 1969; Shockley, 1972). Both radical and conservative scholars tend to develop single-causal theories and explanations during the early phase of ethnic revitalization. The theories and explanations developed by radical theorists tend to focus on racism and other problems in society (Katz, 1975), whereas those developed by conservative researchers usually focus on the characteristics of ethnic students themselves, such as their genetic characteristics and their family socialization (Herrnstein, 1971; Jensen, 1969).

Radical reformers use the research and theory developed by antiegalitarian researchers as evidence to support their arguments that racism is pervasive and institutionalized within the society and that it has permeated much of the research done at some of the nation's most prestigious universities.

Ethnic Revitalization: The Later Phase

During the later phase of ethnic revitalization, ethnic groups search for multiple rather than single causes for their problems; racism as an explanation becomes legitimized but is recognized as only one important cause of the problems of ethnic groups; ethnic rhetoric and polarization lessen; and ethnic groups form coalitions and jointly articulate their grievances.

During the first phase of ethnic revitalization, many researchers and intellectuals who feel committed to ethnic equality but who do not agree with radical reformers on many issues do not freely express their views in public forums because they fear being called racists. These individuals begin to express their views and opinions freely during the later phase of ethnic revitalization (Jencks & Peterson, 1991; Wilson, 1978, 1987). This now becomes possible because emotions cool, thus enabling individuals who disagree to engage in fruitful dialogue without accusations and epithets.

In the United States, a group of conservative intellectuals has emerged who argue that they are committed to ethnic equality and that their views represent another valid way for ethnic groups to attain structural inclusion (Chavez, 1991; Glazer, 1975; Sowell, 1984; Steele, 1990). In general, these intellectuals favor few government intervention programs and encourage ethnic groups to establish businesses and to compete in the market economy of the United States. This group of intellectuals, the neoconservatives, has been highly visible and influential in the national press and has evoked tremendous controversy, especially among ethnic scholars and leaders (Steinfels, 1979). Only a few of these scholars, however, are ethnic minorities (Chavez, 1991; Sowell, 1984; Steele, 1990).

Nation-states facilitate the movement from early to later phases of ethnic revitalization by making symbolic concessions to ethnic groups, such as African American studies programs, the hiring of ethnics in highly visible positions, the establishment of affirmative action policies, and the creation of a middle-class ethnic elite that serves as visible proof that "ethnics can make it" (Carter, 1991). The ethnic elite plays a very important role in moving the nation-state from the early to the later phase of ethnic revitalization. They develop counter arguments to radical reformers, teach balanced and scholarly ethnic studies courses, and search for complex explanations for the causes of the social, economic, and political problems of ethnic groups (Carter, 1991; Wilson, 1987).

Ethnic Revitalization: The Final Phase

During the final phase of ethnic revitalization, many of the reforms born during the early and later phases become institutionalized within the schools and other institutions. Other groups that perceive themselves as oppressed also begin to echo the grievances of ethnic groups and thus broaden the scope of the reform movement. Women, people with disabilities, and other groups articulate their problems and make their special case for entitlements (Banks & Banks, 1993). Conflict tends to develop between these groups and ethnic groups because they compete for the same scarce resources.

Institutions such as the state and federal government, universities, and schools begin to view these groups as a collectivity and to respond to their needs with single programs, projects, and legislation. When women and groups with disabilities began to argue their case for inclusion into the school curriculum in the United States, schools created *multicultural education,* which combined content and information about these diverse groups into a single program. The United States federal government established affirmative action programs designed to help both ethnic minorities and women gain more access to jobs and education.

The final phase of ethnic revitalization is a process that does not end until diverse ethnic and racial groups experience structural inclusion and equality within the nation-state. Consequently, the final phase of ethnic revitalization has not ended in the United States, the United Kingdom, Australia, or Canada because ethnic groups of color are still only partially included within the structures of these societies. Even when ethnic groups attain *inclusion* into institutions, they do not necessarily experience *equality*. Many middle-class African Americans in the United States are discovering, for example, that when they gain access to mainstream U.S. institutions they do not necessarily experience equality within them (Edwards & Polite, 1992; Landry, 1977).

At the same time that the United States is experiencing the final phase of ethnic revitalization, social, political, and economic events are developing that are paving the way for a new ethnic revival that may have many of the same characteristics of the ethnic movement in the 1960s and 1970s. A conservative government and national atmosphere are engendering the kind of alienation, hostility, and poverty that give rise to ethnic revival movements.

Several indicators of the rise of a new ethnic revitalization movement were evident in the United States during the early 1990s. They included the emergence of the Afrocentric movement (Asante, 1990) and a serious race riot that occurred in the Watts district of Los Angeles after a jury found several White police officers not guilty in a controversial case in which Rodney King, an African American man, was seriously beaten. A videotape of King being beaten by the police officers had been shown continually on national television before the trial.

The current situation in the United States suggests that ethnic revitalization movements are cyclic rather than linear. Once an ethnic revival movement has occurred within a nation-state, social, political, and economic conditions tend to arise that give birth to new revivals. As ethnic revitalization movements reach their later and final phases—as in the United States today—events tend to evoke new ones. Ethnic revitalization movements will continue to reemerge in Western democratic societies until racial and ethnic groups attain structural inclusion and equality in their nation-states and societies.

Ethnic Revitalization: Educational Implications

To help nations move from early to later phases of ethnic revitalization, educational institutions at all levels should help minority and majority group students to interpret accurately the current phase of the ethnic revival movement and to respond to it in ways that will help ethnic students satisfy their psychological and academic needs.

During the early phase of ethnic revitalization, such as existed in the United Kingdom in the 1980s, the school should help legitimize racism as a valid explanation of societal realities in the nation-state. Educators who refuse to validate racism as an explanation or to take serious steps to eliminate it will extend the early phase of ethnic revitalization and alienate many ethnic students and radical reformers. Educators who insist, during the early stage of an ethnic revival movement, that the problems of ethnic groups are caused by more complicated variables than racism may be accurate in their views but are not dealing with the subjective reality of marginalized ethnic groups of color. *Racism is the most important or only significant variable for these groups because their daily experiences validate this reality.* When educational and other institutions have validated racism as an important explanation of the problems of ethnic groups of color and have taken meaningful steps to eliminate it, then other causes of their problems can be legitimately explored and validated.

Multiple-causal theories that explain the problems of ethnic groups are developing and becoming legitimate in the United States. Even though racism is still regarded as an important and cogent variable in U.S. society, a few African American scholars, such as Wilson (1978), Patterson (1977), and Sowell (1984), are trying to determine how such variables as class, culture, and values influence the achievement and experiences of ethnic groups. However, the writings of these scholars of color have created considerable controversy and debate within both the minority and majority communities. In general, their writings are less controversial among mainstream White groups than among people of color.

Summary

A large wave of immigrants from Southern, Central, and Eastern Europe entered the United States between 1890 and 1917. The Europeans who already lived in the United States during this period were primarily from Northern and Western Europe. Because of their cultural differences, Catholicism, and competition for jobs with native-born Americans, a nativistic movement arose to halt the immigration of the new immigrants. Nativism became widespread throughout the United States and influenced the nation's institutions, including the schools. The outbreak of World War I in Europe greatly increased nativistic expressions within the larger society and the schools. The schools tried to make the immigrants 100 percent Americans and to exclude all elements of foreignness from the curriculum.

A few philosophers and writers, such as Horace Kallen, Randolph Bourne, and Julius Drachsler, defended the immigrants' rights, stating that cultural democracy should exist in a democratic nation such as the United States. The arguments of these writers, however, influenced few U.S. leaders.

Most institutions within U.S. society, including the schools, remained assimilationist-oriented between World Wars I and II and devoted little serious attention to the educational needs and problems of students of color. However, a number of U.S. educational and scholarly leaders formulated policy and programs for educating students of color during this period. The educational developments in Native American, African American, and Mexican American education between the two wars illustrate the evolutionary nature of ethnic education in the United States.

The intergroup-education movement grew out of the social developments that emerged in response to World War II. Conflict and riots developed in U.S. cities as African Americans and Whites and Anglos and Mexican Americans competed for housing and jobs. The intergroup education movement tried to reduce interracial tensions and to further intercultural understandings. Developments in intergroup education took place at the elementary, secondary, and college level. The intergroup education movement, itself only mildly pluralistic, did not seriously challenge the assimilationist ideology in U.S. life. When the ethnic revitalization movements of the 1960s and 1970s and related educational reform movements emerged, the intergroup education movement had largely faded.

Since 1968, the United States has experienced a major wave of new immigrants primarily from nations in Latin America and Asia. These new immigrants have had a major influence on the social, economic, and educational institutions in the United States. While schools and other social institutions are trying to respond to the needs of these groups—sometimes reluctantly—a renewed movement toward nationalism is advocating national cohesion and identity rather than diversity.

Other Western nation-states, such as the United Kingdom, France, Canada, and Australia, have also become more ethnically diverse since World War II. The ethnic minorities within these societies face problems similar to their counterparts in the United States. Multicultural education has emerged within these nations to respond to the unique needs, problems, and aspirations of ethnic minorities.

Since the 1960s, a series of ethnic revitalization movements have arisen in the various Western nation-states. This chapter presents a typology that describes the major phases of ethnic revitalization movements, particularly as they have developed in the United States and the United Kingdom. The major phases of ethnic revitalization movements can be identified, even though they acquire unique and different characteristics in the various nation-states. Different nation-states are also in different phases of ethnic revitalization.

Nation-states can facilitate the movement from early to later phases of ethnic revitalization by implementing educational policies and programs that promote the integration of structurally excluded ethnic groups into the mainstream society. A curriculum that reflects the cultures, ethos, and experiences of the diverse groups within a nation will reduce ethnic polarization and weaken ethnic revival movements.

References

Alba, R. D. (1990). *Ethnic Identity: The Transformation of White America.* New Haven: Yale University Press.

American Council on Education (1984). Minority Changes Hold Major Implications for U.S. *Higher Education and National Affairs,* 8.

Asante, M. K. (1990). *Kemet, Afrocentricity, and Knowledge.* Trenton, NJ: Africa World Press.

Banks, J. A., & Banks, C. A. M. (1978). *March toward Freedom: A History of Black Americans* (2nd ed.). Belmont, CA: Fearon-Pitman Publishers.

Banks, J. A. & Banks, C. A. M. (Eds.). (1993). *Multicultural Education: Issues and Perspectives* (2nd ed.). Boston: Allyn and Bacon.

Banks, J. A., & Lynch, J. (Eds.). (1986). *Multicultural Education in Western Societies.* London: Cassell.

Bourne, R. S. (1916). Trans-National America. *The Atlantic Monthly, 118,* 95.

Burma, J. H. (Ed.). (1970). *Mexican-Americans in the United States: A Reader.* Cambridge, MA: Schenkman Publishing Company.

Carmichael, S., & Hamilton, C. V. (1967). *Black Power: The Politics of Liberation in America.* New York: Vintage.

Carter, S. L. (1991). *Reflections of an Affirmative Action Baby.* New York: Basic Books.

Carter, T. P., & Segura, R. D. (1979). *Mexican Americans in School: A Decade of Change.* New York: College Entrance Examination Board.

Chavez, L. (1991). *Out of the Barrio.* New York: Basic Books.

Clarke, J. H. (Ed.). with the assistance of A. J. Garvey. (1974). *Marcus Garvey and the Vision of Africa.* New York: Vintage Books.

Cook, L. A. (1947). Intergroup Education. *Review of Educational Research, 17,* 266–278.

Cook, L. A. (Ed.). (1950). *College Programs in Intergroup Relations.* Washington, DC: American Council on Education.

Cosner, L. A. (1977). Robert Ezra Park 1864–1944. In *Masters of Sociological Thought* (2nd ed.) (pp. 357–384). New York: Harcourt Brace.

Cropley, A. J. (1983). *The Education of Immigrant Children.* London: Croom Helm.

Cubberley, E. P. (1909). *Changing Conceptions of Education.* Boston: Houghton Mifflin.

Delpit, L. D. (1988). The Silenced Dialogue: Power and Pedagogy in Educating Other People's Children. *Harvard Educational Review, 58,* 280–298.

Drachsler, J. (1920). *Democracy and Assimilation.* New York: Macmillan.

DuBois, W. E. B. (1961). *The Souls of Black Folk.* New York: Fawcett Publications. (Published originally in 1903.)

Edwards, A., & Polite C. K. (1992). *Children of the Dream: The Psychology of Black Success.* New York: Doubleday.

Eldering, L., & Kloprogge, J. (Eds.). (1989). *Different Cultures, Same School: Ethnic Minority Children in Europe.* Berwyn, PA: Swets North America.

Fuchs, E., & Havighurst, R. J. (1973). *To Live on This Earth: American Indian Education.* Garden City, NY: Doubleday.

Gee, E., et al., (Ed.). (1976). *Counterpoint: Perspective on Asian America.* Los Angeles: Asian American Studies Center, University of California.

Glazer, N. (1975). *Affirmative Discrimination: Ethnic Inequality and Public Policy.* New York: Basic Books.

Gould, B. (1932). Methods of Teaching Mexicans. Master's thesis, University of Southern California.

Harlan, L. R. (1972). *Booker T. Washington: The Making of a Black Leader, 1856–1901.* New York: Oxford University Press.

Heath, S. B. (1983). *Ways with Words: Language, Life, and Work in Communities and Classrooms.* New York: Oxford University Press.

Herrnstein, R J. (1971). I.Q. *Atlantic Monthly, 228,* 43–64.

Higham, J. (1972). *Strangers in the Land: Patterns of American Nativism, 1860–1925.* New York: Atheneum.

Jencks, C., & Peterson, P. E. (1991). *The Urban Underclass.* Washington, DC: The Brookings Institution.

Jensen, A. R. (1969). How Much Can We Boost IQ and Scholastic Achievement? *Harvard Educational Review, 39,* 1–123.

Jones, M. A. (1960). *American Immigration.* Chicago: University of Chicago Press.

Kallen, H. M. (1924). *Culture and Democracy in the United States.* New York: Boni and Liveright.

Katz, M. B. (1975). *Class, Bureaucracy, and Schools: The Illusion of Educational Change in America* (expanded ed.). New York: Praeger Publishers.

Klein, J. W. (1980). *Jewish Identity and Self-Esteem: Healing Wounds through Ethnotherapy.* New York: American Jewish Committee.

Krug, M. (1976). *The Melting of the Ethnics.* Bloomington, IN: Phi Delta Kappa Educational Foundation.

Landry, B. (1987). *The New Black Middle Class.* Berkeley: The University of California Press.

Lemann, N. (1991). *The Promised Land: The Great Migration and How It Changed America.* New York: Knopf.

Lyman, S. M. (1972). *The Black American in Sociological Thought: A Failure of Perspective.* New York: Capricorn Books.

Meriam, L. (Ed.). (1928). *The Problem of Indian Administration.* Baltimore: Johns Hopkins University Press.

Modgil, S., Verma, G. K., Mallick, K., & Modgil, C. (Eds.). (1986). *Multicultural Education: The Interminable Debate.* Philadelphia: The Falmer Press.

Momeni, J. A. (1984). *Demography of Racial and Ethnic Minorities in the United States: An Annotated Bibliography with a Review Essay.* Westport, CT: Greenwood Press.

Moquin, W. (Ed.). (1971). *Makers of America. Hyphenated Americans, 1914–1924.* Vol. 7. Chicago: Encyclopaedia Britannica Educational Corporation.

Novak, M. (1971). *The Rise of the Unmeltable Ethnics: Politics and Culture in the Seventies.* New York: Macmillan.

Novak, M. (Ed.). (1976). *Growing up Slavic in America.* Bayville, NY: Empac.

Pallas, A. M., Natriello, G., & McDill, E. L. (1989). The Changing Nature of the Disadvantaged Population: Current Dimensions and Future Trends. *Educational Researcher, 18,* 16–22.

Patterson, O. (1977). *Ethnic Chauvinism: The Reactionary Impulse.* New York: Stein and Day.

Sanchez, G. I. (1940). *Forgotten People.* Albuquerque: University of New Mexico Press.

Sanchez, G. I. (Ed.). (1946). *First Regional Conference on the Education of Spanish-Speaking People in the Southwest. Inter-American Education Occasional Papers,* No. 1. Austin: The University of Texas Press.

Shockley, W. (1972). Dysgenics, Geneticity, Raceology: A Challenge to the Intellectual Responsibility of Educators. *Phi Delta Kappan, 53,* 297–307.

Sowell, T. (1984). *Civil Rights; Rhetoric or Reality?* New York: William Morrow.

Steele, S. (1990). *The Content of Our Character.* New York: St. Martin's.

Steinfels, P. (1979). *The Neoconservatives: The Men Who Are Changing America's Politics.* New York: Simon & Schuster.

Stewart, E. C. (1972). *American Cultural Patterns: A Cross-Cultural Perspective.* LaGrange Park, IL: Intercultural Network.

Szasz, M. C. (1974). *Education and the American Indian: The Road to Self-Determination, 1928–1973.* Albuquerque: University of New Mexico Press.

Szasz, M. C. (1988). *Indian Education in the American Colonies, 1607–1783.* Albuquerque: University of New Mexico Press.

Taba, H., Brady, E. H., & Robinson, J. T. (1952). *Intergroup Education in Public Schools.* Washington, DC: American Council on Education.

Taba, H., & Wilson, H. E. (1946). Intergroup Education through the School Curriculum. *Annals of the American Academy of Political and Social Science, 244,* 19–25.

Tippeconnic, J. W. III, & Swisher, K. (1992). American Indian Education. In M. C. Alkin (Ed.), *Encyclopedia of Educational Research,* (6th Ed.), Vol. 1, (pp. 75–77). New York: Macmillan.

Tomasi, L. F. (Ed.). (1985). *Italian Americans: New Perspectives in Italian Immigration and Ethnicity.* New York: Center for Migration Studies of New York.

U.S. Bureau of the Census. (1991). *Statistical Abstract of the United States: 1991* (111th Ed.). Washington, DC: U.S. Government Printing Office.

U.S. Senate, Report of the Committee on Labor and Public Welfare, Special Subcommittee on Indian Education. (1969). *Indian Education. A National Tragedy—a National Challenge.* 91st Congress, 1st Session. Washington, DC: U.S. Government Printing Office.

Washington, B. T. (1901). *Up from Slavery: An Autobiography.* New York: Doubleday and Company.

Weinberg, M. (1977). *A Chance to Learn: A History of Race and Education in the United States.* New York: Cambridge University Press.

Wilson, W. J. (1978). *The Declining Significance of Race.* Chicago: University of Chicago Press.

Wilson, W. J. (1987). *The Truly Disadvantaged: The Inner City, the Underclass, and Public Policy.* Chicago: The University of Chicago Press.

Woodson, C. G., & Wesley, C. H. (1922). *The Negro in Our History.* Washington, DC: The Associated Publishers.

Woodson, C. G. (1933). *Mis-Education of the Negro.* Washington, DC: The Associated Publishers.

Chapter 3

Multicultural Education: Nature, Goals, and Practices

The Emergence of Multicultural Education

In the United States, as well as in other Western nations such as the United Kingdom, Canada, Australia, France, and the Netherlands, the emergence of multicultural education has been a gradual and evolutionary process. This chapter describes multicultural education as it developed in the United States. It has also developed in a related but not identical way in the other Western nation-states (Banks & Lynch, 1986; Bullivant, 1981; Eldering & Kloprogge, 1989). Educational developments in nations such as the United Kingdom, Canada, and Australia are often similar to developments in the United States. However, these developments often occur at different times and reflect the cultural, political, and historical context of the nation in which they occur. In both the United States and Australia in the late 1980s, for example, pluralism was strongly challenged by a call for national cohesion and identity. However, in the United States the call for nationalism occurred when a new wave of immigrants was settling in the nation. Australia, like the United Kingdom, had severely restricted new immigration (Encel, 1981).

Phase I: Monoethnic Courses

When the Black civil rights movement began in the mid-1960s in the United States, African Americans demanded that the schools and other institutions respond more adequately to their needs and aspirations. They called for more Black teachers for African American youths, community control of Black schools, and the rewriting of textbooks to make them more accurately reflect African American history and culture. They also demanded African American studies courses.

During the 1970s ethnic minorities, such as African Americans and Asians in the United Kingdom and Canadian Indians, also demanded that educational institutions within their societies respond more directly and positively to their needs and goals.

In time, other ethnic groups in the United States, such as Mexican Americans and American Indians, made demands on schools and colleges similar to those made by African Americans. These institutions responded by establishing courses on specific ethnic groups, such as African American history and literature, and Mexican American history and literature. This phase in the development of multicultural education may be considered Phase 1. It was characterized by monoethnic courses, the assumption that only a member of an ethnic group should teach a course on that group, and a focus on White racism and on how Whites have oppressed ethnic groups of color. A pervasive assumption made during Phase I ethnic studies courses was that Black studies were needed only by African American students and that Asian American studies were needed only by Asian American students.

Phase II: Multiethnic Studies Courses

As more and more ethnic groups in the United States, including White ethnic groups such as Jewish Americans and Polish Americans, began to demand separate courses and the inclusion of their histories and cultures in the curriculum, schools and colleges began to offer multiethnic studies courses that focus on several ethnic cultures and view the experiences of ethnic groups from comparative perspectives. Courses such as Ethnic Minority Music and The History and Culture of Minorities in the United States are taught from comparative perspectives.

We may call the multiethnic studies phase of the development of multicultural education Phase II. Ethnic studies course became more global, conceptual, and scholarly during this period. They also became less politically oriented and began to explore diverse points of view and interpretations of the experiences of ethnic groups in the United States. The recognition emerged and grew that ethnic studies should be designed for all students, and not just for students who were members of particular ethnic groups. Basic assumptions of multiethnic studies courses are that ethnic groups have had both similar and different experiences in the United States and that a comparative study of ethnic cultures can result in useful concepts, generalizations, and theories.

Phase III: Multiethnic Education

As ethnic studies became more global and widespread, more and more educators began to recognize that even though reforming the course of study in schools and colleges was necessary, it was not sufficient to result in effective educational reform. The negative attitudes of many teachers made their use of new ethnic materials and teaching strategies ineffective and in some cases harmful.

Educators also began to recognize that ethnic studies courses alone could not enable students such as African Americans, Latinos, and Native Americans to achieve at levels comparable with the achievement levels of most mainstream White students.

Research emerged that indicated how students of color are often placed in low academic tracts because of middle-class and Anglo-biased IQ tests (Oakes, 1985) and how students who speak a first language other than standard Anglo-American English often fail to achieve in school, in part, because of their language differences (Hakuta, 1990; Krashen, 1991; Ovando & Collier, 1985). Studies that documented the affects of teacher attitudes on student achievement, attitudes, and behavior were published (Kleinfeld, 1975; Rist, 1970). Research also revealed the negative attitudes and interactions that teachers often have with low-income students and students of color (Rist, 1970).

These recognitions and studies convinced many educators involved in minority education that ethnic studies courses and materials, no matter how soundly conceptualized and taught, could not by themselves bring about the kind of substantial educational reform needed to enable students from diverse racial and ethnic groups to experience educational equality. In other words, educators began to realize that ethnic studies were necessary but not sufficient to bring about effective educational reform and equity. Educators began to call for a more broadly conceptualized kind of educational reform, with a focus on the total school environment. Educators began to view the total school as the unit of change, and not any one variable within the educational environment, such as materials or teaching strategies. This more broadly conceptualized reform movement became known as *multiethnic education*, which emerged as Phase III in the development of pluralistic education.

Phase IV: Multicultural Education

Some educators became interested in an educational reform movement that would deal not only with the educational problems of low-income students and students of color but also with the educational problems of cultural groups such as women, people with disabilities, religious groups, and regional groups such as Appalachian Whites. This broader reform movement is known as *multicultural education*, which is Stage IV of the development of pluralistic education.

Multicultural education became the preferred concept in many educational institutions, in part because the concept enabled school districts and universities to pool limited resources and thus to focus on a wide range of groups rather than to limit their focus to racial and ethnic minorities (Banks & Banks, 1993; Sleeter & Grant, 1988). The *Standards* published by the National Council for Accreditation of Teacher Education (NCATE) require teacher-education institutions to implement components, courses, and programs in multicultural education. The NCATE multicultural standards, first published as a part of its general standards in 1977, were reissued in 1987 (National Council, 1987).

Many educators support the multicultural education concept but are concerned that the focus of the movement may become so broad and global that the

issues of *racism* and *racial discrimination,* important concerns of pluralistic education in the 1960s when it emerged, might become lost or de-emphasized (Gay,
1983). Another problem with multicultural education is that the boundaries of the
field are so broad that it is often difficult to determine which cultural groups are
the primary focus or concern in a particular curriculum, publication, or conference. Some authors use the term to refer to groups of color (Baker, 1983; Hernandez, 1989). Increasingly, however, the term is being used to refer to education
related to race, class, gender, social class, exceptionality, and to the interaction of
these variables (Banks & Banks, 1993; Grant & Sleeter, 1986; Sleeter & Grant, 1988).

A Caveat

Because of the historical and evolutionary way in which Phases I through IV of
multicultural education is discussed above, the reader may understandably conclude that when Phase II emerged Phase I disappeared. This is not what in fact
has happened or is happening. As illustrated in Figure 3.1, when Phase II
emerged, Phase I continued, although perhaps in modified form and on a more
limited scale. The earlier phases also begin to take on some characteristics of the
newly emerging phases. Phase I types of ethnic studies courses became more
conceptual and scholarly when Phase II of multicultural education began to

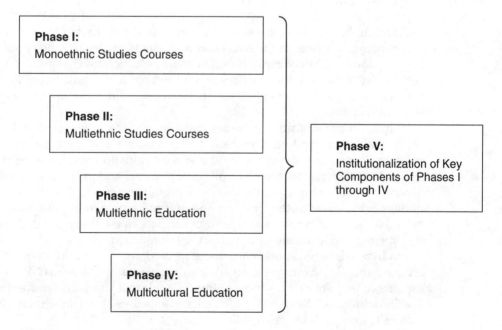

FIGURE 3.1   The Evolution of Multicultural Education

This figure illustrates how the earlier phases of multicultural education continue to exist when new
phases of the movement emerge. However, when the new phases emerge, the earlier phases tend to
assume some of the characteristics of the newer phases and to continue on a more limited scale.

emerge. The assumption also grew that an academically qualified individual, regardless of his or her ethnic group membership, could effectively teach an ethnic studies course on any ethnic group.

Phase V: The Institutionalization Process

I am conceptualizing Phase V of the development of multicultural education as the institutionalization of the key and most effective components of Phases I through IV. Phase V is a *process* that is slowly occurring. Elements of multicultural education are beginning to permeate the curriculum and the total educational environment. However, this process is necessarily a slow one that requires strong support and commitment from boards of education, administrators, and teachers. It took several centuries for the current historical periods (e.g., the Middle Ages, the Renaissance, the European Discovery of America) to be conceptualized and institutionalized. As we try to reconceptualize world and U.S. history and literature, it is reasonable to expect this process to take considerable time and to require continuing effort and commitment by everyone involved in the educational process. Figure 3.2 summarizes the historical development of multicultural education as discussed in this and the previous chapters.

The Goals of Multicultural Education

Multicultural education is a reform movement designed to make major curricular and structural changes in the education of students in the elementary and secondary schools and in colleges and universities. Multicultural education theorists believe that many school practices related to race and ethnicity are harmful to students and reinforce many ethnic stereotypes and discriminatory practices in Western societies.

Multicultural education assumes that ethnicity is a salient part of the United States and other Western societies. It also assumes that ethnic diversity is a positive element in a society because it enriches a nation and increases the ways in which its citizens can perceive and solve personal and public problems. Ethnic diversity also enriches a society because it provides individuals with more opportunities to experience other cultures and thus to become more fulfilled as human beings. When individuals are able to participate in a variety of ethnic cultures, they are more able to benefit from the total human experience.

Individuals who know, participate in, and see the world from only their unique cultural and ethnic perspectives are denied important parts of the human experience and are culturally and ethnically encapsulated. Edwin Kiester, Jr., in *The Shortchanged Children of Suburbia*, tells an anecdote about an economically and culturally encapsulated child (Miel with Kiester, 1967, p. 5):

> *The story is told about a little girl in a school near Hollywood who was asked to write a composition about a poor family. The essay began: "This family was very*

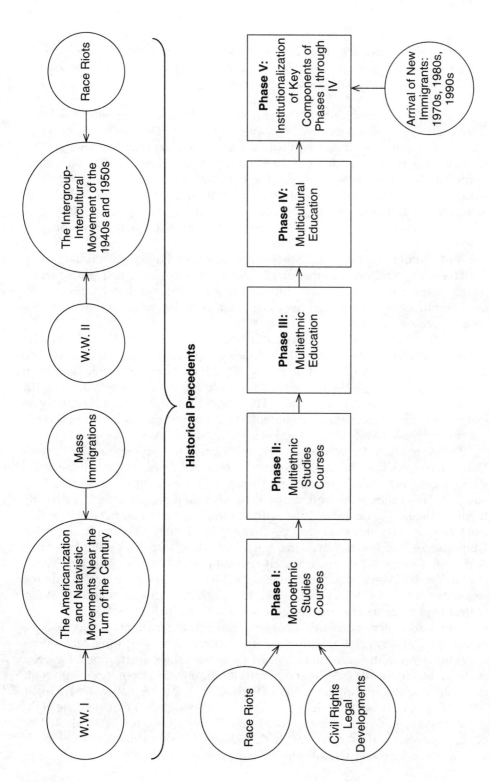

FIGURE 3.2 The Historical Development of Multicultural Education

This figure illustrates the societal and historical forces that resulted in the development of the reforms related to multicultural education.

poor. The Mommy was poor. The Daddy was poor. The brothers and sisters were poor. The maid was poor. The nurse was poor. The butler was poor. The cook was poor. And the chauffeur was poor."

Culturally and ethnically encapsulated individuals are also unable to know fully and to see their own cultures because of their cultural and ethnic blinders. We can get a full view of our own cultures and behaviors only by viewing them from the perspectives of other racial and ethnic cultures. Just as a fish is unable to appreciate the uniqueness of his aquatic environment, so are many mainstream students unable to see and fully appreciate the uniqueness of their cultural characteristics. A key goal of multicultural education is to help individuals gain greater self-understanding by viewing themselves from the perspectives of other cultures.

Multicultural education attempts to acquaint each ethnic and cultural group with the unique cultures of other ethnic groups. It also tries to help ethnic group members see that other ethnic cultures are just as meaningful and valid as their own. Multicultural education assumes that with acquaintance and understanding, respect may follow.

Another major goal of multicultural education is to provide students with cultural and ethnic alternatives. Both the Anglo-American student and the Filipino American student should be provided with cultural and ethnic options in the school. Historically, the U.S. school curriculum has focused primarily on the culture of the Anglo-American child. The school was, and often is, primarily an extension of the Anglo-American student's home and community culture and did not present the student with cultural and ethnic alternatives.

The Anglocentric curriculum, which still exists to varying degrees in most U.S. schools, has harmful consequences for both Anglo-American students and students of color, such as African Americans and Mexican Americans. By teaching Anglo-American students only about their own culture, the school is denying them the richness of the music, literature, values, life-styles, and perspectives that exist among such ethnic groups as African Americans, Puerto Ricans in the United States, and Asian Americans. Anglo-American students should know that African American literature is uniquely enriching, and that groups such as Native Americans and Mexican Americans have values that they may freely embrace. Many of the behaviors and values within these ethnic groups may help White mainstream students to enrich their personal and public lives.

The Anglocentric curriculum negatively affects the student of color because he or she may find the school culture alien, hostile, and self-defeating. Most ethnic minority communities are characterized by some values, institutions, behavior patterns, and linguistic traits that differ in significant ways from those within the dominant society and in the schools (Forbes, 1973; Gay & Baber, 1987; Heath, 1983; Keefe & Padilla, 1987; Philips, 1983; White & Parkham, 1990). Because of the negative ways in which ethnic students and their cultures are often viewed by educators, many of them do not attain the skills they need to function successfully within the wider society (Heath, 1983; Shade, 1989).

One major goal of multicultural education is to provide all students with the skills, attitudes, and knowledge they need to function within their ethnic culture and the mainstream culture, as well as within and across other ethnic cultures. The Anglo-American students should be familiar with Black English; the African American student should be able to speak and write standard English and to function successfully within mainstream U.S. institutions.

Another major goal of multicultural education is to reduce the pain and discrimination members of some ethnic and racial groups experience in the schools and in the wider society because of their unique racial, physical, and cultural characteristics. Groups such as Filipino Americans, Mexican Americans, Asians in the United Kingdom, and Chinese Canadians often deny their ethnic identity, ethnic heritage, and family in order to assimilate and participate more fully in the social, economic, and political institutions of their societies (Rodriguez, 1982). Individuals who are Polish Canadians, Jewish Americans, and Italian Australians also frequently reject parts of their ethnic cultures when trying to succeed in school and in society. As Mildred Dickeman (1973) has insightfully pointed out, schools often force members of these groups to experience "self-alienation" in order to succeed. This is a high price to pay for educational, social, and economic mobility.

When individuals are forced to reject parts of their ethnic cultures in order to experience success, problems are created for both individuals and society. Ethnic peoples of color, such as African Americans and Chinese Canadians, experience special problems because no matter how hard they try to become like Anglos most of them cannot totally succeed because of their skin color.

Some African Americans become very Anglo-Saxon in speech, ways of viewing the world, and in their values and behavior. These individuals become so Anglicized that we might call them "Afro-Saxons." However, such individuals may still be denied jobs or the opportunities to buy homes in all-White neighborhoods because of their skin color. They may also become alienated from their own ethnic communities and families in their attempts to act and be like White mainstream Americans. These individuals may thus become alienated from both their ethnic cultures and the mainstream Anglo culture. Social scientists call such individuals marginal persons.

Individuals who belong to such groups as Jewish Americans and Italian Australians may also experience marginality when they attempt to deny their ethnic heritages and to become Anglo-Americans or Anglo-Australians. Although they can usually succeed in looking and acting like Anglos, they are likely to experience a great deal of psychological stress and identity conflict when they deny and reject family and their ethnic languages, symbols, behaviors, and beliefs (Novak, 1971). Ethnicity plays a cogent role in the socialization of ethnic group members; ethnic characteristics are a part of the basic identity of many individuals. When such individuals deny their ethnic cultures, they are rejecting an important part of self (Klein, 1980).

Marginal ethnic group members are likely to be alienated citizens who feel that they do not have a stake in society. Individuals who deny and/or reject their basic group identity, for whatever reasons, are not capable of becoming fully functioning and self-actualized persons. Such individuals are more likely than other citizens to experience political and social alienation. It is in the best interest of a political democracy to protect the rights of all citizens to maintain allegiances to their ethnic groups and cultural communities (Lynch, 1986, 1989). Research has demonstrated that individuals are quite capable of maintaining allegiance to both their ethnic group and the nation-state (Apter, 1977). Social science research also indicates that individuals have a need for basic group identities, even in highly modernized societies (Isaacs, 1975).

Another important goal of multicultural education is to help students master essential literacy, numeracy, thinking, and perspective-taking skills. Multicultural education assumes that multiethnic content can help students master important skills in these areas. Multiethnic readings and data, if taught effectively, call be highly motivating and meaningful. Students are more likely to master skills when the teacher uses content that deals with significant human problems and issues that relate directly to their lived experiences, identities, hopes, dreams, and struggles. Students are also more likely to master skills when they study content and problems related to the world in which they live. Students in most Western nations live in societies in which ethnic problems are real and salient. Many students live within communities where racial and ethnic tension are salient and are important parts of their lives. Content related to ethnicity in Western societies and to the ethnic communities in which many students live is significant and meaningful to students, especially to those socialized within ethnic communities. Multicultural education theorists believe that skill goals are extremely important.

Cross-Cultural Competency

A key goal of multicultural education is to help students develop cross-cultural competency. However, those of us working in multicultural education have not clarified, in any adequate way, the minimal level of cross-cultural competency we consider appropriate and/or satisfactory for teacher-education students or for elementary and high school students. Nor have we developed valid and reliable ways to assess levels of cross-cultural competency. I think we know what questions to raise about cross-cultural functioning. However, we need to devote considerable time and intellectual energy to resolving these questions.

Is the Anglo-American student, for example, who eats a weekly meal at an authentic Mexican American restaurant and who has no other cross-ethnic contacts during the week functioning cross-culturally? Most of us would probably agree that the act of eating at an ethnic restaurant, in and of itself, is not an instance of meaningful cross-cultural behavior. However, if the Anglo-American student, while eating at the Mexican American restaurant, understands and shares the ethnic symbols in the restaurant, speaks Spanish while in the restaurant, and communicates and interacts positively and comfortably with individuals within the restaurant who are culturally Mexican American, then he or she would be functioning cross-culturally at a meaningful level.

Levels of Cross-Cultural Functioning

I have developed a typology that conceptualizes levels of cross-cultural functioning. Educators need to determine which of these levels are desirable and practical for most students to attain. The typology is presented in Figure 3.3.

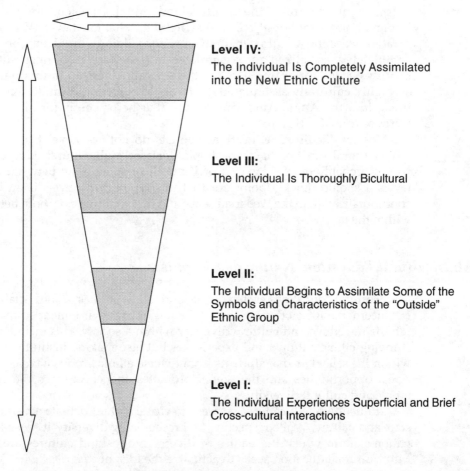

Level IV:
The Individual Is Completely Assimilated into the New Ethnic Culture

Level III:
The Individual Is Thoroughly Bicultural

Level II:
The Individual Begins to Assimilate Some of the Symbols and Characteristics of the "Outside" Ethnic Group

Level I:
The Individual Experiences Superficial and Brief Cross-cultural Interactions

FIGURE 3.3 Levels of Cross-Cultural Functioning

This figure presents a conceptualization of levels of cross-cultural competency. Cross-cultural functioning can range from Level I (brief and superficial contacts with another ethnic culture) to Level IV (in which the individual totally culturally assimilates into a new ethnic culture and consequently becomes alienated from his or her own ethnic culture).

Level I of cross-cultural functioning consists primarily of superficial and brief cross-cultural encounters, such as eating occasionally at a Chinese American restaurant or speaking to the Jewish neighbor who lives across the street when you meet her in the street. Level II of cross-cultural functioning occurs when the individual begins to have more meaningful cross-cultural contacts and communications with members of other ethnic and cultural groups. He or she begins to assimilate some of the symbols, linguistic traits, communication styles, values, and attitudes that are normative within the outside cultural group. Level III of cross-cultural functioning occurs when the individual is thoroughly bicultural and is as comfortable within the adopted culture as he or she is within his or her primordial or first culture. Each of the two cultures is equally meaningful to the bicultural individual. The bicultural individual is bilingual and is adept at cultural-switching behavior. Level IV of cross-cultural functioning occurs when the primordial individual has been almost completely resocialized and assimilated into the foreign or host culture. This process occurs, for example, when the African American individual becomes so highly culturally assimilated (in terms of behavior, attitudes, and perceptions) into the Anglo-American culture that he or she is for all sociological purposes an Afro-Saxon.

Most multicultural education theorists do not see Level I or Level IV of cross-cultural functioning as desirable goals of multicultural education. Most would probably opt for Level II or Level III or some point between these two levels. I should quickly point out that this typology of levels is an ideal-type conceptualization in the Weberian sense and that continua exist both between and within the levels.

Multicultural Education: Nature and Promises

Multicultural education reaches far beyond ethnic studies or the social studies. It is concerned with modifying the total educational environment so that it better reflects the ethnic and cultural diversity within a society. This includes not only studying ethnic cultures and experiences but also making institutional changes within the school so that students from diverse ethnic groups have equal educational opportunities and the school promotes and encourages the concept of ethnic and cultural diversity.

Multicultural education also seeks to create and perpetuate a unified nation-state and culture. While respecting and recognizing diversity, it seeks to create a nation-state in which the values of diverse groups and cultures are reflected. Multicultural education seeks to actualize the idea of *e pluribus unum*, that is, to create a society of diverse people united within a framework of overarching democratic values. The best way to create a unified nation-state in which all groups have strong national identities and allegiances is to structurally include them into the nation-state and the society.

Multicultural education is designed for all students, of all races, ethnic groups, and social classes, and not just for schools that have racially and ethnically mixed populations. A major assumption made by multiculturalists is that multicultural education is needed as much if not more by students who are middle-class members of the dominant, mainstream group as it is by marginalized students of color.

Because multicultural education is a very broad concept that implies total school reform, educators who want their schools to become multicultural must examine their total school environment to determine the extent to which it is monoethnic and promotes dominant group hegemony. They then must take appropriate steps to create and sustain a multicultural educational environment. The ethnic and racial composition of the school staff, its attitudes, the formalized and hidden curricula, the teaching strategies and materials, the testing and counseling programs, and the school's norms are some of the factors that must reflect ethnic diversity within the multicultural school. Figure 3.4 illustrates these and other variables of the school environment that must be reformed in order to make the school multicultural.

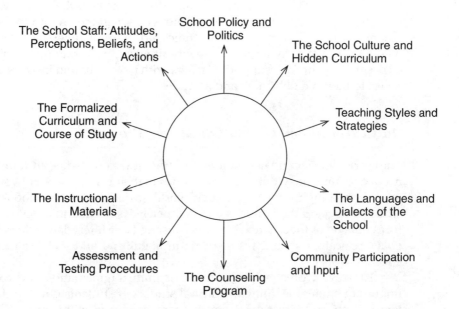

FIGURE 3.4   The Total School Environment

In this figure, the total school environment is conceptualized as a system that consists of a number of major identifiable variables and factors, such as the school culture, school policy and politics, and the formalized curriculum and course of study. In the idealized multicultural school, each variable reflects ethnic pluralism. Even though any one factor may be the focus of initial school reform, changes must take place in each factor in order to create and sustain an effective multicultural educational environment.

The reform must be system-wide or systemic to be effective. Multicultural education is consistent with the notion of *systems thinking* discussed by Senge (1990). To implement multicultural education effectively, the school, college, or university must be conceptualized as a system with highly interrelated components and elements. Each part interacts with and affects the others. Consequently, a change in any one element in the system affects all of the other elements.

Any one of the factors in Figure 3.4 may be the initial focus for school reform, but changes must take place in all of the major school variables in order for multicultural education to be successfully implemented. We learned from the ethnic studies movement of the 1960s that few substantial changes take place when you simply give teachers multicultural materials but do not provide educational opportunities that enable them to acquire new conceptual frameworks for viewing Western society and culture.

The unit of change must be the total school environment rather than any one element, such as materials, teaching strategies, the testing program, or teacher training. Teacher education and empowerment are essential, but other changes must take place in the school environment in order to reform the school. Many teachers attain new insights, materials, and multicultural teaching strategies during summer workshops. They are eager to try them in their schools. However, these teachers often become very discouraged when they return to their schools, where traditional norms toward ethnic and cultural diversity often exist and where they frequently receive no institutional support from their administrators or peers. Without such support, teachers with new skills and insights give up and revert to their old behaviors and attitudes.

Linking Multicultural and Global Education: Promises

The curriculum should help students develop the knowledge, attitudes, and skills needed to function within various cultures in their own society. However, because we live in a highly interdependent world society, the school should also help students develop the attitudes and competencies needed to function within cultures outside of their nation-state. Because of their interrelationships and shared goals, educators should try to relate multicultural and global education more effectively.

A linkage would help reduce curriculum fragmentation and contribute to important student learning in cultural studies. If students develop the ability to view events and situations from the perspectives of ethnic groups in their nation-state, they will be better able to view events within other nations from the perspectives of the major participants in these events. Students who are able to relate positively to and function within a variety of cultures within their own nation are also more likely to function successfully in foreign cultures than are individuals who view domestic ethnic cultures as exotic and strange. We can reduce nonreflective nationalism and ethnocentrism in students by helping them become more ethnically literate and competent citizens in their nation-state.

Linking Multicultural and Global Education: Problems

We should attempt to link and relate multicultural and global education even though each reform movement has unique characteristics that should be respected and maintained in any linkage efforts. We should not assume that multicultural education and global education are identical. This assumption would create new problems and intensify existing ones. Some educators confuse studying about the countries of origin of ethnic groups with the study of these groups in their nation-states. They assume, for example, that when they are teaching about Mexico they are teaching about Mexican Americans.

Other teachers ignore domestic ethnic groups and teach only about their original homelands. Some U.S. teachers are more comfortable teaching about Mexicans who live in Mexico or about Africans than they are teaching about Mexican Americans or African Americans who live in their own communities. They will therefore teach about Mexico and Africa but will rarely teach content related to Mexican Americans and African Americans. Teaching about distant lands is apparently less threatening to some teachers than is teaching about ethnic cultures, problems, and conflicts within their own community. Special ways to solve this problem should be discussed in any attempts to link multicultural and global education.

Even though multicultural and global education should be joined and related, each reform movement has unique contributions to make to the liberal education of students and to educating them for freedom. These unique qualities should be maintained and recognized in any linkage attempts. Ethnic minority cultures within a nation should not be confused with national cultures in other nations.

Linking Multicultural and Global Education by Helping Students Develop Interrelated Identifications

Despite some problems that may emerge, linking multicultural and global education can result in important learning outcomes if proper precautions are taken. Multicultural and global education are related because of the similarity in the skills, attitudes, and behaviors that both reform movements are trying to help students develop. Both multicultural and global education have as major goals helping students develop *cross-cultural competency* (the knowledge, attitudes, and skills needed to function in diverse cultural settings) and helping students develop the ability to view events, situations, and problems from the perspectives of different ethnic and nationality groups.

Multicultural and global education are related in still another important way: students can develop clarified and reflective global identifications only after they have developed clarified and reflective *ethnic* and *national* identifications. The remainder of this chapter discusses the need for the school curriculum to help students develop three interrelated identifications: *ethnic, national,* and *global.*

Ethnic, National, and Global Identification

Identification is "a social-psychological process involving the assimilation and internalization of the values, standards, expectations, or social roles of another person or persons . . . into one's behavior and self-conception" (Theodorson & Theodorson, 1969, pp. 194–195). When an individual develops an identification with a particular group, he or she "internalizes the interests, standards, and role expectations of the group (Theodorson & Theodorson, 1969, p. 195)." Identification is an evolving, dynamic, complex, and ongoing process and not a static or unidimensional conceptualization. All individuals belong to many different groups and consequently develop multiple group identifications. Students have a gender identification, a family identification, a racial identification, as well as identifications with many other formal and informal groups.

A major assumption of this chapter is that all students come to school with ethnic identifications, whether the identifications are conscious or unconscious. Many Anglo-American students are consciously aware of their national identifications as *Americans* but are not consciously aware that they have internalized the values, standards, norms, and behaviors of the Anglo-American ethnic group (Alba, 1990). Students who are African Americans, Jewish Americans, Mexican Americans, and Italian Americans are usually consciously aware of both their ethnic and national identifications. However, many students from all ethnic groups come to school with confused, unexamined, and nonreflective ethnic and national identifications and with almost no global identification or consciousness.

Identity is a concept that relates to all that we are. Societal quests for single, narrow definitions of nationalism have prevented many students from getting in touch with that dimension of their identity that relates to ethnicity. Ethnic identification for many students is a very important part of their personal identity. The individual who has a confused, nonreflective, or negative ethnic identification lacks one of the essential ingredients for a healthy and positive personal identity.

The school should help students develop three kinds of highly interrelated identifications that are of special concern to multicultural educators: an *ethnic*, a *national*, and a *global* identification. These identifications should be *clarified*, *reflective*, and *positive*. Individuals who have *clarified* and *reflective* ethnic, national, and global identifications understand how these identifications developed, are able to examine their ethnic group, nation, and world thoughtfully and objectively and to understand both the personal and public implications of these identifications.

Individuals who have *positive* ethnic, national, and global identifications evaluate their ethnic, national, and global communities highly and are proud of these identifications. They have both the desire and competencies needed to take actions that will support and reinforce the values and norms of their ethnic, national, and global communities. Consequently, the school should not only be concerned about helping students develop reflective ethnic, national, and global identifications, but it should also help them acquire the cross-cultural competencies (which consist of knowledge, attitudes, and skills) needed to function effectively within their ethnic, national, and world communities.

Ethnic Identification

The school within a pluralistic democratic nation should help ethnic students develop clarified, reflective, and positive ethnic identifications. This does not mean that the school should encourage or force ethnic minority students who have identifications with the mainstream ethnic group or who have identifications with several ethnic groups to give up these identifications. However, it does mean that the school will help all students develop an understanding of their ethnic group identifications, objectively examine their ethnic groups, better understand the relationship between their ethnic groups and other ethnic groups, and learn the personal and public implications of their ethnic group identifications and attachments.

A positive and clarified ethnic identification is of primary importance to students beginning in their first years of life. However, rather than help students develop positive and reflective ethnic identifications, historically the school and other social institutions have taught ethnic minority students to be ashamed of their ethnic affiliations and characteristics (Greenbaum, 1974). Social and public institutions have forced many individuals who are Polish Americans, Italian Australian, and Jewish Canadian to experience self-alienation and desocialization and to reject family heritages and cultures. Many members of these ethnic groups have denied important aspects of their ethnic cultures and changed their names in order to attain full participation within their society. Many ethnic individuals consciously denied their family heritages in order to attain social, economic, and educational mobility. However, within a pluralistic democratic society individuals should not have to give up all of their meaningful ethnic traits and attachments in order to attain structural inclusion into society. In democratic, pluralistic nation-states, individuals should be free to publicly affirm their ethnic, cultural, and gender identities.

National Identification

The school should also help each student acquire a clarified, reflective, and positive national identification and related cross-cultural competencies. Each student should develop a commitment to national democratic ideals, such as human dignity, justice, and equality. The school should also help students acquire the attitudes, beliefs, and skills they need to become effective participants in the nation-state and the civic culture. Thus, the development of social participation skills and activities should be major goals of the school curriculum within a democratic pluralistic nation. Students should be provided opportunities for social participation activities whereby they can take action on issues and problems that are consistent with democratic values. Citizenship education and social participation activities are integral parts of a sound school curriculum.

National identification and related citizenship competencies are important for all citizens, regardless of their ethnic group membership and ethnic affiliations. National identification should be acknowledged and promoted in all educational programs related to ethnicity and education. However, individuals can have a wide range of cultural and linguistic traits and characteristics and still be reflective and effective citizens of their nation-states.

Individuals can have ethnic allegiances and characteristics and yet endorse overarching and shared national values and ideals as long as their ethnic values and behaviors do not violate or contradict democratic values and ideals. Educational programs should recognize and reflect the multiple identifications students are developing. I believe students can develop a reflective and positive national identification only after they have attained reflective, clarified, and positive ethnic identifications. This is as true for Anglo-American students as it is for Jewish American, African American, or Italian American students. Often, mainstream individuals do not view themselves as an ethnic group. However, sociologically they have many of the same traits and characteristics of other ethnic groups, such as a sense of peoplehood, unique behavioral values and norms, and unique ways of perceiving the world (Alba, 1990; Gordon, 1964).

Mainstream students who believe that their ethnic group is superior to other ethnic groups and who have highly ethnocentric and racist attitudes do not have clarified, reflective, and positive ethnic identifications. Their ethnic identifications are based on the negative characteristics of other ethnic groups and have not been reflectively and objectively examined. Many mainstream and other ethnic individuals have ethnic identifications that are nonreflective and unclarified. It is not possible for students with unreflective and totally subjective ethnic identifications to develop positive and reflective national identifications because ethnic ethnocentrism is inconsistent with such democratic values as human dignity, freedom, equality, and justice.

Ethnic group individuals who have historically been victims of discrimination must develop positive and reflective ethnic identifications before they will be able to develop clarified national identifications. It is difficult for Polish American, Jewish Australian, or Metis students to support the rights of other ethnic groups or the ideals of the nation-state when they are ashamed of their own ethnicity or feel their ethnic group is denied basic civil rights and opportunities.

Global Identification

It is essential that we help students to develop clarified, reflective, and positive ethnic and national identifications. However, because we live in a global society in which the solutions to the world's problems require the cooperation of all the nations of the world, it is also important for students to develop global identifications and the knowledge, attitudes, and skills needed to become effective and influential citizens in the world community (Anderson, 1990; Lamy, 1990; Tye, 1990). Most students have rather conscious identifications with their communities and nation-states, but they often are only vaguely aware of their status as world citizens. Most students do not have a comprehensive understanding of the full implications of their world citizenship.

There are many complex reasons that most students often have little awareness or understanding of their status as world citizens and rarely think of themselves as citizens of the world (Banks, 1983). This lack of awareness results partly from the fact that most nation-states focus on helping students to develop nationalism rather than to understand their role as citizens of the world. The teaching of nationalism often results in students' learning misconceptions, stereotypes, and myths about other nations and acquiring negative and confused attitudes toward them.

Students also have limited awareness of their roles as world citizens because of the nature of the world community itself. The institutions that attempt to formulate policies for the international community or for groups of nations—such as the United Nations, the Organization of African Unity, and the Organization of American States—are usually weak because of their inability to enforce their policies and recommendations, because of the strong nationalism manifested by their members, and because the international community does not have an effectively mobilized and politically efficacious constituency. Strong nationalism makes most international bodies weak and largely symbolic.

Students find it difficult to view themselves as members of an international community not only because such a community lacks effective governmental bodies, but also because very few heroes or heroines, myths, symbols, and school rituals are designed to help students develop an attachment to and identification with the global community. It is difficult for students to develop identifications with a community that does not have heroes, heroines, and rituals in which they can participate and benefits that can be identified, seen, and touched. We thus must identify and/or create international heroes, heroines, and school rituals to help students develop global attachments and identifications.

When educators attempt to help students develop more sophisticated international understanding and identification, they often experience complex problems. It is difficult to gain public support for programs in international education because many parents view global education as an attempt to weaken national loyalty and undercut nationalism. Many teachers are likely to view global education as an add-on to an already crowded curriculum and thus to assign it a low priority. Some teachers, like many of their students, have misconceptions about and negative attitudes toward other nations that they are likely to perpetuate in the classroom.

Goals for Global Education

When formulating goals and teaching strategies for global education, educators should be aware of the societal and instructional constraints. However, they should realize that it is vitally important for students to develop a sophisticated understanding of their roles in the world community (Anderson, 1990). Students should also understand how life in their communities influences other nations and the cogent influences that international events have on their daily lives. Global education should have as major goals helping students develop an understanding of the interdependence among nations in the modern world, clarified attitudes toward other nations, and a reflective identification with the world community. This latter task is likely to be especially difficult because of the highly ambiguous nature of the international community and the tight national boundaries that exist throughout the world.

The Need for a Delicate Balance of Identifications

Strong nationalism that is nonreflective will prevent students from developing reflective and positive global identifications. Nonreflective and unexamined ethnic identifications and attachments may prevent the development of a cohesive nation and a unified national ideology. Thus, while we should help students to develop reflective and positive ethnic identifications, we must also help them to clarify and strengthen their national identifications—which means that they will develop and internalize such democratic values as justice, human dignity, and equality.

Students need to develop a delicate balance of ethnic, national, and global identifications and attachments. In the past, however, educators have often tried to develop strong national identifications by repressing ethnicity and making ethnic students ashamed of their ethnic roots and families. Schools taught ethnic youths shame, as William Greenbaum (1974) has compassionately written. This is an unhealthy and dysfunctional approach to building national solidarity and reflective nationalism and to shaping a nation in which all of its citizens endorse its overarching values such as democracy and human dignity and yet maintain a sense of ethnic pride and identification.

I hypothesize that ethnic, national, and global identifications are developmental in nature and that an individual can attain a healthy and reflective national identification only when he or she has acquired a healthy and reflective ethnic identification; and that individuals can develop a reflective and positive global identification only after they have a realistic, reflective, and positive national identification. (See Figure 3.5.)

Individuals can develop a commitment to and an identification with a nation-state and the national culture only when they believe that they are a meaningful and important part of that nation and that it acknowledges, reflects, and values their culture and them as individuals. A nation that alienates and does not meaningfully and structurally include an ethnic group into the national culture runs the risk of creating alienation within that ethnic group and of fostering separatism and separatist movements and ideologies (Vallee, Schwartz, & Darkness, 1971). Students will find it very difficult if not impossible to develop reflective global identifications within a nation-state that perpetuates a nonreflective and blind nationalism.

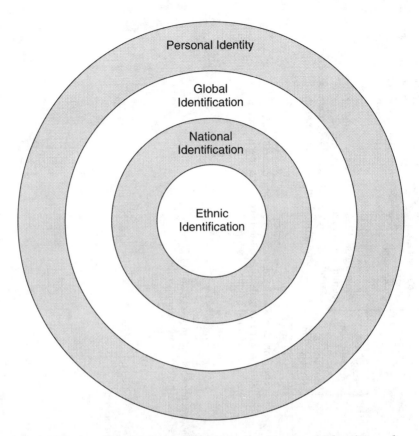

FIGURE 3.5   The Relationship between Personal Identity and Ethnic, National, and Global Identifications

Personal identity is the "I" that results from the lifelong binding together of the many threads of a person's life. These threads include experience, culture, and heredity, as well as identifications with significant others and many different groups, such as one's ethnic group, one's nation, and the global community.

The Expanding Identification of Ethnic Youths: A Typology

A typology of the stages of ethnicity that describes the developmental nature of ethnic, national, and global identifications and clarification is presented in Chapter 12. This typology assumes that individuals can be classified according to their ethnic identification and development. This typology, as summarized in Figure 3.6, illustrates the hypothesis that students must have clarified and positive ethnic identifications (Stage 3) before they can attain clarified and reflective national and global identifications (Stages 5 and 6).

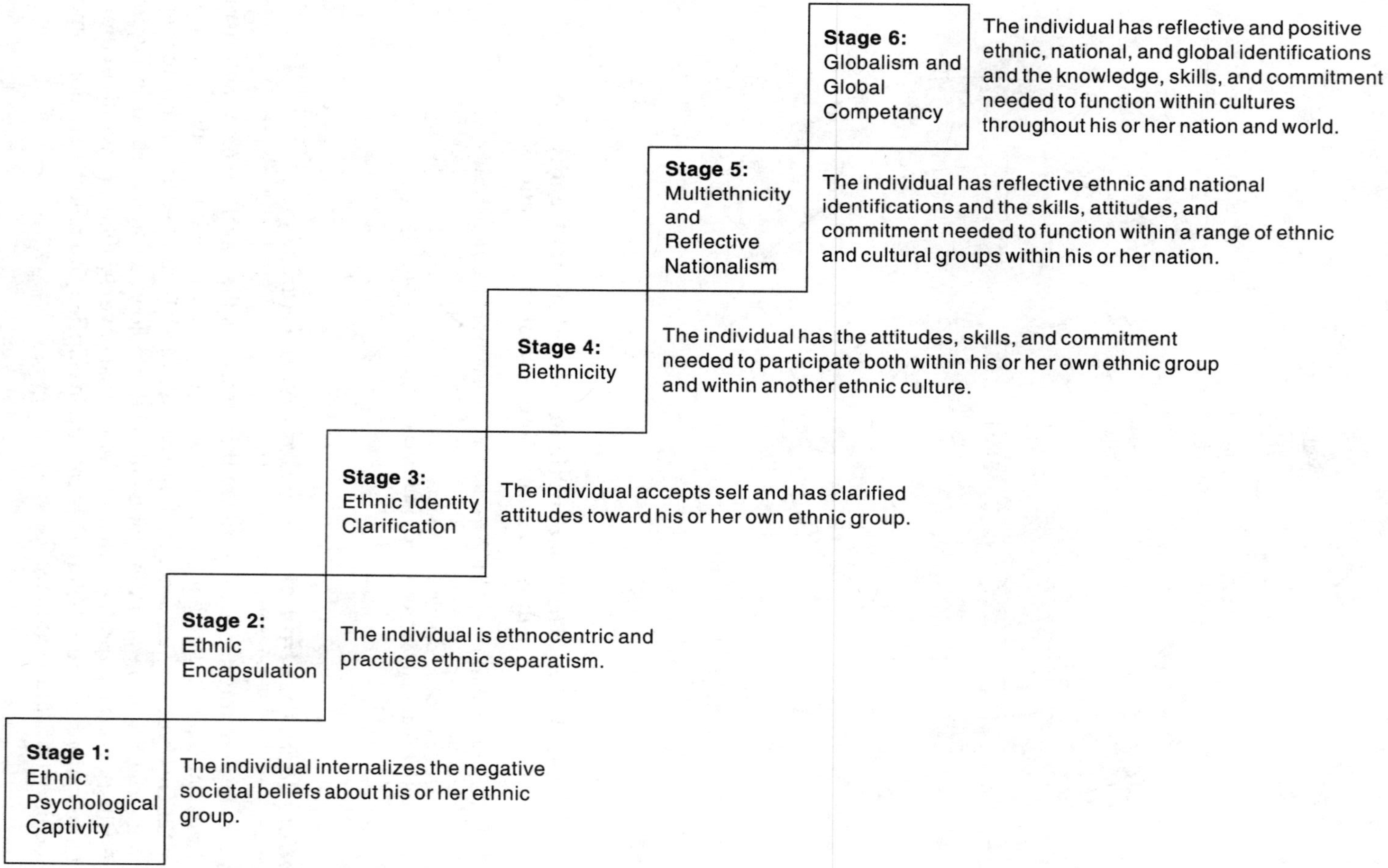

FIGURE 3.6 The Expanding Identifications of Ethnic Youths: A Typology

This figure illustrates the author's hypothesis that students must have clarified and positive ethnic identifications (Stage 3) before they can attain reflective and positive national and global identifications (Stages 5 and 6).

Stage 1:
Ethnic
Psychological
Captivity

The individual internalizes the negative societal beliefs about his or her ethnic group.

Stage 2:
Ethnic
Encapsulation

The individual is ethnocentric and practices ethnic separatism.

Stage 3:
Ethnic Identity
Clarification

The individual accepts self and has clarified attitudes toward his or her own ethnic group.

Stage 4:
Biethnicity

The individual has the attitudes, skills, and commitment needed to participate both within his or her own ethnic group and within another ethnic culture.

Stage 5:
Multiethnicity
and
Reflective
Nationalism

The individual has reflective ethnic and national identifications and the skills, attitudes, and commitment needed to function within a range of ethnic and cultural groups within his or her nation.

Stage 6:
Globalism and
Global
Competency

The individual has reflective and positive ethnic, national, and global identifications and the knowledge, skills, and commitment needed to function within cultures throughout his or her nation and world.

Multicultural Education and Educational Reform

Changing the school so that it reflects the ethnic diversity within a society provides a tremendous opportunity to implement the substantial curriculum reforms that are essential, such as conceptual teaching, interdisciplinary approaches to the study of social issues, value inquiry, and providing students with opportunities to become involved in social action and social participation activities. Thus, multicultural education can serve as a vehicle for general and significant educational reform. This is probably its greatest promise. We can best view multicultural education as a process as well as a reform movement that will result in a new type of schooling that will present novel views of the Western experience and will help students to acquire the knowledge, skills, and commitments needed to make their societies and the world more responsive to the human condition.

Summary

Multicultural education has had an evolutionary development in the United States and in the other major Western nations, such as the United Kingdom, Canada, Australia, France, and Sweden (Banks & Lynch, 1986; Bullivant, 1987; Eldering & Kloprogge, 1989) The development of multicultural education since the 1960s can be conceptualized in the five phases presented in this chapter. This chapter also describes major goals for multicultural education, including (1) helping students gain a greater self-understanding by viewing their cultures from the perspectives of other ethnic groups; (2) providing students with cultural and ethnic alternatives; (3) helping students attain cross-cultural competency; (4) helping students master essential literacy, numeracy, and thinking skills; and (5) helping students to develop clarified and reflective ethnic, national, and global identifications.

Educators should attempt to link and relate multicultural and global education because of the common goals these two educational reform movements are trying to help students attain and because of the widespread fragmentation in the school curriculum. Because both multicultural and global education have unique contributions to make to the general education of students and because they are in many ways distinct, efforts made to link multicultural and global education should maintain the uniqueness of each reform movement. Educators should also take special precautions to assure that domestic ethnic cultures in a nation are not confused with the cultures of nations that are the original homelands of ethnic groups.

During their socialization, students develop multiple group identifications. The school should help students develop three kinds of identifications that are of special concern to multicultural educators: an *ethnic*, a *national*, and a *global* identification.

Multicultural education includes but is much more comprehensive than ethnic studies or curriculum reform related to ethnicity. Multicultural education is concerned with modifying the total school environment so that students from diverse ethnic and cultural groups will experience equal educational opportunities. Educators must reform their total educational environments in order to implement comprehensive multicultural education.

References

Alba, R. D. (1990). *Ethnic Identity: The Transformation of White America.* New Haven: Yale University Press.

Anderson, L. (1990). A Rationale for Global Education. In K. A. Tye (Ed.), *Global Education: From Thought to Action* (pp. 13–34). Arlington, VA: Association for Supervision and Curriculum Development.

Apter, D. E. (1977). Political Life and Cultural Pluralism. In M. M. Tumin & W. Plotch (Eds.), *Pluralism in a Democratic Society* (pp. 58–91). New York: Praeger.

Baker, G. C. (1983). *Planning and Organizing for Multicultural Instruction.* Menlo Park, CA: Addison-Wesley.

Banks, J. A. (1983). Cultural Democracy, Citizenship Education, and the American Dream. National Council for the Social Studies Presidential Address. *Social Education, 47,* 178–179, ff. 222–232.

Banks, J. A., & Banks, C. A. M. (Eds.). (1993). *Multicultural Education: Issues and Perspectives* (2nd ed.). Boston: Allyn and Bacon.

Banks, J. A., & Lynch, J. (Eds.). (1986). *Multicultural Education in Western Societies.* London: Cassell.

Bullivant, B. (1981). *The Pluralist Dilemma in Education: Six Case Studies.* London: George Allen & Unwin.

Bullivant, B. (1987). *The Ethnic Encounter in the Secondary School.* New York: Falmer Press.

Dickeman, M. (1973). Teaching Cultural Pluralism. In J. A. Banks (Ed.), *Teaching Ethnic Studies: Concepts and Strategies* (pp. 5–25). Washington, DC.: National Council for the Social Studies.

Eldering, L., & Kloprogge, J. (Ed.). (1989). *Different Cultures, Same School: Ethnic Minority Children in Europe.* Berwyn, PA: Swets North America.

Encel, S. (1981). *The Ethnic Dimension: Papers on Ethnicity and Pluralism by Jean Martin.* London: George Allen & Unwin.

Forbes, J. D. (1973). Teaching Native American Values and Cultures. In J. A. Banks (Ed.), *Teaching Ethnic Studies: Concepts and Strategies* (pp. 201–225). Washington, DC: National Council for the Social Studies.

Gay, G. (1983). Multiethnic Education: Historical Development and Future Prospects. *Phi Delta Kappan, 64,* 560–563.

Gay, G., & Baber, W. L. (Eds.). (1987). *Expressively Black: The Cultural Basis of Ethnic Identity.* New York: Praeger.

Gordon, M. M. (1964). *Assimilation in American Life: The Role of Race, Religion, and National Origins.* New York: Oxford University Press.

Grant, C. A., & Sleeter, C. E. (1986). Race, Class, and Gender in Education Research: An Argument for Integrative Analysis. *Review of Educational Research, 56,* 195–211.

Greenbaum, W. (1974). America in Search of a New Ideal: An Essay on the Rise of Pluralism. *Harvard Educational Review, 44,* 411–440.

Hakuta, K. (1990). *Bilingualism and Bilingual Education: A Research Perspective.* Occasional Papers in Bilingual Education, No. 3. Washington, DC: National Clearinghouse for Bilingual Education and the Center for Applied Linguistics.

Heath, S. B. (1983). *Ways with Words: Language, Life and Work in Communities and Classrooms.* New York: Cambridge University Press.

Hernandez, H. (1989). *Multicultural Education: A Teacher's Guide to Instruction.* Columbus, OH: Merrill.

Isaacs, H. R. (1975). Basic Group Identity: The Idols of the Tribe. In N. Glazer and D. P.

Moynihan (Eds.), *Ethnicity: Theory and Experience* (pp. 29–52). Cambridge, MA: Harvard University Press.

Keefe, S. E., & Padilla, A. M. (1987). *Chicano Ethnicity.* Albuquerque: University of New Mexico Press.

Klein, J. W. (1980). *Jewish Identity and Self-Esteem: Healing Wounds through Ethnotherapy.* New York: American Jewish Committee.

Kleinfeld, J. (1975). Effective Teachers of Eskimo and Indian Students. *School Review, 83,* 301–344.

Krashen, S. D. (1991). *Bilingual Education: A Focus on Current Research.* Occasional Papers in Bilingual Education, No. 3. Washington, DC: National Clearinghouse for Bilingual Education and the Center for Applied Linguistics.

Lamy, S. L. (1990). Global Education: A Conflict of Images. In K. A. Tye (Ed.), *Global Education: From Thought to Action* (pp. 49–63). Arlington, VA: Association for Supervision and Curriculum Development.

Lynch, J. (1986). Multicultural Education: Agenda for Change. In J. A. Banks and J. Lynch (Eds.), *Multicultural Education in Western Societies* (pp. 178–195). London: Cassell.

Lynch, J. (1989). *Multicultural Education in a Global Society.* New York: The Falmer Press.

Miel, A., with Kiester, E., Jr. (1967). *The Shortchanged Children of Suburbia.* New York: American Jewish Committee.

National Council for Accreditation of Teacher Education. (1987). *Standards, Procedures, and Policies for the Accreditation of Professional Education Units.* Washington, DC: Author.

Novak, M. (1971). *The Rise of the Unmeltable Ethnics.* New York: Macmillan.

Oakes, J. (1985). *Keeping Track: How Schools Structure Inequality.* New Haven: Yale University Press.

Ovando, C. J., & Collier, V. P. (1985). *Bilingual and ESL Classrooms: Teaching in Multicultural Contexts.* New York: McGraw-Hill.

Philips, S. U. (1983). *The Invisible Culture: Communication in Classroom and Community on the Warm Spring Indian Reservation.* New York: Longman.

Rist, R. C. (1970). Student Social Class and Teacher Expectations: The Self-Fulfilling Prophecy in Ghetto Education. *Harvard Educational Review, 40,* 411–451.

Rodriguez, R. (1982). *Hunger of Memory: The Education of Richard Rodriguez.* Boston: David Godine.

Senge, P. M. (1990). *The Fifth Discipline: The Art and Practice of the Learning Organization.* New York: Doubleday/Currency.

Shade, B. J. R. (Ed.). (1989). *Culture, Style and the Educative Process.* Springfield, IL: Charles C Thomas.

Sleeter, C. E., & Grant, C. A. (1988). *Making Choices for Multicultural Education: Five Approaches to Race, Class and Gender.* Columbus, OH: Merrill.

Theodorson, G. A., & Theodorson, A. G. (1969). *A Modern Dictionary of Sociology.* New York: Barnes and Noble Books.

Tye, K. A. (Ed.). (1990). *Global Education: From Thought to Action.* Alexandria, VA: Association for Supervision and Curriculum Development.

Vallee, F. G., Schwartz, M., & Darkness, F. (1971). Ethnic Assimilation and Differentiation in Canada. In B. R. Blishen, F. E. Jones, K. D. Naegele, & J. Porter (Eds.), *Canadian Society: Sociological Perspectives* (3rd ed.) (pp. 390–400). Toronto: Macmillan of Canada.

White, J. L., & Parham, N. (1990). *The Psychology of Blacks: An Afro-American Perspective* (2nd ed.). Englewood Cliffs, NJ.: Prentice-Hall.

Part **II**

Conceptual and Philosophical Issues

Chapter 4
The Complex Nature of Ethnic Groups in Modern Societies

Chapter 5
Culture, Ethnicity, and Education

Chapter 6
Race, Ethnicity, and Educational Paradigms

Chapter 7
Pluralism, Ideology, and Educational Reform

Part II discusses and analyzes some of the major conceptual and philosophical issues and problems related to education and ethnic diversity. It is necessary to formulate precise and valid concepts and to formulate sound philosophical beliefs and positions before effective educational programs related to ethnic and cultural diversity can be implemented. The four chapters in Part II are interrelated by a focus on important conceptual and philosophical issues and their policy and programmatic implications.

Chapter 4 describes the major characteristics of ethnic groups in modernized Western societies and presents a typology for defining and classifying ethnic groups. The United States is used as a case study to describe the salient characteristics of ethnic groups in modernized Western societies. The major concepts related to ethnic and cultural diversity, such as culture, ethnic group, and multicultural education, are described in Chapter 5. The components of culture identified in this chapter are essential for understanding the complex aspects of race, ethnicity, and culture in modernized societies. Chapter 6 presents major paradigms related to race and ethnic diversity that have developed in various Western nation-states.

Chapter 7 describes and clarifies the major philosophical issues and concepts related to education and ethnic diversity. Educators and social scientists with divergent and conflicting ideological positions are recommending a range of educational programs and practices. This chapter presents a typology for classifying ideologies related to ethnicity and schooling and proposes a multicultural ideology to guide educational reform in schools, colleges, and universities. The multicultural ideology is derived by analyzing the nature of ethnic group relations in a modernized democratic society—the United States—and by conceptualizing goals that will enhance cross-cultural competency and interaction.

Chapter 4

The Complex Nature of Ethnic Groups in Modern Societies

During the 1940s and 1950s social scientists predicted that ethnic groups would fade from modernized societies as the people in these groups became culturally assimilated and acculturated. The Black civil rights movement of the 1960s in the United States and the consequent ethnic revival movements in the United States and other parts of the world contravened the predictions of social scientists and indicated that ethnic groups were important parts of modernized pluralistic societies. Ethnic group affiliations and identifications are complex social, political, and psychological processes in modernized societies. Concepts and theories formulated before the 1960s do not adequately describe them (Glazer & Moynihan, 1975; Park, 1950; Wirth, 1945).

This chapter, using ethnic groups in the United States as a case study, describes some of the major characteristics of ethnic groups in modernized societies. Even though the specifics of this chapter are not generalizable to other societies, many of the salient characteristics of ethnic groups in the United States are similar to those of ethnic groups in other Western societies, such as Australia, Canada, and the United Kingdom (Bullivant, 1981; Krauter & Davis, 1978; Watson, 1977; Wilton & Bosworth, 1984).

The final part of this chapter describes a typology for defining and classifying ethnic groups that is consistent with their complex and dynamic characteristics in modernized societies.

Ethnicity in U.S. Society

Ethnicity is a cogent factor in U.S. history, life, and culture. The expressions and manifestations of ethnicity vary with the characteristics of the ethnic group, the nature of its societal experiences, and the sociopolitical climate. Expressions of ethnicity are also related to the ways in which the dominant group responds to various immigrant and immigrant descendant groups, to the objectives that ethnic groups wish to achieve, and to the events that serve as the catalysts for revitalization movements (Franklin, 1991; Glazer & Moyhihan, 1975; Portes & Rumbaut, 1990; Smith, 1981; Sowell, 1981).

Individuals and groups in the United States have often been denied cultural, political, and economic opportunities because of their ethnic group characteristics and their expressions of them. By the beginning of the 1800s, Anglo-Saxon immigrants and their descendants were the most powerful and influential ethnic group in the United States. English cultural traits, values, and behavioral patterns were widespread in colonial America. The English were also strongly committed to Americanizing (Anglicizing) all other immigrant groups, as well as to civilizing (according to the Anglo-Saxon definition of *civilization*) African Americans and various groups of Native Americans.

Through the control of the major social, economic, and political institutions, the English denied to ethnic groups who differed from themselves opportunities to participate fully in the decision-making processes. Only peoples who were culturally and racially like Anglo-Saxons received unqualified rights to total societal participation and social acceptance. Thus, groups such as the French Huguenots, the Germans, the Irish, and the Scotch Irish were victims of much discrimination in colonial America. Southern and Eastern European immigrants, such as the Greeks, the Italians, the Slavs, and the Poles, who came to the United States in massive numbers in the late nineteenth century and the first decades of the twentieth century, were denied total societal participation (Fredrickson & Knobel, 1980; Higham, 1972). Both the original English and the converted Anglo-Saxons saw these new arrivals as ethnically different from themselves and thus undeserving of social acceptance and access to the social, economic, and political systems (Portes & Rumbaut, 1990).

The Assimilation and Inclusion of White Ethnic Groups

Early in America's history, assimilation, or adherence to Anglo-Saxon sociocultural traditions and values, became a prerequisite to social acceptability and access to the political structure. Although in the beginning European immigrants tried desperately to establish and maintain European life-styles and institutions on American soil (Jones, 1960), their efforts were largely doomed because the English controlled the economic and political systems. The English used their power to perpetuate Anglo-Saxon institutions and culture and to discourage the continuation of life-styles and value systems that were non-Anglo-Saxon. Non-English

European immigrants were faced with the decision of either assimilation and inclusion into mainstream society or nonassimilation and exclusion from total participation in the social, economic, and political systems. Most chose assimilation for a variety of reasons (Gleason, 1980; Glazer, 1977). The immigrants from Northern and Western Europe came closest to a complete realization of the goal of total cultural assimilation because they were most like Anglo-Saxons both physically and culturally.

The first generation of Southern, Central, and Eastern European immigrants also tried desperately to conform to society's demands for assimilation and integration. However, the process was not as easy or as successful for them as it had been for their Northern and Western predecessors. Undoubtedly, the degree to which they were physically, culturally, and psychologically unlike Anglo-Saxons partially accounted for their lower level of cultural and structural assimilation (Alba, 1985, 1990; Gordon, 1964). These factors may also partially explain the resurgence of ethnicity among second and third generation White ethnics in the United States, such as the Poles, Czechs, Slovaks, and Greeks, that occurred in the 1970s and their push for the inclusion of their cultural heritages in school ethnic studies programs. This interest became so widespread that many advocates of ethnicity used that concept almost exclusively to refer to White ethnic groups (Novak, 1972). Novak (p. 18) wrote, "the new ethnicity . . . is a movement of self-knowledge on the part of members of third and fourth generations of Southern and Eastern European immigrants to the United States."

The Assimilation and Exclusion of Non-White Ethnic Groups

Non-European ethnic groups of color, such as African Americans, Chinese Americans, and Mexican Americans, faced a much more serious problem than did Southern and Eastern European immigrants. Even though society demanded that they assimilate culturally in order to integrate socially, politically, and economically, it was very difficult for them to assimilate because of their skin color. Even when African Americans, Mexican Americans, and Native Americans succeeded in becoming culturally assimilated, they were still structurally isolated and were denied full, unqualified entry into the organizations and institutions sanctioned by the larger society. They became, in effect, marginal persons, for they were not accepted totally either by their own ethnic group or by the mainstream culture. Their denial of their ethnic cultures made them unacceptable to members of their ethnic communities, and the majority culture denied them full membership because they were people of color. The societal goals for European immigrants, especially those from Northern and Western Europe, were cultural assimilation and structural inclusion, but the goals for non-European immigrants and immigrants of color were cultural assimilation and structural exclusion (Gordon, 1964).

Thus, early in the historical development of the United States Anglo-Saxon values and cultural norms were institutionalized as American norms and as acceptable standards of behavior. They were perpetuated and transmitted through the socialization and enculturation of subsequent generations of Anglo-Saxon European immigrants. Anglo-Saxon customs and values were also perpetuated through the acculturation but structural exclusion of non-White, non-European immigrant groups.

The latter goal was achieved through institutionalizing Anglo-Saxon customs and laws that demanded conformity by groups of color to Anglo-Saxon behavioral patterns, but denied them entry into the social, political, and economic systems. The result, for many groups of color, such as African Americans and Native Americans, was the loss of important aspects of their first cultures. The Anglo-Saxons sought to ensure their dominance and power over these groups by stigmatizing their first cultures and institutions. Thus, when Africans arrived in America, the dominant group ridiculed their languages and punished them for practicing their African customs. Mexican Americans were not allowed to speak Spanish in the schools, even though the Treaty of Guadeloupe Hidalgo guaranteed them the rights to maintain and perpetuate their language and culture (Moquin & Van Doren, 1971). Texas even passed laws that declared Mexican Americans to be Whites. In the 1800s, after most Native Americans had been forced from their lands, subjected to federal controls, and relegated to living on reservations, U.S. policy makers began an aggressive campaign to "Americanize" the Indians (Josephy, 1968).

Distinctive Ethnic Traits in U.S. Society

Undoubtedly, many immigrant groups lost much of the flavor of their original ethnic heritages through the evolutionary processes of assimilation, acculturation, adaptation, and cultural borrowing. Some groups (principally Northern and Western European immigrants, and to a lesser extent Southern, Central, and Eastern European immigrants) voluntarily gave up large portions of their ethnic cultures and became Anglo-Saxonized in return for the privilege of societal participation. Other groups were forced to abandon their original cultural heritages. The structural exclusion to which non-White, non-European immigrants and Native American groups were subjected resulted in the perpetuation of distinctive ethnic traits and the development of unique cultural institutions and traditions (Herskovits, 1941). The cultures of these ethnic minorities differed in degrees from the dominant culture because these groups created values, languages, life-styles, and symbols they needed to survive the oppression, exclusion, and dehumanization to which they were subjected. These cultural traits were institutionalized and transmitted through the generations.

To some extent these cultural components are legacies from the original homelands of ethnic groups of color, modified to accommodate the circumstances of living in America; and to some extent they are new creations designed to meet the needs of particular ethnic groups. The cultural institutions and processes that were created clearly reflect the interactions between original cultural perspectives and the realities of U.S. society. The various ethnic groups developed somewhat different cultural values because their ancestral homes, cultural perspectives, and experiences in the United States were different. The new cultures that emerged undoubtedly have some remnants from the original homelands, but not necessarily in their original forms. Rather, the need to adapt to new surroundings and the effects of cultural sharing gave rise to new cultural forms.

African American churches, survival strategies, language, and civil rights organizations have some African cultural components, although these institutions, without question, were created by Africans in the Americas. They represent aspects of African American cultural life that were created to meet the unique social, economic, and political needs of African Americans. African American modes of communication emerged in response to the need to find viable means of surviving in a hostile environment without jeopardizing physical safety. Words, in addition to being communication devices, became power devices and helped African Americans to survive. African American music has its primordial roots in the African heritage, but it is both an expression of the hopes, fears, aspirations, and frustrations of African Americans and a reflection of their experiences in U.S. society. The forces that gave rise to much of its lyrical content and rhythmic tempo were the prototype life experiences, both physical and psychological, of African Americans as a group.

The ethnic cultures of most European immigrants were largely amalgamated in the United States. The United States became a culturally diffused and a socially and politically stratified society. Northern and Eastern European immigrants were almost totally culturally assimilated and structurally integrated into the dominant Anglo-Saxon society (Alba, 1990). Eastern, Central, and Southern European immigrants were assimilated to a lesser extent, and the political and economic privileges they experienced reflected their lower levels of assimilation. Immigrants of color and Native American groups (i.e., colored, highly visible people) were culturally diffused and largely structurally excluded.

The Nature of Ethnic Groups in Contemporary U.S. Life

Our discussion of cultural and structural assimilation leads us to more complex questions concerning the nature of ethnic groups in contemporary U.S. society, the functions they serve, and the extent to which they exist in the United States today. An ethnic group may be defined as an involuntary collectivity of people with a shared feeling of common identity, a sense of peoplehood, and a shared sense of interdependence of fate. These feelings derive, in part, from a common ancestral origin, a common set of values, and a common set of experiences (Isajiw, 1974). Isajiw (p. 122) defines an ethnic group as "an involuntary group of people who share the same culture or descendants of such people who identify themselves and/or are identified by others as belonging to the same involuntary group."

Identification with and membership in an ethnic group serve many useful functions. The ethnic group provides a network of preferred individual and institutional associations through which primary group relationships are established and personalities are developed. It serves psychologically as a source of self-identification for individuals. It provides a cultural screen through which national cultural patterns of behavior and the value system of other groups are screened, assessed, and assigned meaning (Gordon, 1964). Isajiw suggests that ethnicity is a matter of double boundary building—boundaries from within that are maintained by the socialization process, and boundaries from without, which are established by the process of intergroup relations. The most important question to be considered in analyzing ethnicity in contemporary U.S. society is related less to the extent to which cultural assimilation has occurred and more to how ethnic groups are perceived and identified by other people in the larger society, especially people who exercise political and economic power (Isajiw, 1974).

Ethnicity or ethnic group membership becomes important in relationships with other groups of people when one group discovers it has great actual or potential political and economic power. Such is the case with the Japanese Americans in Hawaii and the Poles and African Americans in Chicago. Ethnicity also becomes important when one is a member of a highly visible minority group, such as African Americans, Asian Americans, and Mexican Americans. It also becomes important when one ethnic group becomes conscious of being surrounded by another ethnic group (Greeley, 1971), such as Anglo-Saxon Protestants in Spanish Harlem and Whites who live in predominantly African American urban areas. Individuals who find themselves in these kinds of situations tend to turn to their own ethnic group for their intimate relationships, for reaffirmation of their identity, and for psychological and emotional support. Attempts to satisfy these kinds of needs often lead to ethnic alliances formed to influence social and political institutions. The individual feels that he or she benefits through the progress of his or her primary group (i.e., a sense of interdependence of fate). Therefore, as Greeley (1971, p. 44) suggests:

> Many ethnic groups have emerged in this country because members of the various immigrant groups have tried to preserve something of the intimacy and familiarity of the peasant village during the transition into urban industrial living. These groups have persisted after the immigrant experience . . . because of an apparently very powerful drive in many toward associating with those who, [they believe], possess the same blood and the same beliefs [they do]. The inclination toward such homogeneous groupings simultaneously enriches the culture, provides for diversity within the social structure and considerably increases the potential for conflict.

Greeley adds (p. 45),

> Visibility, sudden recognition of minority status, or being a large group in an environment where ethnic affiliation is deemed important—these three variables may considerably enhance social-psychological and social-organizational influence of ethnic groups.

Toward the Development of a Typology for Classifying Ethnic Groups

The functions served by ethnic group affiliation suggests that there are several different ways of classifying ethnic groups in contemporary Western societies. Existing definitions of an ethnic group are useful, but they are inadequate for studying the complex characteristics of contemporary ethnic groups in Western societies (Isajiw, 1974). Most of these definitions were formulated when ethnic group characteristics in Western societies were considerably different and before the rise of ethnic revitalization movements during the 1960s and 1970s. New conceptualizations of ethnicity are needed to reflect more accurately the emerging characteristics of ethnic groups in the United States and other Western nations.

It is impossible for a single definition of an ethnic group to adequately describe the multiple and complex dimensions of ethnic groups in contemporary societies. We need to develop a typology that will enable us to identify and classify different types of ethnic groups and to determine the degrees to which various racial and ethnic groups manifest these identified characteristics. We attempt to formulate the basic elements of such a typology in this chapter. It is important for the reader to realize that our typology is an ideal-type construct in the Weberian sense, and that no actual ethnic group will represent a pure type of any of our categories. Rather, various ethnic groups will exhibit the characteristics we identify to a greater or lesser degree. It is also unlikely that any particular ethnic group will completely lack any of the characteristics we describe. The reader should think of each ethnic group category as a continuum.

Each type of ethnic group is an involuntary group whose members share a sense of peoplehood and an interdependence of fate. A *cultural* ethnic group is an ethnic group that shares a common set of values, experiences, behavioral characteristics, and linguistic traits that differ substantially from other ethnic groups within society. Individuals usually gain membership in such a group not by choice but through birth and early socialization. Individuals who are members of cultural ethnic groups are likely to take collective and organized actions to support public policies that will enhance the survival of the group's culture and ethnic institutions. Members of cultural ethnic groups also pass on the symbols, language, and other components of the cultural heritage to the next generation. The individual's ethnic cultural heritage is a source of pride and group identification.

An *economic* ethnic group is an ethnic group that shares a sense of group identity and sees its economic fate tied together. Individual members of the group feel that their economic fate is intimately tied to the economic future of other members of the group. The members of an economic ethnic group respond collectively to societal issues they perceive as critical to determining their economic status, and they work together to influence policies and programs that will benefit the economic status of the group. The individual within an economic ethnic group tends to feel that taking individual actions to improve his or her economic status is likely to be ineffective as long as the economic status of the ethnic group is not substantially improved.

A *political* ethnic group is an ethnic group that has a sense of shared political interests and a feeling of political interdependence. The group responds to political issues collectively and tries to promote those public policies and programs that will enhance the interests of its members as a group. Groups that are political ethnic groups are also usually economic ethnic groups because politics and economics are tightly interwoven in a society. Thus, we can refer to those ethnic groups that work to influence political and economic policies that will benefit their collectivities as *ecopolitical ethnic groups.*

A *holistic* ethnic group is an entire group that has all of the characteristics of the various types of ethnic groups that we have described in their purest forms. Thus, a holistic ethnic group is an involuntary group of individuals who share a sense of peoplehood and an interdependence of fate, a common sense of identity, and common behavioral characteristics. Its members respond collectively to economic and political issues and try to promote public programs and policies that will further the interests of the group as a whole. African Americans and Mexican Americans closely approach the holistic ethnic group. Native Americans, Puerto Ricans in the United States, and Asian Americans are acquiring more characteristics of a holistic ethnic group as the political maturity and collective political action of these groups increase.

Two questions arise from our discussion: What is the structural relationship between ethnic groups and the larger U.S. society? In a pluralistic society such as the United States, is everyone a member of an ethnic group? Our analysis suggests that every American is a member of an ethnic group, that ethnicity exists on a continuum in contemporary American life, and that some individuals and groups are much more ethnic than others (see Chapter 5). *Thus, it is more useful to attempt to describe the degree to which an individual or group is ethnic, rather than to try to determine whether a particular individual or group is ethnic.* The lower-class African individual who lives in an all-Black community, speaks Black English, and who is active in African American political and economic activities is clearly more ethnic than is the highly acculturated African American who tries desperately to avoid any contact with other African Americans.

Third generation Italian Americans who are highly assimilated into the Anglo-Saxon culture may be ethnic only in a cultural sense; that is, they share the values, life-styles, and sense of peoplehood with Anglo-Americans (Alba, 1990). They may do very little, however, to advance the political and economic interests of Anglo-Americans over the interests of non-Anglo-American ethnic groups. African Americans, Puerto Ricans in the United States, and Japanese Americans are all ethnic groups. However, they are structurally different kinds of ethnic groups; and unless we keep the significant differences between these groups in mind when we are deriving generalizations and formulating educational and social policy, our conclusions and recommendations are likely to be misleading.

Of the three groups, African Americans, especially in the mid-1960s, more closely approach what we have described as a holistic ethnic group. Puerto Ricans in the United States, until the 1970s, were primarily a cultural and economic ethnic group but have not been very politically active in a collective sense. However, Puerto Ricans have been becoming more of a political ethnic group since the 1970s. Japanese Americans are probably the least ethnic of the three groups. This is true not only because Japanese Americans are highly culturally assimilated but also because they are not very politically active in an ethnic sense. They are also very economically successful and consequently feel little need to take collective action to influence their economic condition (Daniels, 1988; Takaki, 1989). *The degree to which a particular cultural, nationality, or racial group is ethnic varies over time, in different regions, with social class mobility, and with the pervasive sociopolitical conditions within the society.*

Frequently, third- and fourth-generation descendants of immigrants who came from Northern and Western Europe (e.g., French, Germans, Irish, Dutch, etc.) are thought to have become Anglo-Saxon politically, socially, culturally, and ethnically. The contention is often made that these groups, through the processes of acculturation and assimilation, have lost all traces of their ethnic distinctiveness, internalized Anglo-Saxon values and behaviors, and consider their political and economic interests to be the same as Americans whose origins are Anglo-Saxon (Alba, 1990). The preservation of the original ethnicity of these descendants has been determined on the basis of the presence or absence of overt behaviors attributable to the original ethnic group. When many of these behaviors are not found, conclusions are drawn to the effect that any ethnicity, aside from Anglo-Saxonism, is insignificant in defining the self-identity of descendants of Northern and Western European stock, in determining their primary group relationships, and in governing their social, political, and psychological behaviors. Their ethnic origins have been dismissed as meaningless and dysfunctional, except perhaps on rare occasions when families get together for reunions and to reminisce about "great grandma, the old country, and the old days," fix an ethnic dish, hold an ethnic marriage ceremony, or observe ethnic holidays.

However, the resurgence or rediscovery of ethnicity during the 1970s and the research on White ethnic groups during this period challenged the validity of these contentions. Research by students of the new ethnicity such as Novak (1973, 1974) and Greeley (1974) suggests that ethnicity among Whites is a complex variable that defies such simple explanations and/or dismissals and that it is a persistent, salient factor in the lives of different groups of White Americans, even though they may be fourth-generation immigrants. Greeley (1974, p. 205) explains that White "ethnicity is not a residual social factor that is slowly and gradually disappearing; it is, rather, a dynamic flexible social mechanism and can be called into being rather quickly and transformed and transmuted to meet changing situations and circumstances."

During the 1970s some White ethnic group members became as concerned as groups of color with self-identity, with reestablishing contact with their ethnic and cultural histories, with developing a sense of ethnic unity, and with preserving their cultural heritages. This search for more gratifying responses to the question of "Who am I?" rekindled an interest in ethnic heritage and an awareness of the saliency of ethnicity in their lives. Whites from all sociocultural backgrounds (e.g., Irish, Italian, Polish, German, Czech, Slovak, Greek, etc.) joined African Americans, Latinos, and Native Americans in this search for identity. It is more appropriate to talk about what Greeley (1974, pp. 291–317) calls the process of "ethnicization," or "ethnogenesis," instead of acculturation and assimilation, or Americanization, if we are to understand the cultural diversity and ethnic dynamism in the United States and other Western societies. According to Greeley the so-called new ethnicity among White Americans during the 1970s was not new at all. Rather, it was a rebirth or revival of interest in a persistent force in the history and lives of Americans. Its resurgence was symbolic of the cyclical nature of the ethnicization process.

Unquestionably, a great deal of sociocultural exchange has taken place between the various immigrant groups and the American host society. But this does not mean that either one is any less ethnic. The process of ethnicization leads to the creation of a broader common culture, shared by both the host and immigrant groups. The immigrant groups take on certain attitudes, beliefs, values, and behaviors attributable to Anglo-Saxons, and English Americans adopt some of the immigrants' values, beliefs, customs, and symbols (see Chapter 7). Other immigrant characteristics persist and become more distinctive in response to the challenge of U.S. life. The result for third- and fourth-generation immigrants, such as Italian Americans, Polish Americans, or Irish Americans, is a cultural system that is a combination of commonly shared so-called American traits and distinctive traits preserved from their original ethnic heritages.

To understand ethnicity fully when studying the diverse populations in the United States, attention needs to be given to the interrelationships among *ethnic identification, ethnic heritage,* and *ethnic culture.* This is especially important when studying White ethnic groups because ethnic differences within and between them are often subtle and complex. If identification, heritage, and culture are viewed as discrete dimensions or components of ethnicity, each with different behavioral manifestations, then an individual can proclaim his or her ethnicity by ascribing to any one or to a combination of these. *Ethnic identification* refers to where one places oneself on the ethnic chart (e.g., "I am Irish, German, French, Norwegian, Slovak, Greek, or African American"). *Ethnic heritage* is the specific study and conscious recollection of one's past history, both in the United States and the country of origin. *Ethnic culture* refers to the attitudes, values, personality styles, norms, and behaviors that correlate with ethnic identification (Novak, 1973).

Even though fourth-generation Irish Americans, Polish Americans, or Italian Americans may identify neither physically nor psychosocially with their original ethnic groups and may have little or no consciousness of their ethnic heritage, their "Irishness," "Polishness," or "Italianness" is still very much a part of their lives. Their values, behaviors, perceptions and expectations that differ considerably from those of other Americans, are determined, to a great extent, by the cultural conditioning that persists from the original ethnic experience. These cultural traits are transmitted across generations through family structures and socialization processes and are often so deeply embedded in the subconscious fiber of individuals that they are unaware of their existence. This is why we frequently assume that White ethnic groups, especially those who emigrated from Northern and Western Europe, lose their ethnic identity after three or four generations in the United States.

Undoubtedly, ethnicity is even stronger and more conscious among European descendants who came from Eastern, Southern, and Central Europe than among those from Northern and Western Europe. Such groups as the Poles, Greeks, Italians, Slovaks, Czechs, and Hungarians are more recent arrivals in the United States. Their ties with their original heritages, customs, values, and traditions are stronger, and they share less of a common culture with English Americans than do groups like the French and Germans. Their senses of ethnic identification, heritage, and culture are much more apparent in their daily lives because of the more distinct origins. They are less assimilated culturally and structurally than are other White Americans, and the ethnicization process is less developed. Therefore, their original ethnicity is more highly accentuated, and they are more likely to behave in clearly discernible ways from Anglo-Saxons than are other European immigrants. These groups are likely to support ethnic candidates for public office, live in tightly formed ethnic communities, continue to speak their native languages, marry within their own ethnic groups, conform more rigidly to ethnic values, and perpetuate their ethnic heritages through family structures and socialization. The forces of differentiation acting on them are much stronger and function on more conscious, all-inclusive levels than do the forces of homogenization (Novak, 1973).

The ethnic groups in the United States that are the least assimilated culturally and structurally, and the most visible physically, such as African Americans, Filipino Americans, Mexican Americans, and American Indians, have maintained even stronger senses of cultural identities. To a greater degree than Americans of either Western and Northern, or Southern and Eastern European descent, they feel that their life-styles and political interests conflict with those of the dominant society. They therefore consider themselves to be more ethnic than these other groups. They have created and maintained distinct cultural institutions, values, norms, and languages. Excluded ethnic groups are much more likely than structurally assimilated ethnic groups to emphasize their feelings of kinship, to promote their cultural identities, and to try to influence economic and political institutions so that public policies will be more responsive to their unique group needs. Thus, in the 1970s African Americans tried to gain control of schools located in predominantly African American communities, and Chinese Americans in San Francisco united to oppose efforts to bus their children to schools outside of Chinatown. Mexican Americans are more likely to vote for a Mexican American for public office than for an Anglo-American because they usually feel a Chicano will make decisions more consistent with their ethnic group interests than will an Anglo-American (Litt, 1970).

The preoccupation of both Whites and people of color with their own ethnicity is situational and periodic. It surfaces and assumes a position of prominence in group activities at different times in history and as different aspects of the psychosocial and ecopolitical identification processes demand attention. The nature of the particular identity need determines the way ethnicity is articulated and the activities ethnic groups choose to accentuate their ethnicity. Whether that need is defined as the clarification or reaffirmation of cultural identity, the recollection and reevaluation of historical experiences, the manipulation of social forces to benefit the ethnic group's membership, or gaining political and economic power to advance the social positions of particular ethnic collectives, it determines the "ethnic posture" of the group at any given time. Ethnic needs influence whether an ethnic collectivity functions as an *economic, political,* or *cultural ethnic group.* All ethnic groups assume these various identities at different stages in their developmental processes within the context of U.S. society.

Even though our generalizations are basically valid, they are not applicable to the same degree to all members of all ethnic groups. This is why it is essential, when studying ethnicity, to distinguish ethnic *group* behavior from the behavior of *individual* members of ethnic groups, to consider ethnicity from the perspective of functionality instead of merely as a descriptive trait, and to analyze the behavior of ethnic groups in terms of *ethnic identification, heritage,* and *culture.*

Some members of ethnic groups have little or no sense of ethnic kinship or interdependence of fate. They feel little or no sense of distinction or difference between themselves and the larger society. Some members do not identify with their ethnic group, even though they share its physical and/or cultural characteristics, and the larger society considers them to belong to it. For example, some descendants of Mexican American parentage consider themselves White. They do not speak Spanish, have Anglicized their names, and conform to Anglo-Saxon cultural norms. Some African Americans believe that they are both culturally and structurally assimilated into the larger society. They have inculcated the values and life-styles of the dominant culture, consider themselves totally accepted by the majority society, feel a sense of alienation from African Americans as a group, and find it almost impossible to identify with the cultural and political goals of African Americans (Wortham, 1981).

Summary

The rise of ethnic revival movements in Western societies during the 1960s and 1970s indicated that ethnic groups and ethnic affiliations are integral parts of contemporary societies, despite the contrary predictions social scientists made in previous decades. New concepts and theories are needed to explain adequately the complex nature of ethnic groups in modernized pluralistic societies.

In this chapter, ethnic groups in the United States are used as a case study to describe some of the major characteristics of ethnic groups in Western societies. Ethnic groups in the United States and in such nations as Australia, Canada, and the United Kingdom share many characteristics. This chapter also presents a typology for classifying ethnic groups that is consistent with their complex and changing characteristics in modernized societies. We identified several types of ethnic groups—*cultural, economic, political, ecopolitical,* and *holistic*—and concluded that even though every American is a member of an ethnic group, ethnicity manifests itself in diverse forms in modern U.S. society, and that Americans belong to many different kinds of ethnic groups. The degree to which a particular cultural, national, or racial group is ethnic varies with a number of social, economic, and political conditions within society.

References

Alba, R. D. (1985). *Italian Americans: Into the Twilight of Ethnicity* Englewood Cliffs, NJ: Prentice-Hall.

Alba, R. D. (1990). *Ethnic Identity: The Transformation of White America.* New Haven: Yale University Press.

Bullivant, B. (1981). *The Pluralist Dilemma in Education. Six Case Studies.* Sydney: George Allen & Unwin.

Daniels, R. (1988). *Asian America: Chinese and Japanese in the United States since 1850.* Seattle: University of Washington Press.

Franklin, R. S. (1991). *Shadows of Race and Class.* Minneapolis: University of Minnesota Press.

Fredrickson, G. M., & Knobel, D. T. (1980). A History of Prejudice and Discrimination. In S. Thernstrom, A. Orlov, & O. Handlin (Eds.), *Harvard Encyclopedia of American Ethnic Groups* (pp. 829–847). Cambridge, MA: Harvard University Press.

Glazer, N. (1977). Cultural Pluralism: The Social Aspect. In M. M. Tumin and W. Plotch (Eds.), *Pluralism in a Democratic Society* (pp. 3–24). New York: Praeger.

Glazer, N. (1980). Ethnic Groups in America: From National Culture to Ideology. In M. Berger, T. Abel, & C. H. Page (Eds.), *Freedom and Control in Modern Society* (pp. 158–173). New York: Van Nostrand.

Glazer, N., & Moynihan, D. P. (Eds.). (1975). *Ethnicity: Theory and Experience.* Cambridge, MA: Harvard University Press.

Gleason, P. (1980). American Identity and Americanization. In S. Thernstrom, A. Orlov, & O. Handlin (Eds.), *Harvard Encyclopedia of American Ethnic Groups,* (pp. 31–58). Cambridge, MA: Harvard University Press.

Gordon, M. M. (1964). *Assimilation in American Life: The Role of Race, Religion and National Origins.* New York: Oxford University Press.

Greeley, A. M. (1971). *Why Can't They Be Like Us? America's White Ethnic Groups.* New York: E. P. Dutton and Company.

Greeley, A. M. (1974). *Ethnicity in the United States: A Preliminary Reconnaissance.* New York: Wiley Publishing Co.

Herskovits, M. (1941). *The Myth of the Negro Past.* New York: Harper and Row.

Higham, J. (1972). *Strangers in the Land: Patterns of American Nativism: 1860–1925.* New York: Atheneum.

Isajiw, W. W. (1974). Definitions of Ethnicity. *Ethnicity, 1,* 111–124.

Jones, M. A. (1960). *American Immigration.* Chicago: University of Chicago Press.

Josephy, A. M., Jr. (1968). *The Indian Heritage of American.* New York: Bantam Books.

Krauter, J. F., & Davis, M. (1978). *Minority Canadians: Ethnic Groups.* Toronto: Methuen.

Litt, E. (1970). *Ethnic Politics in America.* Glenview, IL: Scott, Foresman.

Moquin, W., & C. V. Van Doren (Eds.). (1971). *A Documentary History of Mexican Americans.* New York: Bantam Books.

Novak, M. (1972). *The Rise of the Unmeltable Ethnics: Politics and Culture in the Seventies.* New York: Macmillan.

Novak, M. (1973). How American Are You If Your Grandparents Came from Serbia in 1888? In S. TeSelle (Ed.), *The Rediscovery of Ethnicity.* (pp. 1–20). New York: Harper and Row.

Novak, M. (1974a). Cultural Pluralism for Individuals: A Social Vision. In M. M. Tumin and

W. Plotch, *Pluralism in a Democratic Society* (pp. 25–57). New York: Praeger.

Novak, M. (1974b). The New Ethnicity. *Center Magazine, 3,* 18.

Park, R. E. (1950). *Race and Culture.* New York: The Free Press.

Portes, A., & Rumbaut, R. G. (1990). *Immigrant America: A Portrait.* Berkeley: University of California Press.

Smith, A. D. (1981). *The Ethnic Revival in the Modern World.* Cambridge, England: Cambridge University Press.

Sowell, T. (1981). *Ethnic America: A History.* New York: Basic Books.

Takaki, R. (1989). *Strangers from a Different Shore: A History of Asian Americans.* New York: Little, Brown.

Watson, J. L. (1977). *Between Two Cultures: Migrants and Minorities in Britain.* Oxford: Basil Blackwell.

Wilton, J., & Bosworth, R. (1984). *Old Worlds and New Australia: The Post-War Migrant Experience.* Ringwood, Victoria: Penguin Books Australia Ltd.

Wirth, L. (1945). The Problem of Minority Groups. In R. Linton (Ed.), *The Science of Man in the World Crisis* (pp. 347–372). New York: Columbia University Press.

Wortham, A. (1981). *The Other Side of Racism: A Philosophical Study of Black Race Consciousness.* Columbus: Ohio State University Press.

Chapter 5

Culture, Ethnicity, and Education

A wide range of concepts has emerged since the 1960s to describe the diverse programs and practices related to ethnic and cultural diversity. These concepts reflect the many different and often conflicting goals, approaches, and strategies in multicultural education. Concepts such as *multicultural education, multiethnic education, intercultural education,* and *antiracist education* are sometimes used interchangeably and at other times to describe different but interrelated programs and practices. The study of ethnicity and cultural diversity became more legitimate in the schools and universities during the 1960s and 1970s than it had been in previous decades (Bell, 1975; Parsons, 1975).

During the 1980s the national emphasis in the United States and several other nations shifted from international diversity to nationalism and national identity. However, some aspects of the curriculum reforms related to diversity that emerged in the 1960s and 1970s had become partially institutionalized by the late 1980s. More ethnic images in textbooks, various forms of bilingual education, and multicultural education requirements for teachers were found in many educational institutions by the late 1980s. Multicultural curriculum reform continued into the early 1990s, although a heated debate over the canon took place (Bell, 1992; Gates, 1992).

The major concepts in multicultural education, and related practices, are imprecise and ambiguous. Concept clarification within this area is needed so that objectives can be more clearly delineated and strategies for attaining them more appropriately designed. Concepts are very important—they influence our questions, research methods, findings, programs, and evaluation strategies. Multicultural education and multiethnic education, for example, have different programmatic and policy implications. Multicultural education focuses on a wide range of cultural groups, such as ethnic groups, women, and people with disabilities. Multiethnic education focuses on the educational needs of racial and ethnic groups.

In this chapter, I define and delineate the boundaries of some of the major concepts related to education and cultural diversity and suggest their different programmatic and policy implications. This conceptual analysis is designed to help educators at all levels better clarify, specify, and evaluate goals related to cultural and ethnic diversity in Western societies.

Multicultural Education

Of the concepts currently popular, multicultural education is one of the most frequently used, not only in the United States but also in such nations as Australia, the United Kingdom, and Canada. However, the term *intercultural education*, rather than *multicultural education*, is frequently used on the European continent (Batelaan, 1983). Researchers and policy makers who prefer intercultural to multicultural education contend that intercultural implies an education that promotes interaction among different cultures whereas multicultural does not imply such interaction. However, intercultural education is rarely used outside of the European continent.

The use of multicultural education varies widely in different school districts and in the educational literature (Garcia, 1991; Grant, 1979; Nieto, 1992). Sometimes it is used synonymously with ethnic studies; at other times it is used to describe multiethnic education. It is necessary to discuss the meaning of culture in order to describe what multicultural education suggests theoretically since culture is the root of the word *multicultural* and thus of the term *multicultural education.*

The Meaning of Culture

There are many different definitions of culture, but no single definition that all social scientists would heartily accept. Some definitions, however, are fairly widely accepted. During much of this century, the famous definition of culture formulated by Sir E. B. Taylor (1871) was very influential: "Culture . . . is that complex whole which includes knowledge, belief, art, morals, law, custom, and any other capabilities and habits acquired by man as a member of society." Today, Taylor's definition is not popular among social scientists because they believe it is not a very helpful guide for research. They think the definition is too broad and lacks sufficient boundaries. As Dimen-Schein (1977) points out, we can neither observe nor explain everything. Research efforts and policy analyses need to be guided by a definition of culture that is more specific and focused. In recent years, social scientists have formulated definitions of culture that are more precise and functional for modernized societies.

In a comprehensive study of the definitions of culture published in 1952, Alfred L. Kroeber and Clyde Kluckhohn report more than 160. They concluded that most social scientists agreed that (Kroeber & Kluckhohn, 1952, p. 161) "culture consists of patterns, explicit and implicit, of and for behavior acquired and transmitted by symbols, constituting the distinctive achievements of human groups, including their embodiments in artifacts; the essential core of culture consists of traditional (i.e., historically derived and selected) ideas and especially attached values."

In their summary definition of culture, Kroeber and Kluckhohn, like most social scientists today, emphasize the intangible, symbolic, and ideational aspects of group life as the most important aspects of culture. Some social scientists go so far as to exclude material objects (artifacts) from their definition of culture (Theodorson & Theodorson, 1969, p. 95). Even social scientists who view tangible or material objects as a part of culture believe that the interpretation of these objects and the rules governing their use constitute the essence of culture and not the artifacts themselves.

Some social scientists distinguish between the terms *society* and *culture*. These social scientists "reserve the word society for the observable interactions among people, and the word culture for the intangible symbols, rules, and values that . . . people use to define themselves" (Dimen-Schein, 1977, p. 23). Symbolic anthropologists, such as Clifford Geertz and Victor Turner, "study ideology, such as the multiple meaning of words and things, and the role of symbols in ordering social life by unifying opposing meanings" (Dimen-Schein, 1977, p. 23).

Culture is sometimes defined as a strategy or program for survival. In this view of culture, it is created when human groups try to satisfy their survival needs. Bullivant, who views culture as a survival strategy, states that culture is not static, but is subject to the circumstances (environment) in which a society finds itself. He describes three kinds of environments to which human groups respond when creating culture: the geographical environment, the social environment, and the metaphysical environment. Bullivant (1984, p. 4) defines culture as "an interdependent and patterned system of valued traditional and current public knowledge and conceptions, embodied in behaviors and artifacts, and transmitted to present and new members, both symbolically and non-symbolically, which a society has evolved historically and progressively modifies and augments, to give meaning to and cope with its definitions of present and future existential problems."

The Characteristics of Cultures

Most contemporary social scientists view culture as consisting primarily of the symbolic, ideational, and intangible aspects of human societies. Even when they view artifacts and material objects as a part of culture, most social scientists regard culture as the way people interpret, use, and perceive such artifacts and material objects. It is the values, symbols, interpretations, and perspectives that distinguish one people from another in modernized societies and not artifacts, material objects, and other tangible aspects of human societies. Both the Japanese and the Americans use the automobile, but how they organize the making of it and how they interpret it within their societies may differ considerably and thus constitute an essential component of their respective cultures.

Cultures are dynamic, complex, and changing. However, in the schools cultures often are perceived as static, unchanging, and fragmented. Concepts such as "American Indian culture" and "African American culture" often imply static, unchanging life-styles. Native Americans are often described in misleading ways, such as living in tepees. One result of such perceptions and descriptions is the perpetuation of stereotypes about different ethnic, cultural, and racial groups.

Cultures are also systems; they must be viewed as wholes, not as discrete and isolated parts. Any change in one aspect of a culture affects all of its components. For example, the large number of women who entered the work force in the 1970s and 1980s has influenced how women view themselves, how men view women, and the family socialization of children. Many more children today are in child-care facilities at a much younger age than was the case in the 1950s, when fewer women in the United States worked outside the home.

Gilligan (1982) describes caring, interconnection, and sensitivity to the needs of other people as dominant values among women and of the female microculture in the United States. Most of the research she cites was done with women socialized before the women's rights movement of the 1960s and 1970s. Future research might reveal that increased women's rights during the 1960s and 1970s may have had a significant influence on the values held by women, particularly those related to caring and interconnection.

Culture, Macroculture, and Microcultures

The concept of culture as formulated by most social scientists does not deal with variations within the national culture or the smaller cultures within it. However, when dealing with multicultural education, it is necessary to discuss cultural variation within the national culture because multicultural education focuses on equal educational opportunities for different groups within the national culture. Two related concepts can help us deal with cultural variations within the national culture. We can call the national or shared culture of the nation-state or society the big or macroculture. The smaller cultures that constitute it can be called microculture.

Every nation-state has overarching values, symbols, and ideations shared to some degree by all microcultures. Various microcultural groups within the nation, however, may mediate, interpret, reinterpret, perceive, and experience these overarching national values and ideals differently. Figure 5.1 shows the relationship between microcultures and the national macroculture.

The national, overarching ideals, symbols, and values can be described for various nation-states. Myrdal (1944), the Swedish economist, identifies values such as justice, equality, and human dignity as overarching values in the United States. He calls these values the American Creed. Myrdal also describes the "American Dilemma" as an integral part of U.S. society. This dilemma results

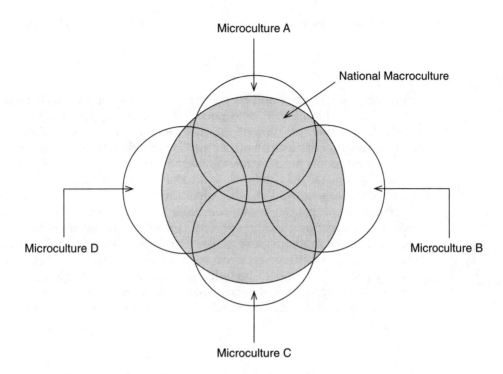

FIGURE 5.1 Microcultures and the National Macroculture

The shaded area represents the national macroculture. All ethnic and cultural groups and citizens of the nation-state share this culture. A, B, C, and D represent microcultures that consist of unique institutions, values, and cultural elements that are nonuniversalized and shared primarily by members of specific ethnic and cultural groups. A major goal of the school should be to help students acquire the knowledge, skills, and attitudes needed to function effectively within the national macroculture, their own microcultures, and within and across other microcultures.

from the fact that even though most U.S. citizens internalize American Creed values, such as justice and human dignity, they often violate them in their daily behavior. Myrdal concludes that a tremendous gap exists between American ideals and American realities. Other U.S. overarching values include the Protestant work ethic, individualism as opposed to a group orientation, distance, and materialism and material progress (Greenbaum, 1974).

The Variables and Components of Culture

As indicated in the previous section, most social scientists today emphasize the intangible components of culture, such as symbols, values, ideations, and ways of interpreting reality. I have identified six major cultural elements or components that are useful for interpreting the behavior of students and teachers and for teaching about various microcultural groups in Western nation-states. Figure

5.2 shows the elements and components of cultures discussed in the following sections.

CULTURAL COMPONENTS/ELEMENTS

① *Values and Behavioral Styles*

Values are abstract, generalized principles of behavior to which members of society attach a high worth or regard. Individuals acquire their values during socialization. Values are one of the most important elements of cultures and microcultures that distinguish one group from another. Values influence behavior and also how people perceive their environment.

Each nation-state has national values that are to some extent shared by all of its microcultural groups; it also has other important values that distinguish one microcultural group from another. In their research on the cognitive styles of students, Ramirez and Castaneda (1974) found that Mexican American and Anglo-American students, as groups, had some different values that are revealed in their cognitive styles or approaches to learning. They found that Mexican Americans tend to be field-sensitive whereas Anglo-Americans are more field-independent. Field-sensitive students prefer to work with other people to achieve a goal; field-independent students prefer to work independently.

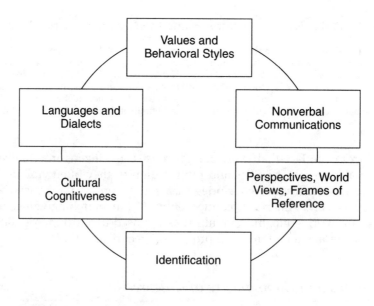

FIGURE 5.2   Elements and Components of Culture

These components of culture, which can be conceptualized as distinct, exist within a holistic and highly interrelated system.

Field-sensitive and field-independent learners also differ in other important ways.

Research on women has revealed that men and women exhibit some significant differences in value orientations. As pointed out previously, individualism is very important to men, whereas relationships, caring, and interconnection tend to be more important to women. Women also experience more problems with competitive achievement and more "fear of success" than do men (Belenky et al., 1986; Horner, 1972).

Languages and Dialects

Languages and dialects are important components of culture. How people view and interpret the world is reflected in their language. Within most nation-states, people speak the national language (or lingua franca) plus many variations of the national language as well as other languages. In the United States, people speak many different varieties of English, including Black English and English with Southern and Eastern regional accents. The first language for many Americans is not English but Spanish, Korean, Chinese, or Vietnamese. People in nations such as the United Kingdom, Australia, and Canada also speak many different dialects and languages in addition to the shared national language or languages. Canada has two national languages, English and French. Many other languages are also spoken in Canada. Cultural differences are both reflected and perpetuated by languages and dialects.

Nonverbal Communications

The way people communicate nonverbally is an important part of culture. How people look at each other and what the particular looks mean often vary within and across different microcultural groups within a society. Philips (1983), in her study of the Indians on the Warm Spring Indian Reservation in Oregon, describes how the communication styles of Indian students and their Anglo teachers—both verbal and nonverbal—differ and often conflict. Nonverbal communication often reveals latent but important components of a culture or microculture. Looking an older person directly in the eye is considered offensive in some U.S. microcultures.

Cultural Cognitiveness

Cultural cognitiveness occurs when individuals or a group are aware of and think about their culture or microculture as unique and distinct from other cultures or microcultures within a society. Cultural cognitiveness involves the process of knowing, including both awareness and judgment.

Cultural cognitiveness differs from cultural identification. An individual may have a strong identification with a culture but little awareness of it as a unique culture, distinct from others. Conversely, an individual may have strong cultural cognitiveness or awareness but little identification with his or her microculture. An individual with strong cultural awareness could be a staunch assimilationist who tries to escape most or all of the symbols of his or her culture.

Perspectives, World Views, and Frames of Reference

Certain perspectives, points of view, and frames of reference are normative within each culture and microcultural group. This does not mean that every individual within a particular cultural or microcultural group endorses a particular point of view or perspective. It does mean, however, that particular views and perspectives occur more frequently within some microcultural groups than do others or within the macroculture. Japanese American perspectives on their World War II internment, African American perspectives on the civil rights movement of the 1960s, and women's perspectives on caring, independence, and individuation (Gilligan, 1982) are various examples of perspectives held by microcultural groups that differ from perspectives within other microcultural groups and the macroculture.

Identification

When an individual identifies with his or her cultural or microcultural group, he or she feels a part of the group; internalizes its goals, interests, and aspirations; and also internalizes its values and standards. An individual's level of identification with his or her cultural group can vary greatly, from practically no identification to almost total identification. An individual African American, Jewish American, or Jamaican in the United Kingdom may have a weak or a strong identification with his or her ethnic group.

Microcultural Groups and Individuals

Individuals are not just African American or White, male or female, or middle or working class. Even though we discuss variables such as race/ethnicity, gender, social class, and exceptionality (member of a special population, such as having a disability or being gifted) as separate variables, individuals belong to these groups at the same time (see Figure 5.3). Each variable influences the behavior of individuals. The influence of these variables is rarely singular; they often interact to influence the behavior of individuals. Gilligan (1982) points out that women are less oriented toward individuation than are men. African American culture tends to be more group oriented than is the mainstream U.S. culture. A reasonable hypothesis is that African American women are even less oriented toward individuation than are White women.

Figure 5.4 illustrates how four major variables—race/ethnicity, gender, social class, and exceptionality—influence student behavior both singly and interac-

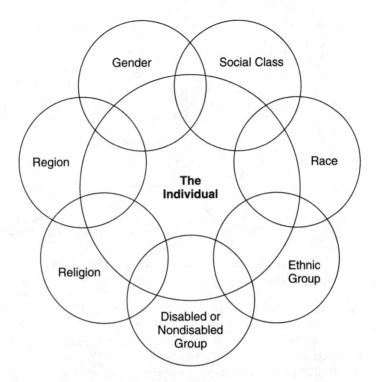

FIGURE 5.3   Individuals Belong to Many Different Microcultural Groups

tively. This figure also shows that many other variables, which are not identified, also simultaneously influence student behavior.

Multicultural Education: Nature and Limitations

Multicultural education suggests a type of education concerned with creating educational environments in which students from a variety of microcultural groups such as race/ethnicity, gender, social class, regional groups, and people with disabilities experience educational equality. The problems of these various groups are highlighted and compared. The total school environment is reformed so that it promotes respect and equity for a wide range of microcultural groups. Multicultural education, conceptualized in this way, is based on the assumption that such concepts as prejudice, discrimination, identity conflicts, and marginalization are common to diverse microcultural groups.

A generic focus within a school reform effort, such as multicultural education, can make a substantial contribution to the liberal education of students. However, school reform efforts should go beyond the level of multicultural education and

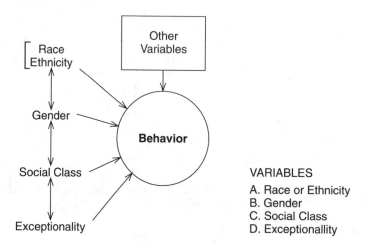

FIGURE 5.4   Multicultural Subvariants

focus on the unique problems that women, African Americans, people with disabilities, and other victimized cultural groups experience in the United States and in other nations. Many problems these groups face are unique and require specialized analyses and strategies.

Multicultural education is a popular concept because it is often interpreted to mean combining the problems of people of color, women, and other groups. Public and school policies that are based primarily on this combining process will prove ineffective and perhaps detrimental to all of the groups concerned. Because of the unique problems of each ethnic and racial group, educational institutions should implement multiethnic education to complement and strengthen multicultural education. These concepts are complementary but not interchangeable.

Because multicultural education is a very broad and inclusive concept, and because it focuses on *cultural differences,* it is not an adequate concept to guide research and policy decisions on problems related to racial and ethnic minorities. It is not clear from the literature on multicultural education, for example, which groups constitute the target populations in multicultural educational reform. Multicultural education also does not deal adequately with the ways in which the needs of the various microcultural groups conflict, interact, and intersect.

Multicultural education theorists sometimes imply that cultural differences and cultural ethnocentrism are the major causes of intergroup tensions and conflicts. *However, racial problems are often more significant in intergroup relations than are cultural differences* (Brooks, 1990; Franklin, 1991; Terkel, 1992). Multicultural education is a useful concept in that it enables the educational reformer to focus on a range of marginalized and victimized groups within society. This is the strength of the concept and is probably why it has so many educational advocates. However, it is not an adequate concept. We need other concepts related to multicultural education, such as race and ethnicity, to guide educational policy that will focus more directly on the unique problems and characteristics of particular groups in society.

Sexism, for example, is very important when dealing with women's issues just as the concepts of race and racism are important for the individual who is researching or designing educational policy for people of color. Concepts such as *ethnic studies, multiethnic education,* and *women studies* are needed to support and enhance the general concept of multicultural education.

The Nature of an Ethnic Group

An ethnic group is a microcultural group with several distinguishing characteristics. Social scientists do not completely agree on one definition of ethnic group. However, we can define an ethnic group as a group that shares a common ancestry, culture, history, tradition, and sense of peoplehood. An ethnic group is primarily an involuntary group, although identification with the group may be optional (Banks et al., 1992). As I point out in Chapter 4, an ethnic group may be economic, political, cultural, or holistic.

This definition suggests that Anglos in the United States and Australia, and the British and French in Canada, are ethnic groups. Pakistanis in the United Kingdom and Mexicans in the United States are ethnic minority groups, a specific type of ethnic group. Members of an ethnic minority group have unique physical and/or cultural characteristics that enable members of other groups to identify its members easily, often for purposes of discrimination (Banks, 1991).

Ethnic Group: A Multidimensional Concept

The definition of an ethnic group just discussed suggests that all people in modernized, culturally pluralistic nation-states are members of ethnic groups. Within a modernized society, however, almost no individuals are totally ethnic, because ethnic characteristics within a modernized society are mediated by technology, acculturation, the physical amalgamation of ethnic groups, and other aspects of modernization. Thus, the appropriate question to ask is not whether an individual is ethnic, but to what extent he or she is ethnic.

Ethnic group membership is a multidimensional concept. The previous discussion and Figure 5.2 identify six major components of culture. These same major variables exist within an ethnic group, which is one type of microcultural group. These separate variables within an ethnic group, although highly interrelated, are conceptually distinct and can be identified. An individual's level of ethnic behavior and characteristics can be determined by ascertaining the extent to which he or she has behavior and characteristics that reflect these ethnic variables.

The Relationship between Physical Characteristics and Ethnic Behavior

It is very important to realize that ethnic behavior and characteristics should not be confused with an individual's biological characteristics and physical traits. It is true that a close relationship often exists between an individual's biological traits and his or her ethnic and cultural characteristics. In premodern societies, there was usually a 100 percent correlation between an individual's biological "ethnic" group and his or her cultural characteristics. This relationship exists to some extent today. Most African Americans, for example, have some "Black" cultural characteristics.

However, some African Americans have so few cultural traits that are Black and so little identification with African Americans as an ethnic group that we might call them Afro-Saxons. This same situation exists for many highly assimilated and upwardly mobile members of ethnic groups such as Mexican Americans, Italian Australians, and Canadian Indians. Americans with an Italian surname may be so totally culturally assimilated in terms of their values, behaviors, and perceptions that they are culturally not Italian Americans but Anglo-Americans. An individual American who is one-eighth each German, Australian, Romanian, Algerian, Chilean, Scotch, Italian, and Korean ancestry, and whose parents did not provide any conscious ethnic influence, is not necessarily without an ethnic identification or ethnic behavior. He or she is most likely culturally an Anglo-American who has an identification with Anglo-Americans as an ethnic group. This identification with Anglo-Americans may be conscious or unconscious. Most frequently, this type of individual will have an unconscious identification with Anglo-Americans as an ethnic group and will offer a self-description as "merely an American."

The Variables of Ethnic Group Behavior

The six major variables of culture identified in Figure 5.2 can be used to conceptualize and determine the level of ethnic behavior of individuals or groups and the level of cross-cultural competency (see Table 5.1). Each of these variables can be conceptualized as existing on a continuum. Measurement techniques can be structured to determine the level of ethnic behavior and traits possessed by individual members of ethnic groups. This multidimensional conceptualization of ethnic behavior can help students understand that an individual may be highly ethnic linguistically but highly assimilated in terms of ethnic values and perspectives. This multidimensional conceptualization of ethnic group can also help students to better understand the complex nature of ethnic group life in Western societies and to mitigate some of the serious and damaging misconceptions about ethnic groups that are pervasive within the schools and the larger society.

The last variable of ethnic group behavior identified in Table 5.1 is the individual's psychological identification with his or her ethnic group. This variable is called *ethnicity*. It is one of the most important variables of ethnic group behavior within a modernized society. In some cases, ethnicity may be the only significant variable of ethnic group behavior possessed by highly assimilated and upper-status members of ethnic groups within a modernized democratic society.

TABLE 5.1 Matrix for Conceptualizing and Assessing Cross-Cultural Behavior

Variables	Understandings and Behavior	Levels of Competency
		1 2 3 4 5 6 7
Values and Behavioral Styles	The ability to understand and interpret values and behavioral styles that are normative within the ethnic group.	◄─────────►
	The ability to express values behaviorally that are normative within the ethnic group.	
	The ability to express behavioral styles and nuances that are normative within the ethnic group.	
Languages and Dialects	The ability to understand, interpret, and speak the dialects and/or languages within the ethnic culture.	◄─────────►
Nonverbal Communications	The ability to understand and accurately interpret the nonverbal communications within the ethnic group.	◄─────────►
	The ability to communicate accurately nonverbally within the ethnic group.	
Cultural Cognitiveness	The ability to perceive and recognize the unique components of one's ethnic group that distinguishes it from other microcultural groups within the society and from the national macroculture.	◄─────────►
	The ability to take actions that indicate an awareness and knowledge of one's ethnic culture.	
Perspectives, World Views, and Frames of Reference	The ability to understand and interpret the perspectives, world views, and frames of reference normative within the ethnic group.	◄─────────►
	The ability to view events and situations from the perspectives, world views, and frames of reference normative within the ethnic group.	
Identification	The ability to have an identification with one's ethnic group that is subtle and/or unconscious.	◄─────────►
	The ability to take overt actions that show conscious identification with one's ethnic group.	

Multiethnic Education

Because an ethnic group is a unique kind of cultural group, multiethnic education is a specific form of multicultural education. Multiethnic education is concerned with modifying the total school environment so that it is more reflective of the ethnic diversity within a society. This includes not only studying ethnic cultures and experiences but also making institutional changes within the school setting so that students from diverse ethnic groups receive equal educational opportunities and the school promotes and encourages the concept of ethnic diversity.

Multiethnic education is a generic concept that implies systemic school reform. Schools that wish to become multiethnic must undertake an institutional analysis to determine the degree to which they are assimilationist oriented and must take effective actions to create and sustain a pluralistic school environment. The staff's attitudes, the testing program, counseling, power relationships, and grouping practices are some of the variables that reflect ethnic diversity within multiethnic schools. (See Figure 3.4 in Chapter 3.)

Ethnic Studies

Ethnic studies can be defined as the scientific and humanistic study of the histories, cultures, and experiences of ethnic groups within a society. It includes but is not limited to a study of ethnic minority groups, such as Chinese Canadians, Australian Aborigines, British Jamaicans, and African Americans. Ethnic studies refers primarily to the objectives, methods, and materials that make up the courses of study within schools and other educational institutions. It constitutes one essential component of multiethnic education. Since the 1960s, many attempts have been made in nations such as the United States, Canada, the United Kingdom, and Australia to infuse ethnic studies into school and university curricula.

The concept of ethnic studies suggests that a wide variety of ethnic groups are studied within a comparative framework. Students are helped to develop concepts, generalizations, and theories that they can use to better understand a range of human behavior. Modernized ethnic studies programs are not only comparative and conceptual but are also interdisciplinary and cut across subject matter lines. Thus, within a globally conceptualized ethnic studies program, teachers of the humanities, the communication arts, and the sciences incorporate ethnic content into the total curriculum. Ethnic content is not reserved for special days, occasions, or courses.

Even though specialized courses such as African American studies, Asian studies, and Canadian Indian studies can help attain specified curricular objectives, a major goal of curriculum reform should be to infuse ethnic content into the core or general curriculum that all students experience. Ethnic content should be for all students, not just for those who are members of ethnic minority groups.

Table 5.2 summarizes the focuses, objectives, and strategies of *multicultural education, multiethnic education,* and *ethnic studies.* Figure 5.5 illustrates how these concepts are related. Efforts to implement each of these ideas should be a major part of reform in schools, colleges, and universities in the Western nation-states.

Race as a Factor in Intergroup Problems

Multicultural education assumes that the intergroup problems in Western nation-states are primarily cultural rather than racial. Widespread cultural assimi-

TABLE 5.2 Programs and Practices Related to Pluralism

Program and Practice	Focus	Objectives	Strategies
Multicultural Education	Cultural groups in a society	To help reduce discrimination against diverse cultural groups and provide them with equal educational opportunities. To present all students with cultural alternatives.	Creating a school atmosphere that has positive institutional norms toward diverse cultural groups within a nation-state.
Multiethnic Education	Ethnic groups within a society	To help reduce discrimination against victimized ethnic groups and to provide all students equal educational opportunities. To help reduce ethnic isolation and encapsulation.	Modifying the total school environment to make it more reflective of the ethnic diversity within a society.
Ethnic Studies	Ethnic groups within a society	To help students develop valid concepts, generalizations, and theories about ethnic groups in a society, to clarify their attitudes toward them, and to learn how to take action to eliminate racial and ethnic problems within a society. To help students develop ethnic literacy.	Modifying course objectives and teaching strategies, materials, and evaluation strategies so they include content and information about ethnic groups in a society.

lation has taken place among ethnic minorities in nations such as the United States and Canada, especially among people who are upwardly mobile. Some research indicates that the values, goals, and aspirations of lower-class African American youths are strikingly similar to those of middle-class Whites in the United States (Valentine, 1971). Thus, even though significant cultural differences exist between Anglo-Americans and most ethnic minorities in the United States, Anglo-Americans and ethnic minorities in the United States share many cultural characteristics. When cultural differences are minimized, conflict between non-White minorities and Whites frequently occurs. The cause of most of this conflict is often racial rather than cultural. Gordon (1964, p. 159) seriously questions the extent of cultural pluralism in the United States.

Structural pluralism . . . is the major key to the understanding of the ethnic makeup of American society, while cultural pluralism is the minor one. . . . The most salient fact . . . is the maintenance of structurally separate subsocieties of

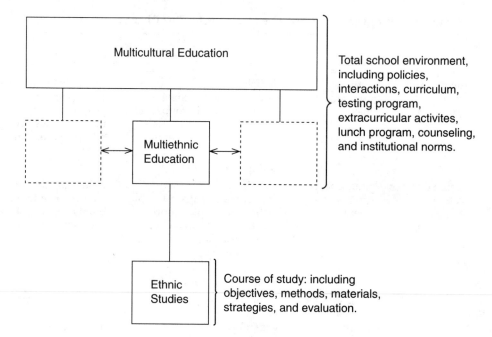

FIGURE 5.5   The Relationships among Multicultural Education, Multiethnic Education, and Ethnic Studies

the three major religious and the racial and quasi-racial groups, and even vestiges of the nationality groups, along with a massive trend toward acculturation of all groups . . . to American culture patterns.

The cultural and ethnic differences among racial groups must be reflected in educational programs designed to reduce intergroup tension and to foster interracial understanding. Overemphasis on cultural differences and cultural pluralism, however, may divert attention from *racial differences* and hostility. We err seriously when we try to understand ethnic conflict in the schools by focusing exclusively on cultural differences between dominant ethnic groups and ethnic minorities. Racism and racial conflict were very evident in the early 1990s, not only in the United States, but also in other Western societies, such as the United Kingdom, Australia, and Canada.

If we develop educational programs and policies designed to make students more accepting of cultural differences but fail to deal seriously with problems caused by racial differences, we will not solve our basic intergroup problems. This is especially true because widespread cultural assimilation is taking place in Western societies, and thus cultural differences between ethnic minorities and dominant ethnic groups will probably be less significant in the future than they are today.

Education for Ethnic and Racial Diversity

Concepts and terms related to ethnicity are the most useful and appropriate for conceptualizing the problems related to the education of ethnic minorities. Most definitions of ethnicity focus on the culture and race of immigrants and immigrant descendant groups. We must concentrate on both variables when designing programs to reduce interethnic and interracial conflict. In his study of definitions of ethnicity, Isajiw (1974, p. 117) found that culture was the second most frequently mentioned attribute of ethnicity, and race (and physical characteristics) was the fourth. Other frequently occurring attributes included common national or geographic origin, religion, language, sense of peoplehood, common values, separate institutions, and minority or subordinate status. Gordon's (1964, pp. 27–28) definition of ethnic group highlights the importance of race: "When I use the term 'ethnic,' I shall mean by it any group which is defined or set off by race, religion, or national origin, or some combination of these categories. . . . However, all of these categories have a common social-psychological referent in that all of them serve to create, through historical circumstances, a sense of peoplehood."

Both racial and cultural differences must be reflected in educational programs designed to reduce intergroup conflict and misunderstanding. Many of our efforts, however, must focus directly on reducing institutional, individual, and cultural racism (Gay, 1973), since racial differences, and not more generalized cultural differences, are the causes of the most serious psychological problems that students of color often experience in the schools and of racial conflict in Western societies.

The relationship between racism and the rejection of the cultures of people of color by dominant groups must also be considered when formulating educational policy to reduce interethnic conflict. Racism is a major reason that many Whites perceive and evaluate the cultures of people of color negatively. Intergroup problems frequently arise not because of the nature of the cultural differences between Whites and people of color, but because of the race of the individual or group who exhibits the specific cultural characteristics. The language of low-income people in the United States is often ridiculed, while the speech of White Boston Brahmins, which is as much a dialect as Black English, is frequently admired by Anglo-Americans. In the 1950s, Mexican American children were often prohibited from speaking Spanish in many schools in the Southwest (U.S. Commisssion on Civil Rights, 1974). However, when Spanish was spoken by Whites it was usually viewed as a useful and esteemed language. Gay (1973, p. 33) has called this phenomenon "cultural racism":

> [Another] form of racism is that which involves the elevation of the White Anglo-Saxon Protestant cultural heritage to a position of superiority over the cultural experiences of ethnic minority groups. It involves elements of both institutional and individual racism. The idea that "White is right" prevails in this expression of racism. Only those values, attitudes, beliefs, traditions, customs, and mores ascribed to by Whites are considered acceptable and normal

prescriptions of behavior. Anything else is labeled deviant, abnormal, degenerate, and pathological. If this belief were to remain in the realm of attitudes, it would be merely ethnocentrism. It becomes racism when Whites use power to perpetuate their cultural heritage and impose it upon others, while at the same time destroying the culture of ethnic minorities.

Because we need to focus our attention on variables related to both race and culture, and the complex interactions and relationships between these two major variables, *ethnic and racial diversity* is a much better concept than is multicultural education to describe and guide research and policy efforts related to the education of people of color.

Reducing Racial Conflict

A number of basic issues and problems related to race, ethnicity, and education warrant immediate and decisive action. A top priority should be to implement programs and practices designed to modify the negative racial attitudes of students. Research indicates that children are aware of racial differences at an early age and often express negative racial attitudes (Katz, 1976; Milner, 1983). Research further suggests that the racial attitudes of students tend to become more negative and crystallized as they grow older if deliberate efforts are not made to influence them (Lynch, 1987; Phinney & Rotheram, 1987).

To modify the racial attitudes of students successfully, experiences designed to influence the racial feelings and perceptions of teachers must be implemented. The attitudes, behavior, and the perceptions of classroom teachers have a profound impact on the social atmosphere of the school and the attitudes of students. Teachers are even more important than the materials they use because the ways in which they present material highly influence how they are viewed by students. Teachers must be strongly committed to a racially tolerant school atmosphere before such a setting can be created and maintained.

Unfortunately, research indicates that many teachers display negative attitudes and behavior toward low-income students and students of color. Studies by Leacock (1969), Rist (1970), and Gay (1974) indicate that many teachers, in both subtle and overt ways, communicate negative feelings to their minority students and have a disproportionate number of negative verbal and nonverbal interactions with them.

These types of studies suggest that teacher in-service education is essential if we are going to reduce institutional racism in the school setting. In-service education for teachers and other school personnel must have at least two major objectives: (1) to help teachers gain a new conceptualization of the history and culture of their societies and (2) to help them confront their own racial feelings, which can be a painful process and, if not handled competently, can be destructive and unsettling. However, despite these risks, it is essential that teachers clarify their racial feelings before they can contribute positively to the reduction of racial prejudice in students and function effectively within a multiethnic setting.

The school can also help reduce cultural racism and ethnocentrism by maximizing the cultural options of mainstream youths and helping them break out of their ethnic encapsulations. These youths need to learn that there are other ways of being, of feeling, and of perceiving. Most individuals are socialized within ethnic enclaves, where they learn one basic life-style. Consequently, they assume that their way is the only way, or that it is the only legitimate cultural style. Other life-styles seem strange, different, and exotic. Most ethnic minority individuals are forced to function within the dominant culture. However, many mainstream individuals are never required to function within other ethnic cultures. The school should provide all students with opportunities to become familiar with other races, life-styles, and cultures and should help young people develop ethnic literacy and become more sophisticated about other cultures. Most people are ignorant about ethnic cultures other than their own.

Mainstream youths should be taught that they have cultural options. We severely limit the potentiality of students when we merely teach them aspects of their own cultures. Anglo-American students should realize that using Black English is one effective way to communicate; that Native Americans have values, beliefs, and life-styles that may be functional for them; and that alternative ways of behaving and of viewing the universe are practiced within the United States that they can freely embrace. By helping mainstream students view the world beyond their limited racial and ethnic perspectives, we will enrich them as human beings and enable them to live more productive and fulfilling lives.

Summary

A wide range of concepts are used to describe programs and practices related to ethnic, cultural, and racial diversity in Western societies. The proliferation of concepts in part reflects the ideological conflicts in multicultural education and the emergent status of educational reform related to ethnic and cultural diversity. Concepts related to multicultural and multiethnic education must be better clarified before pluralistic educational reforms and research can be more effectively designed and implemented.

This chapter examines the major concepts in the field, such as culture, multicultural education, multiethnic education, and ethnic studies. I have tried to clarify the meanings of these concepts and to describe their policy implications.

The issues and problems related to race and education are complex and difficult to diagnose and solve. Many variables influence the relationship between people of color and Whites, such as socioeconomic status, ethnicity, values, languages, and behavioral patterns. Variables related to culture and ethnicity will remain important in explaining interactions between racial groups as long as the groups are socialized within different ethnic communities and have negative attitudes toward the cultural differences exhibited by other racial groups.

However, a focus on ethnic and cultural variables should not divert attention from the role of individual and institutional racism in Western societies. Racism is the basic cause of many of the serious psychological problems that people of color experience in the schools and in the larger society. The interaction of race and culture also explains many interracial problems. Individuals and groups frequently respond negatively to specific cultural behaviors because they are exhibited by racially stigmatized ethnic minorities.

Effective educational policy and programs must be based on research and theory that focus on both race and culture and on the complex interactions between these two major variables, such as socioeconomic status. Programs that focus exclusively on cultural differences are not likely to lead to positive interracial interactions and understandings. An exclusively culture approach is also limited by the extensive degree to which cultural assimilation has taken place in Western societies. Race, however, cannot totally explain interethnic problems because significant cultural differences exist among some minority cultures and mainstream cultures in the various Western societies.

Because of the complexity of the problem, we need to examine multiple variables when trying to determine causes and to devise effective educational programs related to race and education. Further research and analyses are needed to clarify the relationship between culture and race in explaining interracial problems and conflict. Concepts related to race and ethnicity can best guide research and programmatic efforts related to the education of students of color.

References

Banks, J. A. (1991). *Teaching Strategies for Ethnic Studies* (5th ed.). Boston: Allyn and Bacon.

Banks, J. A., Cortes, C., Gay, G., Garcia, R., & Ochoa, A. (1992). *Curriculum Guidelines for Multicultural Education* (Rev. ed.). Washington, DC: National Council for the Social Studies.

Batelaan, P. (1983). *The Practice of Intercultural Education.* London: Commission for Racial Equality.

Belenky, M. F., Clinchy, B. M., Goldberger, N. R., & Tarule, J. M. (1986). *Women's Ways of Knowing: The Development of Self, Voice, and Mind.* New York: Basic Books.

Bell, D. (1975). *Ethnicity and Social Change.* In N. Glazer & D. P. Moynihan (Eds.), *Ethnicity: Theory and Experience* (pp. 141–174). Cambridge, MA: Harvard University Press.

Bell, D. (1992). The Cultural Wars: American Intellectual Life, 1965–1992. *The Wilson Quarterly, 16,* 74–107.

Brooks, R. L. (1990). *Rethinking the American Race Problem.* Berkeley: University of California Press.

Bullivant, B. M. (1984). *Pluralism: Cultural Maintenance and Evolution.* Clevedon, Avon, England: Multilingual Patterns Ltd.

Clark, K. B. (1963). *Prejudice and Your Child* (2nd ed.). Boston: Beacon Press.

Dimen-Schein, M. (1977). *The Anthropological Imagination.* New York: McGraw-Hill.

Franklin, R. S. (1991). *Shadows of Race and Class.* Minneapolis: The University of Minnesota Press.

Garcia, R. L. (1991). *Teaching in a Pluralistic Society: Concepts, Models, Strategies* (2nd ed.). New York: Harper/Collins.

Gates, H. L. (1992). *Loose Canons: Notes on the Culture Wars.* New York: Oxford University Press.

Gay, G. (1973). Racism in America: Imperatives for Teaching Ethnic Studies. In J. A. Banks, (Ed.), *Teaching Ethnic Studies: Concepts and Strategies* (pp. 31–34). Washington, DC: National Council for the Social Studies.

Gay, G. (1974). *Differential Dyadic Interactions of Black and White Teachers with Black and White Pupils in Recently Desegregated Social Studies Classrooms: A Function of Teacher and Pupil Ethnicity.* Washington, DC: National Institute of Education.

Gilligan, C. (1982). *In a Different Voice: Psychological Theory and Women's Development.* Cambridge, MA: Harvard University Press.

Gordon, M. M. (1964). *Assimilation in American Life.* New York: Oxford University Press.

Grant, C. A. (1979). Multicultural Education in the International Year of the Child: Problems and Possibilities. *Journal of Negro Education, 48,* 233–446.

Greenbaum, W. (1974). America in Search of a New Ideal: An Essay on the Rise of Pluralism. *Harvard Educational Review, 44,* 411–444.

Horner, M. S. (1972). Toward an Understanding of Achievement-Related Conflicts in Women. *Journal of Social Issues, 28,* 157–176.

Isajiw, W. W. (1974). Definitions of Ethnicity. *Ethnicity, 1,* 111–124.

Katz, P. A. (Ed.). (1976). *Towards the Elimination of Racism.* New York: Pergamon Press.

Kroeber, A. L., & Kluckhohn, C. (1952). *Culture: A Critical Review of Concepts and Definitions.* New York: Vintage Books.

Leacock, E. B. (1969). *Teaching and Learning in City Schools.* New York: Basic Books.

Lynch, J. (1987). *Prejudice Reduction and the Schools.* London: Cassell.

Milner, D. (1983). *Children and Race: Ten Years On.* London: Ward Lock Educational.

Myrdal, G., with R. Sterner & A. Rose. (1944). *An American Dilemma: The Negro Problem and Modern Democracy.* New York: Harper and Row.

Nieto, S. (1992). *Affirming Diversity: The Sociopolitical Context of Multicultural Education.* White Plains, NY: Longman.

Parsons, T. (1975). Some Theoretical Considerations on the Nature and Trends of Change of Ethnicity. In N. Glazer and D. P. Moynihan (Eds.), *Ethnicity, Theory and Experience.* (pp. 53–83). Cambridge, MA: Harvard University Press.

Philips, S. U. (1983). *The Invisible Culture.* New York: Longman.

Phinney, J. S., & Rotheram, M. J. (Eds.). (1987). *Children's Ethnic Socialization: Pluralism and Development.* Beverly Hills, CA: Sage Publications.

Ramirez, M. III, & Castaneda, A. (1974). *Cultural Democracy, Bicognitive Development and Education.* New York: Academic Press.

Rist, R. C. (1970). Student Social Class and Teacher Expectations: The Self-Fulfilling Prophecy in Ghetto Education. *Harvard Educational Review, 40,* 411–451.

Taylor, E. B. (1871). *Primitive Culture,* Vol. 1. London: John Murray.

Terkel, S. (1992). *Race: How Blacks and Whites Think & Feel about the American Obsession.* New York: The New Press.

Theodorson, G. A., & Theodorson, A. G. (1969). *A Modern Dictionary of Sociology.* New York: Barnes and Noble.

U.S. Commission on Civil Rights. (1974). *Toward Quality Education for Mexican Americans,* Report VI. Washington, DC: Author.

Valentine, C. A. (1971). Deficit, Difference, and Bicultural Models of Afro-American Behavior. *Harvard Educational Review, 41,* 137–157.

Chapter 6

Race, Ethnicity, and Educational Paradigms

The academic and social problems that lower-class and students of color experience in the schools have been discussed widely since the ethnic revival movements of the 1960s. The academic achievement of students of color such as Japanese Americans and Chinese Americans exceeds that of Whites, but the academic achievement of most other groups of students of color in the United States is considerably below that of Whites (Grant, 1992; McCarthy, 1990; Sleeter, 1992; Valencia, 1991). In 1980 the percentage of high school graduates for persons twenty-five years or older was 81.6 for Japanese Americans, 73.3 for Chinese Americans, 69.6 for Whites of non-Spanish origin, and 66.5 for all persons in the United States. However, the percentages for Mexican Americans, Puerto Ricans, and African Americans were 37.6, 40.1, and 51.2, respectively (U.S. Bureau of the Census, 1983). Ethnic minority students in other Western nations, such as the West Indians in the United Kingdom and the Metis in Canada, also achieve below their mainstream peers (Gibson & Ogbu, 1991; Tomlinson, 1989).

A wide range of educational reforms designed to increase equality for students from diverse ethnic, racial, and social-class groups has been implemented since the 1960s. These various educational reforms have emanated from concepts, theories, and paradigms based on different and often conflicting assumptions, values, and goals. In this chapter I identify, describe, and critically analyze the major concepts and paradigms that have been used to explain the low academic achievement of ethnic, racial, and low-income students; the educational programs and practices that exemplify these concepts and paradigms; and their values and assumptions. I also describe how extensively single-factor paradigms are used to guide educational research and practice and what their limitations are and then briefly outline a multifactor, *holistic* theory of multicultural education that can be used to guide educational practice and research.

laws,principles,explanations,theories of a discipline

The Nature of Paradigms

Kuhn (1970, p. 15) uses the term *paradigm* to describe the "entire constellation of beliefs, values, techniques, and so on shared by members of a given [scientific] community." The laws, principles, explanations, and theories of a discipline are also part of its paradigm. Kuhn argues that during the history of a science, new paradigms arise to replace older ones. He calls this phenomenon a "scientific revolution." Kuhn refers primarily to natural science disciplines and draws most of his examples from the natural sciences. It is not clear, in the Kuhnian sense, whether social science has developed true paradigms because of the paucity of universal laws, principles, and theories in social science and because social science is characterized by many competing systems of explanations. Writes Kuhn (1970, p. 15), "It remains an open question what parts of social science have yet acquired such paradigms at all. History suggests that the road to a firm research consensus is extraordinarily arduous." Barnes (1982, p. 17), building on Kuhn's work, defines a paradigm as "an existing scientific achievement, a specific concrete *problem-solution* which has gained universal acceptance throughout a scientific field as a valid procedure, and as a model of valid procedure for pedagogic use." He writes further (pp. 18–19) that

> the culture of an established natural science is passed on in the form of paradigms. The central task of the teacher is to display them. The central task of the students is to assimilate them, and to acquire competence in their routine use. . . . Scientific training . . . demands acceptance of the existing orthodoxy in a given field. Accordingly, it tends to avoid anything which might undermine or offer an alternative to that orthodoxy *[emphasis added]. The history of a field, wherein are found radically variant concepts, problems and methods of problem-solution, is either ignored, or is systematically rewritten as a kind of journey toward, and hence a legitimation of, present knowledge.*

Multicultural Education Paradigms

I am using the word *paradigm* in this chapter to describe an interrelated set of facts, concepts, generalizations, and theories that attempt to explain human behavior or social phenomena and that imply policy and action. A paradigm, which is also a set of explanations, has specific goals, assumptions, and values that can be described. Paradigms compete with one another in the arena of ideas and public policy.

The various problem-solutions or paradigms in multicultural education, like other systems of explanations, have many of the characteristics of paradigms discussed by Kuhn and Barnes, although they are *quasi* or *partial* paradigms in the Kuhnian sense. The *cultural deprivation, language,* and *radical* paradigms in multicultural education constitute constellations of beliefs, values, and techniques and are shared by members of a given scientific community. These conceptions are also problem-solutions that have gained acceptance as valid procedures and explanations.

Each paradigm, such as the cultural deprivation, the language, and the radical, demands acceptance of its orthodoxy and tends to avoid concepts, explanations, and theories that might offer an alternative view or explanation. Each paradigm is also a *partial* theory that provides an incomplete explanation of social reality (Merton, 1968). *Each paradigm is perspectivistic and emanates from specific values, assumptions, and conceptions of the good society.* Paradigms both mirror and perpetuate specific ideologies and lead to different educational policies and practices. Some paradigms, such as the cultural deprivation and the genetic, support dominant ethnic group hegemony and inequality; others, such as the radical and racism, imply reconstruction of the political and economic systems so that excluded ethnic and social-class groups can experience equality.

Response Paradigms: The Schools React to Ethnic Revitalization Movements

When we examine the development of ethnic revitalization movements in Western democratic nations such as the United States, Canada, the United Kingdom, and Australia and the responses that educational institutions have made to them, we can identify and describe specific types and patterns of institutional responses. These patterns and prototypical responses are called *paradigms* in this chapter. These paradigmatic responses do not necessarily occur in a linear or set order in any particular nation, although some of them tend to occur earlier in the development of ethnic revitalization movements than do others. Thus, the response paradigms relate in a general way to the phases of ethnic revitalization movements described in Chapter 2. The ethnic additive and self-concept development paradigms, for example, tend to arise during the first or early phase of an ethnic revitalization movement. Single-explanation paradigms tend to emerge before multiple explanation ones. Single-explanation paradigms usually emerge during the first phase of ethnic revitalization, but multiple-explanation paradigms usually do not emerge or become popular until the later phase.

A sophisticated neoconservative paradigm tends to develop during the final phase of ethnic revitalization, when the groups that are trying to institutionalize pluralism begin to experience success and those committed to assimilationism and to defending the status quo begin to fear that the pluralistic reformers might institutionalize a new ideal and create new goals for the nation-state.

I describe a number of response paradigms that develop when ethnic revitalization movements emerge (see Table 6.1). These multicultural education paradigms might develop within a nation at different times or they may coexist at the same time. Each paradigm is likely to exist in some form in a nation that has experienced an ethnic revitalization movement. However, only one or two are likely to be dominant at any particular time. The leaders and advocates of particular paradigms compete to make their paradigms the most popular in academic, government, and school settings. Proponents of paradigms that can attract

TABLE 6.1 Multicultural Education Paradigms

[handwritten: still in existence in some forms]

Paradigm	Major Assumptions	Major Goals	School Programs and Practices
Ethnic Additive	Ethnic content can be added to the curriculum without reconceptualizing or restructuring it.	To integrate the curriculum by adding special units, lessons, and ethnic holidays to it.	Special ethnic studies units; ethnic studies classes that focus on ethnic foods and holidays; units on ethnic heroes.
Self-Concept Development	Ethnic content can help increase the self-concept of ethnic minority students. Ethnic minority students have low self-concepts.	To increase the self-concepts and academic achievement of ethnic minority students.	Special units in ethnic studies that emphasize the contributions ethnic groups have made to the making of the nation; units on ethnic heroes.
Cultural Deprivation	Many poor and ethnic minority youths are socialized within homes and communities that prevent them from acquiring the cognitive skills and cultural characteristics needed to succeed in school.	To compensate for the cognitive deficits and dysfunctional cultural characteristics that many poor and ethnic minority youths bring to school.	Compensatory educational experiences that are behavioristic and intensive, e.g., Head Start and Follow Through programs in the United States.
Language	Ethnic and linguistic minority youths often achieve poorly in school because instruction is not conducted in their mother tongue.	To provide initial instruction in the child's mother tongue.	Teaching English as a Second Language programs; bilingual-bicultural education programs.
Racism	Racism is the major cause of the educational problems of non-White ethnic minority groups. The school can and should play a major role in eliminating institutional racism.	To reduce personal and institutional racism within the schools and the larger society.	Prejudice reduction; antiracist workshops and courses for teachers; antiracist lessons for students: an examination of the total environment to determine ways in which racism can be reduced, including curriculum materials, teacher attitudes, and school norms.
Radical	A major goal of the school is to educate students so they will willingly accept their social-class status in society. The school cannot help liberate victimized ethnic and cultural groups because it plays a key role in keeping them oppressed.	To raise the level of consciousness of students and teachers about the nature of capitalist, class-stratified societies; to help students and teachers develop a commitment to radical reform of the social and economic systems in capitalist societies.	

Continued

TABLE 6.1 *(continued)*

Paradigm	Major Assumptions	Major Goals	School Programs and Practices
	Lower-class ethnic groups cannot attain equality within a class-stratified capitalist society. Radical reform of the social structure is a prerequisite of equality for poor and minority students.		
Genetic	Lower-class and ethnic minority youths often achieve poorly in school because of their biological characteristics. Educational intervention programs cannot eliminate the achievement gap between these students and majority-group students because of their different genetic characteristics.	To create a meritocracy based on intellectual ability as measured by standardized aptitude tests.	Ability-grouped classes; use of IQ tests to determine career goals for students; different career ladders for students who score differently on standardized tests.
Cultural Pluralism	Schools should promote ethnic identifications and allegiances. Educational programs should reflect the characteristics of ethnic students.	To promote the maintenance of groups; to promote the liberation of ethnic groups; to educate ethnic students in a way that will not alienate them from their home cultures.	Ethnic studies courses that are ideologically based; ethnic schools that focus on the maintenance of ethnic cultures and traditions.
Cultural Difference	Minority youths have rich and diverse cultures that have values, languages, and behavioral styles that are functional for them and valuable for the nation-state.	To change the school so it respects and legitimizes the cultures of students from diverse ethnic groups and cultures.	Educational programs that reflect the learning styles of ethnic groups, that incorporate their cultures when developing instructional principles, and that integrate ethnic content into the mainstream curriculum.
Assimilation-ism	Ethnic minority youths should be freed of ethnic identifications and commit-ments so they can become full participants in the national culture. When schools foster ethnic commitments and identifi-cations, this retards the academic growth of ethnic youths and contributes to the development of ethnic tension and balkanization.	To educate students in a way that will free them of their ethnic characteristics and enable them to acquire the values and behavior of the mainstream culture.	A number of educational programs are based on assimilationist assump-tions and goals, such as cultural deprivation pro-grams, most Teaching English as a Second Language programs, and the mainstream curriculum in most Western nations. Despite the challenges they received during the 1970s, the curricula in the Western nations are still dominated by assimilationist goals and ideologies.

the most government and private support are likely to become the prevailing voices for multicultural education within a particular time or period.

Sometimes one dominant paradigm replaces another, and something akin to what Kuhn calls a "scientific revolution" takes place (Kuhn, 1970). However, what happens more frequently is that a new paradigm will emerge that challenges an older one but does not replace it. During the late 1960s in the United States, the cultural deprivation paradigm dominated the theory, research, and practice related to educating lower-income and minority groups (Bereiter & Engelmann, 1966). This paradigm was seriously challenged by the cultural difference paradigm in the 1970s (Baratz & Baratz, 1970). The cultural difference paradigm did not replace the cultural deprivation paradigm; rather, the two paradigms coexisted. However, the cultural deprivation paradigm lost much of its influence and legitimacy, especially among young scholars of color (Banks, 1984).

The cultural deprivation paradigm was reborn during the late 1980s and early 1990s in the form of a new concept, "at risk" (Richardson et al., 1989). The at-risk paradigm coexists with other paradigms, such as the cultural difference, language, and radical paradigms. However, it is popular and influential in part because it is a funding category for state and federal funding agencies.

The Ethnic Additive and Self-Concept Development Paradigms

Often the first phase of a school's response to an ethnic revitalization movement consists of the infusion of bits and pieces of content about ethnic groups into the curriculum, especially into courses in the humanities, the social studies, and the language arts. Teaching about ethnic heroes and celebrating ethnic holidays are salient characteristics of the ethnic additive paradigm.

This paradigm usually emerges as the first one for a variety of reasons. It develops in part because ethnic groups usually demand the inclusion of their heroes, holidays, and contributions into the curriculum during the first phase of ethnic revitalization. This paradigm also emerges because teachers usually have little knowledge about marginalized ethnic groups during the early phase of ethnic revitalization. It is much easier for them to add isolated bits of information about ethnic groups to the curriculum and to celebrate ethnic holidays than meaningfully to integrate ethnic content into the curriculum or to restructure the curriculum. Thus, Afro-American History Month, American Indian Day, and Asian and Afro-Caribbean feasts and festivals become a part of the curriculum.

The ethnic additive paradigm also arises early because educational institutions tend to respond to the first phase of ethnic revitalization with quickly conceptualized and hurriedly formulated programs that are designed primarily to silence ethnic protest rather than to contribute to equality and to the structural inclusion of ethnic groups into society. In each of the major Western nations, many early programs related to ethnic groups were poorly conceptualized and implemented without careful and thoughtful planning. Such programs are usually attacked and eliminated during the later phases of ethnic revitalization, when the institutionalization of ethnic programs and reforms begins. The weaknesses of these early programs become the primary justification for their elimination. When such programs were attacked and eliminated in the United States in the 1980s many careful and sensitive observers stated that they had been designed to fail.

Two other major goals that educators express during the first phase of ethnic revitalization are to raise the self-concepts of students of color and to increase their racial pride. These goals develop because leaders of ethnic movements try to shape new and positive ethnic identities and because educators assume that members of ethnic groups who have experienced discrimination and structural exclusion have negative self-concepts and negative attitudes toward their own racial and ethnic groups. Much of the social science research before the 1960s reinforced this belief (Clark, 1963; Cross, 1991). Some leaders of ethnic movements also express it. Many educators assume that students need healthy self-concepts in order to do well in school. They also assume that content about ethnic heroes and holidays will enhance the self-concepts and academic achievements of ethnic groups (Asante, 1991). Stone has described some of the serious limitations of the self-concept paradigm (Stone, 1981).

Implications for School Practice

The ethnic additive and self-concept development paradigms often result in policies and school practices that require no fundamental changes in the views, assumptions, and institutional practices of teachers and administrators. These paradigms often lead to the trivialization of ethnic cultures by well-meaning teachers (Moodley, 1986). The emphasis is usually on the life-styles of ethnic groups rather than on reform of the social and political systems so that the opportunities and life chances of low-income and minority students can be substantially improved (McCarthy, 1990).

Policy that emanates from the ethnic additive and self-concept development paradigms often results in educators' doing little more than adding to the curriculum isolated bits of ethnic content designed to enhance the self-concepts of students of color. A fundamental rethinking of the total curriculum does not take place because the assumption is made that only ethnic minorities need to study ethnic content. Much of the ethnic studies curricula in the schools, especially during the early phase of ethnic revitalization movements, reflects the ethnic additive and self-concept development paradigms.

The Cultural Deprivation Paradigm

Cultural deprivation theories, programs, and research often develop during the first phase of an ethnic revitalization movement. Cultural deprivation theorists assume that lower-class youths do not achieve well in school because of family disorganization, poverty, and the lack of effective concept acquisition, and also because of other intellectual and cultural deficits these students experience during their first years of life (Bloom, Davis, & Hess, 1965; Keddie, 1973). Cultural deprivation theorists assume that a major goal of school programs for the so-called culturally deprived students is to provide them with cultural and other experiences that will compensate for their cognitive and intellectual deficits. Cultural deprivation theorists believe that lower-class students can learn the basic skills taught by the schools but that these skills must often be taught using intensive, behaviorally oriented instruction (Bereiter & Engelmann, 1966).

Programs based on cultural deprivation theory, such as most of the compensatory education programs in the United States, are structured in such a way that they require students to make major changes in their behavior. Teachers and other educators are required to make few changes in their behavior or in educational institutions. Such programs also ignore the cultures that students bring to school and assume that low-income and minority children are culturally deprived or disadvantaged. Some of these programs in the United States have been able to help low-income students and students of color to experience achievement gains, but these gains are often not maintained as the students progress through the grades.

Implications for School Practice

Teachers and administrators who accept the cultural deprivations paradigm often blame the victims for their problems and academic failure (Ryan, 1971). These educators argue that low-income students and students of color often do poorly in school because of their cultural and social-class characteristics, not because they are ineffectively taught. They believe that the school is severely limited in what it can do to help these students to achieve because of the culture into which they are socialized.

School programs based on the cultural deprivation paradigm try to alienate students from their first cultures because these cultures are regarded as the primary reason students from specific cultural groups are not achieving well in school (Dickeman, 1973). Students are forced to choose between commitment to their first cultures and educational success.

Educational programs and practices based on the cultural deprivation paradigm reflect and perpetuate the status quo and dominant group hegemony, ideology, and values. They do not question the extent to which dominant group values, assumptions, and societal practices keep lower-class and ethnic youths marginalized and prevent them from becoming empowered and structurally integrated into the mainstream society.

The Language Paradigm

Often during the early stage of ethnic revitalization or when a large number of immigrants settle in a nation and enroll in the schools, educators view the problems of these groups as resulting primarily from their language or dialect differences. When the West Indians and Asians first enrolled in British schools in significant numbers in the 1960s, many British educators believed that if they could solve the language problems of these youths they would experience academic success in British schools. British educators' early responses to the problems of immigrant children were thus almost exclusively related to language (Schools Council, 1970). Special programs were set up to train teachers and to develop materials for teaching English as a second language to immigrant students. French educators also viewed the problems of the North African and Asian students in their schools in the late 1970s as primarily language-related (Banks, 1978).

In the United States, the educational problems of Puerto Ricans and Mexican Americans are often assumed to be rooted in language (Hakuta, 1986; Minami & Kennedy, 1991). Proponents of bilingual education in the United States argued during the 1970s that if the language problems of these students were solved, the students would experience academic success in the schools. As bilingual programs were established in the United States, educators began to realize that many other factors, such as social class, learning styles, and motivation, were also important variables that influenced the academic achievement of Hispanic ethnic groups in the United States (Valencia, 1991; Walsh, 1991).

The experiences with programs based on the language paradigm in the Western nations teach us that an exclusive language approach to the educational problems of ethnic and immigrant groups is insufficient. Languages are integral parts of cultures. Consequently, any attempt to educate students effectively from diverse language and cultural groups must be comprehensive in scope and must focus on variables in the educational environment other than language. An exclusive language approach is unlikely to help language minority students attain educational parity with mainstream students.

The Racism Paradigm

Sometime early during an ethnic revitalization movement, ethnic minority groups and their liberal allies usually state that institutionalized racism is the only or most important cause of the problems of ethnic groups in school and society. This claim by ethnic minorities usually evokes a counterclaim by those who defend the status quo, and an intense debate ensues (Brandt, 1986). This debate usually takes place during the first phase of ethnic revitalization, when ethnic polarization and tension are high. The debate between those who claim that racism is the cause of the problems of ethnic groups and those who deny this claim is usually not productive because each side sets forth extreme and competing claims.

A major goal of the racism advocates is not so much to convince other people that racism does, in fact, cause all of the problems of victimized ethnic groups. Rather, their goals are to legitimize racism as a valid explanation and to convince leaders and people who defend the status quo that racism is an important and tenacious part of Western societies. The debate between radical reformers and conservative defenders of the status quo remains stalemated and single-focused until the dominant group acknowledges the existence of racism and takes meaningful steps to eliminate it. Until this acknowledgment is made in official statements, policies, and actions, radical reformers will continue to state that racism is the single cause of the social, economic, and educational problems of marginalized ethnic groups.

Radical reformers will not search for or find more complex paradigms that explain the problems of marginalized ethnic groups until mainstream leaders acknowledge the existence of institutionalized racism. In other words, institutionalized racism must become legitimized as an explanation, and serious steps must be taken to eliminate it before an ethnic revitalization movement can reach a phase in which other paradigms will be accepted by radical reformers who articulate the interests of groups that are victims of institutionalized racism. Societies and nations are successful in making the racism paradigm less popular when official bodies and leaders validate it, acknowledge that racism exists in the society, and take visible and vigorous steps to eliminate it, such as enacting legislation that prevents discrimination and hiring minorities for influential jobs in the public and private sectors.

The Radical Paradigm

A radical paradigm tends to develop during the early or later stage of ethnic revitalization. It usually has a critical theory or reproductionist orientation (Giroux, 1992; Carthy, 1990). The other paradigms assume that the school can successfully intervene and help ethnic minority youths attain social and political equality, but the radical paradigm assumes that the school is part of the problem and plays a key role in keeping ethnic groups oppressed (Solomon, 1992; Weis, 1988). Thus, it is very difficult for the school to help liberate oppressed groups because one of its central purposes is to educate students so that they will willingly accept their assigned status in society. A primary role of the school is to reproduce the social-class, economic, and political structure (Giroux, 1992).

The radical paradigm stresses the limited role that schools can play to eliminate racism and discrimination and to promote equality for low-income students. Christopher Jencks (1972) is an ineffectiveness of school theorist in the United States. He argues that the most effective way to bring about equality for poor people is to equalize incomes directly rather than to rely on the schools to bring about equality in the adult life of students. He suggests that the schooling route is much too indirect and will most likely result in failure. Bowles and Gintis (1976) wrote a neo-Marxist critique of schools in the United States that copiously documents how schools reinforce the social-class stratification within society and make students politically passive and content with their social-class status.

The radical paradigm argues that multicultural education is a palliative to keep excluded and oppressed groups such as African Americans from rebelling against a system that promotes structural inequality and institutionalized racism (McCarthy, 1990). The radical critics contend that multicultural education does not deal with the real reasons that ethnic and racial groups are oppressed and victimized. It avoids any serious discussion of class, institionalized racism, power, and capitalism. Multicultural education, argue the radical critics, diverts attention from the real problems and issues. They argue that we need to focus on the institutions and structures of society rather than on the characteristics of low-income students or on cultural differences.

Responding to the Radical Critics

Multicultural theorists need to study seriously the critics of the field, evaluate their arguments for soundness and validity, and incorporate their ideas that will contribute to the main goals of multicultural education. These goals include reforming the total school environment so that students from diverse racial, ethnic, and cultural groups will experience educational equality. Realistically, goals for multicultural education must be limited. Educators have little control over the wider society or over students when they leave the classroom. Educators can teach students the basic skills and help them to develop more democratic attitudes by creating school and classroom environments that promote cultural democracy. However, schools alone cannot eliminate racism and inequality in the wider society. They can reinforce democratic social and political movements that take place beyond the school walls and thus contribute in important ways to the elimination of institutional racism and structural inequality. The multicultural curriculum can give students keen insights into racism and inequality within their societies and thus help them develop a commitment to social change.

Multicultural theorists need to think seriously about the radical arguments that multicultural education is a palliative to contain ethnic rage and that it does not deal seriously with the structural inequalities in society and with such important concepts as racism, class, structural inequality, and capitalism (McCarthy, 1990). During the early stages of multicultural education in the United States, when it focused primarily on teaching the cultures and histories of ethnic groups of color, the attention devoted to such concepts as racism and structural inequality was salient. Yet, as the ethnic studies movement expanded to include more and more ethnic groups and eventually to include feminist issues and other cultural groups, increasingly less attention was devoted to racism and to the analysis of power relationships. Gay (1983, pp. 560–563) has expressed concern about the wide boundaries of the field:

> *Another potential threat to multiethnic education comes from within. Although any educational idea must grow and change if it is to stand the test of time, such growth must remain within reasonable boundaries and retain a certain degree of continuity. If many new dimensions are added to an idea too rapidly, the original idea may be distorted beyond recognition. This may be beginning to happen to multiethnic education.*

The radical critique of multicultural education should stimulate multicultural educators to devote more attention to such issues as racism, power relationships, and structural inequality. The radical writers are accurate when they argue that racism and structural inequality are the root causes of many problems of ethnic groups in modernized Western nations such as the United States and the United Kingdom. However, as Green (1982) perceptively points out, multicultural educators must live with the contradiction that they are trying to promote democratic and humane reforms within schools, which are institutions that often reflect and perpetuate some of the salient antidemocratic values pervasive within the wider society. Green writes (p. 34), "Contradiction is the essence of social change."

The school itself is contradictory, because it often expounds democratic values while at the same time contradicting them. Thus, the radical scholars overstate their case when they argue that the schools merely perpetuate and reproduce the inequalities in society. The influence of the schools on individuals is neither as unidimensional nor as cogent as some radical critics claim. The school, both explicitly and implicitly, teaches both democratic and antiegalitarian values, just as the wider society does. Thus, the schools, like the society of which they are a part, create the kind of moral dilemma for people that Gunnar Myrdal (1944) described when he studied U.S. race relations in the forties. Myrdal believed that this moral dilemma made social change possible because most Americans felt a need to make the democratic ideals they inculcated and societal practices more consistent.

The Genetic Paradigm

The ideology and research developed by radical reformers do not go unchallenged. An ideological war takes place between radical reformers and conservatives who defend the status quo. While radical and liberal reformers develop ideology and research to show how the major problems of ethnic groups are caused by institutionalized racism and capitalism, antiegalitarian advocates and researchers develop an ideology and research stating that the failure of ethnic groups in school and society is due to their own inherited or socialized characteristics.

Both radical reformers and conservative scholars tend to develop single causal paradigms during the early phase of ethnic revitalization. The paradigms developed by radical theorists tend to focus on racism and other structural and institutional problems in society, and those developed by conservative researchers usually focus on the characteristics of ethnic students themselves, such as their genetic characteristics and their family socialization.

In the United States the most popular antiegalitarian theories focus on the genetic characteristics of African American and low-income students; these theories were developed by such researchers as Jensen (1969), Shockley (1972), and Herrnstein (1971). Jensen argues that the genetic makeup of African Americans is the most important reason that compensatory educational programs, designed to increase the IQ of African American students, have not been more successful. Shockley developed a theory about the genetic inferiority of African Americans that is less accepted by the academic community than is Jensen's. Herrnstein published his controversial article, which argued that social class reflects genetic differences, in the *Atlantic Monthly*, a widely circulated and highly respected popular magazine. Herrnstein's views evoked more controversy than did Jensen's, perhaps because he argued that social class rather than race was related to heredity. Educators not committed to educational equality for lower-class and students of color often embrace the genetic paradigm. They use it as an alibi for educational neglect.

Implications for School Practice

The assumption that IQ and other tests of mental ability can accurately measure innate mental ability is institutionalized and perpetuated within the schools. Students are assigned to academic tracks based on their performance on tests of mental ability and on other factors such as teacher recommendations and grades. A highly disproportionate number of lower-class students and students of color are assigned to lower-ability tracks. Assignment to lower academic tracks actualizes the self-fulfilling prophecy (Merton, 1968). Research by Oakes (1985, 1992) documents how teacher expectations of students vary in different kinds of tracks. Students in higher academic tracks are expected to learn more and are consequently taught more; those in lower tracks are expected to learn less and are consequently taught less.

The tracking system, which is widespread within U.S. schools, perpetuates social-class and ethnic inequality and teaches students to be content with their social-class status. The genetic paradigm is used to support and justify the tracking system. It perpetuates dominant ethnic group hegemony, inequality, and class and ethnic stratification.

Competing Paradigms

Particularly during the later stage of ethnic revitalization, when aspects of ethnic diversity are being implemented within the schools, an intense clash of ideologies and paradigms is likely to occur between people committed to ethnic pluralism and people who endorse assimilationism and are committed to preserving the status quo. The language paradigm (which often includes a call for bilingual education), the racism paradigm, and the radical paradigm are especially likely to evoke strong responses from assimilationists, who are committed to nationalism and to developing strong national commitments and identifications. In the United States, the call for bilingual education and the federal legislation and court decisions that promoted it stimulated one of the most acid educational debates in recent history (Minami & Kennedy, 1991).

A cultural pluralism paradigm tends to emerge during the first phase of ethnic revitalization. It maintains that a major goal of the schools should be to help students develop commitments and attachments to their ethnic groups so they can participate in its liberation. Cultural pluralists believe that ethnicity and ethnic cultures have a significant influence on the socialization of students and thus should strongly influence the formulation of educational policies and programs (Asante, 1991).

As the ethnic revitalization movement develops, more moderate paradigms emerge, such as the cultural difference and bicultural paradigms. The cultural difference paradigm maintains that ethnic minority youths often do not achieve well in school not because they have a deprived culture, but because their cultures are different from the culture of the school. The school should therefore modify the educational environment in order to make it more consistent with the cultures of ethnic minority youths. If this is done, the students will experience academic gains in the school (Hale-Benson, 1982; Shade, 1989).

Assimilationists often oppose such pluralist programs as bilingual education and ethnic studies because, they argue, these programs prevent students from learning the skills needed to become effective citizens of the nation-state and from developing strong national loyalties. They also argue that pluralist educational programs promote ethnic attachments and loyalties that contribute to ethnic conflict, polarization, and stratification. Assimilationists maintain that the primary goal of the school should be to socialize students so that they attain the knowledge, attitudes, and skills needed to become effective citizens of their nation-states (Schlesinger, 1991). During the final phases of ethnic revitalization, assimilationist paradigms tend to become increasingly conservative. In the United States during the 1980s assimilationism developed into a neoconservative ideology that was strongly nationalistic and reactionary (Steinfels, 1979).

The Need for a Multifactor Paradigm and Holism

Multicultural education is replete with single-factor paradigms that attempt to explain why lower-class students and students of color often do poorly in school. Proponents of these paradigms often become ardent in their views, insisting that one major variable explains the problem of minority students and that their educational problems can be solved if major policies are implemented related to a specific explanation or paradigm. Many existing reforms in multicultural education, such as compensatory education and bilingual programs, are based on single-factor paradigms. Proponents of the ethnic additive and self-concept development paradigms believe that ethnic content and heroes can help minority students increase their academic achievement; cultural deprivation proponents view cultural enrichment as the most important variable influencing academic achievement; radical scholars often view the school as having little possibility of significantly influencing the life-chances of low-income students and students of color.

Experiences in the major Western nations since the late 1960s teach us that the academic achievement problems of ethnic minority students are too complex to be solved with reforms based on single-factor paradigms and explanations (Banks & Lynch, 1986). Education is broader than schooling, and many problems that ethnic minority students experience in the schools reflect the problems in the wider society. The radical critique of schooling is useful because it helps us see the limitations of formal schooling. However, the radical paradigm is limited because it gives us few concrete guidelines about what can be done after we have acknowledged that schools are limited in their ability to bring about equality for low-income students and students of color.

When designing reform strategies, we must be keenly sensitive to the limitations of formal schooling. However, we must also be tenacious in our faith that the school can play a limited but cogent role in bringing about equal educational opportunities for low-income students and students of color, and in helping all students to develop cross-cultural understandings and competencies. To design school programs that will effectively help students of color to increase their academic achievement and help all students develop ethnic literacy and cross-cultural competency, we must conceptualize the school as a system in which all major variables and components are highly interrelated. *A holistic paradigm, which* *conceptualizes the school as an interrelated whole, is needed to guide educational reform.* Viewing the school as a social system can help us derive an idea of school reform that can help students of color and low-income students to increase their academic achievement and help all students develop more democratic attitudes and values. Although our theory and research about multicultural education is limited and developing (Banks, in press), both research and theory indicate that educators can successfully intervene to help students increase their academic achievement and develop more democratic attitudes and values (Katz, 1976; Weinberg, 1977).

Conceptualizing the school as a social system suggests that we must formulate and initiate a change strategy that reforms the total school environment in order to implement multicultural education successfully. Reforming any one variable, such as curriculum materials and the formal curriculum, is necessary but not sufficient. Multicultural and sensitive teaching materials are ineffective in the hands of teachers who have negative attitudes toward different ethnic and cultural groups. Such teachers are not likely to use multicultural materials or to use them in a detrimental way when they do. Thus, helping teachers and other members of the school staff develop democratic attitudes and values is essential when implementing multicultural programs and experiences.

When formulating plans for multicultural education, educators should conceptualize the school as a microculture that has norms, values, roles, statuses, and goals like other cultural systems. The school has a dominant culture and a variety of subcultures. Almost all classrooms in Western societies are multicultural because European American students, as well as African American and Latino students, are socialized within diverse cultures. Teachers in schools in Western societies also come from many different ethnic groups and cultures. Although they may be forgotten and repressed, many teachers were socialized in cultures other than the mainstream one. The school is a microculture in which the cultures of students and teachers meet. *The school should be a cultural environment in which acculturation takes place: both teachers and students should assimilate some of the views, perceptions, and ethos of each other as they interact* (see Figure 6.1). Both teachers and students will be enriched by this process, and the academic achievement of

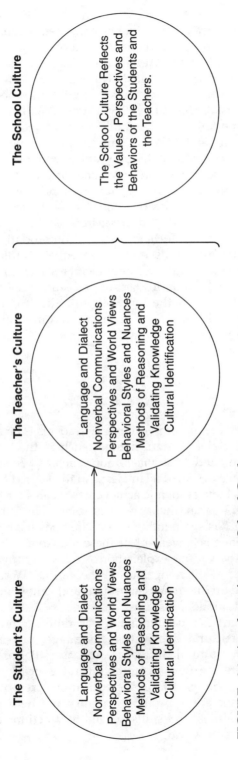

The School Culture

The School Culture Reflects the Values, Perspectives and Behaviors of the Students and the Teachers.

The Teacher's Culture

Language and Dialect
Nonverbal Communications
Perspectives and World Views
Behavioral Styles and Nuances
Methods of Reasoning and
Validating Knowledge
Cultural Identification

The Student's Culture

Language and Dialect
Nonverbal Communications
Perspectives and World Views
Behavioral Styles and Nuances
Methods of Reasoning and
Validating Knowledge
Cultural Identification

FIGURE 6.1 Acculturation as a School Goal

When the student assimilates elements of the teacher's culture and the teacher assimilates elements of the student's culture, the school culture becomes a synthesized cultural system that reflects the cultures of all of its participants.

117

students from diverse cultures will be enhanced because their cosmos and ethos will be reflected and legitimized in the school.

Historically, schools in Western societies have had assimilation rather than acculturation as their major goal. The students were expected to acquire the dominant culture of the school and society, but the school neither legitimized nor assimilated parts of the student's culture. Assimilation and acculturation are different in important ways. Assimilation involves the complete elimination of cultural differences and differentiating group identifications. When acculturation occurs, a culture is modified through contact with one or more other cultures but maintains its essence (Theodorson & Theodorson, 1969).

Both acculturation and accommodation should take place in today's schools in Western democratic societies. *When accommodation occurs, groups with diverse cultures maintain their separate identities but live in peaceful interaction.* However, in order for successful accommodation to take place, various ethnic and cultural groups must have equal status and share power. It is essential that schools in Western democracies acculturate students rather than foster tight ethnic boundaries because all students, including ethnic minority students, must develop the knowledge, attitudes, and skills needed to become successful citizens of their cultural communities, their nation-states, and the global world community.

Summary

The achievement of most ethnic minority students is far below that of mainstream students in the major Western nations, such as the United States, Canada, the United Kingdom, and Australia. Groups such as Mexicans in the United States, Indians and Metis in Canada, Jamaicans in the United Kingdom, and the Australian Aborigines have academic achievement scores far below those of dominant mainstream groups in their societies. Since the ethnic revival movements emerged in the 1960s, a number of explanations have been formulated to posit why the academic achievement of these students is below that of their mainstream peers. The various explanations—called *paradigms* in this chapter—have been formulated at different times in the various Western nations. These paradigms are based on different assumptions and values and imply disparate policy, action, and educational programs.

This chapter describes ten major paradigms: ethnic additive, self-concept development, cultural deprivation, language, racism, radical, genetic, cultural pluralism, cultural difference, and assimilationism. Single-factor paradigms dominate the field of multicultural education. However, multifactor paradigms must be used to guide educational reform and practice if educational institutions are to promote equality and help all students develop the knowledge, attitudes, and skills needed to function effectively in a culturally diverse society and world.

References

Asante, M. K. (1991). The Afrocentric Idea in Education. *The Journal of Negro Education, 60,* 170–180.

Banks, J. A. (1978). Multiethnic Education across Cultures: United States, Mexico, Puerto Rico, France, and Great Britain. *Social Education, 42,* 177–185.

Banks, J. A. (1984). Values, Ethnicity, Social Science Research, and Educational Policy. In B. J. Ladner, (Ed.), *The Humanities in Precollegiate Education, Eighty-third Yearbook of the National Society for the Study of Education,* Part II (pp. 91–111). Chicago: University of Chicago Press.

Banks, J. A. (in press). Multicultural Education: Historical Development, Dimensions, and Practice. In L. Darling-Hammond (Ed.), *Review of Research in Education,* Vol. 19. Washington, DC: American Educational Research Association.

Banks, J. A., & Lynch, J. (Eds.). (1986). *Multicultural Education in Western Societies.* London: Cassell.

Baratz, S. S., & Baratz, J. C. (1970). Early Childhood Intervention: The Social Science Base of Institutional Racism. *Harvard Educational Review, 40,* 29–50.

Barnes, B. (1982). *T. S. Kuhn and Social Science.* New York: Columbia University Press.

Bereiter, C., & Engelmann, S. (1966). *Teaching Disadvantaged Children in the Preschool.* Englewood Cliffs, NJ: Prentice-Hall.

Bloom, B. S., Davis, A., & Hess, R. (1965). *Compensatory Education for Cultural Deprivation.* New York: Holt, Rinehart & Winston.

Bowles, S., & Gintis, H. (1976). *Schooling in Capitalist America.* New York: Basic Books, 1967.

Brandt, G. L. (1986). *The Realization of Anti-Racist Teaching.* London: The Falmer Press.

Clark, K. B. (1963). *Prejudice and Your Child.* Boston: Beacon Press.

Cross, W. E. (1991). *Shades of Black: Diversity in African-American Identity.* Philadelphia: Temple University Press.

Dickeman, M. (1973). Teaching Cultural Pluralism. In J. A. Banks (Ed.), *Teaching Ethnic Studies. Concepts and Strategies* (pp. 5–25).

Washington, DC: National Council for the Social Studies.

Gay, G. (1983). Multiethnic Education: Historical Developments and Future Prospects. *Phi Delta Kappan, 64,* 560–563.

Gibson, M. A., & Ogbu, J. U. (Eds.). (1991). *Minority Status and Schooling: A Comparative Study of Immigrant and Involuntary Minorities.* New York: Garland.

Giroux, H. (1992). *Border Crossing: Cultural Workers and the Politics of Education.* New York: Routledge.

Grant, C. A. (Ed.). (1992). *Research and Multicultural Education: From the Margins to the Mainstream.* Washington, DC: The Falmer Press.

Green, A. (1982). In Defense of Anti-Racist Teaching: A Reply to Recent Critiques of Multicultural Education. *Multiracial Education, 20,* 209.

Hakuta, K. (1986). *Mirror of Language: The Debate on Bilingualism.* New York: Basic Books.

Hale-Benson, J. (1982). *Black Children: Their Roots, Culture, and Learning Styles* (Rev. ed.). Baltimore: The Johns Hopkins University Press.

Herrnstein, R. J. (1971). I.Q. *Atlantic Monthly, 228,* 43–64.

Jencks, C., et al. (1972). *Inequality: A Reassessment of the Effect of Family and Schooling in America.* New York: Basic Books.

Jensen, A. R. (1969). How Much Can We Boost IQ and Scholastic Achievement? *Harvard Educational Review, 39,* 1–123.

Katz, P. A. (Ed.). (1976). *Towards the Elimination of Racism.* New York: Pergamon Press.

Keddie, N. (1973). *The Myth of Cultural Deprivation.* Baltimore: Penguin Books.

Kuhn, T. S. (1970). *The Structure of Scientific Revolutions* (2nd ed.). Chicago: University of Chicago Press.

McCarthy, C. (1990). *Race and Curriculum.* New York: Falmer Press.

Merton, R. K. (1968). *Social Theory and Social Structure* (enlarged ed.). New York: The Free Press.

Minami, M., & Kennedy, B. P. (Eds.). (1991). *Language Issues in Literacy and Bilingual/Multicultural Education,* Reprint Series #22. Cambridge, MA: Harvard Educational Review.

Moodley, K. A. (1986). Canadian Multicultural Education: Promises and Practice. In J. A. Banks & J. Lynch (Eds.), *Multicultural Education in Western Societies* (pp. 51–75). London: Cassell.

Myrdal, G. (1944). *An American Dilemma: The Negro Problem and Modern Democracy.* New York: Harper & Row.

Oakes, J. (1985). *Keeping Track: How Schools Structure Inequality.* New Haven, CT: Yale University Press.

Oakes, J. (1992). Can Tracking Research Inform Practice? Technical, Normative, and Political Considerations. *Educational Researcher, 21,* 12–21.

Richardson, V., Casanova, U., Placier, P., & Guilfoyle, K. (1989). *School Children at Risk.* New York: Falmer.

Ryan, W. (1971). *Blaming the Victim.* New York: Vintage Books.

Schlesinger, A. J., Jr. (1991). *The Disuniting of America: Reflections on a Multicultural Society.* Knoxville, TN: Whittle Direct Books.

Schools Council Working Paper 29. (1970). *Teaching English to West Indian Children: The Research Stage of the Project.* London: Evans Brothers.

Shade, B. J. R. (Ed.). (1989). *Culture, Style, and the Educative Process.* Springfield, IL: Charles C Thomas.

Shockley, W. (1972). Dysgenics, Geneticity, Raceology: A Challenge to the Intellectual Responsibility of Educators. *Phi Delta Kappan, 53,* 297–307.

Sleeter, C. A. (1992). *Keepers of the Dream: A Study of Staff Development and Multicultural Education.* Washington, DC: The Falmer Press.

Solomon, R. P. (1992). *Black Resistance in High School.* Albany: State University of New York Press.

Steinfels, P. (1979). *The Neoconservatives: The Men Who Are Changing America's Politics.* New York: Simon & Schuster.

Stone, M. (1981). *The Education of the Black Child in Britain: The Myth of Multiracial Education.* Glasgow: Fontana.

Theodorson, G. A., & Theodorson, A. G. (1969). *A Modern Dictionary of Sociology.* New York: Barnes and Noble.

Tomlinson, S. (1989). Ethnicity and Educational Achievement in Britain. In L. Eldering & J. Kloprogge (Eds.), *Different Cultures, Same School: Ethnic Minority Children in Europe* (pp. 15–37). Berwyn, PA: Swets North America.

U.S. Bureau of the Census, Census of Population, (1983). *General Social and Economic Characterics,* Part 1, *United States Summary.* Washington, DC: U.S. Government Printing Office, PC80–1–C1.

Valencia, R. R. (Ed.). (1991). *Chicano School Failure and Success: Research and Policy Agendas for the 1990s.* New York: The Falmer Press.

Walsh, C. E. (1991). *Pedagogy and the Struggle for Voice: Issues of Language, Power, and Schooling for Puerto Ricans.* New York: Bergin & Garvey.

Weinberg, M. (1977). *Minority Students: A Research Appraisal.* Washington, DC: U.S. Government Printing Office.

Weis, L. (1988). (Ed.). *Class, Race and Gender in American Education.* Albany: State University of New York Press.

Chapter 7

Pluralism, Ideology, and Educational Reform

Since the 1960s, educational institutions throughout the United States and other Western nations have implemented a variety of programs and projects related to ethnic and cultural diversity. Many of these programs and practices lack clear goals, definitions, and effective staff development components. Some problems in multicultural education result from conceptual ambiguity and ideological polarization. A number of important questions concerning the relationship between educational institutions and ethnicity have not been satisfactorily clarified or resolved. These questions must be better clarified and resolved before we can design and implement more effective and justifiable educational programs related to ethnic diversity in Western societies.

One key question relates to the proper role of public institutions such as schools in the area of ethnicity. Should the schools promote, remain neutral to, or ignore the ethnic characteristics of its students and the ethnic diversity within a society? Many educational leaders believe that the school should not ignore ethnicity and should implement curricular reforms related to ethnic diversity. However, little agreement exists about what kinds of reforms should be initiated and how they can best be implemented. Views on ethnicity and the schools range from beliefs that ethnicity should be an integral and salient part of the school curriculum to cautions that too much emphasis on ethnicity in the schools might be inimical to the shared national culture and might promote divisiveness in society (D'Souza, 1991; Hilliard, Payton-Stewart, & Williams, 1990; Modgil, Verma, Mallick, & Modgil, 1986; Verma, 1989). Views on ethnicity and the schools reflect divergent ideologies and have conflicting policy and programmatic implications. These ideologies and their implications for educational policy merit careful examination and discussion.

I identify two major ideological positions related to race and ethnic diversity that are evident in most theoretical discussions of ethnicity and pluralism in the major Western nation-states such as the United States, the United Kingdom, Canada, Australia, and the Netherlands (Banks & Lynch, 1986; Bullivant, 1987; Husen & Opper, 1983; Moodley, 1992; Porter, 1975; Samuda, Berry, & Laferriere, 1984; Verma, 1989). The major assumptions and arguments of these positions are discussed, and their limitations as guides to educational reform are identified. I then describe an eclectic ideological position that reflects both major ideologies and argue that it can best guide educational policy and reform. The final part of this chapter discusses the implications of this eclectic ideology—called the *multicultural ideology*—for educational policy and practice.

It is very important for the reader to realize that the ideological positions identified and described are ideal types in the Weberian sense. The two major positions in their ideal forms do not accurately describe the views of any particular writer or theorist. However, various views on ethnicity and pluralism can be roughly classified using a continuum that has the two ideologies, in their ideal forms, at the extreme ends.

The two major positions are the *cultural pluralist* ideology and the *assimilationist* ideology. I am not the first observer to structure a typology related to ideologies and theories of ethnic diversity in Westernized societies. Gordon (1964) classifies theories of assimilation into three major categories: Anglo-conformity, the melting pot, and cultural pluralism. Higham (1974) also identifies three ideologies: integrationist, pluralist, and pluralistic integrationist. These two typologies as well as the one presented here are in some ways similar, but they are different conceptualizations.

The Cultural Pluralist Ideology

The cultural pluralist ideology has been formulated in different societies and takes various forms (Asante, 1990; Barton & Walker, 1983; Sizemore, 1972). The pluralist makes various assumptions about the nature of pluralistic democratic societies, the function of the ethnic group in socializing the individual, and the responsibility that the individual member of a presumed oppressed ethnic group has to the liberation struggle of that group. The pluralist also makes certain assumptions about research, learning, teacher training, and the proper goals of the school curriculum.

The pluralist argues that ethnicity and ethnic identities are very important in pluralistic Western societies. Western nation-states, according to the pluralist, consist of competing ethnic groups, each of which champions its own economic and political interests. It is extremely important, argues the pluralist, for individuals to develop a commitment to their ethnic group, especially if that ethnic group is oppressed by more powerful ethnic groups within society. The energies and skills of each member of an ethnic group are needed to help in that group's liberation struggle. Each individual member of an ethnic group has a moral obligation to join the liberation struggle. Thus, the pluralist stresses the rights of the ethnic group over the rights of the individual. The pluralist also assumes that an ethnic group can attain inclusion in and full participation within a society only when it can bargain from a powerful position and when it has closed ranks within (Carmichael & Hamilton, 1967; Sizemore, 1969).

The pluralist views the ethnic group as extremely important in the socialization of the individual within a highly modernized society. It is within their own particular ethnic groups that individuals develop their languages, life-styles, and values and also experience important primary group relationships and attachments. The ethnic community also serves as a supportive environment for individuals and helps to protect them from the harshness and discrimination they might experience in the wider society. The ethnic group thus provides individuals with a sense of identity and psychological support, both of which are extremely important within a highly modernized society controlled primarily by one dominant ethnic group. The pluralist views the ethnic group as important and believes that public institutions such as the school should actively promote the interests of the various ethnic groups in its policies and in the curriculum.

The pluralist makes assumptions about research that differ from those made by the assimilationist. The pluralist assumes that ethnic minority cultures in Western societies are not disadvantaged, deviant, or deficient; rather, they are well ordered and highly structured but *different* from each other and from the mainstream, dominant culture. Thus, the pluralist uses a culture difference model when researching ethnic groups, whereas the assimilationist researcher uses a deficit model or a genetic model (Baratz & Baratz, 1970; Simpkins, Williams, & Gunnings, 1971; Valentine, 1968) (see Chapter 6). Because of their different research assumptions, the cultural pluralist researcher and the assimilationist researcher frequently derive different, and often conflicting, research conclusions. Several researchers who are multiculturalists have used the cultural difference model extensively in their research studies on ethnic groups and have done a great deal to legitimize it within the social science and educational communities (Heath, 1983; Kochman, 1981; Labov, 1970; Mercer, 1989).

The cultural pluralist also assumes that ethnic minorities have unique learning styles and that the school curriculum and teaching strategies should be revised to be more consistent with the cognitive and learning styles of ethnic group students. Ramirez and Castaneda (1974) have written insightfully about the unique learning styles of Mexican American youths. Research summarized by Stodolsky and Lesser (1967) and Banks (1988) also supports the notion that the cognitive, learning, and motivational styles among ethnic groups sometimes differ. After reviewing the research Banks (p. 465) concluded:

> *The research suggests that students come to the classroom with many kinds of differences, some of which may be related to their ethnic group, their social-class status, or social class and ethnicity combined. Research suggests that Afro-American and Mexican American students tend to be more field sensitive in their learning styles than are mainstream Anglo-American students. . . . It is impor-*

tant for teachers to understand that the characteristics of ethnic groups and socioeconomic classes can help us to understand groups but not individuals. All types of learning and motivational styles are found within all ethnic groups and social classes.

Pluralists, because of their assumptions about the importance of the ethnic group in the lives of students, believe the curriculum should be drastically revised to reflect the cognitive styles, cultural history, and present experiences and aspirations of ethnic groups, especially students of color. The cultural pluralist believes that if the school curriculum were more consistent with the experiences of ethnic groups, the learning and adjustment problems students of color experience in the schools would be greatly reduced. Thus, the cultural pluralist argues that learning materials should be culture-specific and that the major goal of the curriculum should be to help the students function more successfully within their own ethnic culture. The curriculum should be structured to stress events from the points of view of the specific ethnic groups (Asante, 1991; Hilliard, Payton-Stewart, & Williams, 1990). The curriculum should promote ethnic attachments and allegiances and should help students gain the skills and commitments that will enable them to help their ethnic group gain power and exercise it within the larger civic culture.

The Assimilationist Ideology

The assimilationist feels that the pluralist greatly exaggerates the extent of the cultural differences within Western societies. However, the assimilationist does not deny that ethnic differences exist within Western societies or that ethnicity is very important to some groups. However, the assimilationist and the pluralist interpret ethnicity in Western societies quite differently. The assimilationist tends to see ethnicity and ethnic attachments as fleeting and temporary within an increasingly modernized world (Patterson, 1977; Schlesinger, 1991). Ethnicity, argues the assimilationist, wanes or disappears under the impact of modernization and industrialization. The assimilationist believes that ethnicity is more important in developing societies than in highly modernized societies and that it crumbles under the forces of modernization and democratization (Apter, 1977). The assimilationist sees the modernized state as being universalistic rather than as being characterized by strong ethnic allegiances and attachments (D'Souza, 1991; Patterson, 1977; Schlesinger, 1991).

Not only do the assimilationists view ethnicity as somewhat noncharacteristic of modernized societies, but they also believe that strong ethnic attachments are rather dysfunctional within a modernized state. Assimilationists believe that the ethnic group promotes group rights over the rights of the individual and that the individual must be freed of ethnic attachments in order to have choices within society. The assimilationist also views ethnicity as a force inimical to the goals of a democratic society. Ethnicity, argues the assimilationist, promotes divisions, exhumes ethnic conflicts, and leads to the Balkanization of society. The assimilationist sees integration as a societal goal in a modernized state and not ethnic segregation and separatism.

The assimilationist believes that the best way to promote the goals of society and to develop commitments to democratic ideals is to promote the full socialization of all individuals and groups into the shared culture. Every society, argues the assimilationist, has national values, ideologies, and norms to which each member of society must develop commitments if it is to function successfully and smoothly. In the United States, these values are embodied in the American Creed and in such documents as the United States Constitution and the Declaration of Independence (Ravitch, 1990). Each society also has a set of common skills and abilities that every successful member of society should master. In the United States these skills include speaking and writing the English language (Porter, 1990).

The primary goal of the school, like other publicly supported institutions, should be to socialize individuals into the common culture and enable them to function more successfully within it. At best, the school should take a position of benign neutrality in matters related to the ethnic attachments of its students (Glazer, 1977). If ethnicity and ethnic attachments are to be promoted, this should be done by private institutions like the church, the community club, and the private school.

The Assimilationist Ideology and Education

Like the cultural pluralists, the assimilationists make assumptions about research related to minorities. Their conclusions reflect their assumptions. Assimilationists usually assume that microcultural groups with characteristics that cause their members to function unsuccessfully in the common culture are deficient, deprived, and pathological and lack needed functional characteristics. Researchers who embrace an assimilationist ideology usually use the genetic, cultural deprivation, or at-risk research models and theories when studying low-income students and students of color (Bereiter & Engelmann, 1966; Jensen, 1969; Richardson, 1990; Shockley, 1972).

The assimilationist learning theorist assumes that learning styles are rather universal across cultures (such as the stages of cognitive development identified by Piaget) and that certain socialization practices, such as those exemplified among middle-class Anglo-Americans, enhance learning, whereas other early socialization practices, such as those found within most lower-class ethnic groups, retard students' abilities to conceptualize and to develop the verbal and cognitive abilities needed for school success. Consequently, assimilationist learning theorists often recommend that ethnic minority youths from lower-class homes enter compensatory educational programs at increasingly early ages. Some theorists have suggested that these youths should be placed in a middle-class educational environment shortly after birth (Caldwell, 1967).

The assimilationist believes that curriculum materials and teaching styles should relate primarily to the common national culture. Emphasis should be on the shared culture within the nation-state because all citizens must learn to participate in a common culture that requires universal skills and competencies. Emphasis on cultural and ethnic differences might promote societal polarization and fail to facilitate socialization into the shared civic culture of the nation-state. The school's primary mission within a democratic society should be to socialize youths into the national civic culture.

The curriculum should stress the commonality of the heritage all people share in the nation-state. It should also help students develop a commitment to the common culture and the skills to participate in social action designed to make the practices in a society more consistent with its professed ideologies. The school should develop within youths a critical acceptance of the goals, assumptions, and possibilities of democratic nation-states.

Attacks on the Assimilationist Ideology

In Chapter 2, I discuss how the assimilationist ideology has historically dominated U.S. intellectual and social thought. In other Western societies such as Australia and Canada, social and public policy has also been most heavily influenced historically by the assimilationist ideology. Multicultural educational policies were not developed in Canada and Australia until the 1970s. The United States still does not have an official multicultural policy, although a number of legal cases and some federal legislation directly or indirectly support education related to cultural and ethnic diversity.

In the United States near the turn of the century, writers such as Horace Kallen (1924), Randolph Bourne (1916), and Julius Drachsler (1920) set forth the concepts of cultural pluralism and cultural democracy, thereby challenging assimilationist policies and practices. When the ethnic revival movements emerged in the various Western societies in the 1960s and 1970s the assimilationist ideology experienced one of its most serious challenges in the history of Western nation-states.

Since the 1960s in the various Western nation-states, both ethnic minority and liberal White scholars and researchers have attacked the assimilationist ideology and the practices associated with it (Hilliard, Payton-Stewart, & Williams, 1990; Ladner, 1973; Verma, 1989). The rejection of the assimilationist ideology by ethnic minority intellectuals and leaders is historically very significant. This rejection represents a major break from tradition within ethnic groups, as Glazer (1977) observes. Traditionally, most intellectuals and social activists, particularly in the United States, have supported assimilationist policies and regarded acculturation as a requisite for full societal participation. Historically, there have been a few staunch separatists among African Americans and other ethnic groups in the United States. However, these leaders have represented a cry in the wilderness. Significant, too, is the fact that many White liberal writers and researchers also began to attack the assimilationist ideology and the practices associated with it in the 1960s. This criticism represented a major break from White liberal tradition in the United States (Baratz & Shuy, 1969; Labov, 1970).

Writers and researchers of color attacked the assimilationist ideology for many reasons. They saw it as a weapon of dominant groups designed to destroy the cultures of ethnic minorities and to make their members personally ineffective and politically powerless. These writers also saw it as a racist ideology that justified damaging school and societal practices that victimized students of color. Many people of color also lost faith in the assimilationist ideology because they had become very disillusioned with what they perceived as its unfulfilled promises. The rise of ethnic awareness and ethnic pride also contributed to the rejection of the assimilationist ideology by many ethnic minorities in the 1960s. Many spokespersons and writers of color searched for an alternative ideology and endorsed some version of cultural pluralism. They viewed the pluralist ideology as much more consistent with the liberation of marginalized ethnic groups than was the assimilationist ideology.

A Critique of the Pluralist and Assimilationist Ideologies

Although both the pluralist and assimilationist positions make some useful assumptions and set forth arguments that curriculum specialists need to ponder seriously as they attempt to revise the school curriculum, neither ideology, in its ideal form, is sufficient to guide educational reform. The pluralist ideology is useful because it informs us about the importance of ethnicity within a society and the extent to which an individual's ethnic group determines his or her life-chances. The assumptions the pluralist makes about the nature of minority cultures, the learning styles of students of color, and the importance of ethnic identity to many students are also useful to the educational reformer.

However, the pluralist exaggerates the extent of cultural pluralism within modern societies and fails to give adequate attention to the fact that high levels of cultural (if not structural) assimilation have taken place in societies such as the United States. Gordon (1964), who seriously questions the extent of cultural pluralism in U.S. society, writes (p. 159), "Structural pluralism . . . is the major key to the understanding of the ethnic makeup of American society, while cultural pluralism is the minor one."

Exaggerating the extent of cultural differences between and among ethnic groups might be as detrimental for school policy as ignoring those that are real. The pluralist also fails to pay adequate attention to the fact that most members of ethnic groups in modern societies participate in a wider and more universalistic culture than the ones in which they have their primary group attachments. Thus the pluralist appears unwilling to prepare youths to cope adequately with the real world beyond the ethnic community. The cultural pluralist also has not clarified, in any meaningful way, the kind of relationship that should exist between antagonistic and competing ethnic groups that have different allegiances and conflicting goals and commitments. In other words, the pluralist has not adequately conceptualized how a strongly pluralistic nation will maintain an essential degree of societal cohesion.

The assimilationist argues that the school within a common culture should socialize youths so they will be effective participants within that culture and will develop commitments to its basic values, goals, and ideologies. The assimilationist also argues that the schools should help youths attain the skills that will enable them to become effective and contributing members of the nation-state in which they live. It is important for educators to realize that most societies expect the common schools to help socialize youths so they will become productive members of the nation-state and develop strong commitments to the idealized societal values. Educators should keep the broad societal goals in mind when they reform the curriculum of the common schools.

However, the assimilationist makes a number of highly questionable assumptions and promotes educational practices that often hinder the success of youths socialized within ethnic communities that have cultural characteristics quite different from those of the school. The assimilationist's assumption that learning styles are universalistic rather than to some extent culture-specific is questionable (Hale-Benson, 1982; Shade, 1989). The assumption that all students can learn equally well from teaching materials that reflect only the cultural experiences of the majority group is also questionable and possibly detrimental to minority group children with strong ethnic identities and attachments (Spencer, 1990).

When assimilationists talk about the common culture, most often they mean the mainstream national culture and are ignoring the reality that most Western societies are made up of many different ethnic groups, each of which has some unique cultural characteristics that are part of the shared national culture. The curriculum builder should seriously examine the common culture concept and make sure that the view of the common national culture promoted in the school is not racist, sexist, ethnocentric, or exclusive, but is multicultural and reflects the ethnic and cultural diversity within society. We need to redefine what the common culture actually is. Our transformed conceptualization should reflect the social realities within a nation-state, not a mythical, idealized view of the life and culture within a particular nation-state.

The Multicultural Ideology

Because neither the cultural pluralist nor the assimilationist ideology can adequately guide educational reform within educational institutions, we need a different ideology that reflects both positions and yet avoids their extremes. We also need an ideology that is more consistent with the realities in Western societies. We might call this position the *multicultural ideology* and imagine that it is found near the center of our continuum, which has the cultural pluralist and the assimilationist ideologies at the extreme ends (see Table 7.1).

The multicultural ideology has not historically been a dominant ideology in Western societies such as the United States and Australia. However, the experiences of some ethnic groups in the United States, the Jews being the most salient example, are highly consistent with the multicultural vision of society. Although

TABLE 7.1 Ideologies Related to Ethnicity and Pluralism in Western Societies

The Cultural Pluralist Ideology	← The Multicultural Ideology →	The Assimilationist Ideology
Separatism	Open society Multiculturalism	Total integration *White mainstream*
Primordial Particularistic	Universalized-primordialism	Universalistic *Dominant Canon*
Minority emphasis	Minorities and majorities have rights.	Majoritarian emphasis
Groups rights are primary	Limited rights for the group and the individual.	Individual rights are primary. *Democratic principles*
Common ancestry and heritage unifies	Ethnic attachments and ideology of common civic culture compete for allegiances of individuals	Ideology of the common culture unifies.
Research Assumption Ethnic minority cultures are well-ordered, highly structured, but different (language, values, behavior, etc.)	*Research Assumption* Ethnic minority cultures have some unique cultural characteristics; however, minority and majority groups share many cultural traits, values, and behavior styles.	*Research Assumption* Subcultural groups with characteristics that make its members function unsuccessfully in the common culture are deprived, pathological, and lack needed functional characteristics.
Cultural difference research model	Bicultural research model.	Social pathology research model and/or genetic research model.
Minorities have unique learning styles	Minorities have some unique learning styles but share many learning characteristics with other groups.	Human learning styles and characteristics are universal.
Curriculum Use materials and teaching styles that are culture specific. The goal of the curriculum should be to help students function more successfully within their own ethnic cultures and help liberate their ethnic groups from oppression.	*Curriculum* The curriculum should respect the ethnicity of the child and use it in positive ways; the goal of the curriculum should be to help students learn how to function effectively within the common culture, their ethnic culture, and other ethnic cultures.	*Curriculum* Use materials and teaching styles related to the common culture; the curriculum should help the students develop a commitment to the common civic culture and its idealized ideologies.
Teachers Minority students need skilled teachers of their same race and ethnicity for role models, to learn more effectively, and to develop more positive self-concepts and identities	*Teachers* Students need skilled teachers who are very knowledgeable about and sensitive to their ethnic cultures and cognitive styles.	*Teachers* A skilled teacher who is familiar with learning theories and is able to implement those theories effectively is a good teacher for any group of students, regardless of their ethnicity, race, or social class. The goal should be to train good teachers of students.

the multicultural ideology is less theoretically developed than the other two positions, it, like the other ideologies, makes a number of assumptions about the nature of modernized society; about what a nation's goals should be; and about research, learning, teacher education, and the school curriculum.

The multicultural theorist feels that the cultural pluralist exaggerates the importance of the ethnic group in the socialization of the individual and that the assimilationist greatly understates the role of ethnic groups in Western societies and in the lives of individuals. Thus, the multicultural theorist believes that both the pluralist and the assimilationist have distorted views of societal realities. He or she assumes that even though the ethnic group and the ethnic community are very important in the socialization of individuals, individuals are also strongly influenced by the common national culture during their early socialization, even if they never leave the ethnic community or enclave. A nation's common culture influences every member of society through such institutions as the school, the mass media, the courts, and the technology that its citizens share. Thus, concludes the multicultural theorist, even though ethnic groups have some unique cultural characteristics, all groups in a society share many cultural traits. As more and more members of ethnic groups become upwardly mobile, ethnic group characteristics become less important—but they do not disappear. Many ethnic group members who are highly culturally assimilated still maintain separate ethnic institutions and symbols (Gordon, 1964).

The multicultural theorist sees neither separatism (as the pluralist does) nor total integration (as the assimilationist does) as ideal societal goals, but rather envisions an open society, in which individuals from diverse ethnic, cultural, and social-class groups have equal opportunities to function and participate. In an open society, individuals can take full advantage of the opportunities and rewards within all social, economic, and political institutions without regard to their own ancestry or ethnic identity. They can also participate fully in the society while preserving their distinct ethnic and cultural traits and are able to "make the maximum number of voluntary contacts with others without regard to qualifications of ancestry, sex, or class" (Sizemore, 1972, p. 281).

In the multiethnic, open society envisioned by the multicultural theorist, individuals would be free to maintain their ethnic identities. They would also be able and willing to function effectively within the common culture and within and across other ethnic cultures. Individuals would be free to act in ways consistent with the norms and values of their ethnic groups as long as they did not conflict with the overarching national idealized values, such as justice, equality, and human dignity. All members of society would be required to conform to these values. *These values would be the unifying elements of the culture that would maintain and promote societal cohesion.*

Because of their perceptions of the nature of Western societies and their vision of the ideal society, multicultural theorists believe that the primary goal of the curriculum should be to help students learn how to function more effectively within their own ethnic culture, within the mainstream national culture, and within other ethnic communities. However, multicultural theorists feel strongly that during the process of education the school should not alienate students from their ethnic attachments but should help them to clarify their ethnic identities and make them aware of other ethnic and cultural alternatives.

The multicultural theorist believes that the curriculum should reflect the cultures of various ethnic groups *and* the shared national culture. Students need to study all of these cultures in order to become effective participants and decision makers in a democratic pluralistic nation. The school curriculum should respect the ethnicity of students and use it in positive ways. However, the students should be given options regarding their political choices and the actions they take regarding their ethnic attachments. The school should not force students to be and feel ethnic if they choose to free themselves of ethnic attachments and allegiances.

The multicultural theorist also assumes that ethnic minorities do have some unique learning styles, although they share many learning characteristics with other students. Educators should be knowledgeable about the aspects of their learning styles that are unique so they can better help minorities attain more success within the school and in the larger society.

Even though the multicultural ideology can best guide educational reform and school policy, difficult questions regarding the relationship between the school and the student's ethnic culture are inherent within this position. The multicultural theorist argues, for example, that the school should reflect both the student's ethnic culture and the common societal culture. These questions emerge: How does the individual function within two cultures that sometimes have contradictory and conflicting norms, values, and expectations? What happens when the ethnic cultures of the students seriously conflict with the goals and norms of public institutions like the school? Do the institutions change their goals? If so, what goals do they embrace? The assimilationist solves this problem by arguing that the student should change to conform to the expectations and norms of public institutions.

Although I support the multicultural ideology and have presented my proposals for curriculum reform within that ideological framework (Banks, 1991), it is very difficult to resolve satisfactorily all the difficult questions inherent within this ideology. However, public institutions like the school can and should allow ethnic group members to practice their culture-specific behaviors as long as they do not conflict with the major goals of the school. One of the school's major goals is to teach students how to read, to write, to compute, and to think. The school obviously cannot encourage ethnic behavior if it prohibits students from reading. On the other hand, some students might be able to learn to read more easily from culturally sensitive readers than from Anglocentric reading materials.

The Canon Debate and the Attack on the Multiculturalists

During the late 1980s and early 1990s, a chorus of strident voices launched a widely publicized and orchestrated attack on the movement designed to infuse content about ethnic groups and women into the school and university curriculum. Much of the debate over multicultural education took place in mass media publications such as *Time* (Gray, 1991), *The Wall Street Journal* (Sirkin, 1990), and the *New Republic* (Howe, 1991), rather than in scholarly journals and forums. The Western traditionalists (assimilationist writers who defend the canon now within the schools and universities) and the multiculturalists rarely engaged in reflective dialogue. Rather, the debate over the canon was forensic social science (Rivlin, 1973). Scholars on each side of the debate marshaled data to support their briefs and ignored facts, interpretations, and perspectives that were inconsistent with their positions and visions of the present and future. Scholars who supported the other side of the debate were required to criticize the positions of their opponents and to present counter evidence and arguments.

D'Souza's (1991) *Atlantic* article—as well as his subsequent book with the same title—was a highly publicized example of a brief written to defend the existing curriculum and structures in higher education and to describe an alarming picture of where multiculturalism is taking the nation. Multiculturalists, because they believe that they must craft convincing counter-briefs to those presented by the Western traditionalists, often failed to describe the significant ways in which the multicultural vision is consistent with the democratic ideals of the West and with the heritage of Western civilization. Little attention has been given in the multicultural literature to the fact that the multicultural education movement emerged out of Western democratic ideals and that one of its major aims is to close the gap between Western democratic ideals such as equality and justice and societal practices that contradict those ideals, such as discrimination based on race, gender, and social class.

Because so much of the debate over the canon has taken place in the popular media, which encourages simplistic explanations, one-liners, and sound-bites, the issues related to the curriculum canon have been overdrawn and oversimplified by advocates on both sides. The results are that the debate has often generated more heat than light and has further polarized various interest groups rather than encouraged a genuine exchange of ideas that might help us to find creative solutions to the problems related to race, ethnicity, gender, and schooling.

As the ethnic texture of the nation deepens, problems related to diversity will intensify rather than diminish. Consequently, we need leaders and educators of good will, from all political and ideological persuasions, to participate in genuine discussions, dialogue, and debates that will help us formulate visionary and workable solutions that will enable us to deal creatively with the challenges posed by the increasing diversity in the United States and the world. We must learn how to transform the problems related to racial and ethnic diversity into opportunities and strengths.

The Multicultural Ideology and Education

The multicultural educational reform movement has had limited but significant success in most of the Western nation-states in which it has developed. Practices such as ethnic studies, bilingual-bicultural education, multicultural education, and intercultural education have not permeated mainstream educational thought and practice in Western societies. An important question that concerns multicultural educators is how to enhance this permeation process and the process of institutionalization. A philosophy of ethnic pluralism must permeate educational institutions before multicultural educational practices can be effectively integrated into the mainstream curriculum. It is important to focus on ways to institutionalize a philosophy of ethnic education while discussing strategies and tactics for implementing change.

We cannot assume that most educators have accepted the idea of multicultural education and are waiting for appropriate strategies and materials to be developed before participating in educational reforms related to multicultural education. I hypothesize that just the opposite is true: that educators are not using many available multicultural strategies and materials because they believe that multicultural strategies and materials will not contribute to their major educational goals and objectives.

Multicultural education has not acquired legitimacy within mainstream educational thought and practice in the United States or in other nations where I have studied multicultural education programs and practices, such as Australia, France, the United Kingdom, and Canada (Banks, 1978). An important question is, How can we legitimize multicultural education within a nation's educational institutions? Once the concept of multicultural education has become legitimized and most educators have internalized a philosophy of ethnic pluralism, the implementation of multicultural education will become a logistical and technical problem.

The Root of the Problem: Ideological Resistance

Educators set forth many reasons to explain the limited response to educational reforms related to ethnic pluralism. These responses include the following:

1. Our students are unaware of racial differences; we will merely create problems that don't exist if we teach ethnic content. All of our students, whether African American or White, are happy and like one another. They don't see colors or ethnic differences.
2. We don't have any racial problems in our school and consequently don't need to teach about ethnic groups.
3. We don't teach about ethnic groups because we don't have any students of color attending our schools.
4. Ethnic studies will negatively affect societal unity and the common national culture. It is divisive and will Balkanize the nation.
5. We don't have time to add more content to what we are already teaching. We can't finish the books and units we already have. Ethnic content will overload our curriculum.
6. We don't teach much about ethnic groups because we don't have the necessary materials. Our textbooks are inadequate.

7. We can't teach ethnic studies in our schools and colleges because most of our teachers are inadequately educated in this area of study. Many of them also have negative attitudes toward ethnic groups. They would probably do more harm than good if they tried to teach about ethnic and racial groups.
8. The local community will strongly object if we teach about race and ethnicity in our schools.
9. We don't teach much about ethnic groups in our schools because scholarship in ethnic studies is not sound. The research in ethnic studies is largely political and polemical.

Some of these explanations, *but not most of them,* have a degree of validity and partially explain why only a few components of multicultural education have become institutionalized within most schools and colleges. Most of these explanations do not reveal the root of the problem, however. *Ideological and philosophical conflicts between pluralistic and mainstream educators (who are basically assimilationists) are the major reasons that educational reforms related to ethnic diversity have not become institutionalized—on a wide scale—within the educational systems in the Western nations.* In other words, the resistance to multicultural education is basically ideological and political.

The Ideological Clash

Mainstream educators, such as the Western traditionalists, are primarily assimilationists. They make most of the major decisions that are implemented and institutionalized within schools and colleges. They are the gatekeepers of the status quo. The multiculturalists are a relatively small but growing group of educators who advocate reforms to make education more ethnically and gender fair. The Western traditionalist and the multiculturalists embrace conflicting and often contradictory ideological positions about the nature of society, the nature of schooling, and the purposes of schooling in a democratic nation.

The Quest for a New Ideology

Neither the *assimilationist* nor the *cultural pluralistic ideology,* in their ideal or pure forms, can effectively guide educational reform in a democratic nation that has a universal culture that is both heavily influenced by and shared by all ethnic groups. Programs based primarily on assimilationist assumptions perpetuate misconceptions about the nature of society and violate the ethnic identities of many students. Curricular practices that reflect an extreme notion of cultural pluralism also distort societal realities and give inadequate attention to the universal culture that strongly influences the behavior of all citizens within a society.

Both the assimilationist and cultural pluralist ideologies emanate from misleading and/or incomplete analyses of the nature of ethnicity in modernized societies such as the United States. The assimilationist ideology in the United States derives primarily from two conceptualizations of ethnicity in U.S. society: *Anglo-conformity* and the *melting pot.* The cultural pluralist ideology emanates from a conceptualization of ethnicity in U. S. society called *cultural pluralism.* I summarize these conceptualizations of ethnicity in the United States and indicate why each is an inadequate and/or misleading conceptualization. I then present my own analysis of ethnicity in U.S. society and derive a new ideology, called the *multicultural ideology,* from my analysis. The multicultural ideology I present is one possible way to reduce the ideological and political resistance to multicultural education.

Anglo-conformity suggests that ethnic groups gave up their cultural attributes and acquired those of Anglo-Saxon Protestants. This concept describes a type of unidirectional assimilation. The *melting pot,* long embraced as an ideal in U.S. society and culture, suggests that the various ethnic cultures in the United States were mixed and synthesized into a new culture, different from any of the original ethnic cultures. *Cultural pluralism* suggests, at least in its extreme form, that the United States is made up of various ethnic subsocieties each of which has a set of largely independent norms, institutions, values, and beliefs.

Each conceptualization presents major problems when one views the reality of ethnicity and race in the United States. The Anglo-conformity conceptualization suggests that Anglo-Saxons were changed very little in the United States and that other ethnic groups did all of the changing. This conceptualization is incomplete, unidirectional, and static. The melting pot conceptualization is inaccurate and misleading because human cultures are complex and dynamic and do not melt like iron. Consequently, the melting pot is a false and misleading metaphor.

The strong cultural pluralist conceptualization denies the reality that there is a universal U.S. culture that every American, regardless of ethnic group, shares to a great extent. This culture includes American Creed values as *ideals,* American English, a highly technological and industrialized civilization, a capitalistic economy, and a veneration of materialism and consumption. Richard Hofstadter (1963) argues convincingly that anti-intellectualism is another key component in the universal U.S. culture. This is not to deny that there are important subcultural variants within the different ethnic subsocieties in the United States or that there are many nonuniversalized ethnic characteristics in U.S. ethnic communities. These nonuniversalized ethnic subvariants are discussed later.

Gordon (1964) believes that *structural pluralism* best describes the ethnic reality in U.S. society. According to Gordon, the ethnic groups in the United States have experienced high levels of cultural assimilation but the nation is characterized by structural pluralism. In other words, ethnic groups are highly assimilated culturally (into the mainstream Anglo-American culture) but have separate ethnic subsocieties, such as African American fraternities, Jewish social clubs, and Chicano theaters.

Multiple Acculturation

Even though Gordon's (1964) notion of structural pluralism is helpful and deals more adequately with the complexity of ethnic diversity in modern U.S. society than the other three concepts, I believe that *multiple acculturation* more accurately describes how the universal U.S. culture was and is forming than does the concept of cultural assimilation. The White Anglo-Saxon Protestant (WASP) culture was changed in the United States, as were the cultures of Africans and of Asian immigrants. African cultures and Asian cultures influenced and changed the WASP culture, just as the WASP culture influenced and modified African and Asian cultures. What was experienced in the United States, and what is still occurring, is multiple acculturation and not a kind of unidirectional type of cultural assimilation whereby the African American culture was influenced by the WASP culture and not the other way around.

The general or universal culture in the United States resulted from this series of multiple acculturations. This culture is still in the process of formation and change (see Figure 7.1). The universal U.S. culture is not just a WASP culture but contains important elements of the wide variety of ethnic cultures that are and/or were part of U.S. society. Those ethnic cultural elements that became universalized and part of the general U.S. culture have been reinterpreted and mediated by the unique social, economic, and political experiences in the United States. *It is inaccurate and misleading to refer to the universal U.S. culture as a WASP culture.*

This notion of U.S. culture has been and often is perpetuated in the school and university curricula. It is, of course, true that the White Anglo-Saxon Protestants have had a more profound influence on the universal U.S. culture than has any other single ethnic group. However, we can easily exaggerate the WASP influence on the general U.S. culture. European cultures were greatly influenced by African and Asian cultures before the European explorers started coming to the Americas in the fifteenth century (Bernal, 1987, 1991; Van Sertima, 1988). The earliest British immigrants borrowed heavily from the American Indians on the East coast and probably would not have survived if they had not assimilated Indian cultural components and used some of their farming methods and tools (Weatherford, 1988).

Ethnic Subsocieties and Nonuniversalized Cultural Components

Figure 7.1 describes the development of U.S. culture by emphasizing multiple acculturation and how ethnic cultural elements became universalized. Other U.S. ethnic realities are not shown in Figure 7.1. These realities include the significant number of ethnic cultural elements that have not become universalized (that are still shared primarily by ethnic subgroups) and the separate ethnic institutions and groups that constitute ethnic subsocieties within the larger U.S. society and culture. The sociocultural environment for most Americans is consequently bicul-

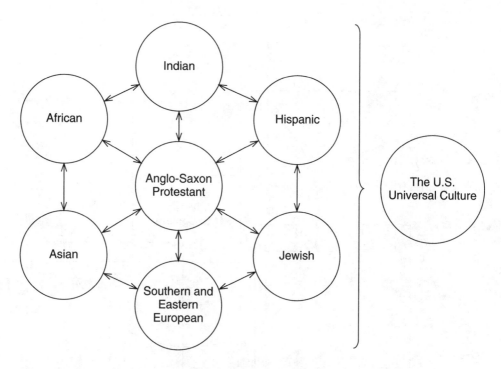

FIGURE 7.1   The Development of U.S. Culture

This figure illustrates how the U.S. universal culture developed through a process conceptualized as *multiple acculturation*. The Anglo-Saxon Protestant culture had the greatest influence on the development of U.S. culture, and each of the various ethnic cultures influenced the Anglo culture and was influenced by it. Each culture was also influenced by and influenced the others. These complex series of acculturations, which were mediated by the U.S. experience and the U.S. sociocultural environment, resulted in the universal U.S. culture. This process is still taking place today.

tural. Almost every American participates both within the universal U.S. culture and society as well as within his or her ethnic subsociety. Like other U.S. ethnic groups, there is a subsociety within the WASP culture that has cultural elements not universal or shared by the rest of society. Patterson (1977) believes that this is a small subsociety in which few individuals participate and that most WASP cultural elements have become universalized. He writes (p. 167), "with the exception of small pockets such as the New England Brahmin elite, the vast majority of WASPs have abandoned the ethnic specificities of their original culture in favor of the elite version of the American universal culture."

Nonuniversalized ethnic cultural characteristics and ethnic subsocieties are realities in contemporary U.S. society. These cultural elements and subsocieties play an important role in the socialization of many Americans and help individual members of ethnic groups satisfy important needs. Figure 7.2 illustrates the relationship between the universal U.S. culture and ethnic subsocieties.

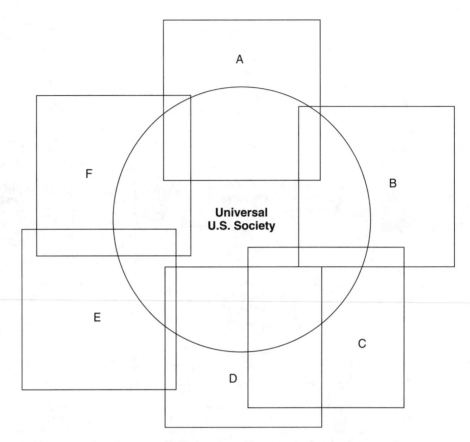

FIGURE 7.2   Ethnic Subsocieties and the Universal U.S. Society

In this figure, the universal U.S. society is represented by the circle. This culture is shared by all ethnic groups within the United States. A, B, C, D, E, and F represent ethnic subsocieties that consist of unique ethnic institutions, values, and cultural elements that are nonuniversalized and shared primarily by members of specific ethnic groups.

The Multicultural Ideology

My analysis of ethnicity in U.S. society leads to a philosophical position that can be called the *multicultural ideology* because one of its key assertions is that Americans function within several cultures, including the mainstream culture and various ethnic subcultures. This multicultural ideology suggests specific goals for curriculum reform related to ethnicity. A major goal of multicultural education derived from my analysis of the nature of ethnicity in the United States is to help students develop cross-cultural competency (discussed in Chapter 3). Edward T. Hall (1977), in his insightful book *Beyond Culture,* underscores the importance of helping students develop the skills and understandings needed to function cross-culturally. He writes (p. 2), "The future depends on man's transcending the limits of individual cultures." Another important goal of multicultural education is to help individuals gain greater self-understanding by viewing themselves from the perspectives of other microcultures within their nation-state.

Establishing Dialogue between Mainstream and Pluralistic Educators

A major implication of my analysis for multicultural education is that personal contact situations and dialogue must be established between mainstream and pluralistic educators so they can resolve their philosophical conflicts and disagreements. Ideological resistance is the root of our problem. Personal contact and dialogue between pluralistic and mainstream educators are essential to derive a basic solution. However, little serious discussion and debate about multicultural education have taken place among educators with divergent beliefs, assumptions, and ideologies about the role of ethnicity in the formal educational process. This is partly because of the highly politicized and racially tense climate that gave birth to the ethnic studies movement and because of the strong emotions that scholars and educators often exemplify when discussing issues related to ethnicity and schooling.

Sharing Power

Another important implication of my analysis is that powerful groups that now dominate educational policy and decisions, such as the Western traditionalists, must be willing to share power with currently excluded and powerless ethnic groups before a multicultural ideology can be developed and educational policy can be shaped that reflects the interests and aspirations of groups of color. Historically in the United States, educational policy for powerless and structurally excluded ethnic groups, such as African Americans and Mexican Americans, has been made by powerful Anglo-American groups that controlled the educational system (Bowles & Gintis, 1976; Katz, 1975). As pointed out in Chapter 2, an Anglocentric education alienates students of color from their ethnic cultures and frequently fails to help them attain the attitudes, skills, and abilities needed to function effectively within the mainstream society and within other ethnic subsocieties.

Powerless and excluded ethnic groups, such as Mexican Americans and Puerto Rican Americans, must participate in shaping educational policy in order for educational reforms related to ethnic diversity to become institutionalized within the U.S. educational system (Walsh, 1991). The groups that exercise power in the U.S. educational establishment design and run the schools so that they reflect their ideology, assumptions, values, and perspectives. The assimilationists who control the schools often see pluralism as a threat to the survival of the United States as they envision it. Ways must be devised for currently excluded ethnic groups to gain power in education and to participate in major educational decisions that affect the education of their youths. Only in this way will a philosophy of ethnic pluralism become institutionalized within the educational system, and the system will become legitimate from the perspectives of people of color. Curricular models that can help lead to a sharing of power by structurally included and excluded groups are conceptualized and discussed in Chapter 11.

Summary

Educational institutions in the various Western nations, stimulated by social forces and supported by private and public agencies, are implementing a wide variety of educational reforms related to pluralism and ethnic diversity in their societies. However, there is widespread disagreement about what these reforms should be designed to attain and about the proper relationship that should exist between the school and the ethnic identities and attachments of students. Educators and social scientists who embrace divergent ideologies are recommending conflicting educational policies and programs.

We can think of these varying ideologies as existing on a continuum, with the cultural pluralist position at one extreme end and the assimilationist position at the other. I argue that neither of these ideologies, in their ideal forms, can effectively guide educational policy in pluralistic democratic societies. Rather, educational policy can best be guided by an eclectic ideology that reflects both the cultural pluralist position and the assimilationist position, but avoids their extremes. I call this the *multicultural ideology.*

The second part of this chapter discusses the multicultural ideology and describes how it derives from an accurate analysis of ethnic and race relations in the United States. The assimilationist ideology, which most mainstream educators in the United States embrace, derives from two misleading and incomplete conceptions of the nature of ethnicity in the United States: Anglo-conformity and the melting pot. Structural pluralism and multiple acculturation accurately describe the nature of ethnic group life in the United States. The multicultual ideology derives from these conceptions of ethnicity and race in the United States. This ideology can be used to help reduce the ideological resistance to pluralistic education and to establish a dialogue between mainstream and pluralistic educators. However, in order for a multicultural ideology to be developed and to influence educational policy, powerful mainstream ethnic and cultural groups must share power with structurally excluded ethnic groups in the various Western nation-states.

References

Apter, A. (1977). Political Life and Pluralism. In M. M. Tumin and W. Plotch (Eds.), *Pluralism in a Democratic Society* (pp. 59–81). New York: Praeger.

Asante, M. K. (1990). *Kemet, Afrocentricity, and Knowledge.* Trenton, NJ: Africa World Press.

Asante, M. K. (1991). The Afrocentric Idea in Education. *The Journal of Negro Education, 60,* 170–180.

Banks, J. A. (1978). Multiethnic Education across Cultures: United States, Mexico, Puerto Rico, France and Great Britain. *Social Education, 42,* 177–185.

Banks, J. A. (1988). Ethnicity, Class, Cognitive, and Motivational Styles: Research and Teaching Implications. *The Journal of Negro Education, 57,* 452–466.

Banks, J. A. (1991). *Teaching Strategies for Ethnic Studies* (5th ed.). Boston: Allyn and Bacon.

Banks, J. A., & Lynch, J. (Eds.). (1986). *Multicultural Education in Western Societies.* London: Cassell.

Baratz, J. C., & Shuy, R. (Eds.). (1969). *Teaching Black Children to Read.* Washington, DC: Center for Applied Linguistics.

Baratz, S. S., & Baratz, J. C. (1970). Early Childhood Intervention: The Social Science Base of Institutional Racism. *Harvard Educational Review, 40,* 29–50.

Barton, L., & Walker, S. (1983). *Race, Class and Education.* London: Croom Helm.

Bereiter, C., & Engelmann, S. (1966). *Teaching Disadvantaged Children in the Preschool.* Englewood Cliffs, NJ: Prentice-Hall.

Bernal, M. (1987, 1991). *Black Athena: The Afroasiatic Roots of Classical Civilization,* Vols. 1 & 2. New Brunswick, NJ: Rutgers University Press.

Bourne, R. S. (1916). Trans-National America. *The Atlantic Monthly, 118,* 95.

Bowles, S., & Gintis, H. (1976). *Schooling in Capitalist America: Educational Reform and the Contradictions of Economic Life.* New York: Basic Books.

Bullivant, B. (1987). *The Ethnic Encounter in the Secondary School.* London: The Falmer Press.

Caldwell, B. (1967). What Is the Optimal Learning Environment for the Young Child? *American Journal of Orthopsychiatry, 37,* 9–21.

Carmichael, S., & Hamilton, C. V. (1967). *Black Power: The Politics of Liberation in America.* New York: Vintage Books.

Drachsler, J. (1920). *Democracy and Assimilation.* New York: Macmillan.

D'Souza, D. (1991). Illiberal Education. *The Atlantic, 267,* 51–79.

Glazer, N. (1977). Cultural Pluralism: The Social Aspect. In M. M. Tumin & W. Plotch, *Pluralism in a Democratic Society* (pp. 3–24). New York: Praeger.

Gordon, M. M. (1964). *Assimilation in American Life: The Role of Race, Religion, and National Origins.* New York: Oxford University Press.

Gray, P. (1991). Whose America? *Time, 138,* 12–17.

Hale-Benson, J. E. (1982). *Black Children: Their Roots, Culture and Learning Styles* (Rev. ed.). Baltimore: The Johns Hopkins University Press.

Hall, E. T. (1977). *Beyond Culture.* Garden City, NY: Doubleday.

Heath, S. B. (1983). *Ways with Words: Language, Life and Work in Communities and Classrooms.* New York: Cambridge University Press.

Higham, H. (1974). Integration vs. Pluralism: Another American Dilemma. *The Center Magazine, 7,* 67–73.

Hilliard, A., Payton-Stewart, L., & Williams, L. O. (Eds.). (1990). *Infusion of African and African American Content in the School Curriculum.* Morristown, NJ: Aaron Press.

Hofstadter, R. (1963). *Anti-Intellectualism in American Life.* New York: Vintage.

Howe, I. (1991). The Value of the Canon. *The New Republic, 204,* 40–44.

Husen, T., & Opper, S. (Eds.). (1983). *Multicultural and Multilingual Education in Immigrant Countries.* New York: Pergamon Press.

Jensen, A. R. (1969). How Much Can We Boost IQ and Scholastic Achievement? *Harvard Educational Review, 39,* 1–123.

Kallen, H. M. (1924). *Culture and Democracy in the United States.* New York: Boni and Liveright.

Katz, M. B. (1975). *Class, Bureaucracy, and Schools: The Illusion of Educational Change in America* (expanded ed.). New York: Praeger.

Kochman, T. (1981). *Black and White Styles in Conflict.* Chicago: The University of Chicago Press.

Labov, W. (1970). The Logic of Nonstandard English. In F. Williams (Ed.), *Language and Poverty: Perspectives on a Theme* (pp. 153–189). Chicago: Markham Publishing Company.

Ladner, J. A. (Ed.). (1973). *The Death of White Sociology.* New York: Vintage.

Mercer, J. R. (1989). Alternative Paradigms for Assessment in a Pluralistic Society. In J. A. Banks & C. A. M. Banks (Eds.), *Multicultural Education: Issues and Perspectives* (pp. 289–304). Boston: Allyn and Bacon.

Modgil, S., Verma, G. K., Mallick, K., & Modgil, C. (Eds.). (1986). *Multicultural Education: The Interminable Debate.* London: The Falmer Press.

Moodley, K. A. (Ed.). (1992). *Beyond Multicultural Education: International Perspectives.* Calgary: Detselig.

Patterson, O. (1977). *Ethnic Chauvinism: The Reactionary Response.* New York: Stein & Day.

Porter, J. (1975). Ethnic Pluralism in Canadian Perspective. In N. Glazer & D. P. Moynihan (Eds.), *Ethnicity: Theory and Experience* (pp. 267–304). Cambridge, MA: Harvard University Press.

Porter, R. P. (1990). The Disabling Power of Ideology: Challenging the Basic Assumptions of Bilingual Education. In G. Imhoff (Ed.), *Learning in Two Languages* (pp. 19–37). New Brunswick, NJ: Transaction Publishers.

Ramirez, R. III, & Castaneda, M. (1974). *Cultural Democracy, Bicognitive Development and Education.* New York: Academic Press.

Ravitch, D. (1990). Multiculturalism: E Pluribus Plures. *The American Scholar, 54,* 337–354.

Richardson, V. (1990). At-Risk Programs: Evaluation and Critical Inquiry. In K. A. Sirotnik, (Ed.), *Evaluation and Social Justice: Issues in Public Education,* No. 45. San Francisco: Jossey-Bass.

Rivlin, A. M. (1973). Forensic Social Science. *Harvard Educational Review, 43,* 61–75.

Samuda, R., Berry, J. W., & Laferriere, M. (Eds.). (1984). *Multiculturalism in Canada: Social and Educational Perspectives.* Toronto: Allyn and Bacon.

Schlesinger, A. R., Jr. (1991). *The Disuniting of America: Reflections on a Multicultural Society.* Knoxville, TN: Whittle Direct Books.

Shade, B. J. R. (Ed.). (1989). *Culture, Style, and the Educative Process.* Springfield, IL: Charles C Thomas.

Shockley, W. (1972). Dysgenics, Geneticity, Raceology: Challenges to the Intellectual Responsibility of Educators. *Phi Delta Kappan, 53,* 297–307.

Simpkins, G., Williams, R. L., & Gunnings, T. S. (1971). What a Culture a Difference Makes: A Rejoinder to Valentine. *Harvard Educational Review, 41,* 535–541.

Sirkin, G. (1990). The Multiculturalists Strike Again. *The Wall Street Journal, 215,* A14.

Sizemore, B. A. (1969). Separatism: A Reality Approach to Inclusion? In R. L. Green (Ed.), *Racial Crisis in American Education* (pp. 249–279). Chicago: Follett Educational Corporation.

Sizemore, B. A. (1972). Is There a Case for Separate Schools? *Phi Delta Kappan, 53,* 281–284.

Spencer, M. B. (1990). Development of Minority Children: An Introduction. *Child Development, 61,* 267–269.

Stodolsky, S. S., and Lesser, G. (1967). Learning Patterns in the Disadvantaged. *Harvard Educational Review, 37,* 546–593.

Valentine C. A. (1968). *Culture and Poverty: Critique and Counter-Proposals.* Chicago: The University of Chicago Press.

Van Sertima, I. V. (Ed.). (1988). *Great Black Leaders: Ancient and Modern.* New Brunswick, NJ: Africana Studies Department, Rutgers University.

Verma, G. K. (Ed.). (1989). *Education for All: A Landmark in Pluralism.* London: The Falmer Press.

Walsh, C. E. (Ed.). (1991). *Pedagogy and the Struggle for Voice: Issues of Language, Power, and Schooling for Puerto Ricans.* New York: Bergin & Garvey.

Weatherford, J. (1988). *Indian Givers: How the Indians of the Americas Transformed the World.* New York: Fawcett Columbine.

$Part$ **III**

Teaching Strategies: Knowledge Construction, Decision Making, and Action

Chapter 8
A Curriculum for Empowerment, Action, and Change

Chapter 9
Teaching Decison-Making and Social Action Skills

Chapter 10
The Curriculum, Ethnic Diversity, and Social Change

To implement multicultural education successfully, teaching strategies must be implemented that help students acquire knowledge from the perspectives of diverse ethnic and cultural groups, clarify and analyze their values, identify courses of action, and act in ways consistent with democratic and humane values. An important goal of multicultural teaching is to help students understand the nature of knowledge, how it is constructed, and how knowledge reflects the values, perspectives, and experiences of its creators.

The three chapters in Part III describe teaching strategies that can be used to help students to better understand how knowledge is constructed, to become knowledge builders themselves, to develop caring, and to take effective personal, social, and civic action. Chapter 8 describes the nature of knowledge and a unit used by a junior high school teacher to help his students understand the nature of knowledge and to learn decision-making and social action skills. Chapter 9 illustrates how teachers can plan and implement units on social issues that have decision-making and social action components. This chapter describes a sample unit that focuses on the question: *Should institutions establish public policies that acknowledge and support racial, ethnic, and cultural diversity?* Chapter 10 describes the extent to which curriculum reform has occurred, how diverse ethnic perspectives enrich the curriculum, and how the teacher can become a cultural mediator and change agent.

Chapter *8*

A Curriculum for Empowerment, Action, and Change

When students are empowered, they have the ability to influence their personal, social, political, and economic worlds. Students need specific knowledge, skills, and attitudes in order to have the ability to influence the worlds in which they live. They need knowledge of their social, political, and economic worlds, the skills to influence their environments, and humane values that will motivate them to participate in social change to help create a more just society and world.

This chapter describes the nature of knowledge and the dominant canons, paradigms, and perspectives that are institutionalized within the school and university curriculum. I contend that the knowledge that is institutionalized within the schools and the larger society neither enables students to become reflective and critical citizens nor helps them to participate effectively in their society in ways that will make it more democratic and just. I propose and describe a curriculum designed to help students to understand knowledge as a social construction and to acquire the knowledge, skills, and values needed to participate in civic action and social change.

Types of Knowledge

I am defining *knowledge* as "familiarity, awareness, or understandings gained through experience or study. The sum or range of what has been perceived, discovered or inferred" (*American Heritage Dictionary*, 1983, p. 384). My conceptualization of knowledge is broad and is used the way in which it is usually used in the sociology of knowledge literature to include ideas, values, and interpretations (Berger & Luckman, 1966; Farganis, 1986).

In another publication, I identify and describe five types of knowledge (Banks, in press): (1) *personal/cultural;* (2) *popular;* (3) *mainstream academic;* (4) *transformative academic;* and (5) *school.* (See Table 8.1.) Personal/cultural knowledge consists of the concepts, explanations, and interpretations that students derive from their personal experiences in their homes, families, and community cultures. The facts, concepts, explanations, and interpretations that are institutionalized within the mass media and in other institutions that are part of the popular culture constitute popular knowledge.

Mainstream academic knowledge consists of the concepts, paradigms, theories, and explanations that constitute traditional Western-centric knowledge in history and in the behavioral and social sciences. Social and behavioral scientists on the margins of the academic establishment create transformative academic knowledge that challenges established paradigms, concepts, and findings in the social, behavioral, natural, and physical sciences (Gould, 1981; Kuhn, 1970). Transformative academic knowledge consists of the facts, concepts, paradigms, themes, and explanations that challenge mainstream academic knowledge and expand and substantially revise established canons, paradigms, theories, explanations, and research methods. When transformative academic paradigms replace mainstream ones, a scientific revolution has occurred (Kuhn, 1970). What is more normal in the social sciences is that transformative paradigms coexist with established ones.

School Knowledge

The facts, concepts, generalizations, and interpretations that are presented in textbooks, teachers' guides, other media forms, and lectures by teachers constitute school knowledge. Students are usually taught school knowledge as a set of facts and concepts to be memorized and later recalled. They are rarely encouraged to examine the assumptions, values, and the nature of the knowledge they are required to memorize or to examine the ways in which knowledge is constructed. Knowledge in the school curriculum is usually viewed as objective, neutral, and immune from critical analysis.

Popular writers such as Hirsch (1987) and Ravitch and Finn (1987) have contributed to the school conception of knowledge as a body of facts not to be questioned, critically analyzed, and reconstructed. Hirsch (1987) writes as if knowledge is neutral and static. His book contains a list of important facts that students should master in order to become culturally literate. Ravitch and Finn (1987) identify and lament the factual knowledge that U.S. high school students do not know. Neither Hirsch nor Ravitch and Finn discuss the limitations of factual knowledge or point out that knowledge is dynamic, changing, and constructed within a social context rather than neutral and static.

I agree with Hirsch and Ravitch and Finn that all people in the United States need to master a common core of shared knowledge. However, the important

TABLE 8.1 Types of Knowledge

Knowledge Type	Definition	Examples
Personal/Cultural	The concepts, explanations, and interpretations that students derive from personal experiences in their homes, families, and community cultures.	Understandings by many African Americans and Hispanic students that highly individualistic behavior will be negatively sanctioned by many adults and peers in their cultural communities.
Popular	The facts, concepts, explanations, and interpretations that are institutionalized within the mass media and other institutions that are part of the popular culture.	Movies such as *Birth of a Nation, How the West Was Won,* and *Dances with Wolves.*
Mainstream Academic	The concepts, paradigms, theories and explanations that constitute traditional Western-centric knowledge in history and the behavioral and social sciences.	Ulrich B. Phillips, *American Negro Slavery;* Frederick Jackson Turner's Frontier theory; Arthur R. Jensen's theory about Black and White intelligence.
Transformative Academic	The facts, concepts, paradigms, themes, and explanations that challenge mainstream academic knowledge and expand and substantially revise established canons, paradigms, theories, explanations, and research methods. When transformative academic paradigms replace mainstream ones, a scientific revolution has occurred. What is more normal is that transformative academic paradigms coexist with established ones.	George Washington Williams, *History of the Negro Race in America;* W. E. B. DuBois, *Black Reconstruction;* Carter G. Woodson, *The Mis-Education of the Negro;* Gerda Lerner, *The Majority Finds Its Past;* Rodolfo Acuna, *Occupied America: A History of Chicanos;* Herbert Gutman, *The Black Family in Slavery and Freedom 1750–1925.*
School	The facts, concepts, generalizations, and interpretations that are presented in textbooks, teacher's guides, other media forms, and lectures by teachers.	Lewis Paul Todd and Merle Curti, *Rise of the American Nation;* Richard C. Brown, Wilhelmena S. Robinson, & John Cunningham, *Let Freedom Ring: A United States History.*

question is: *Who will participate in the formulation of that knowledge and whose interests will it serve?* We need a broad level of participation in the identification, construction, and formulation of the knowledge that we expect all of our citizens to master. Such knowledge should reflect cultural democracy and serve the interests of all of the people within our pluralistic nation and world.

It should contribute to public virtue and the public good. The knowledge institutionalized within our schools and colleges and within the popular culture should reflect the interests, experiences, and goals of all of the nation's citizens and should empower all people to participate effectively in a democratic society.

Knowledge and Empowerment

To empower students to participate effectively in their civic community, we must change the ways in which they acquire, view, and evaluate knowledge. We must engage students in a process of attaining knowledge in which they are required to critically analyze conflicting paradigms and explanations and the values and assumptions of different knowledge systems, forms, and categories. Students must also be given opportunities to construct knowledge themselves so that they can develop a sophisticated appreciation of the nature and limitations of knowledge and understand the extent to which knowledge is a social construction that reflects the social, political, and cultural context in which it is formulated.

Participating in processes in which they formulate and construct various knowledge forms will also enable students to understand how various groups within a society often formulate, shape, and disseminate knowledge that supports their interests and legitimizes their power. Groups without power and influence often challenge the dominant paradigms, knowledge systems, and perspectives that are institutionalized within society. Knowledge and paradigms consistent with the interests, goals, and assumptions of dominant groups are institutionalized within the schools and universities as well as within the popular culture. A latent function of such knowledge is to legitimize the dominant political, economic, and cultural arrangements within society.

The Attempt to Reformulate the Canon

The ethnic studies and women studies movements, which emerged from the civil rights movement of the 1960s and 1970s, have as a major goal a reformulation of the canon that is used to select and evaluate knowledge for inclusion into the school and university curriculum (Banks, 1989). The demand for a reformulation of the curriculum canon has evoked a concerted and angry reaction from established mainstream scholars (D'Souza, 1991; Schlesinger, 1991). They have described the push by ethnic and feminist scholars for a reformulation of the canon as an attempt to politicize the curriculum and to promote special interests. Two national organizations have been formed by established mainstream scholars to resist the efforts by ethnic and feminist scholars to reformulate the canon and transform the school and university curriculum so that it will be more accurately reflect the experiences, visions, and goals of people of color and women. They are the Madison Center and the National Association of Scholars (Heller, 1989). Two organizations that support multicultural issues and concerns have also been organized. Teachers for a Democratic Society focuses on colleges and unviversities. Teacher education and the elementary and secondary schools are the chief concerns of the National Association of Multicultural Education.

The mainstream scholars who have labeled the curricular goals of women and people of color *special interests* view their own interests as universal and in the public good and any claims that challenge their interests as *special interests.* Dominant groups within a society not only view their own interests as identical to the public interest but also are usually able to get other groups, including structurally excluded groups, to internalize this belief. The school and university curriculum help students acquire the belief that the interests, goals, and values of dominant groups are identical to those of the civic community.

School Knowledge and the Dominant Canon

To develop a sense of the need for social change, a commitment to social participation, and the skills to participate effectively in social action that eventuates in change, the knowledge that students acquire must have certain characteristics. It must describe events, concepts, and situations from the perspectives of the diverse cultural, racial, gender, and social-class groups within a society, including those that are politically and culturally dominant as well as those that are structurally excluded from full societal participation. Much of school knowledge as well as knowledge in the popular culture presents events and situations from the perspectives of the victors rather than the vanquished and from the perspectives of those who control the social, economic, and political institutions in society rather than from the points of view of those who are victimized and marginalized.

School and societal knowledge that present issues, events, and concepts primarily from the perspectives of dominant groups tends to justify the status quo, rationalize racial and gender inequality, and to make students content with the status quo. An important latent function of such knowledge is to convince students that the current social, political, and economic institutions are just and that substantial change within society is neither justified nor required.

The ways in which the current social, economic, and political structures are justified in the school and university curricula are usually subtle rather than blatant. These justifications are consequently more effective because they are infrequently suspected, recognized, questioned, or criticized. These dominant perspectives emanate from the canon that is used to define, select, and evaluate knowledge in the school and university curriculum in the United States and in other Western nations. This canon is European-centric and male-dominated. It is rarely explicitly defined or discussed. It is taken for granted, unquestioned, and internalized by writers, researchers, teachers, professors, and students.

The Western-centric and male-centric canon that dominates the school and university curriculum often marginalizes the experiences of people of color, Third World nations and cultures, and the perspectives and histories of women. It results in the Americas being called the "New World," in the notion that Columbus "discovered" America, in the Anglo immigrants to the West being called "settlers" rather than "immigrants," and in the description of the Anglo immigrants' rush to the West as the "Westward Movement." Calling the Americas "The New World" subtly denies the nearly 40,000 years that Native Americans have lived in this land. The implication is that history did not begin in the Americas until the Europeans arrived. From the perspectives of the Lakota Sioux, the Anglo settlers in the West were invaders and conquerors. The Westward Movement is a highly Eurocentric concept. The Lakota Sioux did not consider their homeland the West but the center of the universe. And, of course, it was the Anglos who were moving West and not the Sioux. From the perspective of the Lakota Sioux it was not a Westward Movement but the Great Invasion.

Concepts such as The New World, The Westward Movement, hostile Indians, and lazy welfare mothers not only justify the status quo and current social and economic realities, but they also fail to help students understand why there is a need to substantially change current social, political and economic realities or help them develop a commitment to social change and political action. These Anglo-centric and Euro-centric notions also fail to help students of color and female students develop a sense of empowerment and efficacy over their lives and their destinies.

Both the research by Coleman et al. (1966) and the research on locus of control (Lefcourt, 1976) indicate that people need a sense of control over their destiny in order to become empowered to achieve or to act. Many students of color and female students are victimized and marginalized by the knowledge that results from the Eurocentric canon because they are made to believe that problems such as racism and sexism either do not exist in any substantial way or that such problems result from their own actions or shortcomings. In his book *The Closing of the American Mind*, Bloom (1987) states that African American students are not well integrated into the structure of predominantly White university campuses because of their own resistance to social integration. This is a classic example of "blaming the victim" (Ryan, 1971) and contradicts the scientific findings by Fleming (1985). Fleming attributes the structural exclusion of African American students on predominantly White campuses to an inhospitable environment that fails to meet the needs of African American students.

The Dominant Canon and the Popular Culture

The popular culture frequently reinforces and extends the dominant canon and paradigms taught in the school and university curriculum. An example is the popular film, *Mississippi Burning*. This film presents several dominant-group perspectives on the civil rights movement of the 1960s that are notable. In actual history, African Americans were the real heroes of the civil rights movement. They were the primary architects of the movement, lead the first demonstrations and sit-ins, and showed tremendous efficacy in the movement. The FBI (Federal

Bureau of Investigation), under the leadership of J. Edgar Hoover, was at best a reluctant protector of civil rights and played a major role spying on and under-cutting the civil rights movement and civil rights leaders. Martin Luther King was a frequent victim of Hoover's tactics and undercover agents (Garrow, 1986). Despite these realities, *Mississippi Burning* presents African Americans as shad-owy figures who were primarily victims and two FBI agents as the real heroes and defenders of Black rights in the civil rights movement. The depiction of the civil rights movement in *Mississippi Burning* is a travesty on history, but it was a popular film that was believable and credible to many Americans because it is consistent with the canon that is institutionalized and taught within the school and university curriculum.

A Transformative Curriculum for Empowerment

In the previous section of this chapter, I describe the nature and goals of the dominant Eurocentric curriculum in the nation's schools and colleges. This cur-riculum reinforces the status quo, makes students passive and content, and en-courages them to acquiescently accept the dominant ideologies, political and economic arrangements, and the prevailing myths and paradigms used to ration-alize and justify the current social and political structure.

A transformative curriculum designed to empower students, especially those from victimized and marginalized groups, must help students develop the knowledge and skills needed to critically examine the current political and eco-nomic structure and the myths and ideologies used to justify it. Such a curriculum must teach students critical thinking skills, the ways in which knowledge is constructed, the basic assumptions and values that undergird knowledge sys-tems, and how to construct knowledge themselves.

A transformative curriculum cannot be constructed merely by adding content about ethnic groups and women to the existing Eurocentric curriculum or by integrating or infusing ethnic content or content about women into the main-stream curriculum. When the curriculum is revised using either an additive or an infusion approach, the basic assumptions, perspectives, paradigms, and values of the dominant curriculum remain unchallenged and substantially unchanged, despite the addition of ethnic content or content about women. In such a revised curriculum, the experiences of women and of people of color are viewed from the perspectives and values of mainstream males with power.

When the meeting of the Lakota Sioux and the Anglos from the East is conceptualized as The Westward Movement, adding content about the Lakota and about women neither changes nor challenges the basic assumptions of the curriculum or the canon used to select content for inclusion into it. The Lakota and women heroes selected for study are selected using the Western-centric, male-dominated paradigm. When the dominant paradigm and canon are used to select ethnic and women heroes for inclusion into the curriculum, the heroes selected for study are those who are valued by dominant groups and not necessarily those considered heroes by victimized and nonmainstream groups. Ethnic heroes selected for study and veneration are usually those who helped Whites conquer or oppress powerless people rather than those who challenged the existing social, economic, and political order. Consequently, Sacajawea and Booker T. Washington are more likely to be selected for inclusion into the mainstream curriculum than are Geronimo and Nat Turner.

Critical Thinking and Multiple Voices

A curriculum designed to empower students must be transformative in nature and must help students develop the knowledge, skills, and values needed to become social critics who can make reflective decisions and implement their decisions in effective personal, social, political, and economic action. In other words, reflective decision making and personal and civic action must be the primary goals of a transformative and empowering curriculum.

The transformative curriculum must help students reconceptualize and rethink the experiences of people in both the United States and the world, to view the human experience from the perspectives of a range of cultural, ethnic, and social-class groups, and to construct their own versions of the past, present, and future. In the transformative curriculum multiple voices are heard and legitimized: the voices of textbook, literary, and historical writers, the voices of teachers, and the voices of other students. Students can construct their own versions of the past, present, and future after listening to and reflecting on the multiple and diverse voices in the transformative classroom. Literacy in the transformative curriculum is reconceptualized to include diverse voices and perspectives and is not limited to literacy in the Hirsch (1987) sense, that is, to the mastering of a list of facts constructed by authorities. Writes Starrs (1988),

> In the new definition literacy should be seen as a struggle for voice. As such the presence of different voices is an opportunity and a challenge. All students will deal with the fact that their voices differ from one another's, from their teachers', from their authors'. All learners will somehow cope with the issue of translating their many voices, and in the process they will join in creating culture—not simply receiving it.

The transformative curriculum teaches students to think and reflect critically on the materials they read and the voices they hear. Baldwin (1985), in a classic essay, "A Talk to Teachers," states that the main goal of education is to teach students to think: "The purpose of education . . . is to create in a person the ability to look at the world for himself, to make his own decisions, to say to himself this is black or this is white, to decide for himself whether there is a God in heaven or not. To ask questions of the universe, and then to live with those questions, is the way he achieves his identity" (p. 326). Although Baldwin believed that thinking was the real purpose of education, he also believed that no society was serious about teaching its citizens to think. He writes further: "But no society is really anxious to have that kind of person around. What society really, ideally, wants is a citizenry which will simply obey the rules of society. If a society succeeds in this, that society is about to perish" (p. 326).

The transformative curriculum can teach students to think by encouraging them, when they are reading or listening to resources, to consider the author's purposes for writing or speaking, his or her basic assumptions, and how the author's perspective or point of view compares with that of other authors and resources. Students can develop the skills to critically analyze historical and contemporary resources by being given two accounts of the same event or situation that present different perspectives and points of view.

A Lesson with Different Voices

In a lesson I developed for a junior high school U.S. history textbook (Banks with Sebesta, 1982) entitled "Christopher Columbus and the Arawak Indians," the students are presented with an excerpt from Columbus's diary that describes his arrival in an Arawak community in the Caribbean in 1492. These are among the things that Columbus (Jane, 1930) writes about the Arawaks:

> *They took all and gave all, such as they had, with good will, but it seemed to me that they were a people very lacking in everything. They all go naked as their mothers bore them, and the women also, although I saw only one very young girl . . . They should be good servants and quick to learn, since I see that they very soon say all that is said to them, and I believe that they would easily be made Christians, for it appeared to me that they had no religious beliefs. Our Lord willing, at the time of my departure, I will bring back six of them to Your Highnesses, that they may learn to talk. I saw no beast of any kind in this island, except parrots.*

The students are then encouraged to view Columbus's voice from the perspective of the Arawaks. The Arawaks had an aural culture and consequently left no written documents. However, archaeologist Fred Olsen studied Arawak artifacts and used what he learned from them to construct a day in the life of the Arawaks, which he describes in his book, *On the Trail of the Arawaks* (Olsen, 1974). The students are asked to read an excerpt from Olsen's account of a day in the life of the Arawaks and to respond to these questions:

> *Columbus wrote in his diary that he thought the Arawaks had no religious beliefs. You read about Arawak life in the report by Fred Olsen. Do you think Columbus was correct? Why?*
>
> *Accounts written by people who took part in or witnessed (saw) an historical event are called primary sources. Can historians believe everything they read in a primary source? Explain.* (Banks with Sebesta, 1982, p. 43)

Key Concepts and Issues

In addition to helping students view events and situations from diverse ethnic, gender, and social-class perspectives, a transformative curriculum should be organized around key concepts and social issues. The conceptual-issue-oriented curriculum facilitates the teaching of decision-making and social action skills in several important ways. First, a conceptual curriculum helps students understand the ways in which knowledge is constructed, enables them to formulate concepts themselves, and to understand the ways in which the concepts formulated reflect the values, purposes, and assumptions of the conceptualizers. In an inquiry-oriented conceptual curriculum, students are not passive consumers of previously constructed knowledge, but are encouraged to formulate new ways to organize, conceptualize, and think about data and information.

The conceptual approach also allows the teacher to rethink the ways that topics, periods, and literary movements are structured and labeled. Periodization in history, literature, and art tend to reflect a Eurocentric bias, such as the Middle Ages, the Renaissance, and the Westward Movement. When content is organized around key interdisciplinary concepts such as culture, communication, and values, the teacher can structure lessons and units that facilitate the inclusion of content from diverse cultures as well as content that will help students develop the knowledge, values, commitments, and skills needed to participate in effective personal, economic, and civic action.

In the U.S. junior high school textbook I authored that was cited earlier (Banks with Sebesta, 1982), I used a key concept, *revolution,* to organize a unit rather than focus the unit exclusively on the revolution in the English colonies in 1776. By organizing the unit around the concept of revolution rather than a particular revolution, the students were able to examine three American revolutions, to study each in depth, and to derive generalizations about revolutions in general. They were also able to identify ways in which these three revolutions were alike and different. They also used the definition and generalizations they derived about revolutions from this unit to determine whether events such as the civil rights movement of the 1960s and 1970s and the women rights movement of the 1970s could accurately be called "revolutions." The three American revolutions they studied were the (1) The Pueblo Revolt of 1680, in which Pope lead a resistance against the conquering Spaniards; (2) The Revolution in the British Colonies, 1776; and (3) The Mexican Revolution of 1810, the aim of which was to acquire Mexico's independence from Spain.

The Moral Component of Action

After students have mastered interdisciplinary knowledge related to a concept or issue such as racism or sexism, they should participate in value or moral inquiry exercises. The goal of such exercises should be to help students develop a set of consistent, clarified values that can guide purposeful and reflective personal or civic action related to the issue examined. This goal can best be attained by teaching students a method or process for deriving their values within a democratic classroom atmosphere. In this kind of democratic classroom, students must be free to express their value choices, determine how those choices conflict, examine alternative values, consider the consequences of different value choices, make value choices, and defend their moral choices within the context of human dignity and other American creed values. Students must be given an opportunity to derive their own values reflectively in order to develop a commitment to human dignity, equality, and to other democratic values. They must be encouraged to reflect on values choices within a democratic atmosphere in order to internalize them (Banks with Clegg, 1990).

I have developed a value inquiry model that teachers can use to help students to identify and clarify their values and to make reflective moral choices. It consists of these steps (Banks with Clegg, 1990, p. 445):

Value Inquiry Model - STEPS:

1. Defining and recognizing value problems
2. Describing value-relevant behavior
3. Naming values exemplified by the behavior
4. Determining conflicting values in behavior described
5. Hypothesizing about the possible consequence of the values analyzed
6. Naming alternative values to those described by behavior observed
7. Hypothesizing about the possible consequences of values analyzed
8. Declaring value preferences; choosing
9. Stating reasons, sources, and possible consequences of value choice: justifying, hypothesizing, predicting

I illustrate how Mr. Carson, a junior high school social studies teacher, used this model while teaching a unit on the civil rights movement. Mr. Carson wanted his students to acquire an understanding of the historical development of the civil rights movement, to analyze and clarify their values related to integration and segregation, as well as to conceptualize and perhaps take some kinds of actions related to racism and desegregation in their personal life, the school, or the local community. Mr. Carson is a social studies teacher in a predominantly White suburban school district near a city in the Northwest that has a population of about 1 million. The metropolitan area in which Mr. Carson's school is located has a population of about 2 million.

The Long Shadow of Little Rock

Mr. Carson used the Banks value inquiry model to help his students analyze the value issues revealed in Chapter 8 of *The Long Shadow of Little Rock* by Daisy Bates (1987). In this excellently written and moving chapter, Mrs. Bates describes the moral dilemma she faced when serving as head of the National Association for the Advancement of Colored People (NAACP) in Little Rock when Central High School was desegregated by nine African American high school students. The desegregation of Central High school began during the 1957–58 school year.

Mrs. Bates was the leading supporter and organizer for the nine students. Her husband, L. C. Bates, was a journalist. They owned a newspaper, *The States Press*. In Chapter 8 of *The Long Shadow of Little Rock*, Mrs. Bates describes how a middle-aged White woman came to her home at 3:00 in the afternoon and told her to call a press conference and announce that she was withdrawing her support for the nine students and advising them to withdraw from Central High School and return to the Negro schools. The woman said she represented a group of "Southern Christian women." Mrs. Bates asked the woman what would happen if she didn't do what she told her to do. She looked at Mrs. Bates straight in the eye and said, "You'll be destroyed—you, your newspaper, your reputation . . . Everything."

During her long, anguished night, Mrs. Bates wondered whether she had the right to destroy sixteen years of her husband's work—the newspaper. Yet she felt that she could not abandon a cause to which she and many other African Americans were deeply committed. By morning Mrs. Bates had made her difficult and painful decision. She called her visitor and said, "No." Later, she told her husband, L. C., what she had done. He said, "Daisy, you did the right thing." Mrs. Bates's visitor kept her promise. *The State Press* was closed because advertising from it was withdrawn by all of the major stores and businesses in Little Rock. The Bates family suffered financial and personal turmoil because of the closing of *The State Press* and because of threats and attempts on Mrs. Bates's life.

Using the Banks value inquiry model, these are some of the questions Mr. Carson asked his students:

Defining and Recognizing Value Problems
1. What value problem did Mrs. Bates face after she was visited by the woman?

Naming Values Exemplified by Behavior Described
2. What did the visitor value or think was important? What did Mrs. Bates value? What did Mr. Bates value?

Hypothesizing about the Sources of Values Analyzed
3. How do you think Mrs. Bates's visitor developed the values she had? How do you think Mr. and Mrs. Bates developed the values they showed in this selection?

Declaring Value Preferences: Choosing
4. Try to put yourself in Mrs. Daisy Bates's place on October 29, 1959. What decision would you have made?

Stating Reasons, Sources, and Possible Consequences of Value Choice
5. Why should Mrs. Bates have made the decision you stated above? What were the possible consequences of her saying "no" and saying "yes" to her visitor?

Give as many reasons as you can about why Mrs. Bates should have made the decision you stated above.

Keep in mind that Mrs. Bates knew that if she said yes to her visitor she would probably have been able to keep her property but that the nine students would have probably had to return to Black schools and that segregation would have been maintained in Little Rock. One the other hand, by saying no, she risked losing all of her property and her husband's property, including his newspaper. Also, consider the fact that she did not involve him in making her decision.

Decision Making and Citizen Action

After Mr. Carson's students had derived knowledge about the civil rights movement of the 1950s and 1960s and clarified their values regarding these issues, he asked them to list all of the possible actions they could take to increase desegregation in their personal lives as well as in the life of the school and the community. Mr. Carson was careful to explain to the students that action should be broadly conceptualized. He defined action in a way that might include a personal commitment to do something, such as making an effort to have more friends from different racial and ethnic groups, making a commitment to see the videotape *Roots* and discuss it with a friend, as well as reading a play or book that will help you to better understand another racial or ethnic group, such as *A Raisin in the Sun* by Lorraine Hansberry or *Beloved* by Toni Morrison. Among the possible actions the students listed that they could take were these:

1. Making a personal commitment to stop telling racist jokes.
2. Making a commitment to challenge our own racial and ethnic stereotypes either before or after we verbalize them.
3. Compiling an annotated list of books about ethnic groups that we will ask the librarian to order for our school library.
4. Asking the principal to order sets of photographs that show African Americans and other people of color who have jobs that represent a variety of careers. Asking the principal to encourage our teachers to display these photographs on their classroom walls.
5. Observing television programs to determine the extent to which people of color, such as African Americans and Asian Americans, are represented in such jobs as news anchors and hosts of programs. Writing to local and national television stations to express our concern if we discover that people of color are not represented in powerful and visible roles in news or other kinds of television programs.
6. Contacting a school in the inner city to determine if there are joint activities and projects in which we and they might participate.
7. Asking the principal or the board of education in our school district to require our teachers to attend in-service staff development workshops that will help them

learn ways in which to integrate content about ethnic and racial groups into our courses.

8. Sharing some of the facts that we have learned in this unit, such as that by the year 2000, one out of three Americans will be a person of color, with our parents and discussing these facts with them.

9. Making a personal commitment to have a friend from another racial, ethnic, or religious group by the end of the year.

10. Making a personal commitment to read at least one book a year that deals with a racial, cultural, or ethnic group other than my own.

11. Do nothing, take no actions.

The Decision-Making Process

After the students had made a list of possible actions they could take regarding the issues studied in the unit (including no actions), Mr. Carson asked them to consider the possible consequences of each of the actions identified, such as:

If I Take No Actions
Then I will be doing nothing to improve race relations in my personal life, in my school, my community or nation.

But I will not risk trying to do something that could fail. I will also be indicating to others, by my behavior, that I am not concerned about improving race relations in my personal life, my family, school, or community.

If I Make a Personal Commitment to Tell No More Racist Jokes
Then I will be improving my personal behavior that relates to other racial, ethnic, and cultural groups. I will also demonstrate to others that I am concerned about improving race relations in my personal life.

But I will be doing little directly to improve the behaviors of other people in my family, school, and community.

After the students had worked in groups of five to identify and state the possible consequences of various courses of actions, Mr. Carson asked them to continue working in their groups and to select one or two personal or group actions they would like to take related to the problems they had studied in the unit. Mr. Carson also asked the students to be prepared to defend and/or explain the course of action or actions they chose, to tell whether it was feasible for them to carry out the action or actions, and to provide a time-line for its initiation and completion (if possible). These are among the actions the students chose:

- Kathy and Susan decided to read the play *A Raisin in the Sun* by Lorraine Hansberry to try to get a better understanding of the experience of African Americans in the United States.
- Clay's group, which included Clay, Pete, Tessie, Rosie, and Maria, decided that it would prepare a list of books on ethnic cultures and ask the school librarian to order them for the school library. Clay's group planned to ask

Mr. Carson to help them find resources for the preparation of the annotated list of books.

- Roselyn decided that she wanted to improve her understanding of ethnic cultures by reading. She decided to read these books during the year: *Let the Circle Be Unbroken* by Mildred D. Taylor, *A Jar of Dreams* by Yoshiko Uchida, and *America Is in the Heart* by Carlos Bulosan.
- Aralean's group, which included Juan, James, Angela, and Patricia, decided that it wanted to develop a proposal that would require teachers in the district to attend multicultural education workshops. They will develop their plan with Mr. Carson and present it to the principal and then to the Board of Education for possible adoption.

The Role of the Teacher in an Empowerment and Transformative Curriculum

An effective transformative and empowerment curriculum must be implemented by teachers who have the knowledge, skills, and attitudes needed to help students understand the ways in which knowledge is constructed and used to support power group relationships in society. Teachers are human beings who bring their cultural perspectives, values, hopes, and dreams to the classroom. They also bring their prejudices, stereotypes, and misconceptions to the classroom. The teacher's values and perspectives mediate and interact with what they teach and influence the way that messages are communicated and perceived by their students. A teacher who believes that Christopher Columbus discovered America and one who believes that Columbus came to America when it was peopled by groups with rich and diverse cultures will send different messages to their students when the European exploration of America is studied.

Because the teacher mediates the messages and symbols communicated to the students through the curriculum, it is important for teachers to come to grips with their own personal and cultural values and identities in order for them to help students from diverse racial, ethnic, and cultural groups to develop clarified cultural identities and to relate positively to each other. I am hypothesizing that self-clarification is a prerequisite to dealing effectively with and relating positively to outside ethnic and cultural groups. An Anglo-American teacher who is confused about his or her cultural identity and who has a nonreflective conception of the ways that Anglo-American culture relates to other groups in the United States will have a difficult time relating positively to outside ethnic groups such as African Americans and Mexican Americans.

Effective teacher education programs should help pre- and in-service teachers explore and clarify their own ethnic and cultural identities and develop more positive attitudes toward other racial, ethnic, and cultural groups. To do this, such programs must recognize and reflect the complex ethnic and cultural identities and characteristics of the individuals within teacher education programs (Banks, 1988). Teachers should also learn how to facilitate the identity quest among students and help them become effective and able participants in the common civic culture.

Effective teachers in the transformative curriculum must not only have clarified personal and cultural identifications, they must also be keenly aware of the various paradigms, canons, and knowledge systems on which the dominant curriculum is based and those that it eschews. Because teacher-education students attain most of their knowledge without analyzing its assumptions and values or engaging in the process of constructing knowledge themselves, they often leave teacher-education programs with many misconceptions about culturally and racially different groups and with conceptions about their national history and culture that are incomplete, misleading, and chauvinistic. Consequently, the knowledge that many teachers bring to the classroom contributes to the mystification rather than to the clarification of social, historical, and political realities. This knowledge also perpetuates inequality and oppression rather than contributes to justice, liberation, and empowerment.

In order to educate teachers so that they will convey images, perspectives, and points of view in the curriculum that will demystify social realities and promote cultural freedom and empowerment, we must radically change the ways in which they acquire knowledge. We must engage them in a process of attaining knowledge in which they are required to analyze the values and assumptions of different paradigms and theories. Teachers must also be given the opportunity to construct concepts, generalizations, and theories so that they can develop an understanding of the nature and limitations of knowledge and comprehend the extent to which knowledge reflects the social and cultural context in which it is formulated.

Participating in processes in which they formulate and construct knowledge forms will also help teachers to understand how various groups in society who formulate, shape, and disseminate knowledge often structure and disseminate knowledge that supports their interests and legitimizes their power. This knowledge often legitimizes dominant institutions and helps to make victimized groups politically passive and content with their marginalized status. Teachers must not only understand how the dominant paradigms and canon help keep victimized groups powerless but also must be committed to social change and action if they are to become agents of liberation and empowerment.

References

The American Heritage Dictionary. (1983). New York: Dell Publishing.

Baldwin, J. (1985). *The Price of the Ticket: Collected Nonfiction, 1948–1985.* New York: St. Martin's Press.

Banks, J. A. (1989). The Battle over the Canon: Cultural Diversity and Curriculum Reform. *Allyn and Bacon Educators' Forum, 1,* 11–13.

Banks, J. A. (in press). The Canon Debate, Knowledge Construction, and Multicultural Education. *Educational Researcher, 21.*

Banks, J. A., with Sebesta, S. (1982). *We Americans: Our History and People,* Vol. 1 & 2. Boston: Allyn and Bacon.

Banks, J. A., with A. A. Clegg, Jr. (1990). *Teaching Strategies for the Social Studies: Inquiry, Valuing and Decision-Making* (4th ed.). White Plains, NY: Longman.

Bates, D. (1987). *The Long Shadow of Little Rock.* Fayetteville: The University of Arkansas Press.

Berger, P., & Luckman, T. (1966). *The Social Construction of Reality.* New York: Doubleday.

Bloom, A. (1987). *The Closing of the American Mind.* New York: Simon & Schuster.

Coleman, J. S., et al. (1966). *Equality of Educational Opportunity.* Washington, DC: U.S. Government Printing Office.

D' Souza, D. (1991). *Illiberal Education: The Politics of Race and Sex on Campus.* New York: The Free Press.

Farganis, S. (1986). *The Social Construction of the Feminine Character.* Totowa, NJ: Russell & Russell.

Fleming, J. (1985). *Blacks in College: A Comparative Study of Students' Success in Black and White Institutions.* San Francisco: Jossey-Bass Publishers.

Garrow, D. J. (1986). *Bearing the Cross: Martin Luther King and the Southern Christian Leadership Conference.* New York: Vintage.

Gould, S. J. (1981). *The Mismeasure of Man.* New York: Norton.

Heller, S. (1989). Press for Campus Diversity Leading to More Closed Minds, Say Critics. *The Chronicle of Higher Education, 35,* pp. A13, ff A22.

Hirsch, E. D., Jr. (1987). *Cultural Literacy: What Every American Needs to Know.* Boston: Houghton Mifflin.

Jane, L. C. (1930). *The Voyages of Christopher Columbus.* London: The Argonaut Press.

Kuhn, T. S. (1970). *The Structure of Scientific Revolutions* (2nd ed.). Chicago: The University of Chicago Press.

Lefcourt, H. M. (1976). *Locus of Control: Current Trends in Theory and Research.* New York: John Wiley.

Olsen, F. (1974). *On the Trail of the Arawaks.* Norman: University of Oklahoma Press.

Ravitch, D., & Finn, C. E., Jr. (1987). *What Do Our 17-Year-Olds Know? A Report on the First National Assessment of History and Literature.* New York: Harper and Row.

Ryan, W. (1971). *Blaming the Victim.* New York: Vintage.

Schlesinger, A. M. (1991). *The Disuniting of America: Reflections on a Multicultural Society.* Knoxville, TN: Whittle Direct Books.

Starrs, J. (1988). Cultural Literacy and Black Education. "A paper submitted to James A. Banks as a partial requirement for the course EDC&I 469, University of Washington.

Chapter 9

Teaching Decision-Making and Social Action Skills

The multicultural curriculum should help students develop the ability to make reflective decisions so they can resolve personal problems, and through social action influence public policy and develop a sense of political efficacy (Banks with Clegg, 1990; Lewis, 1991). In many ethnic studies units and lessons, emphasis is on the memorization and testing of isolated historical facts about shadowy ethnic heroes of questionable historical significance. In these types of curricula ethnic content is merely an extension of the traditional curriculum.

The multicultural curriculum should have goals that are more consistent with the needs of an ethnically and culturally diverse global society. We live in a world society that is beset with momentous social and human problems. Effective solutions to these tremendous problems can be found only by an active and informed citizenry capable of making sound public decisions that will benefit the world community. It is imperative that the school play a decisive role in educating citizens capable of making reflective decisions on social issues and taking effective actions to help solve them.

Elements of Reflective Decision Making

Decision making consists of several components, including the derivation of knowledge, prediction, value analysis and clarification, the synthesis of knowledge and values, and the affirmation of a course of action (see Figure 9.1). All decisions consist of knowledge, valuing, and prediction components, but reflective decisions must also satisfy other requirements. To make a reflective decision, the decision maker must use the scientific method to attain knowledge. The knowledge must not only be *scientific*, but it must also be *interdisciplinary* and cut

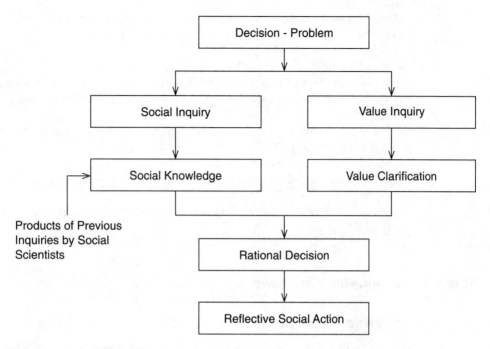

FIGURE 9.1   The Decision-Making Process

(*Source:* Adapted from *Teaching Strategies for the Social Studies: Inquiry, Valuing, and Decision-Making*
4/e by James A. Banks, with Ambrose A. Clegg, Jr. Copyright © 1990 by Longman Publishing Group.)

across disciplinary lines. Knowledge from any one discipline is insufficient to
help us make reflective decisions. To make reflective decisions about social issues,
such as busing to achieve school desegregation and reducing interracial conflict,
the individual must view these problems from the perspectives of such disciplines as sociology, economics, political science, and anthropology. The perspectives of any one discipline are too limited to guide thoughtful decision making
and reflective social action.

This chapter consists of a teaching unit based on the decision making
model described in Figure 9.1. The key question in this sample unit is, *Should
institutions establish public policies that acknowledge and support racial, ethnic, and
cultural diversity?*

Some Subissues Related to the Major Problem

There is a wide range of questions related to racial, ethnic, and cultural diversity
in a pluralistic society that students can state and research. Open housing, ethnic
separatism, interracial marriage, and affirmative action are some of the key issues

and problems the class can explore when studying about ethnicity and race. Specific problems related to the major question in this unit include:

- Should students of color be judged by different criteria than Whites when applying for employment and admission to colleges and universities?
- Should institutions establish quotas for hiring and admitting persons of color?
- Should persons of color be permitted to establish separate facilities and organizations in publicly supported institutions?
- Should busing be used to desegregate public schools?
- Should interracial and interethnic marriage be encouraged and socially accepted?
- Should all-male African American academies be supported with public funds?

Stages in Considering This Issue

Gathering Scientific Data

To make an intelligent decision on a social issue such as *Should institutions establish public policies that acknowledge and support racial, ethnic, and cultural diversity?* the students need to acquire knowledge. However, decisions can be no better than the knowledge on which they are based. To make reflective decisions, students must study high-level concepts and master key generalizations. Generalizations can be taught in a variety of ways. However, it is necessary for students to use the *scientific method* to derive generalizations needed for decision making. When planning lessons to help students gain knowledge, the teacher should identify social science and related generalizations that will help them make reflective decisions. Concepts should be selected from several disciplines, such as sociology, anthropology, history, and geography. *Discrimination, assimilation, ethnic group, culture, powerlessness,* and *separatism* are key concepts related to racial, ethnic, and cultural diversity. After key concepts are identified, organizing (or key) generalizations related to the concepts are identified, and subideas related to the organizing generalizations and to the content chosen for study are stated. A detailed example of this type of curriculum planning is not presented here because I discuss it at considerable length in other publications (Banks, 1991; Banks with Clegg, 1990).

Value Inquiry

After the students have had an opportunity to derive social science generalizations related to a social issue, they should undertake lessons that will enable them to *identify, analyze,* and *clarify* their values related to them. Value lessons should be conducted in an open classroom atmosphere so the students will be willing to express their beliefs freely and to examine them openly. If the teacher is authoritarian, the students will not express their actual feelings and attitudes. Beliefs that are unexpressed cannot be examined. Because of how teachers are viewed by most students, it is a good idea for teachers to withhold their views on controversial issues until the students have had an opportunity to express their beliefs.

When teachers reveal their position on a social issue, many students then make statements they believe teachers want them to make rather than say things they actually believe. The teacher who opens a discussion on interracial marriage or open housing by saying that everybody should have the right to marry whomever they please or that open housing laws violate a seller's constitutional rights, cannot expect the students to state opposing beliefs. Some students will openly disagree with the teacher, but most will not. I am not suggesting that teachers should not state their positions on issues. However, experience suggests that when teachers openly express their views early in class discussions, the dialogue usually becomes stifled or slanted in one direction.

Decision Making and Social Action

After the students have derived social science generalizations and clarified their values regarding the social issue, the teacher should ask them to list all the possible actions they could take regarding racial, ethnic, and cultural diversity in their school and community and to predict the possible consequences of each alternative. It is imperative that the alternatives and consequences the students identify and state are realistic and based on the knowledge they have mastered during the scientific phase of the unit. Alternatives and consequences should be thoughtful, predictive statements and not ignorant guesses or wishful thinking. After the students have discussed and weighed all alternative courses of action, they should decide on courses of action most consistent with their own values and implement them within their school or community. For example, the students, or some of them, may decide that racial, ethnic, and cultural diversity should be important public policy goals in a pluralistic society but that it does not exist within their school. They might design and implement a plan to increase ethnic and racial harmony and interactions in their school. Figure 9.2 summarizes the major steps I have discussed for studying a social issue.

The Origin of the Issue

The teacher can begin a study of the key issues discussed in this chapter by asking the students to cut out newspaper items that deal with such issues as open housing, affirmative action programs, job discrimination, and the experiences of students of color on predominantly White school and university campuses.

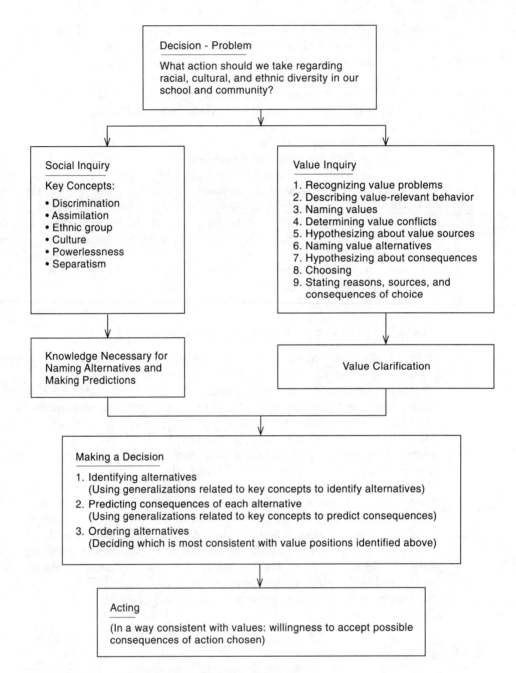

FIGURE 9.2   The Decision-Making Process

(*Source:* Adapted from *Teaching Strategies for the Social Studies: Inquiry, Valuing, and Decision-Making*
4/e by James A. Banks, with Ambrose A. Clegg, Jr. Copyright © 1990 by Longman Publishing Group.)

The Definition of Key Concepts

When studying problems related to racial, ethnic, and cultural diversity, the class should clarify the definitions of key terms and reach general agreement about what they mean. Terms such as *integration, race, desegregation, separatism, racism, discrimination,* and *cultural pluralism* are some key concepts that should be defined when policies related to racial, ethnic, and cultural diversity are studied. Several of these terms are discussed below.

Some writers make a distinction between *integration* and *desegregation*. They define *desegregation* as the mere physical mixing of different racial and ethnic groups. *Integration*, for these writers, means much more. It occurs only when mutual respect and acceptance develop between different racial and ethnic groups that are members of the same institutions.

Separatism is sometimes said to exist when ethnic groups that are excluded from the mainstream society establish ethnic organizations and institutions to meet their exclusive needs. Students can explore other definitions of separatism and identify instances of it within their communities. When discussing separatism, the class should try to distinguish *separatism* and *segregation*. These terms are highly related and are often confused. Separatist institutions are designed to help an ethnic group attain self-determination and political power and to enhance its ethnic culture. Segregated institutions in *minority communities* are usually created by the dominant society in order to keep minorities subjugated. These types of institutions are designed and controlled by the powerful groups in a society and not by the ethnic minority community. Thus, *separatist* and *segregated* institutions in minority communities are fundamentally different in structure and function.

Students will also need to define a *culturally pluralistic society*. We *can* define a culturally pluralistic society as an open society in which individuals are able to take full advantage of the social, economic, and educational advantages of a society, and yet are able to maintain their unique ethnic identities and allegiances. Individuals would not necessarily have to become assimilated into the dominant culture in order to satisfy their survival needs.

The examples above merely suggest the kinds of working definitions students can formulate for some of the key concepts in this chapter. Many other examples and definitions could be given. It is extremely important for students to know how the concepts they are using are defined by themselves and other people. Without a clear understanding of the key terms they are using, their most diligent research efforts will be frustrated.

Hypotheses

Students can formulate an infinite number of hypotheses related to racial, ethnic, and cultural diversity when studying public policies related to these concepts. What follows is a list of *possible* hypotheses.

If persons of color are required to meet the same qualifications as Whites, then most institutions and firms will remain predominantly White and segregated. This hypothesis is based on the assumption that most persons of color, perhaps for a variety of reasons, will be unable to compete successfully with Whites for jobs and in educational institutions if present criteria and methods are used to screen and select employees and students. An opposing hypothesis might state that if persons of color are required to have the same qualifications as Whites, they would eventually be able to satisfy them because persons of color could and would obtain the experiences and knowledge needed to do so.

If institutions and firms establish quotas for persons of color, some qualified minorities and Whites will be discriminated against. This hypothesis assumes that there are more qualified persons of color for positions and slots than quotas would provide for, that some nonqualified persons of color may be hired in preference to qualified ones, and that if a White and a person of color are equally qualified, firms with quotas would hire the individuals of color until their quotas had been attained. It also assumes that qualified persons of color would not be hired once such quotas were reached. A different hypothesis might suggest that firms and schools will recruit and hire persons of color only if they are required to fulfill quotas.

If open housing laws are enacted and enforced, then Whites will be forced to sell their homes at a tremendous loss. This hypothesis assumes that property values are greatly reduced when individuals of color move into predominantly White neighborhoods. A related hypothesis might state that if open housing laws are not enacted and enforced, housing segregation will increase.

If busing is not used to desegregate the public schools, most African Americans and Whites will continue to attend racially segregated schools. This hypothesis assumes that because of the housing patterns of African American and Whites busing is necessary to desegregate the public schools. Another hypothesis might state that if open housing laws were enacted and enforced, neighborhood schools would become voluntarily integrated.

Testing the Hypotheses

The students will need to gather data to test the hypotheses they have formulated. Because of the nature of the hypotheses formulated above and the short history of most civil rights programs and legislation, limited historical data are available about the effects of laws that prohibit segregation and discrimination. Also, like any other problems related to human behavior, problems in race relations are exceedingly complex. It is difficult to establish causal relationships with a high degree of certainty, such as if A then B, or if there is forced school desegregation (A), conflict (B) will develop between African Americans and Whites. There are too many other variables that may influence either A or B and thus affect the outcome of busing in a particular community. How forced desegregation affects the relationships between African Americans and Whites in a particular community may depend on who made the legal decision, whether a local or federal court, the extent of racial hostility within the community before the court order, the percentage of African Americans and Whites in the community involved in the busing program, the types of African Americans and White leaders in the community, and many other variables.

When students are gathering data to test hypotheses related to racial, ethnic, and cultural diversity, they should be helped to see how difficult it is to establish relationships with a high degree of reliability. Another caveat is in order. Much information and data related to ethnic and racial problems are highly emotional and biased. They are often presented to support or invalidate a particular position or point of view. Examples of these types of studies abound in the literature on race relations. Rivlin (1973) has perceptively called this kind of research "forensic" social science.

Studies written in the forensic tradition include D'Souza (1991) and Schlesinger (1991). African American perspectives are presented in Asante (1987) and Lomotey (1990). The perspectives of other ethnic groups are found in these sources: Asian Americans (Takaki, 1989; Uchida, 1981); Mexican Americans (Acuña, 1988; Mirande, 1985); Puerto Ricans in the United States (Rodriguez, 1989; Walsh, 1991). One partial way to solve the problem of forensic social science is to present the students with readings that support several positions on an issue and then present data that support specific viewpoints.

Some Tentative Conclusions

The students *might* reach these four tentative conclusions after they have studied issues and policies related to racial, ethnic, and cultural diversity and examined their values regarding race relations.

 1. Persons of color should be required to have the same qualifications for jobs and to enter college as any other persons. However, the ways in which these qualifications are determined should be modified so they reflect ethnic diversity and so that individuals of color will not be victimized by discriminatory tests and other selective devices based exclusively on the dominant culture. Institutions and firms should aggressively recruit minorities to increase the pool from which they can select. This type of policy will, in the long run, result in the hiring of individuals of color who are as qualified as their White counterparts. In the short run, however, it might mean that industries and universities will not be able to increase the numbers of individuals of color in their populations at a very rapid rate.

 2. Institutions should not establish quotas for persons of color, but should implement affirmative action programs that will enable them to recruit minorities aggressively and give preference to them if persons of color and Whites are equally qualified. The goal should be to have an integrated staff or student body that includes people who represent diverse ethnic and racial groups, and not to get a specific number from each ethnic group. This policy will result in the employment of minorities but will not restrict their number or encourage the hiring of individuals of color who are less qualified than White employees, or the admission of minority students who cannot succeed in college.

3. Open housing laws should be enacted in all communities to assure that every person has the opportunity to buy the house he or she wants and can afford regardless of race or ethnic group. If effectively enforced, open housing laws are not likely to result in many interracial communities because Whites usually move out of neighborhoods when minorities move into them. No legal actions should be taken to prevent freedom of movement by Whites. However, planned interracial communities should be established because people who grow up in interracial communities have more positive racial attitudes and are more likely to live in interracial neighborhoods and to send their children to interracial schools.

4. The establishment of interracial schools should be a major societal goal. Any reasonable plans, including those requiring busing, should be implemented if they are needed to establish and maintain desegregated schools. Parents opposed to interracial schools and/or busing should have the right to take their children out of the public schools. However, they should not be allowed to dictate or unduly influence school policy. Major societal goals and democratic values (such as equality and justice) should take precedence over the whims of special interest and pressure groups. If a school district takes a strong position vis-à-vis interracial schools and busing, hostile pressure groups, which are usually small but vocal minorities, will eventually accept the school's policy and lose both community support and wide public forums for their views.

Suggested Methods for Teaching about Racial, Ethnic, and Cultural Diversity and Public Policies

Initiating the Unit

The teacher can begin a study of racial, ethnic, and cultural diversity and public policies by reading the class a current *case* study taken from the newspaper or a news magazine that deals with a controversial policy and/or issue related to racial, ethnic, or cultural diversity. An example of such a case study taken from a newspaper (NEA Constitution, 1974) and questions the class can discuss follow.

NEA Constitution, By-Laws Are Racist, Illegal, Anti-Defamation League Says

Palm Beach, Fla. *The Anti-Defamation League of B'nai B'rith has condemned as "unlawful, undemocratic and racist" the new constitution and by-laws of the National Educational Association. . . .*

According to Peirez, the NEA Constitution specifically designates as ethnic minorities, blacks, Mexican-Americans, other Spanish-speaking groups, Asian Americans and Indians. The NEA authorizes those minorities alone to nominate minority candidates for its board of directors and executive committees. It further requires that there be a minimum of 20 percent ethnic minority representation on the NEA board, executive committee and all other committees and that delegates to its national representative assembly from state and local affiliates be allocated on the basis of the ethnic minority percentage of the population or be denied credentials.

The NEA Constitution also provides that nominations for NEA president be restricted to certain ethnic minority groups if, after 11 years, no member of such a group has been elected.

Questions

1. Do the quotas established by the NEA Constitution constitute reverse discrimination? Why or why not?
2. Should institutions and organizations practice reverse discrimination when trying to compensate for past injustices? Why or why not?
3. Does the NEA Constitution violate the civil rights of Whites? Why or why not?
4. What effects do you think the NEA Constitution and bylaws will have on persons of color in the organization? On Whites in the organization? Why?

Social Science Inquiry

When the teacher has initiated a study of racial, ethnic, and cultural diversity with a case study such as the one above, the students should study *historical* information that will enable them to understand the forces that have shaped public policy regarding racial, ethnic, and cultural diversity. Attention should be given to the legalization of segregation that took place in the decades after the Civil War in the United States. Ask individual students to prepare and present reports on the following topics:

- the Black codes
- the poll tax
- the grandfather clause
- the Dred Scott Decision
- *Plessy* v. *Ferguson*

When these reports are presented to the class, the students should discuss these questions: Why did segregation become widespread in the post-Civil-War period? Why was it legalized? How did these laws affect African Americans? White Americans? Other groups of Americans?

1. Ask the students to pretend they are the Supreme Court in 1896 and are hearing the case of Homer Plessy, a mulatto who complains that he has to sit in separate cars on trains passing through his native state of Louisiana. Plessy argues that this type of segregation violates protection guaranteed to him by the Fourteenth Amendment to the Constitution. Ask individual students to role play the roles of the Supreme Court justices, Homer Plessy, and the prosecuting and defense attorneys. After the arguments on both sides have been presented to the

Court, the judges should deliberate and then rule on the case. After the role-play situation, the class should discuss:

   a. ways in which their simulated court was similar to and different from the actual Supreme Court in 1896.

   b. whether the role-players were successfully able to assume the attitudes and viewpoints of people who lived in 1896.

   c. what the "separate but equal" doctrine meant in 1896 and what it means today.

  2. At the turn of the century, two major civil rights organizations were formed to fight for the rights of African Americans: the National Association for the Advancement of Colored People (NAACP) and the National Urban League. Also during this period two major civil rights leaders became nationally eminent, Booker T. Washington and W. E. B. DuBois. Washington and DuBois became staunch opponents because they held opposing views about racial equality and the ways in which African Americans should be educated. Ask the class to read Washington's biography, *Up from Slavery*, and selections from W. E. B. DuBois's *The Souls of Black Folks*. The class should discuss the views of these two men and determine which of their ideas were valid and which were not. After the class has discussed the views of Washington and DuBois, ask two students to role-play a debate between the two men regarding steps African Americans should take to achieve racial equality.

  3. Most national civil rights organizations in the early 1900s were interracial. Ask the students to do required readings on the history and development of the NAACP and the National Urban League. When they have completed the readings, they should compare and contrast these two organizations with the Niagara Movement and earlier Black protest movements, such as the Negro Convention Movement and the African Civilization Society. Particular attention should be paid to (1) reasons the organizations emerged, (2) who made policy and held key positions within them, (3) types of problems that arose within the organizations, (4) the major goals of the organizations, and (5) ways in which the organizations succeeded or failed and why.

  4. Black separatist movements developed early in U.S. history. Some of the earliest were led by such African Americans as Martin R. Delaney and Paul Cuffee. Ask the students to research the lives of these men and to present dramatizations that show ways in which they were advocates of Black nationalism. Marcus Garvey, another Black separatist, attained eminence in the 1930s. Ask the class to read his biography, *Black Moses*, by E. D. Cronon, and to list ways in which Garvey was similar to and different from earlier Black nationalist leaders.

  5. In the 1930s, 1940s, 1950s, and 1960s racial segregation received a number of severe blows that culminated in the *Brown* decision of 1954 and the Civil Rights Act of 1964. Ask the students to develop a chronology that lists the major civil rights legislation enacted between 1930 and 1964. After the chronology is developed, the students should discuss these two questions:

a. What were the major social and political factors that led to the passage of each of these bills?

b. Why has racial segregation actually increased in U.S. society since the 1960s even though so many civil rights bills have been enacted?

6. The major goal of the civil rights movement in the 1950s was to desegregate public accommodation facilities and other institutions. Action tactics and court battles achieved much desegregation. However, by 1965, many African Americans, especially young African American activists, were disillusioned with the attainments of the movement and realized that integration alone would not eliminate the African Americans' major social, economic, and political problems. These young activists felt that both the goals and tactics of the movement should be changed. They issued a call for "Black Power!" The students can gain an understanding of the concept of Black power by reading *Black Power: The Politics of Liberation in America* by Stokely Carmichael and Charles V. Hamilton. Many Black integrationists rejected the views of Black power advocates. Ask the class to research the views of the men and women listed below and to simulate a national convention of African American civil rights leaders in which they discuss the problem, "What should be the future course of African Americans: Integration or Separatism?"

(a)	Martin Luther King, Jr.	(i)	Shirley Chisholm
(b)	Roy Wilkins	(j)	Bobby Seale
(c)	Roy Innis	(k)	Huey Newton
(d)	Angela Davis	(l)	Imamu Amiri Baraka
(e)	Stokely Carmichael	(m)	Richard G. Hatcher
(f)	H. Rap Brown	(n)	Julian Bond
(g)	Vernon Jordan	(o)	Ronald V. Dellums
(h)	Rev. Jesse Jackson	(p)	Barbara Jordan

Individual students should be asked to research and play the roles of each leader in the convention. After the major question has been discussed, the convention participants should then develop an action agenda for African Americans in the 1990s that they all can endorse.

Value Inquiry

After the students have had an opportunity to gather factual data related to racial, ethnic, and cultural diversity, they should examine their values, attitudes, and beliefs. A wide variety of strategies and materials can be used to help students examine and clarify their values. Some valuing exercises appropriate for studying about racial, ethnic, and cultural diversity are given below. These strategies are adapted from techniques developed by Simon, Howe, and Kirschenbaum (1978).

Spread of Opinion

The teacher should divide the class into several small groups and give each group a piece of paper with one of these issues written on it:

- forced busing
- interracial marriage
- open housing laws
- reverse discrimination
- separatism
- quotas
- interracial adoptions
- interracial dating
- segregated fraternities and sororities
- African American all-male academies and schools

Each group should identify a number of positions that can be taken on its issue. Each group member should write a statement defending one position, whether in agreement or not. When the statements have been completed, the students should discuss each issue and state their own positions on it.

Unfinished Sentences

The teacher should duplicate the following list of statements and give a copy to each student. The students should be asked to complete the statements with the words and phrases they first think of when they read each statement. After the students have completed the statements, the teacher should divide the class into small groups and ask the students to discuss, "What I learned about myself from this exercise."

1. If I were African American (or White, Mexican American, etc.) I would . . .
2. Most African Americans are . . .
3. If an African American (or a Mexican American, etc.) family moved into my neighborhood, I would . . .
4. If I were forced to ride a bus to a desegregated school each day, I would . . .
5. If my sister married an African American (or a White, etc.), I would . . .
6. People of other races make me feel . . .
7. A *racist is* a person who . . .
8. If I were called a *racist,* I would . . .
9. Most Whites are . . .
10. Special programs created for people of color are . . .
11. Persons of color who participate in special programs are . . .
12. People who are opposed to interracial marriage are . . .
13. People of color who score poorly on IQ tests are . . .

Strongly Agree/Strongly Disagree

The teacher should duplicate the following list of statements and give a copy to each student. Ask the students to indicate the extent to which they agree or disagree with the statements by writing one of the following letter combinations in front of each statement:

- SA = Strongly agree
- AS = Agree somewhat
- DS = Disagree somewhat
- SD = Strongly disagree

After the students have responded to each statement, divide the class into small groups and ask the students to discuss their responses in their groups.

_____ **1.** I am prejudiced toward some racial and ethnic groups.
_____ **2.** I would not live in a predominantly African American (or White, etc.) neighborhood.
_____ **3.** Most Mexican Americans are poor because they are lazy.
_____ **4.** Most Whites are racists.
_____ **5.** I would encourage my sister to marry an African American (or a White, etc.) if she wanted to.
_____ **6.** Persons of color should meet the same college admission requirements as Whites.
_____ **7.** IQ tests are unfair to persons of color and should be abandoned.
_____ **8.** Students should not be required to be bused to desegregated schools.
_____ **9.** Only African Americans should teach Black Studies.
_____ **10.** Universities and firms should establish quotas for persons of color.
_____ **11.** White fraternities and sororities should be required to admit African Americans, Mexican Americans, Asian Americans, and other persons of color.

Values Grid

An effective summary valuing activity for this unit is the valuing grid. Place Table 9.1 on a ditto stencil and make copies for each student.

Ask the students to make brief notes about how they feel about each of the eleven issues listed in the table. Each issue will have been discussed during earlier parts of the unit. The following seven questions are taken from the valuing strategy developed by Simon et al. (1978). List the following questions on the board and explain each one to the students.

1. Are you proud of (do you prize or cherish) your position?
2. Have *you publicly affirmed* your position?
3. Have you chosen your position from *alternatives?*
4. Have you chosen your position after *thoughtful consideration* of the pros and cons and consequences?
5. Have you chosen your position *freely?*
6. Have you *acted on* or done anything about your beliefs?
7. Have you acted with *repetition,* pattern, or consistency on this issue?

TABLE 9.1

Issue	1	2	3	4	5	6	7
1. Forced busing							
2. Interracial housing							
3. Interracial marriage							
4. Interracial dating							
5. Racial quotas							
6. Segregated schools							
7. Black separatism							
8. White racism							
9. Affirmative-action programs							
10. Black English							

Ask the students to write *Yes* or *No* in each square in the chart to indicate their responses to each of the seven questions for each issue. When the students have individually completed the grid, they should break up into groups of threes and discuss as many of their responses as they would like to discuss.

Decision Making and Social Action

When the students have gathered scientific data and clarified their values, they should identify *alternative courses of actions* they can take regarding racial, ethnic, and cultural diversity in a pluralistic society, and the *possible consequences* of each course of action. Individual and/or groups should then formulate plans to implement courses of action that are most consistent with their values. Below are possible action projects that some students may decide to implement.

Action Projects

1. Conducting a survey to determine the kinds of jobs most persons of color have in local hotels, restaurants, and firms, and, if necessary, urging local businesses to hire more minorities in top-level positions. Conducting boycotts of local businesses that refuse to hire persons of color in top-level positions.

2. Conducting a survey to determine the treatment of ethnic groups in all courses and textbooks in the school and recommending ways in which the school curriculum can become more integrated; suggesting that a permanent review board be established to examine all teaching materials and determine how they present ethnic groups. Presenting these recommendations to appropriate school officials and pressuring them to act on the recommendations.

3. Conducting a survey to determine what local ethnic organizations and leaders are within the community. Inviting some of them to participate in school programs and projects, such as assemblies and classes.

4. Conducting a survey to determine whether the school and public libraries have adequate collections of books and materials about ethnic groups. If necessary, recommending books and materials to be purchased and pressuring the libraries to buy them.

5. Conducting a survey to determine what local laws exist (and how they are enforced) regarding open housing and discrimination in public accommodations, and, if necessary, developing recommendations regarding changes to be made in the laws or in how they should be implemented. Presenting these recommendations to appropriate public officials and pressuring them to act on the recommendations.

6. If the school is racially segregated: Developing plans for exchange activities and programs with a school whose population is predominantly of another race.

7. Conducting a survey to determine the racial and ethnic composition of the school staff (including secretaries, teachers, janitors, etc.) and, if necessary, recommending appropriate action to take to make the school more racially integrated. Presenting these recommendations to appropriate school officials and pressuring them to act on the recommendations.

8. Conducting a survey to determine whether the posters, bulletin boards, photographs, and school holidays reflect the ethnic diversity within society and, if necessary, implementing a plan to make the total school environment more integrated and multiethnic.

9. If the school is interracial: Conducting a survey to determine if there are examples of racial conflict and tension within the school. If there are, formulating and implementing plans to alleviate these problems.

Summary

This chapter illustrates how the teacher can help students develop decision-making and social action skills by studying the possible consequences of the establishment public policies related to racial, ethnic, and cultural diversity. The decision-making model illustrated in this chapter consists of social science inquiry, value inquiry, the synthesis of knowledge and values, and reflective decision making and social action. The sample unit illustrates how each component of the decision-making model can be implemented in the classroom. Possible actions the students might take related to racial, ethnic, and cultural diversity in their school and community are also described.

References

Acuña, R. (1988). *Occupied America: A History of Chicanos* (3rd ed.). New York: Harper & Row.

Asante, M. K. (1987). *The Afrocentric Idea.* Philadelphia: Temple University Press.

Banks, J. A. (1991). *Teaching Strategies for Ethnic Studies* (5th ed.). Boston: Allyn and Bacon.

Banks, J. A., with Clegg, A. A., Jr. (1990). *Teaching Strategies for the Social Studies: Inquiry, Valuing, and Decision-Making* (4th ed.). White Plains, NY: Longman.

D'Souza, D. (1991). *Illiberal Education: The Politics of Race and Sex on Campus.* New York: The Free Press.

Lewis, B. A. (P. Espeland, Ed.). (1991). *The Kid's Guide to Social Action.* Minneapolis: Free Spirit Publishing.

Lomotey, K. (Ed.). (1990). *Going to School: The African-American Experience.* Albany: State University of New York Press.

Mirande, A. (1985). *The Chicano Experience: An Alternative Perspective.* Notre Dame, IN: University of Notre Dame Press.

NEA Constitution. (1974). By-Laws Are Racist, Illegal, Anti-Defamation League Says. *New York Teacher.*

Rivlin, A. M. (1973). Forensic Social Science. *Harvard Educational Review, 43,* 61–75.

Rodriguez, C. E. (1989). *Puerto Ricans Born in the USA.* Boston: Unwin Hyman.

Schlesinger, A. M., Jr. (1991). *The Disuniting of America: Reflections on a Multicultural Society.* Knoxville, TN: Whittle Direct Books.

Simon, S. B., Howe, L. W., & Kirschenbaum, H. (1978). *Values Clarification. A Handbook of Practical Strategies for Teachers and Students.* New York: Hart Publishing. (Reprinted with permission of A & W Publishers, Inc. Copyright 1972; copyright 1978 by Hart Publishing Co., Inc., pp. 35–37, 241–257, 252–254.)

Takaki, R. (1989). *Strangers from a Different Shore: A History of Asian Americans.* Boston: Little, Brown.

Uchida, Y. (1982). *Desert Exile: The Uprooting of a Japanese-American Family.* Seattle: University of Washington Press.

Walsh, C. E. (1991). *Pedagogy and the Struggle for Voice: Issues of Language, Power, and Schooling for Puerto Ricans.* New York: Bergin & Garvey.

Chapter *10*

The Curriculum,
Ethnic Diversity,
and Social Change

The Ethnic Revival Movements

The Black civil rights movement that emerged in the 1960s stimulated the rise of ethnic revival movements throughout the United States as well as in other parts of the world. A major goal of these ethnic movements was to change the social, economic, and political systems so that structurally excluded and marginalized ethnic groups would attain social and economic mobility and educational equality. The demand for changes in the educational system was a major goal of the ethnic revival movements throughout the Western world (Banks & Lynch, 1986; Gipson & Obgu, 1991; Solomon, 1992). Ethnic groups demanded changes in the educational system because they believed the school could be an important instrument in their empowerment and liberation. Most ethnic groups have a tenacious faith in the school to help them attain social-class mobility and structural inclusion (Clark, 1973; Edmonds et al., 1973) despite the arguments by revisionists such as Jencks et al. (1972) and Bowles and Gintis (1976) that the school merely reproduces the social structure and depoliticizes powerless ethnic groups.

Educational Responses to Ethnic Revival Movements

In the various Western societies in which ethnic revival movements have taken place, such as the United States, Canada, the United Kingdom, and Australia, educators have responded with a wide range of programs, projects, and curricular innovations to silence ethnic protest, increase the achievement of ethnic groups, and close the gap between their expressed democratic ideals and practices (Banks & Lynch, 1986, Eldering & Kloprogge, 1989; Moodley, 1992). The social studies (history in particular) was one of the first curricular areas to be scrutinized and criticized by ethnic reformers (Banks, 1973; Fitzgerald, 1979). Major goals of the ethnic revival movements were to shape new identities of ethnic groups and to highlight the roles that various ethnic groups had played in the development of their nations. Ethnic reformers saw history as an important part of the curriculum that perpetuated old images and stereotypes and that therefore needed radical revision and reconstruction (Blassingame, 1971).

Almost three decades have passed since the ethnic protest and revival movements first emerged in the United States. This period has been characterized by intense ethnic polarization and debate, rapid and often superficial curriculum changes and innovations, the birth and death of promising ideas, progress and retrenchment, hope and disillusionment, and a flurry of activity related to ethnic and immigrant groups. The late 1980s was characterized by conservatism and a back-to-the-basics ideology ushered in partly by the movement for academic excellence, which devoted scant attention to equality and the needs of victimized ethnic groups (Johnston, 1985; National Commission on Excellence in Education, 1983).

The early 1990s were characterized by a bitter debate over the literacy and social science canons used to select books, concepts, and theories for the school, university, and college curricula (Asante, 1989; Gates, 1992; Schlesinger, 1991). While multicultural education was seriously challenged by neoconservative and Western traditionalists, it experienced tremendous growth in terms of the number of textbooks published, enrollments in multicultural teacher education courses, and the number of conferences, workshops and textbooks (Cushner, McClelland, & Safford, 1992; Garcia, 1991; Nieto, 1992).

In this chapter, I describe the visions and goals that ethnic reformers had for multiethnic studies when the ethnic revival movements emerged more than two decades ago and the limited extent to which these goals have been realized; I also identify the factors that have restrained significant curriculum reform. Finally, I propose a reform strategy that views the teacher as a change agent and cultural mediator. Such a teacher interprets ethnic and majority cultures for mainstream students and students of color and helps them see why social change is essential if we are to close the gap between our nation's democratic ideals and its social, economic, and political realities.

Life-Style versus Life-Chance Approaches

During the early phases of ethnic revitalization movements in the United States as well as in other Western nations, ethnic leaders demanded that ethnic heroes and cultures become a part of the school curriculum. Educators often responded to these demands quickly and without careful planning and sufficient teacher in-service education. As a result, ethnic heroes such as Crispus Attucks and Martin Luther King, Jr., were inserted into the curriculum along with bits and pieces of content about ethnic cultures and traditions (Cuban, 1968). This additive approach to the study of ethnic content emanates from several assumptions that preclude substantial curriculum reform, perpetuate stereotypes and misconceptions of ethnic cultures and life-styles, and prevent teachers from dealing effectively and comprehensively with such concepts as racism, class stratification, powerlessness, and the reforms needed to empower ethnic groups.

When educators add ethnic heroes and bits and pieces of ethnic content to the curriculum, the assumption is made that ethnic heroes and content are not integral parts of the mainstream U.S. experience. Consequently, it is also assumed that it is sufficient to add special units and festivals to teach about ethnic groups and their cultures. Particularly in the elementary grades, ethnic content is taught primarily with special lessons and pageants on holidays and birthdays. African Americans often dominate lessons during Afro-American History Month or on Martin Luther King's birthday but are largely invisible in the curriculum during the rest of the year. Even though African Americans and other groups of color are now a more integral part of textbooks than they were before the 1960s, their presence is neither comprehensive nor sufficiently integrated into the total curriculum (Sleeter & Grant, 1991).

The infusion of bits and pieces of ethnic content into the curriculum not only reinforces the idea that groups of color are not integral parts of U.S. society, but it also results in the trivialization of ethnic cultures. The study of the foods eaten by Mexican Americans or of Indian tepees will not help students develop a sophisticated understanding of Mexican American culture and of the tremendous cultural diversity among Native Americans. This kind of teaching about ethnic cultures often perpetuates misconceptions and stereotypes about ethnic cultures and leads well-meaning but misinformed teachers to believe they have integrated their curricula with ethnic content and helped their students better understand ethnic groups.

Superficial teaching about ethnic groups and ethnic cultures may do more harm than good. Excluding a study of ethnic cultures in the curriculum might be preferable to the trivialization and marginalization of ethnic cultures and life-styles. The distortion of ethnic cultures that has taken place in the schools has led some critics of multicultural education to argue that teaching about ethnic groups in the schools should focus on their life-chances rather than on their life-styles (Bullivant, 1986b; McCarthy, 1988).

A curriculum that focuses on life-chances describes the ways structurally excluded ethnic groups are victimized by social, economic, and political variables such as institutionalized racism, class stratification, and political powerlessness. Critics of multicultural education who make this argument are concerned that a focus on cultures and life-styles not only trivializes the cultures of ethnic groups, but also diverts attention from the real causes of ethnic group victimization and poverty. They believe that a focus on life-styles might cause majority groups to blame the victims for their victimization and thus help entrench institutionalized stereotypes. Writes Moodley (1986, p. 62):

> *Given the complexity of cultures, they are frequently trivialized in presentation in the elementary curriculum. Werner et al. refer to the common isolated use of artifacts and other aspects of the material culture, without a holistic interpretation, as the "museum approach." It reinforces the "us"—"them" differences and highlights a "hierarchy of cultures" based on the way the outsider perceives the minority.*

Teachers do not need to decide whether they will approach the teaching of ethnic content from a life-style or life-chance perspective. Both cultural knowledge and knowledge about why many ethnic groups are victimized by institutionalized racism and class stratification are needed in a sound curriculum that accurately and sensitively reflects the experience of ethnic groups. Both perspectives are needed to help students gain a comprehensive and sophisticated understanding of the experiences of ethnic groups in the United States and in other nations. However, teaching accurately about the cultures of ethnic groups is a complex and difficult task.

To teach about ethnic cultures accurately, teachers must help students understand that ethnic cultures, especially within a modernized society such as the United States, are dynamic, holistic, and changing processes (Beals, with Spindler, & Spindler, 1967). Students also need to understand that a culture consists of many aspects or variables, such as symbols, language, and behavior, and that an individual member of a culture may exemplify the characteristics of a group completely or hardly at all. Consequently, knowing what have been called African American cultural characteristics may give an individual few clues about the behavior of a particular African American individual and reinforce stereotypes and misconceptions (White & Parham, 1990).

The Search for New Perspectives

Major goals of the ethnic revival movements of the 1960s and 1970s were not only to include more information about the cultures and history of ethnic groups in the curriculum, but also to infuse the curriculum with new perspectives, frames of reference, and values. However, in textbooks and in teaching, even though ethnic events and heroes are often added to the curriculum, the interpretations and perspectives on these events and heroes often remain those of mainstream historians and scholars (Banks, in press). When concepts, events, and situations in the curriculum are viewed only or primarily from the perspectives of mainstream scholars and historians, students obtain a limited view of social reality and an incomplete understanding of the human experience. As James Baldwin (1985) perceptively points out in several trenchant essays, White Americans cannot fully understand their history unless they study African American history from myriad perspectives because the history of African Americans and Whites is intricately interwoven.

In an important essay on the sociology of knowledge published in the midst of the civil rights movement, Merton (1972) discusses *insiders* and *outsiders* and their competing knowledge claims. Both insiders and outsiders claim that only they can obtain valid knowledge about group life. Insiders claims that only a member of their group can formulate accurate and valid knowledge about the group because of the special insights that result from being socialized within the group. Outsiders claim that valid knowledge results only when they study groups because of the dispassionate objectivity they bring to the study of group life. Merton concludes that both insiders and outsiders can make important contributions to understanding group life, and that insiders and outsiders should unite in their quests for knowledge.

Social and historical knowledge reflects the values, experiences, times, and social structure in which scholars are socialized and work. In an ethnically and racially stratified society such as the United States, ethnic and racial microcultures also influence the formulation of knowledge. Social scientists and historians who are insiders in the African American community and those who are outsiders are likely to agree on many observations about African American life and behavior; they also are likely to formulate some findings and interpretations that differ in significant ways. Many mainstream social scientists conducted studies of African Americans before the civil rights movements of the 1960s that were strongly attacked by African American social scientists in the 1970s (Ladner, 1973). Much of this controversy focused on historical interpretations of such topics as slavery and the Civil War, sociological interpretations of the African American family, and descriptions and interpretations of Black English and African American culture. Mainstream social scientists frequently described African American culture and life as disorganized, pathological, and deviant (Ladner, 1973). African American students were often labeled *culturally deprived* (Reisman, 1962). Traditional research assumptions, methods, and conclusions of mainstream social scientists often differed sharply from those of the new African American social scientists during this period (Banks, 1984; Banks, 1992; Ladner, 1973).

Even though ethnicity and race often influence the knowledge claims, research, and perspectives of social scientists and historians, these influences are complex and difficult to describe precisely. Individual White, Mexican American, or African American scholars may be influenced more by their own class interests, commitment to scholarly objectivity, or other values than they are by race or ethnicity (Chavez, 1991; Steele, 1990). The revisionist and sensitive studies of African Americans by White social scientists such as Baratz (1970), Gutman (1964), and Genovese (1974) during the 1960s and 1970s are cases in point, as are the more conservative analyses of the African American experience written by African American scholars such as Sowell (1984), Steele (1990), and Carter (1991).

Even though the influences of race, ethnicity, and class on social knowledge are complex and difficult to describe precisely, they are nonetheless significant and far-reaching. Insider perspectives on such important social and historical events as the Holocaust, the internment of Japanese Americans, and the civil rights movements of the 1960s provide students with insights, perspectives, and feelings about these events that cannot be gained from reading source materials or accounts by individuals who have experienced these events only from a distance (Farmer, 1985; Nakano & Nakano, 1980; Raines, 1977). Scholars who are socialized within ethnic cultures in which these events are important parts of the social and cultural history are also likely to have perspectives on them that differ from those of mainstream scholars (Anzaldúa, 1987; Collins, 1990).

It is important for students to experience a curriculum that not only presents the experience of ethnic and cultural groups in accurate and sensitive ways, but that also enables them to see the experiences of both mainstream and minority groups from the perspectives of different cultural, racial, and ethnic groups. A curriculum that includes the experiences of different ethnic groups *and* presents these experiences from diverse perspectives and points of view is needed to help students understand the complexity of the human experience and how a nation's various groups have strongly influenced each other culturally and interacted within the social structure. Table 10.1 summarizes the dominant and desirable characteristics of multiethnic studies described above.

The Ideological Resistance to Multicultural Education

After nearly three decades of debates and attempts to reform the school and the curriculum to reflect ethnic and cultural diversity in the United States, multicultural reforms remain on the periphery of the mainstream curriculum in most U.S. schools, colleges, and universities. Most examples of blatant racism and stereotypes of ethnic groups have been deleted from textbooks and teaching materials, but content about racial and ethnic groups is not yet thoroughly integrated into mainstream textbooks and teaching materials. Instead, materials about racial and ethnic groups are often relegated to special units and holidays and are appendages to the main story about the development of U.S. society. However, much progress was made in integrating ethnic and cultural content into the mainstream curriculum from the 1960s to the early 1990s.

Most content about African Americans is studied when topics such as slavery, Reconstruction, and the civil rights movement of the 1960s are covered (Sleeter & Grant, 1991). A unilinear, Eurocentric approach is used most frequently to teach about the development of U.S. history and society. The story of the development of the United States is often told by describing the sojourn of the Europeans across the Atlantic to the Americas and then from the Atlantic to the Pacific oceans. The focus of the story is on European settlers, on the way they shaped America in their image, created a nation that promised freedom for all people, and made the United States a world power. Groups of color such as African Americans, Mexican Americans, and Indians are discussed primarily at points at which they interacted with the Europeans in North America.

TABLE 10.1 Dominant and Desirable Characteristics of Multiethnic Studies

Dominant Characteristics	Desirable Characteristics
Focuses on isolated aspects of the histories and cultures of ethnic groups.	Describes the history and cultures of ethnic groups holistically.
Trivializes the histories and cultures of ethnic groups.	Describes the cultures of ethnic groups as dynamic wholes and processes of change.
Presents events, issues, and concepts primarily from Anglocentric and mainstream perspectives and points of view.	Presents events, issues, and concepts from the perspectives and points of view of diverse racial and ethnic groups.
Is Eurocentric—shows the development of America primarily as an extension of Europe into the Americas.	Is multidimensional and geocultural—shows how peoples and cultures came to America from many different parts of the world, including Asia and Africa, and the important roles they played in the development of U.S. society.
Content about ethnic groups is an *appendage* to the regular or core curriculum.	Content about ethnic groups is an *integral part* of the regular or core curriculum.
Ethnic minority cultures are described as deprived or pathological.	Ethnic minority cultures are described as *different* from mainstream Anglo culture but as normal and functional.
Concepts such as institutional racism, class stratification, powerlessness, and the victimization of ethnic and racial groups are given scant attention.	An important focus is on such concepts as institutional racism, class stratification, powerlessness, and the victimization of ethnic and racial groups.
The curriculum is dominated by the assimilationist ideology. Pluralist and radical ideologies are either ignored or depicted as undesirable.	The curriculum reflects a pluralistic ideology, with some attention given to radical ideas and conceptions.
Focuses on lower-level knowledge, ethnic heroes, holidays, and the recall of factual information	Focus on higher-level knowledge, such as concepts, generalizations, and theories.
Emphasizes the mastery of knowledge and cognitive outcomes.	Emphasizes decision making and citizen action. Knowledge formulation, value analysis, and citizen action are important components of the curriculum. Knowledge is synthesized with clarified values in order to make reflective decisions that guide action.
Encourages acceptance of existing ethnic, class, and racial stratification.	Focuses on social criticism and social change.

A number of reasons have been set forth to explain why the school curriculum remains Anglocentric and Eurocentric after nearly three decades of attempted reform. Many teachers and principals state they have not reformed the curriculum to reflect ethnic diversity in their schools because they do not have students of color in their school populations and consequently have no racial or ethnic problems. These educators believe that ethnic content is needed only by students of color or to help reduce ethnic conflict and tension within schools that have racial problems. This assumption is widespread within the schools and has existed at least since the early 1950s, when Hilda Taba and her colleagues did their pioneering work in intergroup education (Taba, Brady, & Robinson, 1952).

Other reasons often given for the lack of progress in substantially reforming the curriculum to reflect ethnic and cultural diversity since the 1960s include the lack of effective teaching materials, ambivalent teacher attitudes toward ethnic diversity, lack of effective in-service education, and the lack of administrative support. Each of these reasons explains in part why multicultural content has not permeated the school curriculum in the last two decades, but as a group they do not reveal the basic reason that multicultural content has not permeated, in any meaningful way, the U.S. school, college, and university curriculum. I believe the resistance to multicultural content is basically *ideological*.

An ideology is a system of ideas, beliefs, traditions, principles, and myths held by a social group or society that reflects, rationalizes, and defends its particular social, political, and economic interests (Bullivant, 1986a). Dominant ethnic and cultural groups develop ideologies to defend and rationalize their attitudes, goals, and social structure. Writes Bullivant (p. 103):

> *In an analysis of ethnoculturally pluralistic societies the term ideology can be used to refer to the system of beliefs and values employed by a dominant ethnocultural group to legitimize its control over the life chances of subordinate ethnocultural groups.*

Bullivant calls this situation a form of *ethnic hegemony*.

The dominant ideology related to ethnic and racial pluralism within the United States has been described with several different concepts, including the *melting pot, Anglo-conformity,* and *cultural assimilation* (Gordon, 1964). This ideology states that the diverse ethnic and racial groups within the United States not only should but eventually will surrender their unique cultural and ethnic characteristics and acquire those of Anglo or mainstream Americans. Robert E. Park (Coser, 1977), the eminent U.S. sociologist who played a key role in the development of the Chicago School of Sociology (Bulmer, 1984), believed that race and ethnic relations were characterized by four inevitable phases: *contact, conflict, accommodation, assimilation.*

Park's notion about inevitable cultural assimilation dominated U.S. social science until the ethnic revival movements emerged in the 1960s (Glazer & Moynihan, 1975). The assimilationist envisions a society and nation-state in which ethnic characteristics die of their own weight. Group affiliations within a modernized society, argues the assimilationist, are related to social class, occupation, education, and to other voluntary and achieved statuses. The assimilationist believes that ethnic affiliations and attachments are antithetical to a modernized democratic society because they promote primordial affiliations, groups rights over the rights of the individual, and particularistic concerns rather than the overarching goals of the nation-state (Patterson, 1977).

The assimilationist conception is not so much wrong as it is flawed and incomplete (Apter, 1977). Groups of color such as African Americans, Mexican Americans, and Indians realized by the late 1960s that no matter how culturally assimilated they became, they were often unable to attain structural assimilation and full participation in U.S. society. During most of their histories in the United States these groups had worked diligently to become culturally assimilated and full participants in U.S. society (Glazer, 1977). In the late 1960s most ethnic groups of color had become disillusioned with assimilation as a societal goal and with the assimilationist ideology. They began seriously to question not only its desirability but also its latent function. Many leaders and scholars of color began to view it as a tool of dominant ethnic groups used to rationalize and maintain their power and to keep victimized ethnic groups content with the status quo and yet striving to attain implausible goals (Sizemore, 1973).

During the ethnic revival movements of the 1960s and 1970s, ethnic minority scholars and leaders stridently attacked the assimilationist ideology and began to exhume, fashion, and shape a pluralist ideology that they saw as more consistent with their social, economic, political, and educational aspirations (Ladner, 1973). This ideology maintains that the assimilationist claims about individual opportunity in the United States are a myth and that U.S. citizens are judged first as members of groups and only secondarily as individuals. The pluralists argue that individuals are rarely able to experience social and economic mobility that is beyond that of their ethnic or cultural group (Dickeman, 1973). Pluralists envision a curriculum that will strengthen family and ethnic attachments and help students develop a commitment to the liberation of their ethnic group.

Assimilationists contend that they oppose a pluralist curriculum because it is un-American, will undercut U.S. patriotism, will create ethnic Balkanization, and will prevent students of color from attaining the knowledge, attitudes, and skills they need to become effective participants in mainstream U.S. society and culture (D'Souza, 1991; Schlesinger, 1991). Pluralists maintain that mainstream Americans are strongly opposed to a pluralistic curriculum that reinterprets the U.S. experience and represents diverse ethnic perspectives on the development of U.S. society. They fear it will undercut their dominant position in society and legitimize the quest of excluded ethnic groups for empowerment and significant social change (Asante, 1989; Sizemore, 1973).

Teaching for Social Change

A major goal of education has traditionally been to socialize students so they would unquestionably accept the existing ideologies, institutions, and practices within their society and nation-state (Giroux, 1992; Newmann, 1968). Political education within the United States has traditionally fostered political passivity rather than political action. Although several experimental political studies courses designed to foster political action were developed for students during the flurry of social studies curricular activity during the 1970s (Gillespie & Patrick,

1974), these projects have not substantially changed the nature of political education in the nation's schools. Students are taught to vote and to participate in the political systems in ways that will not significantly reform U.S. society. Writes Newmann (p. 536):

> *By teaching that the constitutional system of the U.S. guarantees a benevolent government serving the needs of all, the schools have fostered massive public apathy. Whereas the protestant ethic calls for engagement (to survive economically one must earn a living), the political creed breeds passivity. One need not struggle for political rights, but only maintain a vague level of vigilance, obey the laws, make careful choices in elections, perform a few duties (taxes, military service), and his political welfare is assured.*

Even though the schools teach students the expressed ideals about justice and equality that are dominant within U.S. society, rarely do we *deliberately* educate students for social change and help them acquire the knowledge, attitudes, and skills needed to help close the gap between our democratic ideals and societal realities. *A major goal of the curriculum should be to help students acquire the knowledge, values, and skills they need to participate in social change so that marginalized and structurally excluded ethnic, racial, gender, and cultural groups can become full participants in their societies.* To participate effectively in social change, students must be taught social criticism and must be helped to understand the inconsistency between our ideals and social realities, the work that must be done to close this gap, and how they can, as individuals and groups, become empowered to influence the social and political systems of their societies.

When conceptualizing a curriculum designed to promote civic action and social change, we need to ponder seriously the arguments by the revisionists and radical scholars (Giroux, 1992; Katz, 1975; McCarthy, 1988). They contend that the schools are incapable of teaching students to be change agents because two of their major roles are to reproduce the social structure and to socialize students so they will passively accept their position in our class- and ethnically stratified society. The radical critics of the schools, especially those in the United Kingdom, have been keenly critical of multicultural education as a strategy to promote social change (Modgil, Verma, Mallick, & Modgil, 1986). They argue that multicultural education is a palliative to keep excluded and oppressed groups from rebelling against a system that promotes structural inequality and institutionalized racism (Carby, 1980). The radical scholars also claim that multicultural education avoids any serious analysis of class, racism, power, capitalism, and other systems that keep excluded ethnic groups powerless (McCarthy, 1988). Multicultural education, they argue, diverts attention from the real problems and issues. Instead, it focuses on the victim as the problem.

It is difficult to reject completely the argument that one of the school's major roles is to socialize students so they will fit into the existing social order. However, the revisionists and other radical scholars overstate the case when they argue that the schools *merely* socialize students into the existing social order. The school itself is contradictory, because it often expounds democratic values while at the same time contradicting them. The school does socialize students into the existing social structure; it also enables some students to acquire the knowledge, attitudes, and skills needed to participate effectively in social action and social change.

The Teacher as Cultural Mediator and Change Agent

Whether they are deliberate goals of the school or not, many students learn compassion and democratic ideals and develop a commitment to participate in social change from powerful and influential classroom teachers. These teachers are also cultural mediators who interpret the mainstream and ethnic cultures to students from diverse cultural groups and help students understand the desirability of and possibility for social change. Many such teachers participated in social action in the 1960s and 1970s to promote social justice and human rights. Today, many teachers are deeply concerned about apartheid in South Africa, the possibility of a nuclear holocaust, and the widening gap between the rich and the poor in the United States. In 1989, the top 4 percent of individuals and families in the United states earned $452 billion in wages and salaries, the same amount as the bottom 51 percent of individuals and families (Barlett & Steele, 1992).

The school—primarily through the influence of teachers who have clarified and reflective commitments to democratic values, knowledge, and pedagogical skills and who have the charisma to inspire other people—can play a significant role in teaching social criticism and in motivating students to become involved in social change (see Figure 10.1). Some teachers have a significant influence on the values, hopes, and dreams of their students. The classroom should be a forum of open inquiry, where diverse points of view and perspectives are shared and analyzed reflectively. Teachers who are committed to human freedom should feel free to express their views in the classroom, provided that students have first had an opportunity to express freely and to defend their own beliefs and that teachers defend their beliefs reflectively and in ways consistent with democratic values (Oliver & Shaver, 1966). In the democratic classroom, both students and teachers should have the freedom to express their values and beliefs but should be required to defend them and to point out ways in which their moral choices are related to overarching democratic ideals, such as human dignity, justice, and equality (Engle & Ochoa, 1988).

In a democratic society, students and teachers should freely express morally and intellectually defensible values and beliefs about human freedom (Shaver & Strong, 1982). Teaching, like social science inquiry, is not a value-neutral activity (Harding, 1991). This is especially the case in multicultural

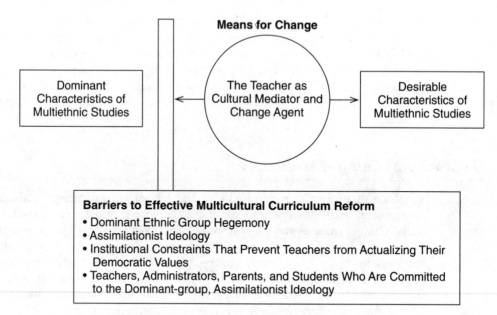

Barriers to Effective Multicultural Curriculum Reform

- Dominant Ethnic Group Hegemony
- Assimilationist Ideology
- Institutional Constraints That Prevent Teachers from Actualizing Their Democratic Values
- Teachers, Administrators, Parents, and Students Who Are Committed to the Dominant-group, Assimilationist Ideology

FIGURE 10.1   The Teacher as Cultural Mediator and Social Change Agent

studies, where teachers and students must deal with human problems, conflicts, and dilemmas toward which it is impossible to remain neutral. Both teachers and social scientists have often been admonished to strive for objectivity in their work. Teachers should not use the classroom as a forum to promote partisan political beliefs, but they should, like caring social scientists, become *involved observers* to borrow Kenneth B. Clark's (1965) apt phrase. They should support and defend moral and ethical positions that are consistent with democratic values and ideals. Clark (p. xxi) eloquently states his creed as a social scientist. It is an appropriate one for teachers:

> *An important part of my creed as a social scientist is that on the grounds of absolute objectivity or on a posture of scientific detachment and indifference, a truly and serious social science cannot ask to be taken seriously by a society desperately in need of moral and empirical guidance in human affairs. . . . I believe that to be taken seriously, to be viable, and to be relevant social science must dare to study the real problems of men and society, must use the real community, the market place, the arena of politics and power as its laboratories, and must confront and seek to understand the dynamics of social action and social change.*

Teachers who support human freedom, justice, and equality can motivate students to engage in social action to improve the human condition (Lewis, 1991). It is individual teachers—and not schools per se—who can and do help students develop the ideals, knowledge, and skills needed to reform society. They do this by exemplifying a commitment to democratic values in the content they select, in their interpretations of social and historical events, and in their words and deeds. Teachers, while respecting the beliefs and diversity of their students and helping them develop social science inquiry skills, can support democracy, equality, and the empowerment of marginalized racial and ethnic groups (Cummins, 1986).

If teachers are to be the primary agents for change in schools, when we select and educate individuals for teaching we must keep democratic values, teaching, and commitments foremost in mind. A major goal of our selection and professional education process must be to place in the classroom teachers who have strong and clarified democratic values and the knowledge and skills to implement a curriculum that will enable students to acquire the content, commitment, and competencies needed to participate in democratic social change. Teacher education programs that are designed to help teachers become effective cultural mediators and change agents must help them to acquire (a) social science knowledge, derived using a process in which the goals, assumptions, and values of knowledge are learned; (b) clarified cultural identifications; (c) positive intergroup and racial attitudes; and (d) pedagogical skills (see Figure 10.2). To select and educate teachers successfully is probably the most challenging and difficult task that lies ahead for those of us who would like to see the schools—and the multicultural curriculum in particular—become a vehicle for social change and human betterment.

Summary

A series of ethnic revival movements emerged in Western societies, such as the United States, Canada, the United Kingdom, and Australia, during the 1960s and 1970s. A major goal of these movements was to reform the school curriculum so that the images of ethnic groups and the roles people of color had played in the development of their nation-states and societies would be accurately and comprehensively depicted.

This chapter describes the curricular visions and goals of the ethnic revival movements, the limited extent to which these goals have been realized, and the factors that have prevented significant curriculum reform. This chapter also proposes a reform strategy that conceptualizes the teacher as a cultural mediator and change agent and a curriculum that promotes social criticism and civic action to improve the human condition.

Knowledge

• Has:

Social Science Knowledge
(Derived using a process in
which the goals,
assumptions, and values of
knowledge are learned.)

Pedagogical Knowledge
Knowledge of the
characteristics of students
from diverse ethnic, racial,
cultural, and social class
groups; of prejudice and
prejudice reduction theory
and research; and of
teaching strategies and
techniques.

**Clarified Cultural
Identification**

• Has a reflective and
clarified understanding of
his or her cultural
heritage and experience
and knowledge of how it
relates to and interacts
with the experiences of
other ethnic and cultural
groups.

**Positive Intergroup and
Racial Attitudes**

• Has clarified and positive
attitudes toward different
racial, ethnic, cultural,
and social-class groups.

Pedagogical Skills

• Has the skills to:

–Make effective
instructional decisions;

–Reduce prejudice and
intergroup conflict; and

–Formulate and devise a
range of teaching
strategies and activities
that will facilitate the
acedmic achievement of
students from diverse
racial, ethnic, cultural,
and social-class groups.

**The Effective
Multicultural
Teacher**

FIGURE 10.2 Characteristics of the Effective Teacher in a Multicultural Society

References

Anzaldúa, G. (1987). *Borderlands: La Frontera The New Mestiza*. San Francisco: Spinseters/Aunt Lute.

Apter, D. E. (1977). Political Life and Cultural Pluralism. In M. M. Tumin and W. Plotch (Eds.), *Pluralism in a Democratic Society* (pp. 58–91). New York: Praeger.

Asante, M. K. (1989). *Afrocentricity*. Trenton, NJ: Africa World Press.

Baldwin, J. (1985). *The Price of the Ticket: Collected Nonfiction 1984–1985*. New York: St. Martin's.

Banks, J. A. (Ed.). (1973). *Teaching Ethnic Studies: Concepts and Strategies*. Washington, DC: National Council for the Social Studies.

Banks, J. A. (1984). Values, Ethnicity, Social Science Research, and Educational Policy. In B. Ladner (Ed.), *The Humanities in Precollegiate Education*, 83rd Yearbook of the National Society for the Study of Education (pp. 91–111). Chicago: University of Chicago Press.

Banks, J. A. (1992). African American Scholarship and the Evolution of Multicultural Education. *Journal of Negro Education, 61*, 1–14.

Banks, J. A. (in press). The Canon Debate, Knowledge Construction, and Multicultural Education, *Educational Researcher*.

Banks, J. A., & Lynch, J. (Eds.). (1986). *Multicultural Education in Western Societies*. New York: Praeger.

Baratz, J. C. (1970). Teaching Reading in an Urban Negro School System. In F. Williams (Ed.), *Language and Poverty: Perspectives on a Theme* (pp. 11–24). Chicago: Markham Publishing Co.

Barlett, D. L., & Steele, J. B. (1992). *America: What Went Wrong?* Kansas City: Andrews and McMeel.

Beals, A. R., with G. Spindler & L. Spindler (1967). *Culture In Process*. New York: Holt, Rinehart and Winston.

Blassingame, J. W. (Ed.). (1971). *New Perspectives on Black Studies*. Urbana: University of Illinois Press.

Bowles, S., & Gintis, H. (1976). *Schooling in Capitalist America*. New York: Basic Books.

Bullivant, B. (1986a). Multicultural Education in Australia: An Unresolved Debate. In J. A. Banks & J. Lynch (Eds.), *Multicultural Education in Western Societies* (pp. 98–124). New York: Praeger.

Bullivant, B. (1986b). Towards Radical Multiculturalism: Resolving Tensions in Curriculum and Educational Planning. In S. Modgil, G. K. Verma, K. Malick, & C. Modgil (Eds.), *Multicultural Education: The Interminable Debate* (pp. 33–47). London: The Falmer Press.

Bulmer, M. (1984). *The Chicago School of Sociology: Institutionalization, Diversity, and the Rise of Sociological Research*. Chicago: The University of Chicago Press.

Carby, H. V. (1980). *Multicultural Fictions*, Stenciled Occasional Paper, Race Series, SP No. 58. The University of Birmingham (England).

Carter, S. L. (1991). *Reflections of an Affirmative Action Baby*. New York: Basic Books.

Chavez, L. (1991). *Out of the Barrio*. New York: Basic Books.

Clark, K. B. (1965). *Dark Ghetto: Dilemmas of Social Power*. New York: Harper Torchbooks.

Clark, K. B. (1973). Social Policy, Power and Social Science Research. *Harvard Educational Review, 43*, 113–121.

Collins, P. H. (1990). *Black Feminist Thought: Knowledge, Consciousness, and the Politics of Empowerment*. New York: Routledge.

Coser, L. A. (1977). *Masters of Sociological Thought: Ideas in Historical and Social Context* (2nd ed.). New York: Harcourt.

Cuban, L. (1968). Black History, Negro History, and White Folk. *Saturday Review*, 64–65.

Cummins, J. (1986). Empowering Minority Students: A Framework for Intervention. *Harvard Educational Review, 56*, 18–36.

Cushner, K., McClelland, A., & Safford, P. (1992). *Human Diversity in Education: An Integrative Approach*. New York: McGraw-Hill.

Dickeman, M. (1973). Teaching Cultural Pluralism. In J. A. Banks (Ed.), *Teaching Ethnic Studies: Concepts and Strategies*, 43rd Yearbook (pp. 5–25). Washington, DC: National Council for the Social Studies.

D'Souza, D. (1991). Illiberal Education. *The Atlantic, 267*, 51–79.

Edmonds, R. E., et al. (1973). A Black Response to Christopher Jencks' Inequality and Certain

Other Issues. *Harvard Educational Review, 43,* 76–91.

Eldering, L., & Kloprogge, J. (1989). *Different Cultures, Same School: Ethnic Minority Children in Europe.* Berwyn, PA: Swets North America.

Engle, S. H., & Ochoa, A. S. (1988). *Education for Democratic Citizenship: Decision Making in the Social Studies.* New York: Teachers College Press.

Farmer, J. (1985). *Lay Bare the Heart: An Autobiography of the Civil Rights Movement.* New York: Arbor House.

Fitzgerald, F. (1979). *America Revisited: History Textbooks in the Twentieth Century.* New York: Vintage Books.

Garica, R. L. (1991). *Teaching in a Pluralistic Society* (2nd ed.). New York: Harper/Collins.

Gates, H. L. (1992). *Loose Canons: Notes on the Culture Wars.* New York: Oxford University Press.

Genovese, E. D. (1974). *Roll, Jordan Roll: The World the Slaves Made.* New York: Pantheon.

Gillespie, J. A., & Patrick, J. J. (1974). *Comparing Political Experiences.* Washington, DC: The American Political Science Association.

Gipson, M. A., & Ogbu, J. U. (Eds.). (1991). *Minority Status and Schooling: A Comparative Study of Immigrant and Involuntary Minorities.* New York: Garland.

Giroux, H. A. (1992). *Border Crossing: Cultural Workers and the Politics of Education.* New York: Routledge.

Glazer, N. (1977). Cultural Pluralism: The Social Aspect. In M. M. Tumin & W. Plotch (Eds.), *Pluralism in a Democratic Society* (pp. 3–24). New York: Praeger.

Glazer, N., & Moynihan, D. P. (Eds.). (1975). *Ethnicity: Theory and Experience.* Cambridge, MA.: Harvard University Press.

Gordon, M. M. (1964). *Assimilation in American Life.* New York: Oxford University Press.

Gutman, H. G. (1964). *The Black Family in Slavery and Freedom, 1750–1925.* New York: Oxford University Press.

Harding, S. (1991). *Whose Knowledge? Whose Science? Thinking from Women's Lives.* Ithaca, NY: Cornell University Press.

Jencks, C., et al. (1972). *Inequality: A Reassessment of the Effect of Family and Schooling in America.* New York: Basic Books.

Johnston, W. J. (Ed.). (1985). *Education on Trial.* San Francisco: Institute for Contemporary Studies.

Katz, M. B. (1975). *Class, Bureaucracy, and Schools: The Illusion of Educational Change in America* (expanded ed.). New York: Praeger.

Ladner, J. A. (Ed.). (1973). *The Death of White Sociology.* New York: Vintage Books.

Lewis, B. A. (1991). *The Kids' Guide to Social Action.* by P. Espeland (Ed.). Minneapolis: Free Spirit Publishing.

McCarthy, C. (1988). Rethinking Liberal and Radical Perspectives on Racial Inequality in Schooling: Making the Case for Nonsynchrony. *Harvard Educational Review, 58,* 265–279.

Merton, R. K. (1972). Insiders and Outsiders: A Chapter in the Sociology of Knowledge. *The American Journal of Sociology, 78.* 9–47.

Modgil, S., Verma, G. K., Mallick, K., & Modgil, C. (Eds.). (1986). *Multicultural Education: The Interminable Debate.* London: The Falmer Press.

Moodley, K. A. (1986). Canadian Multicultural Education. In J. A. Banks & J. Lynch (Eds.), *Multicultural Education in Western Societies* (pp. 51–75). New York: Praeger.

Moodley, K. A. (Ed.). (1992). *Beyond Multicultural Education: International Perspectives.* Calgary: Detselig.

Nakano, T. U., & Nakano, L. (1980). *Within the Barbed Wire Fence: A Japanese Man's Account of His Internment.* Seattle: University of Washington Press.

National Commission on Excellence in Education. (1983). *A Nation at Risk.* Washington, DC: U.S. Department of Education.

Newmann, F. M. (1968). Discussion: Political Socialization in the Schools. *Harvard Educational Review, 38,* 536–545.

Nieto, S. (1992). *Affirming Diversity: The Sociopolitical Context of Multicultural Education.* White Plains, NY: Longman.

Oliver, D. W., & Shaver, J. P. (1966). *Teaching Public Issues in the High School.* Boston: Houghton Mifflin.

Patterson, O. (1977). *Ethnic Chauvinism: The Reactionary Impulse.* New York: Stein and Day.

Raines, H. (1977). *My Soul Is Rested: Movement Days in the Deep South Remembered.* New York: Putnam's.

Reisman, F. (1962). *The Culturally Deprived Child.* New York: Harper and Row.

Schlesinger, A. M., Jr. (1991). *The Disuniting of America: Reflections on a Multicultural Society.* Knoxville, TN: Whittle Direct Books.

Shaver, J. P., & Strong, W. (1982). *Facing Value Decisions: Rationale-Building for Teachers* (2nd ed.). New York: Teachers College Press.

Sizemore, B. A. (1973). Shattering the Melting Pot Myth. In J. A. Banks (Ed.), *Teaching Ethnic Studies: Concepts and Strategies* (pp. 73–101). Washington, DC: National Council for the Social Studies.

Sleeter, C. E., & Grant, C. A. (1991). Race, Class, Gender, and Disability in Current Textbooks. In M. W. Apple & L. K. Christian-Smith (Eds.), *The Politics of the Textbook* (pp. 78–110). New York: Routledge.

Solomon, R. P. (1992). *Black Resistance in High School.* Albany: State University of New York Press.

Sowell, T. (1984). *Civil Rights: Rhetoric or Reality?* New York: William Morrow.

Steele, S. (1990). *The Content of Our Character.* New York: St. Martin's.

Taba, H., Brady, E. H., & Robinson, J. T. (1952). *Intergroup Education in Public Schools.* Washington, DC: American Council on Education.

White, J. L., & Parham, T. A. (1990). *The Psychology of Blacks: An African-American Perspective* (2nd ed.). Englewood Cliffs, NJ: Prentice-Hall.

Part *IV*

Curriculum Issues, Models, and Reform

Chapter 11
The Multicultural Curriculum: Issues, Approaches, and Models

Chapter 12
The Stages of Ethnicity: Implications for Curriculum Reform

A major goal of the ethnic revival movements of the 1960s and 1970s was to change the curriculum so it would more accurately reflect the ethnic and cultural diversity within Western societies. The two chapters in Part IV describe the efforts made to reform the curriculum within the last three decades, the limited extent to which curriculum reform has occurred, the nature and goals of the multicultural curriculum, factors that inhibit curriculum reform, and how the curriculum can reflect the ethnic characteristics of students.

The problems involved in changing the curriculum to reflect ethnic diversity, the nature of the multicultural curriculum, approaches to multicultural curriculum reform, and curricular models that can help create an open society are discussed in Chapter 11. The ways in which the curriculum can be designed to reflect the stages of ethnic development of students are described in Chapter 12.

Chapter *11*

The Multicultural Curriculum: Issues, Approaches, and Models

Several widespread assumptions about teaching ethnic content have adversely affected the development of the multicultural curriculum in educational institutions. We need to examine and to challenge these assumptions and related practices and to formulate new assumptions and goals for the multicultural curriculum if integrating the curriculum with ethnic content is to become a vehicle for general curriculum reform. If we merely add ethnic content to the traditional curriculum, which has many problems, our efforts to modify the curriculum with ethnic content are likely to lead to a dead end. We need to reform the total school curriculum.

Assumptions about Ethnic Content

Ethnic Content as Ethnic Minority Studies

One pervasive assumption many educators embrace is that ethnic content deals exclusively or primarily with ethnic groups of color, such as the Jamaicans in Britain, the Indians in Canada, and African Americans. This assumption is widespread within the schools of Western societies, such as the United Kingdom, Canada, and the United States. The multicultural curriculum is often based on and reflects it. The multicultural curriculum of many schools in the United States, for example, devotes little or no attention to the experiences of European American ethnic groups, such as Jewish Americans, Polish Americans, and Italian

Americans. This narrow conceptualization of ethnic content emerged out of the social forces that gave rise to the ethnic studies movement in the 1960s and 1970s (Blassingame, 1971; Duran & Bernard, 1982).

As pointed out in Chapter 2, during the 1960s African Americans staged a struggle for their civil rights that was unprecedented in U.S. history. They demanded control of various social, economic, and political institutions within the African American community. They also demanded that the school curriculum be reformed so it would more accurately reflect their historical and cultural experiences in the United States. Other ethnic minority groups, both in the United States and other Western societies, such as the Asians in the United Kingdom, Mexicans in the United States, and the Metis in Canada, became acutely aware of their own ethnic identity and struggles, in part, because of the Black civil rights movement (Banks & Lynch, 1986; Moodley, 1992). These groups also called for new versions of school and college history that would more accurately reflect their experiences.

The types of ethnic studies courses, curricula, and experiences formulated during the 1960s and 1970s often reflected the political and social demands made within local communities. Responding largely to crises and public pressures, curriculum specialists often developed ethnic studies units and courses without giving serious thought to the basic issues that should be considered when curriculum changes are made. The nature of learning, the social and psychological needs of students, and social science theory and research are the types of problems and issues that received little if any attention in many of the hurriedly formulated ethnic studies units and courses created during the 1960s and 1970s. Rather, the overriding consideration was to create some kinds of curricula and courses so that ethnic demands would be met and militant ethnic students and faculty would be silenced. Consequently, during the 1960s and 1970s ethnic studies often became defined as the study of ethnic minority groups. Many curricula and courses formulated were parochial in scope and fragmented and were structured without careful planning and clear rationales. Even though ethnic studies courses and curricula today are often more global in scope, scholarly, and educationally sound than they were in the 1960s and 1970s, they are frequently haunted by their early history and problems (Gay, 1992). The problems ethnic studies experienced increased in the 1980s because of the push for conservatism and nationalism in Western nations such as the United States, the United Kingdom, and Australia.

Ethnic Studies as an Addition to the Curriculum

Many educators assume that ethnic studies is essentially additive in nature and that we can create a valid multicultural curriculum by leaving the present curriculum essentially intact; we can simply add a list of people of color and events to the list of mainstream people and events already studied in schools and colleges. These educators believe we should teach about the heroic deeds of Booker T. Washington and Geronimo just as we teach about the heroic deeds of Betsy Ross and Abraham Lincoln and that pictures of African American and Native American heroes and heroines should be added to those of eminent mainstream Americans already in the textbooks and hanging in the school corridors and classrooms. In additive types of ethnic studies curricula, students are required to memorize isolated facts about mainstream history and ethnic minority history.

Conceptualizing ethnic content as essentially additive in nature is problematic for several reasons. A large body of educational literature has documented the traditional and nonstimulating nature of many school courses and has stated why reform in classroom teaching is sorely needed (Goodlad, 1984). Even though much curriculum reform took place in the teaching of school subjects in the United States during the 1970s, especially in textbooks, in many classrooms teachers continue to emphasize the mastery of low-level facts and do not help students master high-level concepts, generalizations, and theories.

Modifying the curriculum to include ethnic content provides a rich opportunity to reexamine the assumptions, purposes, and nature of the curriculum and to formulate a curriculum with new assumptions and goals. Merely adding low-level facts about ethnic content to a curriculum already bulging with discrete and isolated facts about mainstream history will result in an overkill. Isolated facts about Crispus Attucks do not stimulate the intellect any more than isolated facts about Betsy Ross and Abraham Lincoln. To integrate content about ethnic groups meaningfully into the total curriculum we must undertake more substantial and innovative curriculum reform.

Ethnic Studies as the Study of Strange Customs

Other assumptions are made about ethnic studies, and many school practices reflect them. Some teachers, especially in the primary grades, believe ethnic studies should deal primarily with the tangible elements of minority cultures that seem strange and different to themselves and their students. Consequently, experiences in the primary grades often focus on the foods and unique customs and artifacts of minority cultures, such as soul food, tepees, igloos, and chow mein. Focusing on the customs within ethnic minority groups that seem strange to teachers and their students is likely to reinforce stereotypes and misconceptions rather than to help students develop cultural sensitivity and knowledge of other cultures, which is usually the goal teachers state when they plan these types of learning experiences.

Because many primary grade teachers are unlikely to approach the study of cultural differences from an anthropological and sensitive perspective, their students are likely to conclude that cultural characteristics that are different from their own are indeed strange and unusual and therefore that people of color share few characteristics with them. The multicultural curriculum should emphasize the intangible aspects of culture discussed in Chapter 5 (such as values, cultural cognitiveness, perspectives, and world views), and not strange customs or tangible cultural elements like matzo and sombreros. Ethnic content should be used to help students learn that all human beings have common needs and characteristics, although the ways in which these traits are manifested frequently differ cross-culturally.

Ethnic Studies as the Celebration of Ethnic Holidays

Some teachers, again usually in the primary and elementary grades, see ethnic studies as the celebration of ethnic holidays, such as Martin Luther King's birthday and Cinco de Mayo. In many schools, lessons about ethnic groups are limited primarily to these types of special days and holidays. Some schools set aside particular days or weeks of the year for African American history and culture, Afro-Caribbean feasts and celebrations, and Asian history and culture. The long-range effects of these kinds of special ethnic days might be detrimental and serve to reinforce the notion that ethnic groups, such as African Americans, Jamaicans in the United Kingdom, and the Aborigines in Australia, are not integral parts of their national society and culture. This is especially likely to happen if ethnic groups are studied only on special days or in special units and lessons. The students are likely to conclude that U.S. history and African American history, for example, are separate and mutually exclusive entities.

The notion that Asians in Britain, Mexicans in the United States, and Aborigines in Australia are integral parts of their national societies should be reflected in how the multicultural curriculum is organized and in all activities and teaching strategies. Special units and days might prevent the students from developing the notion that these groups are integral parts of their national societies. However, if ethnic groups of color are integral parts of the school curriculum, highlighting the experiences of a particular ethnic group is less likely to result in negative learnings by students. The danger of negative learnings occurring is greatly increased when these types of experiences are isolated and are not integral parts of the total school curriculum.

Expanding the Definition of Ethnic Studies

Each major assumption discussed and criticized here, although widespread and in some cases understandable, is intellectually indefensible and continues to have adverse effects on the teaching of ethnic content.

The assumption that ethnic studies is equivalent to ethnic minority studies is one of the most widespread beliefs held by educators. It is both inaccurate and educationally unsound to assume that ethnic studies should be limited to a study of ethnic minority groups. Ethnic studies should be, in part, the scientific and humanistic examination of the variables related to ethnicity that influence human behavior. Any individual or group whose behavior can be totally or partially explained by variables related to ethnicity is an appropriate subject in the multicultural curriculum.

A definition of ethnic group can help us determine the parameters of ethnic studies and the curricular implications of the concept. In Chapter 5, I define an *ethnic group* as a group that shares a common ancestry, culture, history, tradition, and sense of peoplehood and that is a political and economic interest group. These characteristics of an ethnic group suggest that all individuals in Western pluralistic societies can be considered members of ethnic groups. However, individual members of an ethnic group vary widely in their levels of ethnic identification and ethnic behavior (see Chapter 5).

Our definition of ethnic groups indicates that Anglo-Australians, Italian Australians, German Americans, Jewish Americans, as well as African Americans and Australian Aborigines, should be studied within a comparative multicultural curriculum. Members of each group exhibit behavioral characteristics that can be partially explained by variables related to ethnicity.

The multicultural curriculum should include but not be limited to a study of ethnic minority groups. An ethnic minority group is a particular type of ethnic group with the distinguishing characteristics described in Chapter 5. Jewish Americans are an ethnic minority group with unique cultural characteristics; African Americans have unique physical and cultural characteristics. Ethnic minorities are frequently a numerical minority and are often politically and economically powerless within a society. However, this is not always the case. In the Republic of South Africa, the Blacks are politically and economically powerless but are a numerical majority. However, they are considered a sociological minority.

To conceptualize ethnic studies as the study of ethnic minorities is inconsistent with how sociologists define ethnicity and prevents the development of a broadly conceptualized multicultural curriculum that compares and contrasts the experiences of all of the diverse groups within a society and that helps students fully understand the complex role of ethnicity in modern Western societies such as the United States, the United Kingdom, Canada, and Australia. Conceptualizing ethnic studies exclusively as the study of ethnic minority groups also promotes a kind of we-they attitude among mainstream students and teachers. Many students believe that ethnic studies is the study of "them," whereas other historical and cultural studies in the school is the study of "us." Some teachers assume that because ethnic studies is the study of "them," it should be taught only when there are students of color within the school.

Ethnic Studies: A Process of Curriculum Reform

Ethnic studies should not be limited to the study of ethnic minority groups although it should definitely include them. It should not be an addition or an appendage to the regular curriculum. Rather, ethnic studies should be viewed as a process of curriculum reform that will result in the creation of a new curriculum based on new assumptions and new perspectives. This new curriculum will help students gain novel views of the experiences of Western societies and new conceptions of what it means to be American, British, Australian, or Canadian. Since the English immigrants gained control over most economic, social, and political institutions early in the national histories of nations such as the United States and Australia, to become American or Australian has meant to become Anglicized. Especially during the height of nativism in the United States in the late 1800s and early 1900s, the English Americans defined Americanization as Anglicization. This notion of Americanization is still widespread within U.S. society and schools today. When many Americans think of American history and American literature they tend to think of Anglo-American history and Anglo-American literature.

Reconceptualizing Western Societies

Because the assumption that only what is Anglo-Australian is Australian and what is Anglo-American is American is so deeply ingrained in curriculum materials and in the hearts and minds of many students and teachers, we cannot significantly change the curriculum by merely adding a unit or a lesson here and there about Aborigine, Italian Australian, or African American history. Rather, we need to examine seriously the conception of Australian or American perpetuated in the curriculum and its basic purposes and assumptions.

We need to reconceptualize how we view Western societies and cultures in the school curriculum. We should teach the history of the Western nation-states from diverse ethnic perspectives rather than primarily or exclusively from the point of view of mainstream historians, writers, and artists. Most courses in the school curriculum in the major Western nations are taught from mainstream perspectives. These types of courses and experiences are based on what I call the Mainstream Centric Model or Model A (see Figure 11.1). Ethnic studies, as a process of curriculum reform, can and often does proceed from Model A to Model B, the ethnic additive model. In courses and experiences based on Model B, ethnic content is an additive to the major curriculum thrust, which remains mainstream centric. Many schools and other educational institutions have implemented Model B types of curricular changes. African American studies courses, Asian studies courses, and special units on ethnic groups in the elementary grades are examples of Model B types of curricular experiences.

However, I am suggesting that curriculum reform proceed directly from Model A to Model C, the multiethnic model. In courses and experiences based on Model C, the students study concepts, themes, issues, and events from several ethnic perspectives and points of view. Mainstream perspectives are only one group of several and are neither superior nor inferior to other ethnic perspectives. I view Model D, the Ethnonational Model, types of courses and curricula as the ultimate goal of curriculum reform. In this curriculum model, students study historical and social events from the perspectives of different ethnic groups within other nations. Since we live in a global society, students need to learn how to become effective citizens of the world community. This is unlikely to happen if they study historical and contemporary social events primarily from the perspectives of the ethnic and cultural groups within their own nation.

Teaching Multicultural Perspectives

When studying a period in U.S. history, such as the colonial period, in a course organized on the Multiethnic Model (Model C), the inquiry does not end when students view the period from the perspectives of mainstream historians and writers. Rather, they ponder these kinds of questions: Why did Anglo-American

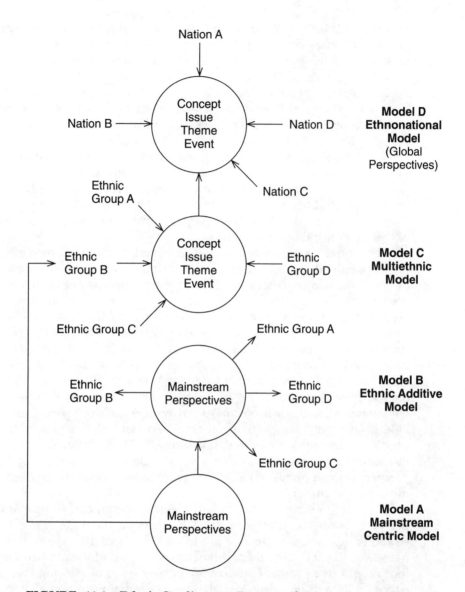

FIGURE 11.1 Ethnic Studies as a Process of Curriculum Reform

Ethnic studies is conceptualized as a process of curriculum reform that can lead from a total mainstream perspective on a society's history and culture (Model A), to multiethnic perspectives as additives to the major curriculum thrust (Model B), to a completely multiethnic curriculum in which every event, concept, and issue is viewed from the perspectives of different ethnic groups (Model C). In Model D, the ultimate goal of curriculum reform, students view events, concepts, and issues from the perspectives and points of view of various groups within different nations.

historians name the English immigrants *colonists* and the other nationality groups *immigrants?* How do Native American historians view the colonial period? Do their views of this period differ in any substantial ways from the views of Anglo-American historians? Why or why not? What was life like for the Jews, African Americans, and other ethnic groups in America during the seventeenth and eighteenth centuries? How do we know? In other words, in courses and curricula organized on Model C, students view historical and contemporary events from the perspectives of different ethnic and cultural groups.

I am not suggesting that we eliminate or denigrate mainstream history or mainstream perspectives on historical events. I am suggesting that mainstream perspectives should be among many different ethnic and cultural perspectives taught in the school. Only by approaching the study of society in this way will students get a global rather than an ethnocentric view of the history and culture of their nation and other societies.

A historian's experience and culture, including his or her own ethnic culture, cogently influences his or her views of the past and present. However, it would be simplistic to argue that there is one mainstream view of history and contemporary events or one African American and Mexican American view. Wide differences in experiences and perceptions exist both within and across ethnic groups. However, people who have experienced a historical event or social phenomenon, such as racial bigotry or internment, often view the event differently than do those who have watched it from a distance. There is no one mainstream American perspective on the internment of Japanese Americans during World War II and no one Japanese American view of it. However, accounts written by people who were interned, such as Takashima's powerful *A Child in Prison Camp,* often provide insights and perspectives on the internment that cannot be provided by people who were not interned (Takashima, 1971). Individuals who viewed the internment from the outside can also provide us with unique and important perspectives and points of view. Both perspectives should be studied in a sound multicultural curriculum.

Only by looking at events, such as the internment, from many different perspectives can we fully understand the history and culture of a society. Various ethnic groups within a society are often influenced by events differently and perceive and respond to them differently. One goal of the multicultural curriculum should be to present students with new ways of viewing the history and culture of their society. Any goals that are less ambitious, although important, will not result in the substantial curricular reform I consider imperative.

Approaches to Multicultural Curriculum Reform

The Contributions Approach

Four approaches to the integration of ethnic content into the curriculum have evolved since the 1960s. The Contributions Approach to integration is one of the most frequently used and is often used extensively during the first phase of an ethnic revival movement. This approach is characterized by the addition of ethnic heroes into the curriculum that are selected using criteria similar to those used to select mainstream heroes for inclusion into the curriculum. The mainstream curriculum remains unchanged in terms of its basic structure, goals, and salient characteristics.

The Heroes and Holidays Approach is a variant of the Contributions Approach. In this approach, ethnic content is limited primarily to special days, weeks, and months related to ethnic events and celebrations. Cinco de Mayo, Martin Luther King's Birthday, and African American History Week are examples of ethnic days and weeks that are celebrated in the schools. During these celebrations, teachers involve students in lessons, experiences, and pageants related to the ethnic groups being commemorated. When this approach is used, the class studies little or nothing about the ethnic groups before or after the special event or occasion.

The Contributions Approach is the easiest approach for teachers to use to integrate the curriculum with ethnic content. However, it has several serious limitations. Students do not attain a global view of the role of ethnic and cultural groups in U.S. society. Rather, they see ethnic issues and events primarily as an addition to the curriculum, and consequently as an appendage to the main story of the development of the nation and to the core curriculum in the language arts, the social studies, the arts, and to other subject areas. The teaching of ethnic issues with the use of heroes, holidays, and contributions also tends to gloss over important concepts and issues related to the victimization and oppression of ethnic groups and their struggles against racism and for power. Issues such as racism, poverty, and oppression tend to be evaded in the Contributions Approach to curriculum integration. The focus, rather, tends to be on success and the validation of the Horatio Alger myth that every American who is willing to work hard can go from rags to riches and pull himself or herself up by the bootstrap.

The Contributions Approach often results in the trivialization of ethnic cultures, the study of their strange and exotic characteristics, and the reinforcement of stereotypes and misconceptions. When the focus is on the contributions and unique aspects of ethnic cultures, students are not helped to understand them as complete and dynamic wholes.

The Ethnic Additive Approach

Another important approach to the integration of ethnic content to the curriculum is the addition of content, concepts, themes, and perspectives to the curriculum without changing its basic structure, purposes, and characteristics. The Additive Approach is often accomplished by the addition of a book, a unit, or a course to the curriculum without changing it substantially.

The Additive Approach allows the teacher to put ethnic content into the curriculum without restructuring it, which takes substantial time, effort, training, and rethinking of the curriculum and its purposes, nature, and goals. The Additive Approach can be the first phase in a more radical curriculum reform effort designed to restructure the total curriculum and to integrate it with ethnic content, perspectives, and frames of reference. However, this approach shares several disadvantages with the Contributions Approach. Its most important shortcoming is that it usually results in the viewing of ethnic content from the perspectives of mainstream historians, writers, artists, and scientists because it does not involve a restructuring of the curriculum. The events, concepts, issues, and problems selected for study are selected using Mainstream-Centric and Eurocentric criteria and perspectives. When teaching a unit such as *The Westward Movement* in a fifth-grade U.S. History class, the teacher may integrate her unit by adding content about the Lakota (Sioux) Indians. However, the unit remains Mainstream Centric and focused because of its perspective and point of view. A unit called *The Westward Movement* is Mainstream and Eurocentric because it focuses on the movement of European Americans from the eastern to the western part of the United States. The Lakota Indians were already in the West and consequently were not moving West. The unit might be called *The Invasion from the East* from the point of view of the Lakota. An objective title for the unit might be *Two Cultures Meet in the Americas.*

The Additive Approach also fails to help students to view society from diverse cultural and ethnic perspectives and to understand the ways in which the histories and cultures of the nation's diverse ethnic, racial, cultural, and religious groups are inextricably bound.

The Transformation Approach

The Transformation Approach differs fundamentally from the Contributions and Additive Approaches. This approach changes the basic assumptions of the curriculum and enables students to view concepts, issues, themes, and problems from several ethnic perspectives and points of view. The key curriculum issue involved in the Transformation Approach is not the addition of a long list of ethnic groups, heroes, and contributions, but the infusion of various perspectives, frames of reference, and content from various groups that will extend students' understandings of the nature, development, and complexity of U.S. society. When students are studying the Revolution in the British colonies, the perspectives of the Anglo Revolutionaries, the Anglo Loyalists, African Americans, Indians, and the British are essential for them to attain a thorough understanding of this significant event in U.S. history. Students must study the various and sometimes divergent meanings of the Revolution to these diverse groups to fully understand it.

When studying U.S. history, language, music, arts, science, and mathematics, the emphasis should not be on the ways in which various ethnic and cultural groups have contributed to mainstream U.S. society and culture. The emphasis, rather, should be on how the common U.S. culture and society emerged from a complex synthesis and interaction of the diverse cultural elements that originated within the various cultural, racial, ethnic, and religious groups that make up U.S.

society. One irony of conquest is that those who are conquered often deeply influence the cultures of the conquerors.

The Decision-Making and Social Action Approach

This approach includes all of the elements of the Transformation Approach but adds components that require students to make decisions and to take actions related to the concept, issue, or problem they have studied in the unit. In this approach, students study a social problem such as, "What actions should we take to reduce prejudice and discrimination in our school?" They gather pertinent data, analyze their values and beliefs, synthesize their knowledge and values, and identify alternative courses of action, and finally decide what, if any, actions they will take to reduce prejudice and discrimination in their school. Major goals of the Decision-Making and Social Action Approach are to teach students thinking and decision-making skills, to empower them, and to help them acquire a sense of political efficacy.

Mixing and Blending the Approaches

The four approaches to the integration of ethnic content into the curriculum that I have described are often mixed and blended in actual teaching situations. One approach, such as the Contributions Approach, can also be used as a vehicle to move to other and more intellectually challenging approaches, such as the Transformation and the Decision-Making and Social Actions Approaches. It is not realistic to expect a teacher to move directly from a highly Mainstream-Centric curriculum to one that focuses on decision making and social action. Rather, the move from the first to the higher levels of ethnic content integration into the curriculum is likely to be gradual and cumulative (see Figure 11.2).

Curricular Models for an Open Society

The multicultural curriculum should do more than help students view concepts, events, and situations from diverse cultural and ethnic perspectives. It should also help students acquire the knowledge, skills, and attitudes needed to promote and participate in an open society. We can define an *open society* as one in which individuals from diverse ethnic, cultural, and social-class groups have equal opportunities to participate. Individuals can take full advantage of the opportunities and rewards within all social, economic, and political institutions without regard to their ancestry or ethnic identity. They can also participate in the society while preserving their distinct ethnic and cultural traits and can "make the maximum number of voluntary contacts with others without regard to qualifications of ancestry, sex, or class." (Sizemore, 1972a, p. 281). This kind of society has never existed in the human experience, but it is an ideal toward which we should strive.

Levels of Integration of Ethnic Content

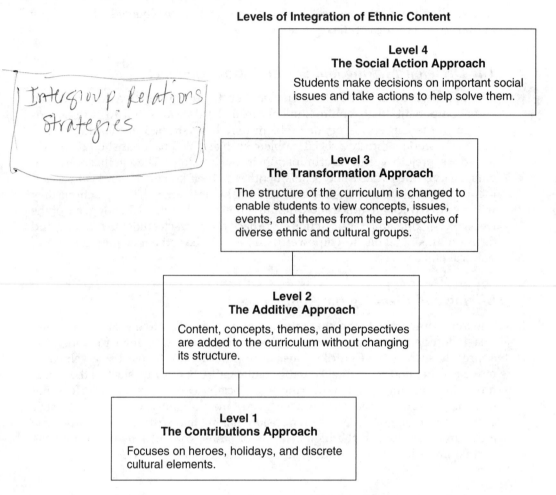

Intergroup Relations Strategies [handwritten note]

Level 4
The Social Action Approach

Students make decisions on important social issues and take actions to help solve them.

Level 3
The Transformation Approach

The structure of the curriculum is changed to enable students to view concepts, issues, events, and themes from the perspective of diverse ethnic and cultural groups.

Level 2
The Additive Approach

Content, concepts, themes, and perpsectives are added to the curriculum without changing its structure.

Level 1
The Contributions Approach

Focuses on heroes, holidays, and discrete cultural elements.

FIGURE 11.2   Approaches to Multicultural Curriculum Reform

Powerful and Excluded Ethnic Groups

In every past and present society, individuals have had and still have widely unequal opportunities to share fully in the reward systems and benefits of their society. The basis for the unequal distribution of rewards is determined by elitist groups in which power is centered. Powerful groups decide which traits and characteristics are necessary for full societal participation. They determine traits on the basis of the similarity of such traits to their own values, physical characteristics, life-styles, and behavior. At various times in history, powerful groups have used celibacy, gender, sexual orientation, ethnicity, race, religion, as well as many other variables, as determinants of which individuals and groups would be given or denied opportunities for social mobility and full societal participation. In colonial

America, for example, White Anglo-Saxon male Protestants with property control-led most social, political, economic, and military institutions. They excluded from full participation in decision making peoples, such as Native Americans and African Americans, who were different from themselves. They both invented and perpetuated stereotypes and myths about groups that were politically, economically, and socially excluded to justify their exclusion (Franklin, 1976).

Creating an Open Society

To create the kind of open society I have defined, we will either have to redistribute power so that groups with different ethnic and cultural characteristics will control entry to various social, economic, and political institutions, or we will have to modify the attitudes and actions of individuals who will control future institutions so they will become less ethnocentric and permit people who differ from themselves culturally and physically to share in society's reward system on the basis of the real contributions they can make to the functioning of society. We can conceptualize these two means to an open society as models.

Curricular Models

Model I can be called a *Shared Power Model*. The goal of this model would be to create a society in which currently excluded ethnic groups would share power with dominant ethnic groups. They would control a number of social, economic, and political institutions. The methods used to attain the major ends of this model would be an attempt to build group pride, cohesion, and identity among excluded ethnic groups and to help them develop the ability to make reflective political decisions, to gain and exercise political power effectively, and to develop a belief in the humanness of their own groups.

The alternative means to an open society can be called Model II, *Enlightening Powerful Groups Model*. The major goal of this model would be to modify the attitudes and perceptions of dominant ethnic groups so that they would be willing, as adults, to share power with excluded ethnic groups. They would also be willing to regard victimized ethnic groups as human beings, unwilling to participate in efforts to continue their oppression, willing to accept and understand the actions by marginalized ethnic groups to liberate themselves, and willing to take action to change the social system so it would treat powerless ethnic groups more justly. The major goals within this model focus on helping dominant ethnic groups expand their conception of who is human, develop more positive attitudes toward ethnic minorities, and be willing to share power with excluded ethnic groups. Figures 11.3 and 11.4 summarize these two models.

Characteristics of Model I: Shared Power Model

Most individuals who are aware of the extent to which marginalized ethnic groups are powerless in Western societies will probably view the shared power model as more realistic than Model II. The shared power model, if successfully

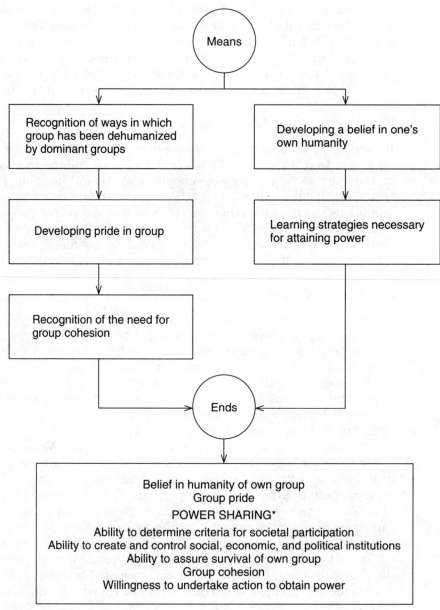

*Major end of model.

FIGURE 11.3   Model I—Shared Power Model

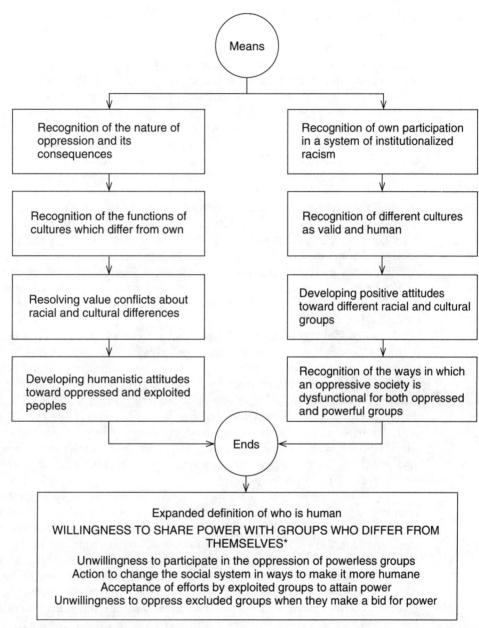

FIGURE 11.4   Model II—Enlightening Powerful Groups Model

implemented, would result in the redistribution of power so that excluded ethnic groups in Western societies would control such institutions as schools, courts, industries, health facilities, and the mass media. They would not necessarily control all institutions within their society, but they would control those in which they participated and that are needed to fulfill their individual and group needs. These groups would be able to distribute jobs and other rewards to persons who, like themselves, are denied such opportunities by present powerful ethnic groups. Elements within this model have been used by such groups as Jews and Catholics to enable them to participate more fully in shaping public policy in the United States (Greeley, 1975; Dinnerstein, Nichols, & Reimers, 1979).

In a society in which different ethnic groups share power, victimized ethnic groups would control and determine the traits and characteristics necessary for sharing societal rewards and opportunities. IQ test scores may cease to be an important criterion, but the ability to relate to people of color may become an essential one. A major assumption of this model is that presently excluded ethnic groups, if they attained power, would, like present powerful groups, provide opportunities for those persons who are most like themselves physically and culturally. This assumption may or may not be valid because ethnic group individuals sometime have ambivalent attitudes toward their own ethnic group (Milner, 1983).

If this model is used to achieve an open society, we will have to think of how a shared power model can be implemented without violence directed against ethnic minority groups, and how essential societal cohesion can be maintained without conflict between competing powerful groups that would totally disrupt a nation's social system. There are valid reasons to believe that educators and policy makers should seriously consider both concerns if we intend to create societies in which a number of competing ethnic groups share power. Writes Clark (1965, p. xv), "No human being can easily and graciously give up power and privilege. Such change can come only with conflict and anguish and the ever-present threat of retrogression."

Translating the shared power model into curriculum goals and strategies, our attention would focus primarily on the victims of structural and political exclusion, such as Australian Aborigines, Canadian Indians, British Asians, and African Americans. We would try to help these students attain the skills, attitudes, abilities, and strategies needed to attain power while maintaining an essential degree of societal cohesion. We would help these students see, through valid content samples, how previously excluded and politically powerless ethnic groups in history have attained power and how certain nonreflective actions and inactions can result in further exclusion and victimization.

The Assumptions of Model II: Enlightening Powerful Groups Model

Model II, whose primary goal is to help mainstream students develop more positive attitudes toward marginalized ethnic groups, rests on several assumptions. We have little evidence to support the validity of these assumptions. If anything, current data give us little hope in this model as an effective way to achieve an open society (Allport, 1979). This model assumes that most members of the mainstream experience a moral dilemma that results from the inconsistency between the ideals about equality they hold and the discrimination that ethnic minorities experience in society. Myrdal, in his classic study of race relations in the United States, stated that most White Americans in the United States experienced such a dilemma (Myrdal, 1962). It is possible that such a dilemma does not exist for many mainstream individuals in Western nation-states, including the United States.

It may be unrealistic to assume that teaching mainstream students about the harsh experiences ethnic minorities have experienced will cause them to become more willing to regard ethnic minorities as fellow human beings with certain entitlements in order to resolve their moral dilemmas related to democracy and inequality. Revisionist historians argue that discriminatory policies toward ethnic minorities are deliberate (Carnoy, 1974; Katz, 1975). If their arguments are valid, then teaching mainstream students about the brutalities of slavery or the denial of land rights to the Australian Aborigines cannot be expected to influence significantly how mainstream students perceive or treat marginalized ethnic minorities.

Purposes of Models I and II

Even though these two models represent what I feel are the basic ways by which we can create an open society, they are ideal-types concepts. Like any ideal-type concepts or models, they are best used for conceptualizing and thinking about issues and problems. The laws in Western nation-states, the current organization of schools, and the types of student populations in many schools make it difficult, in many cases, to implement either Model I or Model II in pure form. However, these models can help the curriculum specialist determine the kinds of emphases necessary for the curricula for different student populations. The curricula for excluded and dominant ethnic groups should have many elements in common, but I also believe that the central messages these groups receive in the curriculum should in some cases differ.

Using the two models as departure points, I discuss the kinds of emphases I believe should constitute the curriculum for excluded and powerful ethnic groups in order to create and sustain an open society. I consider the limitations of each model in my recommendations and suggest how they can be reduced. In situations in which teachers have students from both powerful and excluded ethnic groups, it will be necessary for them to combine elements from both models in order to structure an effective curriculum.

The Curriculum for Excluded Groups: Curriculum Implications of Model I

The curriculum I recommend for victimized ethnic groups will include most of the elements of Model I. However, it will also include elements from Model II because a pure, shared power model curriculum may result in a totally fragmented and dehumanized society.

The curriculum for marginalized ethnic groups should recognize their feelings toward self, help them clarify their racial attitudes, liberate them from psychological captivity, and convince them of their humanness, since the dominant society often makes them believe they are less than human. Ethnic minorities will be able to liberate themselves from psychological and physical oppression only when they know how and why the myths about them emerged and were institutionalized and validated by the scholarly community and the mass media. A curriculum that has as one major goal the liberation of excluded ethnic groups must teach these groups how social, political, and economic institutions in the mainstream society, including the schools, the academic community, and the mass media, have contributed to their feelings of inferiority and powerlessness.

They should be taught how social science knowledge often reflects the norms, values, and goals of the powerful ethnic and cultural groups in society, and how it often validates those belief systems that serve the needs of powerful groups and are detrimental to ethnic minorities (Sizemore, 1972b). When teaching students about how social knowledge has served to validate the stereotypes and beliefs about them, the teacher can use as examples historical and current textbook descriptions of groups of color.

Studying about how they have been psychologically and physically dehumanized is necessary to help victimized ethnic groups liberate themselves, but it is not sufficient. They must also be helped to develop the ability to make reflective public decisions so they can gain power and shape public policies that affect their lives. They must develop a sense of political efficacy and be given practices in social action strategies that teach them how to get power without violence and further exclusion. In other words, excluded ethnic groups must be taught the most effective ways to gain power. The school should help them become both effective and reflective political activists.

I define *reflective decision-making* and *social action* as the kinds of decisions and social action that will enable ethnic minorities to attain power but will at the same time ensure their existence as a group and their essential societal cohesion. A curriculum designed to help liberate marginalized ethnic groups should emphasize opportunities for social action, in which students have experience obtaining and exercising power (Banks, with Clegg, 1990; Newmann, 1975).

The curriculum for marginalized ethnic groups should not only help release them from psychological captivity and focus on social action, but it should also help them develop humanistic attitudes toward their own ethnic group, other victimized ethnic groups, and members of the mainstream society. The school should make an effort, when teaching victimized ethnic groups how to attain power and clarify their ethnic identity, to prevent them from becoming chauvinistic and ethnocentric. Marginalized ethnic groups should learn to value their own cultures, try to attain power, and develop group solidarity and identity in order to participate fully in society. However, they should also become effective citizens of their nation-states and acquire the knowledge, attitudes, and skills required to participate fully and effectively within it. The multicultural curriculum should acknowledge and respect the national culture and the need for national identity. The humanistic emphasis, which is a Model II component, must be incorporated into a curriculum for victimized ethnic groups to prevent them from developing ethnocentric attitudes, perceptions, and behaviors.

The Curriculum for Dominant Ethnic Groups: Curriculum Implications of Model II

Because we have no reliable ways of knowing that a Model I type curriculum would lead to an open society as I have defined it, the curriculum builder should also implement elements of Model II in appropriate settings, that is, in settings that contain both dominant and mainstream ethnic groups. What I suggest is that because both models have serious limitations, and because we know little about how to create an open society because we have never made a serious effort to create one, we should take a multiple approach to the problem. Also, the two models are complementary and not contradictory. If we succeed in enlightening or changing the attitudes of mainstream and dominant ethnic groups so that they become more willing to share power with excluded ethnic groups, then the struggle for power among victimized ethnic groups would consequently be less intense and thus less likely to lead to violence and societal chaos.

The elements that constitute Model II have been among the most widespread methods used by educators and policy makers to create a more just society. This approach is suggested by such terms as *intergroup education, human relations, race relations,* and *intercultural education*. In the 1940s in the United States, Hilda Taba and her colleagues (Taba, Brady, & Robinson, 1952) did pioneering work in intergroup education. A major assumption of intergroup education is that because negative intergroup attitudes are learned, they can be unlearned if students experience a curriculum specifically designed for that purpose. A seminal study by Trager and Yarrow supports the assumption that democratic attitudes can be taught to children if a deliberate program of instruction is designed for that purpose (Trager & Yarrow, 1952).

The primary goal of intergroup education (Model II elements) is to enlighten dominant ethnic groups by changing their attitudes toward and perceptions of victimized ethnic minorities. Intergroup education attempts to enlighten dominant ethnic group members by creating experiences for them in which they read or hear about prejudice, discrimination, and institutionalized racism. The participants are frequently encouraged to examine their own racial and ethnic attitudes, perceptions, and behaviors (Epstein, 1968).

It is difficult to determine how much potential Model II approaches have for changing the racial attitudes, beliefs, and behaviors of individuals. These methods have never been extensively implemented. Individuals are often not exposed to Model II type experiences until they are adults. Such adults usually attend a two- or three-week workshop, or a course in race relations for a quarter or a semester. Evidence suggests that these experiences usually have little permanent impact on adults' racial attitudes, although other kinds of experiences (used in conjunction with lectures and readings) seem to have some lasting influence on the racial attitudes of adults (Banks, 1991). It is predictable that a short workshop would have limited affect on adults' racial attitudes since an experience of twenty hours or less cannot be expected to change attitudes and perceptions an individual has acquired over a 20-year period, especially when the basic institutions in which they live reinforce their pre-experimental attitudes.

Because of the meager results obtained from Model II approaches, some educators feel that this model should be abandoned and that a shared power model is the only realistic way in which to achieve an open society. As an individual who has conducted many race relations workshops, I greatly respect individuals who endorse this point of view. However, I feel that Model II approaches should be continued, but that how they are implemented should be greatly modified. They should be continued and expanded because (1) we have no assurance that a shared power model will succeed in this period of history (however, we also have no assurance that it will not); (2) Model II strategies have never been extensively implemented; rather, they are usually used in experiments with students or with teachers when a racial crisis develops in a school; (3) research suggests that children's racial attitudes can be modified by curriculum intervention, especially in the earliest years; the younger children are, the greater the impact that curriculum intervention is likely to have on their racial feelings (Katz & Rosenberg, 1978); and (4) racism is a serious, dehumanizing pathology in Western societies that the school has a moral and professional responsibility to help eradicate.

Earlier I discuss the severe limitations of Model II and the questionable assumptions on which it is based. I argue that elements of this model should be implemented in appropriate settings. I do not see these two positions as contradictory; rather, I feel that when curriculum builders are aware of the limitations of their strategies, they can better use, evaluate, and modify them. A knowledge of the limitations of a curriculum strategy will also prevent the curriculum builder from expecting unrealistic outcomes. For example, a knowledge of the limitations of Model II will help teachers realize that a unit on race relations during African American history month will most likely have little influence on the racial attitudes of their students. They will know that only a modification of their total curriculum is likely to have any significant impact on their students' racial attitudes and beliefs, and that even with this kind of substantial curriculum modification, the chances for modification of racial attitudes will not be extremely high, especially if they are working with older students or adults. Curricular experiences are more likely to change students' racial *beliefs* than their racial *attitudes* (Allport, 1979).

Increasing the Effectiveness of Model II Approaches

Despite the severe limitations of Model II as it is currently used in the schools and in teacher education, I believe that substantial modifications in the implementation of Model II components can significantly increase this model's impact on the racial attitudes and perceptions of dominant ethnic group individuals. The ultimate result of an effective implementation of the model may be that children of dominant ethnic groups, as adults, will be more likely to perceive excluded ethnic groups as human beings and thus more likely to share power with them and allow them to participate more fully in society. These statements are, at best, promising hypotheses, but I base them on experience, gleanings from research, and faith. Below, I suggest ways in which the implementation of a Model II type curriculum can have maximum opportunity to enlighten or modify the racial attitudes, beliefs, and perceptions of students.

By the time children enter school, they have already absorbed the negative attitudes toward ethnic groups of color that are pervasive within the larger society. Although this fact has been documented since Lasker's pioneering research in 1929 (Lasker, 1929), teachers are often surprised to learn in workshops that even kindergarten pupils are aware of racial differences and assign different values to Blacks and Whites. This fact alone gives us little hope for effective intervention. However, a related one does. The racial attitudes of kindergartners are not as negative or as crystallized as those of fifth graders (Glock et al., 1975). As children grow older and no systematic efforts are made to modify their racial feelings, they become more bigoted. The curriculum implications of this research are clear. To modify children's racial attitudes, a deliberate program of instruction must be structured for that purpose in the earliest grades. The longer we wait, the less our chances are for success. By the time the individual reaches adulthood, the chances for successful intervention become almost—but not quite—nil.

Effective intervention programs must not only begin in the earliest grades; but the efforts must also be sustained over a long period of time, and material related to cultural differences must permeate the entire curriculum. Also, a variety of media and materials enhances chances for successful intervention. A unit on Native Americans in the second grade and a book on Mexican Americans in the third grade will do little to help students understand or accept cultures different from their own. A hit-and-miss approach to the study of cultural differences may do more harm than good. There may be times when a separate in-depth unit on an ethnic minority culture is educationally justified in order to teach a concept, such as acculturation or separatism. Most often, however, when ethnic groups are studied in this way the students are likely to get the impression that ethnic minorities have not played an integral and significant role in shaping the history and culture of their society.

Summary

Several widespread assumptions about the nature of ethnic studies and the multicultural curriculum are adversely affecting the teaching of ethnic studies in educational institutions. This chapter examines and challenges these assumptions. It also describes the characteristics of an effective multicultural curriculum. The multicultural curriculum should be based on a broad definition of ethnic group and should include the study of both ethnic groups and ethnic minorities.

Ethnic studies should also be viewed as a process of curriculum reform. By restructuring their curriculum when integrating it with ethnic content, educators can create a new curriculum based on fresh assumptions and perspectives. This new curriculum will enable students to gain novel views of the human experience and new conceptions of Western societies.

Four approaches to multicultural curriculum reform used by schools, colleges, and universities can be identified: (1) Contributions, (2) Additive, (3) Transformation, and (4) Decision-Making and Social Action. The transformation and social-action approaches should be the goal of curriculum reform. These approaches can best help students to acquire the knowledge, attitudes, and skills needed to become effective citizens in a pluralistic democratic society.

The multicultural curriculum should also help create and sustain an open society. To create an open society, it is necessary to define such a social system clearly and to design a curriculum specifically to achieve and perpetuate it. An open society is a social system in which individuals from diverse ethnic, cultural, and social-class groups can freely participate and have equal opportunities to gain the skills and knowledge the society needs in order to function. Rewards within an open society are based on the contributions each person, regardless of his or her ancestry or social class, makes to the fulfillment of the society's functional requirements.

Two models by which we can achieve an open society are presented in this chapter. Model I, the Shared Power Model, focuses on helping marginalized ethnic groups attain power so they can control a number of social, economic, and political institutions and can determine who may participate in them. These groups would also determine how rewards would be distributed. A second model, the Enlightening Powerful Groups Model, focuses on changing the attitudes, beliefs, perceptions, and behaviors of members of powerful ethnic groups so they will share power with marginalized ethnic groups, regard them as groups that deserve human rights, and take actions to eliminate institutionalized racism and discrimination.

The complexity of modern Western societies makes it impossible for either model to be implemented in pure form. Also, both models are ideal-type concepts based on a number of unverified assumptions. However, these models can help the curriculum builder determine the kinds of emphases that would constitute an open-society curriculum for excluded, powerful, and mixed groups, for planning programs, and for ascertaining the effectiveness of various curriculum strategies.

References

Allport, G. W. (1979). *The Nature of Prejudice* (25th anniv. ed.). Reading, MA.: Addison-Wesley.

Banks, J. A. (1991). Multicultural Education: Its Effects on Students' Racial and Gender Role Attitudes. In J. P. Shaver (Ed.), *Handbook of Research on Social Studies Teaching and Learning* (pp. 459–469). New York: Macmillan.

Banks, J. A., & Lynch, J. (Eds.). (1986). *Multicultural Education in Western Societies*. New York: Praeger.

Banks, J. A., with Clegg, A. A., Jr. (1990). *Teaching Strategies for the Social Studies: Inquiry, Valuing and Decision-Making* (4th ed.). New York: Longman.

Blassingame, J. W. (Ed.). (1971). *New Perspectives on Black Studies.* Urbana: University of Illinois Press.

Carnoy, M. (1974). *Education as Cultural Imperialism.* New York: David McKay.

Clark, K. B. (1965). Introduction: The Dilemma of Power. In T. Pasons & K. B. Clark (Eds.), *The Negro American* (pp. xi–xviii). Boston: Houghton Mifflin.

Dinnerstein, L., Nichols, R. L., & Reimers, D. M. (1979). *Natives and Strangers: Ethnic Groups and the Building of America.* New York: Oxford University Press.

Duran, L. I., & Bernard, H. (Eds.). (1982). *Introduction to Chicano Studies* (2nd ed). New York: Macmillan.

Epstein, C. (1968). *Intergroup Relations for the Classroom Teacher.* Boston: Houghton Mifflin.

Franklin, J. H. (1976). *Racial Equality in America.* Chicago: University of Chicago Press.

Gay, G. (1992). The State of Multicultural Education in the United States. In K. A. Moodley (Ed.), *Beyond Multicultural Education: International Perspectives* (pp. 41–65). Calgary, Alberta: Detselig Enterprises Ltd.

Glock, C. Y., et al. (1975). *Adolescent Prejudice.* New York: Harper and Row.

Goodlad, J. I. (1984). *A Place Called School: Prospects for the Future.* New York: McGraw-Hill.

Greeley, A. M. (1975). *Why Can't They Be Like Us? America's White Ethnic Groups.* New York: Dutton.

Katz, M. B. (1975). *Class, Bureaucracy, and Schools: The Illusion of Educational Change in America* (expanded ed.). New York: Praeger.

Katz, P. A., & Rosenberg, S. (1978). Modification of Children's Racial Attitudes. *Developmental Psychology, 14,* 447–461.

Lasker, B. (1929). *Race Attitudes in Children.* New York: Henry Holt.

Milner, D. (1983). *Children and Race: Ten Years On.* London: Ward Lock Educational.

Moodley, K. A. (Ed.). (1992). *Beyond Multicultural Education: International Perspectives.* Calgary, Alberta: Detselig Enterprises Ltd.

Myrdal, G. (1962). *An American Dilemma: The Negro Problem and Modern Democracy,* Vols. 1 & 2. New York: Harper and Row.

Newmann, F. M. (1975). *Education for Citizen Action: Challenge for Secondary Curriculum.* Berkeley, CA: McCutchan.

Sizemore, B. A. (1972a). Is There a Case for Separate Schools? *Phi Delta Kappan, 53,* 281–284.

Sizemore, B. A. (1972b). Social Science and Education for a Black Identity. In J. A. Banks & J. D. Grambs (Eds.). *Black Self-Concept: Implications for Education and Social Science* (pp. 141–170). New York: McGraw-Hill.

Taba, H, Brady, E. H., & Robinson, J. T. (1952). *Intergroup Education in Public Schools.* Washington, DC: American Council on Education.

Takashima, S. (1971). *A Child in Prison Camp.* Montreal: Tundra Books.

Trager, H. G., & Yarrow, M. R. (1952). *They Learn What They Live: Prejudice in Young Children.* New York: Harper and Brothers.

Chapter 12

The Stages of Ethnicity: Implications for Curriculum Reform

Assumptions about Ethnic Students

When planning multicultural experiences for students, we tend to assume that ethnic groups are monolithic and have rather homogeneous needs and characteristics. We often assume, for example, that individual members of ethnic minority groups, such as Jewish Americans and African Americans, have intense feelings of ethnic identity and a strong interest in learning about the experiences and histories of their ethnic cultures. Educators also frequently assume that the self-images and academic achievement of ethnic minority youths will be enhanced if they are exposed to a curriculum that focuses on the heroic accomplishments and deeds of their ethnic groups and highlight the ways in which ethnic groups have been victimized by the mainstream society.

Ethnic Groups Are Complex and Dynamic

These kinds of assumptions are highly questionable and have led to some disappointments and serious problems in programs and practices related to ethnic diversity. In designing multicultural experiences for students, we need to consider seriously the psychological needs and characteristics of ethnic group members and their emerging and changing ethnic identities. Ethnic groups, such as African Americans, Italian Australians, and Anglo-Canadians, are not monolithic but are dynamic and complex groups (see Chapter 4).

Many of our curriculum development and teacher education efforts are based on the assumption that ethnic groups are static and unchanging. However, ethnic groups are highly diverse, complex, and changing entities. Ethnic identity, like other ethnic characteristics, is also complex and changing among ethnic group members. Thus there is no one ethnic identity among African Americans that we can delineate, as social scientists have sometimes suggested, but many complex and changing identities among them.

During the 1960s and 1970s social scientists frequently suggested, for example, that African Americans had confused racial identities and ambivalent, negative attitudes toward their own ethnic group. The typology I have developed, however, suggests that only a segment of African Americans can be so characterized and that those African Americans are functioning at Ethnicity Stage 1. See Kardiner and Ovesey (1951) for the classical social pathology interpretation of the African American personality.

In recent years researchers such as Cross (1991) and Spencer (1985) have developed concepts, theories, and research that seriously challenge the negative self-concept hypothesis. These researchers make a useful distinction between *personal identity* (self-concept, self-esteem) and *group identity* or reference group orientation. In a series of pioneering studies, Spencer (1982, 1984) has marshaled significant support for the postulate that young African American children are able to distinguish their personal identity from their group identity, can have high self-esteem and yet express a White bias, and that the expression of a White bias results from a cognitive process that enables young children to perceive accurately the norms and attitudes toward Whites and African Americans that are institutionalized within society.

Effective educational programs should help students explore and clarify their own ethnic identities. To do this, such programs must recognize and reflect the complex ethnic identities and characteristics of the individual students in the classroom. Teachers should learn how to facilitate the identity quests among ethnic youths and help them become effective and able participants in the common civic and national culture.

The Stages of Ethnicity: A Typology

To reflect the myriad and emerging ethnic identities among teachers and ethnic youths, we must attempt to identify them and to describe their curricular and teaching implications. The description of a typology that attempts to outline the basic stages of the development of ethnicity among individual members of ethnic groups follows. The typology is a preliminary ideal-type construct in the Weberian sense and constitutes a set of hypotheses based on the existing and emerging theory and research and on the author's study of ethnic behavior.

This typology is presented to stimulate research and the development of concepts and theory related to ethnicity and ethnic groups. Another purpose of the typology is to suggest preliminary guidelines for teaching about ethnicity in the schools and colleges and for helping students and teachers to function effectively at increasingly higher stages of ethnicity. Ford (1979) developed an instrument to measure the first five of these six stages of ethnicity and administered it to a sample of classroom teachers. She concluded that her study demonstrated that teachers are spread into the five stages that I had hypothesized. The sixth stage of the typology was developed after the Ford study was completed.

Stage 1: Ethnic Psychological Captivity

During this stage the individual absorbs the negative ideologies and beliefs about his or her ethnic group that are institutionalized within the society. Consequently, he or she exemplifies ethnic self-rejection and low self-esteem. The individual is ashamed of his or her ethnic group and identity during this stage and may respond in a number of ways, including avoiding situations that bring contact with other ethnic groups or striving aggressively to become highly culturally assimilated. Conflict develops when the highly culturally assimilated psychologically captive ethnic is denied structural assimilation or total societal participation.

Individuals who are members of ethnic groups that have historically been victimized by cultural assaults, such as Polish Americans and Australian Aborigines, as well as members of highly visible and stigmatized ethnic groups, such as African Americans and Chinese Canadians, are likely to experience some form of ethnic psychological captivity. The more that an ethnic group is stigmatized and rejected by the mainstream society, the more likely are its members to experience some form of ethnic psychological captivity. Thus, individuals who are members of the mainstream ethnic group within a society are the least likely individuals to experience ethnic psychological captivity.

Stage 2: Ethnic Encapsulation

Stage 2 is characterized by ethnic encapsulation and ethnic exclusiveness, including voluntary separatism. The individual participates primarily within his or her own ethnic community and believes that his or her ethnic group is superior to other groups. Many individuals within Stage 2, such as many Anglo-Americans, have internalized the dominant societal myths about the superiority of their ethnic or racial group and the innate inferiority of other ethnic groups and races. Many individuals who are socialized within all-White suburban communities in the United States and who live highly ethnocentric and encapsulated lives can be described as Stage 2 individuals. Alice Miel (with Kiester, 1967) describes these kinds of individuals in *The Shortchanged Children of Suburbia.*

The characteristics of Stage 2 are most extreme among individuals who suddenly begin to feel that their ethnic group and its way of life, especially its privileged and ascribed status, are being threatened by other racial and ethnic groups. This frequently happens when African Americans begin to move into all-White ethnic communities. Extreme forms of this stage are also manifested among individuals who have experienced ethnic psychological captivity (Stage 1) and who have recently discovered their ethnicity. This new ethnic consciousness is usually caused by an ethnic revitalization movement. This type of individual, like the individual who feels that the survival of his or her ethnic group is threatened, is likely to express intensely negative feelings toward outside ethnic and racial groups.

However, individuals who have experienced ethnic psychological captivity and who have newly discovered their ethnic consciousness tend to have highly ambivalent feelings toward their own ethnic group and try to confirm, for themselves, that they are proud of their ethnic heritage and culture. Consequently, strong and verbal rejection of outgroups usually takes place. Outgroups are regarded as enemies and racists and, in extreme manifestations of this stage, are viewed as planning genocidal efforts to destroy their ethnic group. The individual's sense of ethnic peoplehood is escalated and highly exaggerated. The ethnic individual within this stage of ethnicity tends to reject strongly members of his or her ethnic group who are regarded as assimilationist-oriented and liberal, who do not endorse the rhetoric of separatism, or who openly socialize with members of outside ethnic groups, especially with members of a different racial group.

The Stage 2 individual expects members of the ethnic group to show strong overt commitments to the liberation struggle of the group or to the protection of the group from outside and "foreign" groups. The individual often endorses a separatist ideology. Members of outside ethnic groups are likely to regard Stage 2 individuals as racists, bigots, or extremists. As this type of individual begins to question some of the basic assumptions of his or her culture and to experience less ambivalence and conflict about ethnic identity, and especially as the rewards within the society become more fairly distributed among ethnic groups, he or she is likely to become less ethnocentric and ethnically encapsulated.

Stage 3: Ethnic Identity Clarification

At this stage the individual is able to clarify personal attitudes and ethnic identity, to reduce intrapsychic conflict, and to develop clarified positive attitudes toward his or her ethnic group. The individual learns self-acceptance, thus developing the characteristics needed to accept and respond more positively to outside ethnic groups. Self-acceptance is a requisite to accepting and responding positively to other people. During this stage, the individual is able to accept and understand both the positive and negative attributes of his or her ethnic group. The individual's pride in his or her ethnic group is not based on the hate or fear of outside groups. Ethnic pride is genuine rather than contrived. Individuals are more likely to experience this stage when they have attained a certain level of economic and psychological security and have been able to have positive experiences with members of other ethnic groups.

Stage 4: Biethnicity

The individual within this stage has a healthy sense of ethnic identity and the psychological characteristics and skills needed to participate successfully in his or her own ethnic culture as well as in another ethnic culture. The individual also has *a strong desire to function effectively in two ethnic cultures.* We can describe such an individual as *biethnic.* Levels of biethnicity vary greatly. Many African Americans, in order to attain social and economic mobility, learn to function effectively in Anglo-American culture during the formal working day. The private lives of these individuals, however, may be highly African American and monocultural.

People of color in the United States are forced to become biethnic to some extent in order to experience social and economic mobility. However, members of mainstream groups, such as Anglo-Americans, can and often do live almost exclusive monocultural and highly ethnocentric lives.

Stage 5: Multiethnicity and Reflective Nationalism

The Stage 5 individual has clarified, reflective, and positive personal, ethnic, and national identifications; positive attitudes toward other ethnic and racial groups; and is self-actualized. The individual is able to function, at least beyond superficial levels, within several ethnic cultures within his or her nation and to understand, appreciate, and share the values, symbols, and institutions of several ethnic cultures within the nation. Such multicultural perspectives and feelings, I hypothesize, help the individual live a more enriched and fulfilling life and formulate creative and novel solutions to personal and public problems.

Individuals within this stage have a commitment to their ethnic group, an empathy and concern for other ethnic groups, and a strong but *reflective* commitment and allegiance to the nation state and its idealized values, such as human dignity and justice. Thus, such individuals have reflective and clarified ethnic and national identifications and are effective citizens in a democratic pluralistic nation. Stage 5 individuals realistically view the United States as the multiethnic nation that it is. They have cross-cultural competency within their own nation and commitment to the national ideals, creeds, and values of the nation-state.

The socialization that most individuals experience does not help them attain the attitudes, skills, and perspectives needed to function effectively within a variety of ethnic cultures and communities. Although many people participate in several ethnic cultures at superficial levels, such as eating ethnic foods and listening to ethnic music (called Level I in Chapter 3), few probably participate at more meaningful levels and learn to understand the values, symbols, and traditions of several ethnic cultures and are able to function within other ethnic cultures at meaningful levels (Level II through III, see Chapter 3).

Stage 6: Globalism and Global Competency

The individual within Stage 6 has clarified, reflective, and positive ethnic, national, and global identifications and the knowledge, skills, attitudes, and abilities needed to function within ethnic cultures within his or her own nation as well as within cultures outside his or her nation in other parts of the world. The Stage 6 individual has the ideal delicate balance of ethnic, national, and global identifications, commitments, literacy, and behaviors. This individual has internalized the universalistic ethical values and principles of humankind and has the skills, competencies, and commitment needed to take action within the world to actualize personal values and commitments.

Characteristics of the Stages of Ethnicity Typology

This typology is an ideal-type construct (see Figure 12.1) and should be viewed as dynamic and multidimensional rather than as static and linear. The characteristics within the stages exist on a continuum. Thus, within Stage 1, individuals are more or less ethnically psychologically captive; some individuals are more ethnically psychologically captive than are others.

The division between the stages is blurred rather than sharp. Thus, a continuum also exists between as well as within the stages. The ethnically encapsulated individual (Stage 2) does not suddenly attain clarification and acceptance of his or her ethnic identity (Stage 3). This is a gradual and developmental process. Also, the stages should not be viewed as strictly sequential and linear. I am hypothesizing that some individuals may never experience a particular stage. However, I hypothesize that once an individual experiences a particular stage, he or she is likely to experience the stages above it sequentially and developmentally. I hypothesize, however, that individuals may experience the stages upward, downward, or in a zigzag pattern. Under certain conditions, for example, the biethnic (Stage 4) individual may become multiethnic (Stage 5); under new conditions the same individual may become again biethnic (Stage 4), ethnically identified (Stage 3), and ethnically encapsulated (Stage 2). Note, for example, the extent to which Jewish Americans, who tend to express more positive attitudes toward groups of color than do other White ethnic groups in the United States, became increasingly in-group-oriented as Israel become more threatened and as the expressions of anti-Semitism escalated in the 1970s and 1980s (Forster & Epstein, 1974). Northern White ethnic groups became increasingly more ethnically encapsulated as busing for school desegregation gained momentum in northern cities in the 1970s (Glazer, 1983).

Figure 12.1 illustrates the dynamic and multidimensional characteristics of the development of ethnicity among individuals. Note especially the arrowed lines that indicate that continua exist both horizontally and vertically.

Preliminary Curricular Implications of the Stages of Ethnicity Typology

The discussion that follows on the curricular implications of the stages of ethnicity typology should be viewed as a set of tentative hypotheses that merit testing by educators and researchers interested in ethnicity and education. The reader should keep foremost in mind the tentative and exploratory nature of the following discussion.

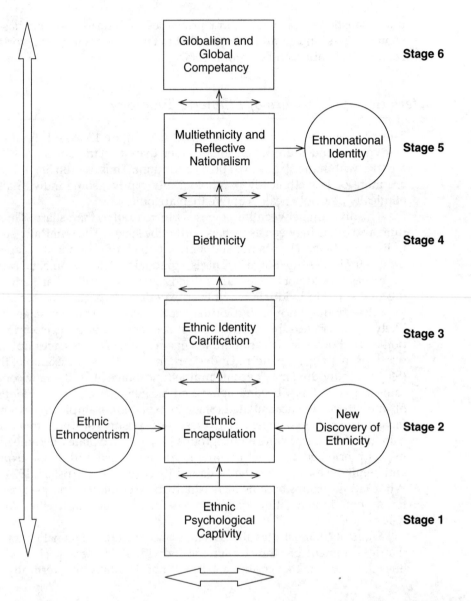

FIGURE 12.1   The Stages of Ethnicity: A Typology

Curricular Implications of Ethnicity: Stage 1

The student within this stage of ethnicity can best benefit from monoethnic content and experiences that will help him or her to develop ethnic awareness and a heightened sense of ethnic consciousness (see Chapter 10). Such monoethnic experiences should be designed to help the individual come to grips with personal ethnic identity and to learn how his or her ethnic group has been victimized by the larger society and by institutions, such as the media and the schools, which reinforce and perpetuate dominant societal myths and ideologies. African American studies, Chinese Canadian studies, and Australian Aboriginal studies courses conceptualized in *interdisciplinary* and *humanistic* ways, and other monoethnic experiences can help the individual within this stage to raise his or her level of ethnic consciousness. Strategies that facilitate moral development and decision-making skills should be an integral part of the curriculum for the ethnically psychologically captive individual (Banks with Clegg, 1990).

Curricular Implications of Ethnicity: Stage 2

Individuals within this stage can best benefit from curricular experiences that accept and empathize with their ethnic identities and hostile feelings toward outside groups. The teacher should accept the individual's hostile feelings and help him or her express and clarify them. A strong affective curricular component that helps students clarify their negative ethnic and racial feelings should be a major part of the curriculum. The students should be helped to deal with their hostile feelings toward outside groups in constructive ways. The teacher should help the individual begin the process of attaining ethnic identity clarification during the later phases of this stage.

Curricular Implications of Ethnicity: Stage 3

Curricular experiences within this stage should be designed to reinforce the student's emerging ethnic identity and clarification. The student should be helped to attain a balanced perspective on his or her ethnic group. A true acceptance of one's ethnic group involves accepting its glories as well as its shortcomings. The individual in this stage of ethnicity can accept an objective view and analysis of his or her ethnic group, whereas an objective analysis is often very difficult for Stage 1 and Stage 2 individuals to accept. Value clarification and moral development techniques should be used to enhance the individual's emerging ethnic identity clarification.

Curricular Implications of Ethnicity: Stage 4

Curricular experiences should be designed to help the student master concepts and generalizations related to an ethnic group other than his or her own and to help the student view events and situations from the perspective of another ethnic group. The student should be helped to compare and contrast his or her own ethnic group with another ethnic group. Strategies should also be used to enhance the individual's moral development and ability to relate positively to his or her own ethnic group and to another ethnic group.

Curricular Implications of Ethnicity: Stage 5

The curriculum at this stage of ethnicity should be designed to help the student develop a global sense of ethnic literacy and to master concepts and generalizations about a wide range of ethnic groups. The student should also be helped to view events and situations from the perspectives of different ethnic groups within the United States as well as within other nations. The student should explore the problems and promises of living within a multiethnic cultural environment and discuss ways in which a multiethnic society may be nurtured and improved. Strategies such as moral dilemmas and case studies should be used to enable the individual to explore moral and value alternatives and to embrace values, such as human dignity and justice, that are needed to live in a multiethnic community and global world society.

Curricular Implications of Ethnicity: Stage 6

At this stage, the student has acquired three levels of identifications that are balanced: an ethnic, national, and global identification and related cross-cultural competencies. Because the typology presented in this chapter constitutes a continuum, the process of acquiring an effective balance of ethnic, national, and global identifications and related cross-cultural competencies is a continuous and *ongoing process.* Thus, the individual never totally attains the ideal ethnic, national, and global identifications and related cross-cultural skills for functioning within his or her ethnic group, nation, and world. Consequently, a major goal of the curriculum for the Stage 6 individual is to help the student function at Stage 6 more effectively.

Knowledge, skills, attitudes, and abilities that students need to function more effectively within their ethnic group, nation, and world should be emphasized when teaching students at Stage 6. This includes knowledge about the individual's own ethnic group, other ethnic groups, the national culture, and knowledge about other nations in the world. Valuing strategies, such as moral dilemmas and case studies that relate to the individual's ethnic group, nation, and world, should also be effectively used at this stage to enhance the student's developing sense of ethnic, national, and global identifications. A major goal of teaching students within this stage is to help them understand how to determine which particular allegiance—whether ethnic, national, or global—is most appropriate within a particular situation. Ethnic, national, and global attachments should be given different priorities within different situations and events. The student within Stage 6 should learn how to determine which identification is most appropriate for particular situations, settings, and events.

Summary

When planning multicultural experiences for students and teachers, we need to consider the ethnic characteristics of individuals. In designing curricula related to ethnicity, we often assume that ethnic groups are monolithic and have rather homogeneous needs and characteristics. However, students differ greatly in their ethnic identities and characteristics just as they differ in their general cognitive and affective development (Kohlberg & Mayer, 1972; Piaget, 1972). Consequently, some attempt should be made to individualize experiences for students within the multicultural curriculum.

The description of a typology that attempts to outline the basic stages of the development of ethnicity among individual members of ethnic groups is presented in this chapter. This typology is a preliminary ideal-type construct in the Weberian sense and constitutes a set of hypotheses based on the existing and emerging theory and research and the author's study of ethnic behavior. The six stages within the typology are:

Stage 1: Ethnic Psychological Captivity
Stage 2: Ethnic Encapsulation
Stage 3: Ethnic Identity Clarification
Stage 4: Biethnicity
Stage 5: Multiethnicity and Reflective Nationalism
Stage 6: Globalism and Competency.

It is hypothesized that individuals within these different stages should be exposed to curricular experiences consistent with their levels of ethnic development. The curricular implications of each of the stages of ethnicity are discussed.

References

Banks, J. A., with Clegg, A. A., Jr., (1990). *Teaching Strategies for the Social Studies* (4th ed.). New York: Longman.

Cross, W. E., Jr. (1991). *Shades of Black: Diversity in African-American Identity.* Philadelphia: Temple University Press.

Ford, M. (1979). The Development of an Instrument for Assessing Levels of Ethnicity in Public School Teachers, Ed.D. diss., University of Houston.

Forster, A., & Epstein, B. R. (1974). *The New Anti-Semitism.* New York: McGraw-Hill.

Glazer, N. (1983). *Ethnic Dilemmas 1964–1982.* Cambridge, MA.: Harvard University Press.

Kardiner, A., & Ovesey, L. (1951). *The Mark of Oppression: A Psychosocial Study of the American Negro.* New York: Norton.

Kohlberg, L., & Mayer, R. (1972). Development as the Aim of Education. *Harvard Educational Review, 42,* 449–496.

Miel, A., with Kiester, E., Jr. (1967). *The Short-changed Children of Suburbia.* New York: Institute of Human Relations Press, The American Jewish Committee.

Piaget, J. (1972). *Six Psychological Studies.* New York: Random House.

Spencer, M. B. (1982). Personal and Group Identity among Black Children: An Alternative Synthesis. *Genetic Psychology Monographs, 106,* 59–84.

Spencer, M. B. (1984). Black Children's Race Awareness, Racial Attitudes, and Self-Concept: A Reinterpretation. *Journal of Child Psychology and Psychiatry, 25,* 433–441.

Spencer, M. B. (1985). Cultural Cognition and Social Cognition as Identity Correlates of Black Children's Personal-Social Development. In M. B. Spencer, G. K. Brookins, & W. R. Allen (Eds.), *Beginnings: The Social and Affective Development of Black Children* (pp. 215–230). Hillsdale, NJ: Lawrence Erlbaum Associates.

Instructional Issues and Guidelines

Chapter 13
Reducing Prejudice in Students: Theory, Research, and Strategies

Chapter 14
Language, Ethnicity, and Education

Chapter 15
Curriculum Guidelines for Multicultural Education

The three chapters in Part V focus on several important and continuing issues in effective multicultural educational reform: (1) helping students to develop more democratic racial attitudes and values; (2) language issues in multicultural education; and (3) guidelines for establishing effective multicultural education classrooms and schools.

A key goal of multicultural education is to help students attain more positive racial attitudes. The research, theory, and strategies related to reducing student prejudice are described in Chapter 13. The characteristics of the effective multicultural teacher are also described in this chapter. Many students in the multicultural classroom speak languages and dialects that differ from those fostered by the school and the mainstream society. Chapter 14 presents information and insights about language diversity that teachers will find useful when working with students from diverse language groups. The final chapter, Chapter 15, describes guidelines that teachers and other practicing educators can use to create multicultural curricula and learning environments. This last chapter also summarizes some of the major issues, problems, and recommendations discussed in this book.

Chapter 13

Reducing Prejudice in Students: Theory, Research, and Strategies

The Causes of Prejudice

We cannot reduce racial prejudice unless we acquire an understanding of its causes. First, however, we need to define prejudice. The literature on race relations is replete with efforts to define *prejudice*. Even though the definitions differ to some extent, most suggest that prejudice is a set of rigid and unfavorable attitudes toward a particular group or groups that is formed in disregard of facts. Prejudiced individuals respond to perceived members of these groups on the basis of preconceptions, tending to disregard behavior or personal characteristics that are inconsistent with their biases. Simpson and Yinger (1985, p. 21) have provided a lucid and useful definition of *prejudice*.

> Prejudice is an emotional, rigid attitude (a predisposition to respond to a certain stimulus in a certain way) toward a group of people. They may be a group only in the mind of the prejudiced person; that is, he categorizes them together, although they may have little similarity or interaction. Prejudices are thus attitudes, but not all attitudes are prejudices.

Although social scientists have attempted for years to derive a comprehensive and coherent theory of prejudice, their efforts have not been totally successful. A number of theories explain various components of prejudice, but none sufficiently describes its many dimensions. Social scientists have rejected some of the older, more simplistic theories of prejudice; other theories are too limited in scope to be functional. Still others are extremely useful in explaining certain forms of prejudice directed toward specific groups but fail to account for its other facets. A serious study of the theories of prejudice reveals the complexity of this configuration of attitudes and predispositions; thus, simplistic explanations of prejudice only hinder our understanding of it.

Theories of Prejudice

Arnold M. Rose (1962) has critically reviewed both the older, simpler theories of prejudice and the more complex modern psychological explanations. A summary of his analysis is presented below in order to illuminate the strengths and weaknesses of the various theories.

The *racial and cultural difference theory* maintains that people have an instinctive fear and dislike of individuals who are physically and culturally different from themselves. Rose dismisses this theory as untenable, since research indicates that children are tolerant of other races and groups until they acquire the dominant cultural attitudes toward ethnic minorities. Children must be *taught* to dislike different races and ethnic groups. Rose (1962, p. 78) writes that this theory "should be thought of as a rationalization of prejudice rather than as an explanation of it."

The *economic competition theory* holds that prejudice emanates from antagonism caused by competition among various groups for jobs and other economic rewards. Although this theory sheds light on many historical examples of racial prejudice and discrimination, it has some serious limitations. It fails to explain why a group continues to practice discrimination when it no longer profits economically from doing so. A number of studies document the severe financial losses attributable to discrimination against ethnic groups.

The *social control theory* maintains that prejudice exists because individuals are forced to conform to society's traditions and norms; thus, they dislike certain groups because they are taught to do so by their culture. This theory helps explain why prejudice may be perpetuated when it is no longer functional, but it does not consider how it originates.

The *traumatic experience theory* states that racial prejudice emerges in an individual following a traumatic experience involving a member of a minority group during early childhood. This theory is inadequate because young children do not associate an unpleasant experience with a particular racial group unless they have already been exposed to the concept of racial differences. In noting another limitation of this theory, Harley (1968) writes:

> *This idea can be discounted because persons can hold extreme prejudice with no contact with persons of the discriminated class, and the traumatic experiences reported by persons as reason for their prejudice are very often found to be either imagined by them or elaborated and embellished beyond recognition.*

The *frustration-aggression theory* is a modern psychological explanation of prejudice. It suggests that prejudice results when individuals become frustrated because they are unable to satisfy real or perceived needs. Frustration leads to aggression, which may then be directed toward minority groups because they are highly visible targets and are unable to retaliate. Displacing aggression on stigmatized groups is much safer than attacking the real source of the frustration. Rose (1962) illuminates two basic weaknesses in this theory: (1) it fails to explain why certain groups are selected as targets rather than others, and (2) it assumes that all frustration must be expressed. However, a number of writers and researchers have relied heavily on this theory to help explain the emergence and perpetuation of prejudice.

The *projection theory* states that "people attribute to others motives that they sense in themselves but that they would not wish to acknowledge openly" (Rose, 1962, p. 83). This theory is severely limited because it fails to explain motives for prejudice or why certain characteristics are attributed to specific groups.

In attempting to derive a comprehensive theory of prejudice, Rose (1962) suggests that the modern psychological theories are the most useful explanations. He (pp.92–93) writes:

> *The central theories today which seriously attempt to explain prejudice are based on the concepts of frustration-aggression, projection, and symbolic substitution. These theories have a good deal in common despite the differing kinds of evidence which lead to their formation. All of them postulate (1) a need to express antagonism (2) toward something which is not the real object of antagonism. Not only is there an essential similarity among the three theories, but they complement each other at their weakest points. The symbolic theory does most to explain which group is selected for prejudice and why. The frustration-aggression theory does most to explain the strength behind prejudice. The projection theory offers a plausible explanation of the psychological function of prejudice as a cleansing agent to dissolve inner guilt or hurt.*

A Comprehensive Theory of Prejudice

Simpson and Yinger (1965, p. 49) have formulated a comprehensive theory of prejudice "around three highly interactive but analytically distinct factors, each the convergence of several lines of theory and evidence." The first factor is the personality requirements of the individual. As a result of both constitutional and learned needs, some people develop personalities that thrive on prejudices and irrational responses. This theory has been offered by a number of other writers and researchers. We later review some research on which it is based.

An individual may also develop prejudices based not on personality needs but on the way society is structured. The power structure of society is especially important to this concept, which is similar to the economic competition theory

Rose discusses. Simpson and Yinger (1965, p. 50) write, "It is impossible to interpret individual behavior adequately without careful attention to the social dimension."

The third basic cause of prejudice suggested by Simpson and Yinger (p. 50) is society itself.

> *In almost every society . . . each new generation is taught appropriate beliefs and practices regarding other groups. Prejudices are, in part, simply a portion of the cultural heritage; they are among the folkways.*

This explanation is identical to the social control theory summarized by Rose.

Simpson and Yinger (1965, p. 50) stress that all three of these factors interact: "Any specific individual, in his pattern of prejudice, almost certainly reflects all of the causes." Both they and Rose emphasize that multiple explanations are needed to account for the complexity of racial prejudice.

Personality Theories of Prejudice

In his review of the theories of prejudice, Rose discusses personality explanations. As we have seen, Simpson and Yinger cite the individual's personality needs as one basic cause of prejudice; earlier researchers considered personality *the* most important variable in the formation of bigotry. The latter attributed different types of personalities to differences in child-rearing practices, some of which were thought to produce personalities intolerant of different races and groups, whereas others helped develop racial tolerance and acceptance in the child. Else Frenkel-Brunswik (1948) and her associates conducted the pioneering research on the role of personality in the formation of prejudice.

In one of a series of studies, Frenkel-Brunswik (1948) compared the racial attitudes and personality characteristics of 1,500 children. Interviews were conducted with the subjects and their parents; both personality and attitude tests were administered. Frenkel-Brunswik concluded that there were significant differences in the personalities of prejudiced and unprejudiced children. She found that prejudiced children evidenced more rejection of out-groups, a blind acceptance of the in-group, a greater degree of aggression, and a strong rejection of persons perceived as weak. The more prejudiced children also displayed a greater resentment of the opposite sex and an admiration for strong figures. They were more willing to submit to authority, more compulsive about cleanliness, and more moralistic. The unprejudiced children were (p. 305) "more oriented toward love and less toward power than the ethnocentric child . . . and more capable of giving affection." In summarizing her study, Frenkel-Brunswik (p. 296) notes, "It was found that some children tend to reveal a stereotyped and rigid glorification of their own group and an aggressive rejection of outgroups and foreign countries."

Frenkel-Brunswik and her associates also studied the relationship between personality and prejudice in adults (Adorno et al., 1950). They concluded that certain individuals, because of their early childhood experiences, have insecure personalities and a need to dominate and to feel superior to other individuals.

These individuals possess an *authoritarian personality*, which is manifested not only in racial prejudice but also in their sexual behavior and religious and political views. The authors write (Adorno et al., p. 971):

> *The most crucial result of the present study, as it seems to the authors, is the demonstration of close correspondence in the type of approach and outlook a subject is likely to have in a great variety of areas, ranging from the most intimate features of family and sex adjustments through relationships to other people in general, to religion and to social and political philosophy. Thus a basically hierarchical, authoritarian, exploitive parent-child relationship is apt to carry over into a power-oriented, exploitively dependent attitude toward one's sex partner and one's God and may well culminate in a political philosophy and social outlook which has no room for anything but a desperate clinging to what appears to be a strong and disdainful rejection of whatever is relegated to the bottom.*

Flaws in Personality Research

Even though the research by Frenkel-Brunswik and her associates contributed greatly to the literature on the origins of prejudice, other researchers have severely criticized it because of its methodological flaws and weak theoretical base. We defer a discussion of the theory on which the research is based and review a number of its methodological weaknesses.

Simpson and Yinger (1965) have written one of the most perceptive critiques. They point out that the inadequate attention given to sampling techniques limits the generalizability of the findings. The research is also weakened by heavy reliance on the subjects' memories of childhood; the inadequate control of variables, such as education and group membership; and the low reliability of the measuring instruments. The F Scale used by the researchers measured many variables simultaneously, failing to measure well any one variable. However, Simpson and Yinger (p. 66) conclude that the flaws in the research do not substantially diminish its import. "Despite the seriousness of such methodological problems, they do not refute, in the judgment of most observers, the significance of personality research for the student of prejudice."

Other Personality Studies

Other researchers have also attempted to explain the emergence of racial prejudice as a personality variable. Lindzey (1950) studied the personalities of 22 individuals judged "high in prejudice" and 22 judged "low in prejudice." The subjects were divided into experimental and control groups. After exposing members of the experimental groups to a frustration experience, Lindzey (p. 39) concluded that the individuals high in prejudice evidenced more "frustration susceptibility—and "more overt disturbance in response to frustration than those low in minority group prejudice." The subjects high in prejudice also received higher scores on an instrument that measured "conservative nationalistic statements." Writes Lindzey (p. 33):

> *We have pointed to certain evidence in our data suggesting that the high in prejudice are more "frustratable," somewhat more aggressive, and more conforming to authority norms than the low in prejudice. Further, we have proposed that early exposure to strict norms is one means by which we might account for the behavior patterns that appear to characterize the high in prejudice in this study.*

Allport and Kramer (1946) found that the more prejudiced persons in a sample of college students maintained closer ties with their families, whereas the least prejudiced students reacted against their parents' attitudes. The former also had more negative memories of childhood, were better able to identify racial and ethnic groups, were more religious, and expressed more hostility and aggression. "From all these results," Allport and Kramer (p. 35) write, "we conclude that *prejudice is woven into the very fabric of personality* [emphasis added]. A style of life is adopted. It proceeds by rule of thumb." The subjects who reported that they had studied "scientific facts about race" in school were more often classified as "less prejudiced." However, only 8 percent of the subjects could recall studying racial facts in school.

Like Frenkel-Brunswik, Allport and Kramer believe that prejudice can be explained largely as a product of personality. However, both research teams compared extreme bigots with individuals who manifested few negative racial attitudes, whereas most people exhibit only an average amount of racial prejudice and do not have seriously disorganized personalities. Thus, there are severe limitations implicit in an exclusive personality approach to the study of prejudice.

Social Structure Theories of Prejudice

Herbert Blumer (1966) seriously questions attempts to attribute prejudice and discrimination to personality variables. He almost completely dismisses the role of attitudes in influencing behavior. Blumer asserts that the *social setting* rather than *racial attitudes* is the prime determinant of behavior. In trying to understand discrimination against minority groups, he contends that we should analyze social settings and norms instead of the personal attitudes of the individual. Blumer reviews a number of studies indicating the frequently occurring discrepancy between an individual's verbalized attitudes and actual behavior.

Saenger and Gilbert (1950) found that prejudiced individuals will patronize a racially mixed store when their desire to shop exceeds their antipathy toward African Americans. Research by Blalock (1956) suggests that discrimination is not always a correlate of racial prejudice. In certain situations, prejudiced individuals may not discriminate, since the prevailing norms may affect their behavior more than will their personal attitudes. Merton (1949) presents a useful typology for illustrating the relationship between prejudice and discrimination. He identifies four ideal-types:

1. The unprejudiced nondiscriminator.
2. The unprejudiced discriminator.
3. The prejudiced nondiscriminator.
4. The prejudiced discriminator.

Blumer (1966, pp. 112–113) summarizes an important study by Lohman and Reitzes (1952):

> *In a study of race relations in a large city . . . the same set of whites behaved entirely differently toward [African Americans] in three situations—working establishment, residential neighborhood and shopping center; no prejudice or discrimination was shown in the working establishment where the whites and [African Americans] belonged to the same labor union, whereas prejudice and discrimination toward [African Americans] by the same whites was pronounced in the case of residential neighborhood.*

Blumer seriously underestimates the role of attitudes and personality as determinants of racial discrimination and prejudice. *An adequate theory of prejudice must take into account both personality variables and the social structure.* Explaining prejudice and discrimination as totally a product of a disorganized personality ignores the facts that human beings are social beings and that their reactions in a social setting reflect not only their individual idiosyncrasies and biases but also the prevailing norms and expectations. Thus, bigoted teachers will be less inclined to manifest their true attitudes toward African American students when African American parents are visiting the room than those teachers would be inclined to do when they and the students are alone.

However, social setting alone cannot completely explain racial discrimination; neither can it, as Blumer implies, totally diminish the importance of racial attitudes. If the same bigoted teachers were transferred to an all–African American school in which there was little tolerance for racial discrimination, their behavior would probably become more consistent with the dominant norms of the new setting, but their attitudes would most likely be revealed to their students in subtle ways and perhaps affect them just as profoundly. *The most equalitarian social setting cannot cause an intense bigot to exhibit behavior identical to that of a person free of racial prejudice.*

Much of the research Blumer relies on to support his hypothesis is subject to serious criticism, particularly the study by Lohman and Reitzes (1952). These authors found that their White subjects behaved (Blumer, p. 112) *"entirely differently toward [Blacks] in different social settings"* [emphasis added] and showed "no prejudice toward them at work." However, I seriously question whether the African American factory workers would have endorsed these conclusions, believing instead that they most likely could have cited examples of discrimination directed against them by their White coworkers. It is highly unlikely that persons who are so bigoted that they would exclude African Americans from their neighborhoods could treat them with full equality at work or indeed in any other setting.

The *social setting* explanation of prejudice and discrimination presents other difficulties. In trying to explain an individual's reactions in a given situation, we must consider not only the group norms but also the importance the individual attaches to the group and setting. Research suggests that a group or situation must be important to an individual before he or she accepts its norms and values. Pearlin (1954) classified a random sample of 383 college students into "acceptors" and "rejectors" on the basis of their attitudes toward African Americans. A majority of the subjects who accepted African Americans in different situations had broken their own close family ties and developed identifications with campus groups. The more prejudiced individuals indicated that they had maintained close ties with their families and developed few associations with campus groups. Students who became more racially liberal as a result of their college experience considered college group norms more important than their parents' attitudes, whereas the more prejudiced subjects deemed family norms more important. Thus, simply placing individuals in new settings with different norms and values does not necessarily change their behavior and attitudes. Pearlin (1954, p. 50) writes:

> *These findings indicate that when a person holds membership in groups having conflicting views on an issue, his own attitudes will be influenced by the relative importance of the groups to him. Generally, in such a situation the attitudes of the individual will approximate most nearly the norms of the groups to which he most closely refers himself; . . . attitude change cannot be reckoned solely in terms of exposure to new ideas. Whether or not an individual will undergo modification of his attitude depends in large part on the nature of his relationship to groups holding the opposing sentiments and opinions.*

The social setting hypothesis also fails to consider that individuals collectively determine the group norm. Whether a group sanctions racial discrimination or racial tolerance thus depends on the attitudes of its members. Clearly, then, we must consider both individual attitudes and social norms when attempting to explain the genesis and perpetuation of racial discrimination and prejudice. The most important variables that affect the formation of racial prejudice are summarized in Figure 13.1.

Micro Approaches to Prejudice Reduction

Both personality characteristics and the social structure of institutions influence the degree to which individuals are prejudiced and the extent to which they act

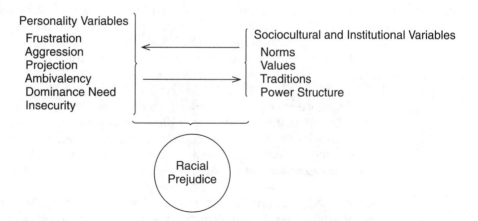

FIGURE 13.1   Variables That Cause Racial Prejudice

on their prejudices, that is, *discriminate*. However, few researchers have studied the effects of changes in social structure on the racial attitudes of students. Most researchers have examined the effects of particular components of the school, such as materials, films, interracial contact, and special units on the racial attitudes of students. It is very difficult to identify and manipulate all of the major variables within an institution, such as a school, in an experimental situation.

Studies that have been conducted using materials, interracial contact, and special units on minority groups indicate that children's racial attitudes can be modified by school experiences specifically designed for that purpose. One of the most frequently cited studies on the effects of teaching materials on children's racial attitudes is the study reported by Trager and Yarrow (1952). Their curricula had significant effects on children's racial feelings. All changes were in the expected directions. Children exposed to a democratic curriculum expressed more positive racial attitudes; those exposed to an ethnocentric curriculum developed more negative racial feelings. Trager and Yarrow summarize their study (p. 341):

> *The changes achieved in the experiment demonstrate that democratic attitudes and prejudiced attitudes can be taught to young children. The experiment contributes to an understanding of some of the important conditions which are conducive to learning attitudes. Furthermore, it is apparent that children learn prejudices not only from the larger environment but from the content of the curriculum and its value. If democratic attitudes are to be learned they must be specifically taught and experienced.*

Research by Johnson (1966) and by Litcher and Johnson (1969) confirms the Trager and Yarrow findings. Both studies support the postulate that teaching materials affect children's racial attitudes toward ethnic groups and themselves.

Johnson (1966) studied the effects of a special program in Black history on the racial attitudes and self-concepts of a group of African American children. The course had a significant effect on the boys' attitudes. However, the effect on the girls' attitudes and self-perceptions was not significant. Writes Johnson (1966, p. 129):

> *The Freedom School . . . seemed to have some effect on the boys in the areas of self attitudes, equality of Negroes and whites, attitudes toward Negroes, and attitudes toward civil rights. That is, they became more confident in themselves, more convinced that Negroes and whites are equal, more positive toward Negroes, and more militant toward civil rights.*

Litcher and Johnson (1969) investigated the effects of multiethnic readers on the racial attitudes of White elementary students. On all posttest measures, the children who had studied multiethnic as opposed to all-White readers expressed significantly more positive racial feelings toward African Americans. The authors write convincingly (p. 151): "The evidence is quite clear. Through the use of a multiethnic reader, white children developed markedly more favorable attitudes toward [African Americans]."

Katz and Zalk (1978) studied the effects of four short-term intervention techniques for modifying the racial attitudes of White elementary school children. The techniques were (1) increased positive racial contact, (2) vicarious interracial contact, (3) reinforcement of the color black, and (4) perpetual differentiation of minority group faces. The children were posttested after two weeks and again four to six months later. The authors conclude (p. 447):

> *Results revealed a significant short-term reduction in prejudice for all experimental groups on combined measures. Vicarious contact and perceptual approaches were more effective than the other two. Some interaction effects with grade and race of examiner were found. Long-term treatment effects were less pronounced, although some gains were maintained in the vicarious contact and perceptual differentiation groups.*

In a comprehensive review of the literature on changing intergroup attitudes and behaviors, Stephan (1985) concluded that several techniques and approaches are effective in reducing racial prejudice. A number of the studies he reviewed indicate that cooperation in multiethnic groups is one of the most effective ways to help students attain more positive racial attitudes. Workshops—especially when they help Whites understand the discrepancies between the reality and the ideals related to race in the United States—can help adults attain more positive racial attitudes. The use of multiethnic school curricula has resulted in the reduction of prejudice in seven studies reported by Stephan, including those by Leslie, Leslie, and Penfield (1972) and those by Yawkey and Blackwell (1974). Several studies discussed by Stephan reported that students developed more positive racial attitudes when they took the role of people from other racial groups.

Stephan (1985) derived the following thirteen tentative principles about ways to reduce prejudice:

1. Cooperation within groups should be maximized and competition between groups should be minimized.
2. Members of the in-group and the out-group should be of equal status both within and outside the contact situation.
3. Similarity of groups members on nonstatus dimensions (beliefs, values, etc.) appears to be desirable.
4. Differences in competence should be avoided.
5. The outcomes should be positive.
6. Strong normative and institutional support for the contact should be provided.
7. The intergroup contact should have the potential to extend beyond the immediate situation.
8. Individuation of group members should be promoted.
9. Nonsuperficial contact (e.g., mutual disclosure of information) should be encouraged.
10. The contact should be voluntary.
11. Positive effects are likely to correlate with the duration of the contact.
12. The contact should occur in a variety of contexts with a variety of in-group and out-group members.
13. Equal numbers of in-group and out-group members should be used.

In their important study of adolescent prejudice, Glock, Wuthnow, Piliavin, and Spencer (1975) found that youths who are cognitively sophisticated exemplify less prejudice and discrimination than do students who lack cognitive sophistication. By *cognitive sophistication* Glock et al. mean the ability to think clearly about prejudice, to reason logically about it, and to ask probing questions. They write:

> The findings suggest that the best way for the schools to combat prejudice is simply for them to do their fundamental job of education more effectively. This at least appears to be the message of the consistent finding that the most effective armor against prejudice is cognitive sophistication. Presumably, if the general level of cognitive sophistication were raised, without necessarily any specific instruction about prejudice, the incidence of prejudice would be reduced.

Although subject to the limitations of the research, a number of guidelines can be derived from the research on changing children's racial attitudes, some of which is reviewed above. The research suggests that children's racial attitudes can be modified if the school designs specific objectives and strategies for that purpose and if it increases students' cognitive sophistication. Most research studies indicate that specific instructional objectives must be clearly formulated; incidental teaching of race relations is usually not effective. Also, clearly defined teaching strategies must be structured to attain the objectives. Attitude changes induced by experimental intervention will persist through time, although there is a tendency for modified attitudes to revert to the pre-experimental ones.

However, the effects of the experimental treatment do not completely diminish. This finding suggests that intergroup education programs should not consist of one-shot treatments. *Systematic experiences must be structured to reinforce and perpetuate the desired attitudes.* Cooperative rather than competitive cross-ethnic situations should be fostered. A multicultural curriculum will enhance the possibility for students to develop more positive attitudes toward different racial and ethnic groups, as will equal-status contact situations.

Visual materials such as pictures and films greatly enhance the effectiveness of attempts to change racial attitudes (Cooper & Dinerman, 1951). Contact with minority groups does not in itself significantly affect children's racial attitudes. The prevalent attitude toward different races and groups in the social situation is the significant determinant of children's racial feelings. The attitudes and predispositions of the classroom teacher are important variables in a program designed to foster positive racial feelings (Banks, 1972). Students who are able to reason at a high level and to think critically tend to show less prejudice than do students who reason at lower levels and think less critically.

Macro Approaches to Prejudice Reduction

Most approaches to the reduction of prejudice in the schools have focused on limited factors in the school environment, such as instructional materials and cooperative learning (Slavin, 1977), and on aspects of the formalized curriculum, such as courses and increasing levels of cognitive sophistication (Gabelko & Michaelis, 1981). Although it is necessary to focus on these aspects of the school environment, this approach is clearly insufficient because the school is an interrelated social system, each part of which shapes and influences the racial attitudes and behavior of students. The social structure of institutions has a cogent impact on the racial attitudes, perceptions, and behavior of individuals. Thus, intervention designed to reduce prejudice among students should be institutional and comprehensive in nature. It is necessary to use multiethnic instructional materials to increase the cognitive sophistication of students, but to focus exclusively on instructional materials and increasing the cognitive sophistication of students is too narrow and will not substantially reduce institutional prejudice and discrimination.

To reduce prejudice, we should attempt institutional or systemic reform of the total school and try to reform all of its major aspects, including institutional norms, power relationships, the verbal interactions between teachers and students, the culture of the school, the curriculum, extracurricular activities, attitudes toward minority languages, and the counseling and testing programs. The latent or hidden values within an institution like a school often have a more cogent impact on students' attitudes and perceptions than does the formalized course of study. Educators who have worked for years in curriculum reform know that helping teachers attain new skills and then placing these teachers in an institutional environment whose norms contradict and do not support the teachers' use of those newly acquired skills frequently lead to frustration and failure. Thus, any approach to school reform that is likely to succeed must focus on each major element of the school environment identified earlier in Figure 3.4.

Prejudice among students is reinforced by many aspects of the student's environment, including the school. Cortes (1981) uses the concept of the "societal curriculum" to describe the societal factors that influence and shape students' attitudes toward different ethnic and racial groups, such as television, newspapers, and popular books.

Often the negative images of ethnic groups that children learn in the larger society are reinforced and perpetuated in the school. Rather than reinforcing children's negative feelings toward ethnic groups, the school should counteract children's negative societal experiences and help them develop more positive attitudes toward a range of ethnic and racial groups. It is not possible for the school to avoid playing a role in the ethnic education of students. This is so because many children come to school with stereotypes of different racial and ethnic groups and negative attitudes toward these groups. Either the school can do nothing deliberate to intervene in the formation of children's racial attitudes (which means that the school would unwittingly participate in the perpetuation of racial bias), or it can attempt to intervene and influence the development of children's racial attitudes in a positive direction.

To take this latter course, it is imperative that the school do more than merely devise a few units or teaching strategies to reduce prejudice and focus on the histories and cultures of ethnic groups on particular days or weeks of the school year. Specialized units and teaching strategies are clearly insufficient. Teaching about ethnic groups only at particular times may do more harm than good because these kinds of activities and rituals may reinforce the idea that ethnic groups, such as Asians and Indians, are not integral parts of their societies.

The school environment consists of both a manifest and a hidden curriculum. The manifest curriculum consists of such discernable environmental factors as curriculum guides, textbooks, bulletin boards, and lesson plans. These aspects of the school environment are important and must be reformed in order to create a school environment that promotes positive attitudes toward diverse ethnic and racial groups. However, the school's latent or hidden curriculum is often a more cogent factor than is its manifest or overt curriculum. The latent curriculum has been defined as the curriculum that no teacher explicitly teaches but that all students learn. It is the powerful part of the school experience that communicates to students the school's attitudes toward a range of issues and problems, including how the school views them as human beings and its attitudes toward diverse racial and ethnic groups.

How does the school communicate its cogent, latent messages to students? These messages are communicated to students in a number of subtle but powerful ways, including the following:

1. By the kind of verbal and nonverbal interactions teachers have with students from different racial and ethnic groups; by the kinds of statements teachers make about different ethnic groups; and by teachers' nonverbal reactions when issues related to ethnic groups are discussed in class. Research by Gay (1974), Rist (1970), and the U.S. Commission on Civil Rights (1973) indicates that teachers often have more positive verbal and nonverbal interactions with middle-class, Anglo students than with students of color and lower-class students.

2. How teachers respond to the languages and dialects of children from different ethnic and racial groups. Some research suggests that teachers are often biased against the languages and dialects of children who are members of particular ethnic and racial groups (Saville-Troike, 1981).

3. Grouping practices used in the school. Research by Mercer (1989) and Samuda (1975) indicates that members of some ethnic groups in the United States are disproportionately placed in lower ability groups because of their performance on IQ and other standardized aptitude tests that discriminate against these groups because they are normed on middle-class Anglo-Americans.

4. Power relationships in the schools. Often in schools, most of the individuals who exercise the most power belong to dominant ethnic groups. Students acquire important learning by observing which ethnic groups are represented among the administrators, teachers, secretaries, cooks, and bus drivers in the school.

5. The formalized curriculum also makes statements about the values the school has toward ethnic diversity. The ethnic groups that appear in textbooks and in other instructional material teach students which groups the school considers important and unimportant.

6. The learning styles, motivational systems, and cultures promoted by the school express many of the school's important values toward cultural differences. The educational environments of most schools are more consistent with the learning patterns and styles of mainstream students than with those of ethnic minority students, such as African Americans, Indians, and Puerto Ricans. Ramirez and Castaneda (1974) have found that Mexican American youths tend to be more field-sensitive than field-independent in their cognitive styles. Anglo-American students tend to be more field-independent. Field-sensitive and field-independent students differ in a number of characteristics and behavior. Field-sensitive students tend to work with others to achieve a common goal and are more sensitive to the feelings and opinions of other people than are field-independent students. Field-independent students prefer to work independently and to compete and gain individual recognition. Students who are field-independent are more often preferred by teachers and tend to get higher grades, although learning style is not related to IQ.

An Interdisciplinary Conceptual Curriculum

It is essential that educators take an institutional approach to school reform when intervening to reduce prejudice in students; the formalized curriculum is a vital element of the school. Hence, curriculum reform is imperative. The curriculum within a school designed to help reduce prejudice in students should be interdisciplinary, focus on higher levels of knowledge, and help students view events and situations from diverse ethnic and national perspectives.

Many ethnic studies units, activities, and programs emphasize factual learning and the deeds of ethnic heroes. These types of experiences use ethnic content but traditional teaching methods. Isolated facts about Martin Luther King do not stimulate the intellect or help students increase their levels of cognitive sophistication any more than do discrete facts about George Washington or Thomas Jefferson. The emphases in sound multicultural programs must be on *concept attainment, value analysis, decision making,* and *social action* (Banks, 1991). Facts should be used only to help students attain higher-level concepts and skills. Students need to master higher-level concepts and generalizations in order to increase their levels of cognitive sophistication.

Concepts taught in the multicultural curriculum should be selected from several disciplines and, when appropriate, be viewed from the perspectives of such disciplines and areas as the various social sciences, art, music, literature, physical education, communication, the sciences, and mathematics. It is necessary for students to view ethnic events and situations from the perspectives of several disciplines because any one discipline gives them only a partial understanding of problems related to ethnicity. When students study the concept of *culture,* they can attain a global perspective of ethnic cultures by viewing them from the perspective of the various social sciences and by examining how they are expressed in literature, music, dance, art, communication, and foods. The other curriculum areas, such as science and mathematics, can also be included in an interdisciplinary study of ethnic cultures.

Concepts such as *culture* can be used to organize interdisciplinary units and activities related to ethnicity. Other concepts, such as *communication* and *interdependence,* can also be analyzed and studied from an interdisciplinary perspective (see Figure 13.2). However, it is neither possible nor desirable to teach each concept in the curriculum from the perspectives of several disciplines and curricular areas. Such an attempt would result in artificial relationships and superficial learnings by students. However, the many excellent opportunities that exist within the curriculum for teaching concepts from an interdisciplinary perspective should be fully explored and used.

Interdisciplinary teaching requires the strong cooperation of teachers in the various content areas. Team teaching will often be necessary, especially at the high school level, to organize and implement interdisciplinary units and lessons.

The Role of the Teacher in Prejudice Reduction

Teachers are human beings who bring their own cultural perspectives, values, hopes, and dreams to the classroom. They also bring their own prejudices, stereotypes, and misconceptions (Rist, 1970). The teacher's values and perspectives

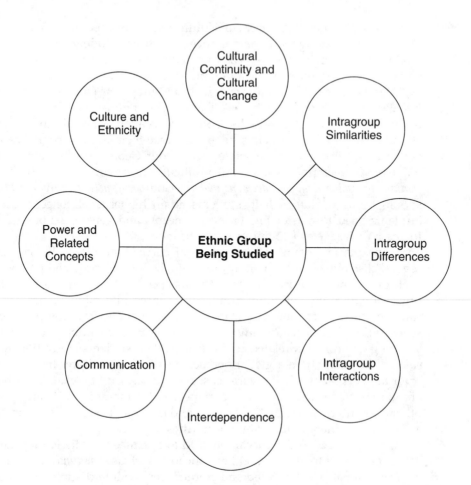

FIGURE 13.2   Interdisciplinary Concepts for Studying Ethnic Groups

mediate and interact with what they teach and influence how messages are communicated to and perceived by their students. Because the teacher mediates the messages and symbols communicated to the students through the curriculum, it is important for teachers to understand their own personal and cultural values and identities in order for them to help students from diverse racial, ethnic, and cultural groups to develop clarified identities and relate positively to each other. Research by Rubin (1967) indicates that increases in self-acceptance are associated with a reduction in prejudice.

Effective teachers in a multicultural society must have (1) democratic attitudes and values, (2) a multicultural philosophy, (3) the ability to view events and situations from diverse ethnic perspectives and points of view, (4) an understanding of the complex and multidimensional nature of ethnicity in Western societies, (5) knowledge of the stages of ethnicity and their curricular and teaching implications, and (6) the ability to function increasingly at higher stages of ethnicity. Figure 13.3 summarizes these characteristics.

Changing Teacher Attitudes and Behaviors

What can teachers do to change their racial attitudes, perceptions, and behaviors? Even though researchers have amply documented the nondemocratic attitudes and interactions teachers frequently have with students of color and low-income students, little work has been done on effective techniques that can be used to change teachers' racial attitudes and behavior. Smith (1947) concluded that the racial attitudes of adults can be significantly modified in a positive direction by contact with and involvement in minority group cultures. Bogardus (1948) found that a five-week intergroup education workshop, which consisted of lectures on

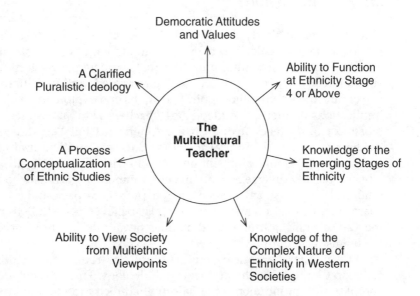

FIGURE 13.3   Characteristics of Effective Teachers in a Multicultural Society

To function effectively in ethnically pluralistic environments, the teacher must have democratic attitudes and values, a clarified pluralistic ideology, a process conceptualization of ethnic studies, the ability to view society from diverse ethnic perspectives and points of view, knowledge of the emerging stages of ethnicity, knowledge of the complex nature of ethnicity in Western societies, and the ability to function at Ethnicity Stage 4 or above. Reformed teacher-education programs should be designed to help teachers acquire these attitudes, conceptual frameworks, knowledge, and skills.

racial problems, research projects, and visits to community agencies, had a significantly positive effect on the participants' racial attitudes.

An extensive review of the research suggests that changing the racial attitudes of adults is a difficult task (Banks, 1972; Stephan, 1985) To maximize the chances for successful intervention programs, experiences must be designed specifically to change attitudes. Courses with general or global objectives are not likely to be successful. Courses that consist primarily or exclusively of lecture presentations have little impact. Diverse experiences, such as seminars, visitations, community involvement, committee work, guest speakers, films, multimedia materials, and workshops, combined with factual lectures, are more effective than is any single approach. Community involvement and cross-cultural interactions (with the appropriate norms in the social setting) are the most cogent techniques. Psychotherapy is also promising. Individuals who express moderate rather than extreme attitudes are the most likely to change. This is encouraging since few individuals exemplify extreme prejudice.

A Multicultural Philosophy

Teachers need to clarify their own philosophical positions regarding the education of students of color and to endorse an ideology consistent with the multiple acculturation and structural pluralism that characterize Western societies. Teachers should be aware of the major ideologies related to ethnic pluralism and be able to examine their own philosophical positions and explore the policy and teaching implications of alternative ideologies. Teachers with an assimilationist ideology will most likely teach a unit on the American Civil War differently than will teachers with a multicultural ideology. Effective multicultural teachers should embrace a philosophical position that will facilitate their effectiveness in culturally and racially diverse educational environments. Teachers who endorse a multicultural ideology as defined in Chapter 7 respect and value the ethnic characteristics of students of color but also believe these students need to acquire the values, skills, attitudes, and abilities needed to function successfully within the mainstream culture.

Effective teachers in the multicultural classroom must endorse what I describe in Chapter 7 as the multicultural ideology. This ideology derives from the complex and multidimensional nature of ethnicity in modern Western societies. However, because most classroom teachers were socialized within a society, schools, and teacher-education institutions that had mainstream-centric norms and were assimilationist oriented, many teachers are therefore likely to embrace an assimilationist ideology and to view pluralistic ideologies (whether weak or strong) as radical and unpatriotic. It is very difficult for individuals to change their philosophical orientations or even to question their currently held ideological beliefs. Most people have a great deal of affective and intellectual commitment to their ideological orientations and values. These ideologies are deeply held and result from years of informal and formal socialization.

Teachers should first examine their currently held ideological positions related to race and ethnicity. If they feel they need to change their ideological orientations in order to become effective multicultural teachers (the teacher who is a strong pluralist is probably as ineffective in a multicultural classroom as is the teacher who is a strong assimilationist), they should enroll in courses and seek other educational experiences related to race and ethnicity. Vicarious as well as direct experiences with other cultures, if they are open to these experiences, will help teachers examine their philosophical beliefs. The caveats about cross-cultural functioning discussed later in this chapter should be studied by teachers who seek cross-cultural experiences as a way to help them examine their philosophical beliefs. With these kinds of cross-cultural experiences, teachers will have opportunities to interact with individuals with widely differing ideologies and value positions about pluralism and race.

Teachers should also examine the *possible consequences* of embracing various philosophical beliefs. They should discuss how different philosophical orientations toward race and ethnic group life may influence their behavior in the classroom and the academic achievement and emotional growth of ethnic students. A number of researchers have observed that African American students tend to be more action-oriented and expressive in their learning styles than are Anglo-American students (Abrahams & Gay, 1972; Gay, 1978). Mexican American and Anglo youths tend to differ in their learning styles (Ramírez & Castañeda, 1974). Mexican American students also tend to be less individually competitive than are Anglo students (Vasquez, 1979). The ideological positions and commitments of teachers, whether conscious or unconscious, influence how they respond to the different cultural learning styles and characteristics of African American and Mexican American students. Teachers who are staunch assimilationists are likely to regard these different behaviors of African Americans and Mexican American students as negative and pathological characteristics that should be eradicated. Teachers who are more multicultural in their philosophical orientations are more likely to perceive these behaviors of African Americans and Mexican American students as legitimate and functional cultural behaviors that they should build on and use when planning and teaching.

Assimilationism and Mainstream-Centricism: Problems for Teachers

I am often asked in workshops what are the greatest problems teachers face when they try to plan and implement a multicultural curriculum and school environment. Are they lack of sensitive and effective multicultural teaching materials, lack of administrative support, student resistance, lack of adequate planning time, parental resistance, or some other problems? I have given this question much serious thought in the years that I have been working with teachers in multicultural education. Even though the factors mentioned are problems for many teachers who want to implement multicultural education, I do not believe they are the most difficult problems faced in multicultural teaching.

The two most serious problems faced when planning and implementing multicultural education are the strong *assimilationist ideology* many teachers have (discussed above) and their inability to view society from diverse ethnic perspectives and points of view. These problems are no doubt related to other societal problems. Many teachers, for example, might hold tenaciously to an assimilationist ideology or be unable to view their society from the perspectives of writers and social scientists of color because of racist attitudes or the fear that new ideologies and new conceptualizations of society will lead to a sharing of power by dominant and marginalized ethnic groups (see Chapter 11).

Whatever the root causes of these problems, and many reasonable hypotheses can be stated, the strong assimilationist ideology many teachers embrace and their inability to view their society from diverse ethnic perspectives are, in my view, the most difficult problems that must be overcome when the multicultural curriculum is designed and implemented.

Viewing Society from Diverse Ethnic Perspectives

Teachers need to acquire a conceptualization of their society that is based on novel assumptions and on accurate knowledge about its role and place in the world today. Textbooks, the mass media, and other parts of a nation's culture perpetuate many myths about it that are culturally encapsulating and ethnocentric. Teachers need to acquire new perspectives about the nature and development of the society and develop the ability to view it from the perspectives of ethnic groups that have historically been victimized.

I do not mean to suggest that mainstream perspectives and views on history and contemporary society should be excluded from the school curriculum. However, students can gain a sophisticated understanding of the complex nature of a society only by viewing events, situations, and concepts from the perspectives of the diverse ethnic groups that have shaped and are shaping it.

Teachers should not only be able to view society and culture from diverse ethnic perspectives and points of view, but they should also be able to teach history, science, literature, and other disciplines from the perspectives of different ethnic groups. The school and the teacher education curriculum should be organized on what I call Models C and D (see Chapter 11). In these models, students are helped to view events, concepts, and situations from the perspectives of different ethnic groups within their society as well as within other nations.

The Complex Nature of Ethnicity

Classroom teachers need a better understanding of the complex nature of ethnicity within Western societies. Misconceptions about the nature of ethnicity within Western societies are widespread among the general population, teachers, and their students. When many teachers think of an ethnic group, they think of groups of color such as African Americans and Japanese Canadians. They therefore confuse an *ethnic* group with a *racial* group. Teachers can better understand the complex nature of ethnicity if they learn to distinguish several concepts that are often confused, such as ethnic group, ethnicity, ethnic minority group, race, and culture. These concepts are defined in Chapter 5.

The Teacher and the Stages of Ethnicity

To work successfully with students from diverse ethnic backgrounds, teachers should be knowledgeable about the ethnic characteristics of their students. Students differ in their ethnic identities and characteristics just as they differ in their cognitive and affective development (Kohlberg & Mayer, 1972; Piaget, 1968). Consequently, the teacher should make some attempt to individualize multiethnic experiences for students.

These three hypothetical students might need somewhat different curricular experiences related to race and ethnicity. Juan was socialized within a rather conservative Mexican American community in the Southwest. Jessie Mae, who is African American, spent Saturday afternoons during her early years in a Black awareness school. John is an Anglo-American student who has never had any firsthand experiences with persons of color. These students are now in the same eighth-grade social studies class. The teacher is beginning a unit on race relations in the United States. Each student will need some unique experiences tailored to his or her complex and emerging ethnic identities. Chapter 12 presents a typology that outlines the basic stages of the development of ethnicity among individual members of ethnic groups that teachers can use as a guide when trying to identify the ethnic characteristics of students.

To become more effective multicultural educators, teachers should try to determine their own stage of ethnicity and become sensitive to their ethnic behaviors and characteristics. Teachers should not only try to help students function at higher stages of ethnicity but should also try to function at higher stages of ethnicity themselves. Teachers who are functioning primarily at Stages 1 and 2 cannot realistically be expected to help students develop positive racial attitudes toward different ethnic and racial groups or to help students to function at higher stages of ethnicity. Once teachers are aware of their own ethnic attitudes, behaviors, and perceptions, they can begin an action program designed to change their behavior if necessary. Such a program may consist of individual readings, taking courses at the local college or university, or participating in cross-cultural experiences either in their own or other nations.

Cross-Cultural Experiences: Problems and Promises

Teachers who plan to have cross-cultural experiences should be aware of both the problems and promises of functioning in a different culture. Functioning cross-culturally, in the final analysis, is usually rewarding and personally revealing. Because enculturation into our own cultures is primarily a subconscious process, we can learn a great deal about our norms, values, behaviors, and perceptions by functioning in other cultural environments.

To acquire the maximum benefits from cross-cultural functioning, individuals must be able to interpret their experiences accurately and develop a sophisticated level of *cross-cultural awareness.* Despite its positive long-range outcomes, individuals functioning within another culture frequently experience cultural shock and confusion and make embarrassing cultural mistakes. All individuals are likely to experience cultural shock during their first experiences in another culture. The greater the differences between the new culture and their own ethnic and/or national culture, the greater the cultural shock individuals are likely to experience.

Americans can experience cultural shock within ethnic cultures in their nation as well as in other nations. Anglo-Americans who have had few experiences with African American culture and have not traveled outside the United States are likely to experience cultural shock when they first visit a traditional Black Baptist Church as well as when they first visit a nation such as Mexico.

Some preparation before experiencing another culture may help reduce cultural shock and enable the individual to function more successfully within it. Such preparation may consist of readings, (especially literary works because literature often conveys the nuances and subtleties of a culture), viewing films, and interacting with individuals socialized within the culture. However, no amount of preparation will totally eliminate cultural shock and cultural mistakes during an individual's first experience with a culture. If teachers are knowledgeable about the rewards as well as the problems of cross-cultural functioning, they will be better able to interpret their cross-cultural experiences accurately and will therefore benefit more from them in the long run.

Hypotheses Regarding Cross-Cultural Behavior

I have developed some hypotheses regarding cross-cultural behavior based on my own functioning in other cultures (such as Guam, Mexico, Japan, and the United Kingdom, and different ethnic cultures within the United States), on my observations of and conversations with other individuals who have functioned cross-culturally, and on my reading of the literature related to cross-cultural functioning (Stewart, 1972). These hypotheses should be helpful to individuals who are planning cross-cultural experiences and to those who are trying to interpret their cross-cultural interactions and behavior or the cross-cultural behaviors of others.

- The weaker the ethnic boundaries are between ethnic cultures, the more likely cross-cultural functioning will occur between these cultures.
- The weaker the ethnic boundaries between ethnic cultures, the easier cross-cultural functioning will be for individuals in those cultures. Individuals who

have weak ethnic cultural characteristics and ethnic identities are more likely to participate in cross-cultural behavior than are individuals with strong ethnic characteristics and ethnic identities.

- Psychological discomforts and confusion are so potentially high in cross-cultural functioning that cross-cultural behavior will occur only when motivation is high for functioning cross-culturally and the potential rewards are substantial.

- Subethnic boundaries (within an ethnic group) are often distinct and tight. Consequently, individuals who are socialized within one subethnic culture may experience problems and conflicts when functioning within another subethnic culture within his or her ethnic group.

- As an individual becomes more competent in functioning within an outside ethnic culture, his or her personal ethnicity and ethnic behavior changes and/or reduces in intensity.

- The response to the individual who is functioning cross-culturally by the outside ethnic group influences the depth and nature of his or her cross-cultural behavior and his or her psychological interpretation of his or her cross-cultural behavior.

Summary

Major goals of the multicultural curriculum should be to reduce prejudice and to help students acquire more democratic racial attitudes and values. Racial incidents in which negative racial attitudes were blatantly and sometimes violently expressed increased in the major Western nations such as the United Kingdom, the United States, and Canada in the late 1980s and the early 1990s. Racial incidents on college and university campuses in the United States attracted national attention. The schools in Western societies need to act decisively to help students acquire more democratic attitudes and values.

This chapter critically discusses theories that explain the causes of prejudice. Various theories focus on the personality of the individual, on group norms, and on the social structure as the primary cause of prejudice. A comprehensive theory that incorporates each variable is needed to explain the complex nature of prejudice in contemporary societies.

Research reviewed in this chapter suggests that the school can help students become less prejudiced and acquire more democratic attitudes and values. However, instruction must be designed specifically for this purpose and must take place in a social environment that has a number of identifiable characteristics, including the promotion of cooperation rather than competition, a multicultural curriculum, and situations in which students experience equal status. The teacher is an important variable in a curriculum that fosters democratic attitudes and values. The final part of this chapter describes the characteristics of the effective teacher in a multicultural society.

References

Abrahams, R. D., & Gay, G. (1972). Black Culture in the Classroom. In R. D. Abrahams & R. C. Troike (Eds.), *Language and Cultural Diversity in American Education* (pp. 67–84). Englewood Cliffs, NJ.: Prentice-Hall.

Adorno, T. W., Frenkel-Brunswik, E., Levinson, D. J., & Sanford, R. N. (1950). *The Authoritarian Personality.* New York: Harper and Row.

Allport, G., & Kramer, B. (1946). Some Roots of Prejudice. *The Journal of Psychology, 22,* 9–39.

Banks, J. A. (1972). Racial Prejudice and the Black Self-Concept. In J. A. Banks and J. D. Grambs (Eds.), *Black Self-Concept: Implications for Education and Social Science* (pp. 5–35). New York: McGraw-Hill.

Banks, J. A. (1991). *Teaching Strategies for Ethnic Studies* (5th ed.). Boston: Allyn and Bacon.

Blalock, H. (1956). Economic Discrimination and Negro Increase. *American Sociological Review, 21,* 584–588.

Blumer, H. (1966). United States of America. In *Research on Racial Relations* (pp. 87–133). New York: Unesco.

Bogardus, E. S. (1948). The Intercultural Workshop and Racial Distance. *Sociology and Social Research, 32,* 798–802.

Cooper, E., & Dinerman, H. (1951). Analysis of the Film 'Don't Be a Sucker': A Study of Communication. *Public Opinion Quarterly, 15,* 243–264.

Cortes, C. E. (1981). The Societal Curriculum: Implications for Multiethnic Education. In J. A. Banks (Ed.), *Education in the 80s: Multiethnic Education* (pp. 24–32). Washington, DC: National Education Association.

Frenkel-Brunswik, E. (1948). A Study of Prejudice in Children. *Human Relations, 1,* 295–306.

Gabelko, N., & Michaelis, J. U. (1981). *Reducing Adolescent Prejudice: A Handbook.* New York: Teachers College Press.

Gay, G. (1974). *Differential Dyadic Interactions of Black and White Teachers with Black and White Pupils in Recently Desegregated Social Studies Classrooms: A Function of Teacher and Pupil Ethnicity.* Washington, DC: National Institute of Education.

Gay, G. (1978). Viewing the Pluralistic Classroom as a Cultural Microcosm. *Educational Research Quarterly, 2,* 45–59.

Glock, C., Wuthnow, R., Piliavin, J. A., & Spencer, M. (1975). *Adolescent Prejudice.* New York: Harper and Row.

Harley, D. (1968). Prejudice in Whites. Unpublished paper, Michigan State University.

Johnson, D. W. (1966). Freedom School Effectiveness: Changes in Attitudes of Negro Children. *The Journal of Applied Behavioral Science, 2,* 325–330.

Katz, P., & Zalk, S. R. (1978). Modification of Children's Racial Attitudes. *Developmental Psychology, 14,* 447–461.

Kohlberg, L., & Mayer, R. (1972). Development as the Aim of Education. *Harvard Educational Review, 42,* 449–496.

Leslie, L. L., Leslie, J. W., & Penfield, D. A. (1972). The Effects of a Student Centered Special Curriculum upon the Racial Attitudes of Sixth Graders. *Journal of Experimental Education, 41,* 63–67.

Lindzey, G. (1950). Differences between High and Low in Prejudice and their Implications for the Theory of Prejudice. *Personality, 19,* 16–40.

Litcher, J., & Johnson, D. (1969). Changes in Attitudes toward Negroes of White Elementary School Students after Use of Multiethnic Readers. *Journal of Educational Psychology, 60,* 148–152.

Lohman, J., & Reitzes, D. C. (1952). Note on Race Relations in Mass Society. *American Journal of Sociology, 58,* 241–246.

Mercer, J. R. (1989). Testing and Assessment Practices in Multiethnic Education. In J. A. Banks (Ed.), *Education in the 80's: Multiethnic Education* (pp. 93–104). Washington, DC: National Education Association.

Merton, R. K. (1949). Discrimination and the American Creed. In R. M. MacIver (Ed.),

Discrimination and the National Welfare (pp. 99–126). New York: Harper and Row.

Pearlin, L. I. (1954). Shifting Group Attachments and Attitudes toward Negroes. *Social Forces, 33*, 41–47.

Piaget, J. (1968). Six *Psychological Studies*. New York: Random House.

Ramirez, M. III, & Castaneda, A. (1974). *Cultural Democracy, Bicognitive Development and Education*. New York: Academic Press.

Rist, R. C. (1970). Student Social Class and Teacher Expectations: The Self-Fulfilling Prophecy in Ghetto Education. *Harvard Educational Review, 40*, 411–451.

Rose, A. (1962). The Causes of Prejudice. In M. L. Barron (Ed.), *American Cultural Minorities. A Textbook in Intergroup Relations.* New York: Alfred A. Knopf.

Rubin, I. (1967). The Reduction of Prejudice through Laboratory Training. *Journal of Applied Behavioral Science, 3*, 29–50.

Saenger, G., & Gilbert, E. (1950). Customer Reactions to Integration of Negro Sales Personnel. *International Journal of Opinion and Attitude Research, 4*, 57–76.

Samuda, R. J. (1975). *Psychological Testing of American Minorities.* New York: Dodd, Mead.

Saville-Troike, M. (1981). Language Diversity in Multiethnic Education. In J. A. Banks (Ed.), *Education in the 80s: Multiethnic Education* (pp. 72–81). Washington, DC: National Education Association.

Simpson, G. E, & Yinger, J. M. (1965). *Racial and Cultural Minorities.* New York: Harper and Row.

Simpson, G. E., & Yinger, J. M. (1985). *Racial and Cultural Minorities: An Analysis of Prejudice and Discrimination* (5th ed.). New York: Plenum Press.

Slavin, R. (1977). How Student Learning Teams Can Integrate the Desegregated Classroom. *Integrated Education, 15*, 56–58.

Smith, F. T. (1947). An Experiment in Modifying Attitudes toward the Negro. Summarized in A. M. Rose, *Studies in the Reduction of Prejudice* (p. 9). Chicago: American Council on Race Relations.

Stephan, W. G. (1985). Intergroup Relations. In G. Lindzey & E. Aronson (Eds.), *The Handbook of Social Psychology*, Vol. 2 (3rd ed.) (pp. 599–658). Hillsdale, NJ.: Lawrence Erlbaum Associates.

Stewart, E. C. (1972). *American Cultural Patterns: A Cross-Cultural Perspective.* LaGrange Park, IL: Intercultural Network.

Trager, H. G., & Yarrow, M. R. (1952). *They Learn What They Live*. New York: Harper.

U.S. Commission on Civil Rights, (1973). *Teachers and Students. Differences in Teacher Interaction with Mexican American and Anglo Students.* Washington, DC: U.S. Government Printing Office.

Vasquez, J. A. (1979). Bilingual Education's Needed Third Dimension. *Educational Leadership, 38*, 166–168.

Yawkey, T. D., & Blackwell, J. (1974). Attitudes of 4-year-old Urban Black Children toward Themselves and Whites Based upon Multiethnic Social Studies Materials and Experiences. *Journal of Educational Research, 67*, 373–377.

Chapter 14

Language, Ethnicity, and Education

All teachers teach language. In the United States, teachers teach the full range of school-English language arts on a daily basis. Yet, most teachers rarely think of themselves as language teachers. They go about their daily classroom activities encouraging students to listen, follow directions, take good notes, and to think before speaking or writing. Communicating, thinking, and knowing are universal instructional aims taught through the medium of the English language. This is as it should be—the better the students use the English language, the better they know, think, and communicate. And, if all students were fully literate in school-English, there would be little need for most of this chapter. The reality is that we live in a multilingual society.

Many students enter school speaking a non-English language or a dialect of American English. These students are variously described as linguistically different, linguistic minorities, bilingual, bidialectal, or as LEP, the federal government's term for students who are "limited-English proficient." Being linguistically different involves more than merely speaking a foreign language or a different English dialect. Speaking a language or dialect links one to particular ethnic and cultural groups that hold values and attitudes that may or may not conflict with the prevailing values and attitudes held by teachers and other people in a school's community. Whether student's prefer "ain't" over "isn't" is inconsequential. No one is too concerned if a student speaks with a Hoosier twang. Or, if a student from Boston says "Cuba" as though it were pronounced "Cuber," no one seems to worry about the mispronunciation. But if an African American student prefers to say "I be sick" rather than "I am sick," or if a

This chapter is contributed by Ricardo L. Garcia, College of Education, University of Idaho, Moscow, Idaho.

Hispanic student pronounces "sit" as though it were "seat," then concern about the student's purported language deficiencies emerge.

Some differences are not innocuous, especially if they cause communication breakdowns between teachers and students. Problems for both teachers and students arise when the classroom communication system—couched in the culture reflected by speakers of school-English—conflicts with the student's communication system. Subtle but potent instances of miscommunication can lead to larger problems of student alienation, discontent, and academic failure. In effect, students who experience communicative conflict may retreat or withdraw from the school's society.

The Relationship between Language and National Policy

Does linguistic diversity impede national cohesion? Is it possible to have a nation when everyone speaks a different language, as in the *Old Testament*'s Tower of Babel? Nationalism and ethnicity are similar group phenomena. Both involve group identity, a sense of peoplehood, and an interdependence of fates, requiring allegiance to some group. At times, the two phenomena conflict. Countries throughout the world have had to deal with the issue of how to build national unity while allowing ethnic group diversity. If ethnic groups are given too much autonomy, national unity is threatened; if ethnic groups are suppressed too much, then ethnic group dissent emerges, again threatening national cohesion.

Central to a nation's development of nationalism is the designation of an official language. An official language serves the functions of political and psychological integration on a national scope. A nation's official language(s) embodies, carries, and conveys the nation's symbols. National anthems, slogans, and oaths of allegiance in the national language(s) meld a nation's spirit. The national language(s) act as the political unification agent and communication medium among the nation's citizens.

Most nations have one or more languages stipulated as their official language(s). Some nations, such as France, have an official language regulated by a language academy. Other nations have an official bilingual policy, such as Canada, allowing for English and French to coexist as official languages. Some nations (India and Russia, for example) have one official language that is used nationally and allow regional languages and dialects to be used and taught within their respective regions. Due to the centrality of language to nationalism, the selection as to which language or languages to use in a nation's school as the medium(s) of instruction is a critical national decision.

Language Policy in the United States

The United States has no official legal language policy; it has an informal national standard, American English. Social customs and usages, rather than governmental agencies, tend to regulate languages in the United States. Non-English languages are allowed in public documents and institutions; their use is limited by varying state laws. To a great extent the United States is still an English-centric language nation. Non-English languages are considered foreign languages. Even the languages indigenous to the United States, the languages of Native Americans, are viewed as foreign by some people in the United States.

Within the United States, some ethnic groups developed dual or multiple dialects of English. Almost everyone in U.S. society is somewhat bidialectal in the sense that everyone speaks their individual idiolects as well as a group dialect. However, here the term *bidialectalism* is used to mean the ability to speak two distinctively different American English regional or cultural group dialects. For example, as a group, African Americans speak the Black English dialect as well as standard English. However, not all African Americans speak Black English.

Some groups developed bilingual abilities. *Bilingualism* is used here to mean the ability to speak with two distinctively different language systems, such as Spanish and English, or German and English. At one time, German Americans were the most literate bilinguals in the United States. Bilingual German newspapers, periodicals, radio programs, and books attested to a high level of German-English bilingualism (Fishman, 1966). However, the anti-Germanic feelings sparked by World War I and inflamed by World War II with Germany substantially doused German-English bilingualism. Currently, Puerto Ricans, as a group, speak Spanish and English. In Puerto Rico, Spanish is considered the native language, but a speaking knowledge of U.S. English is required for high school graduation.

Again, as with bidialectalism, not all members of a group need to be bilingual for the group to be considered bilingual. In the above illustration, Puerto Ricans as a group are Spanish-English bilingual, but not all Puerto Ricans are bilingual. The level of bilingualism varies within different bilingual groups. Some groups, such as many Native American tribes, are attempting to restore their native language. Other groups (e.g., Greek Americans) are working diligently to teach their youth the native language. Other groups use two languages for daily transactions (e.g., Chinese Americans and Cuban Americans).

More than 25 European languages are spoken in the United States. Some of these languages are Spanish, Italian, German, Polish, French, Yiddish, Russian, Swedish, Hungarian, and Norwegian. Add these languages to the Asian and Middle Eastern languages now spoken as well as the historically spoken Native American languages, and it is obvious that the United States is multilingual. The most recent additions are the languages of the Hmong, Vietnamese, Laotian, Cambodian, and ethnic Chinese people. Referred to as *Indochinese*, these people come from an area of the world that is culturally diverse. In Laos, Cambodia, and Vietnam at least 20 languages are spoken.

It is important that Indochinese peoples be recognized as culturally diverse. They should not be lumped together as a single group. What they have in common is that they are refugees in an industrialized Western nation and have relocated from Asia to the United States. More than these few words are necessary to describe these new groups. Curriculum materials describing their language and cultural characteristics have been developed (Center for Applied Linguistics, 1981; Whitemore, 1979).

The languages cited here are evidence of linguistic pluralism, a legacy that permeates the development of language policy in the United States (Ferguson & Heath, 1981; Fishman, 1966; Laird, 1970). Through social, economic, and political forces, American English was established as the nation's common language. Yet, the Constitution provided religious freedom, which fostered religious pluralism and the notion that the United States was a diversified nation. As immigrants settled in urban and rural parts of the United States they often adhered to their native religions, cultures, and languages. Neighborhoods in cities thus became ethnic enclaves, providing the individual a buffer zone that eased assimilation into the new culture. Often small settlements evolved into villages and towns peopled by one or several ethnic groups. In the urban enclaves and rural settlements, native, non-English languages were used in business affairs, schools, and religious institutions.

Government interference in language planning was minimal during the nation's beginning stages. Thomas Jefferson believed the mark of an educated person was bilingualism. He taught himself Spanish and spoke French. Benjamin Franklin, however, decried the use of German by so many Pennsylvania residents. He feared that German might supplant English as the nation's language. Yet, he assisted the development of Pennsylvania's German language schools. John Adams proposed the establishment of English as the nation's official language with a national academy to regulate and standardize English. The proposal was rejected by Congress as antidemocratic (Heath, 1981). Noah Webster's dictionaries and spellers attempted to regulate and standardize American English. His efforts, along with the efforts of other lexicographers, did much to standardize American English spelling but did not result in making English the nation's official language (Laird, 1970).

By the middle 1800s a bilingual tradition existed in schools. As the public school movement spread, so did the idea that local communities could conduct school in their native languages, especially since the antecedent schools—the religious schools—had taught native religions, cultures, and languages. Also, to encourage immigrant parents to place their children in school rather than the workplace, some public schools ensured that the home language and culture would be taught in the public schools. School districts in Milwaukee, New York, St. Louis, and Cleveland provided native language and, sometimes, bilingual instruction in elementary grades as recruitment inducements (Zeydel, 1964). Through the Civil War a govermental noninterference attitude prevailed, accommodating linguistic pluralism and often encouraging public school attendance. After the Civil War era and into the era of the Industrial Revolution, the need for a common language emerged to conduct business and governmental affairs. English language ethnocentrism began to prevail.

English language ethnocentrism started as a matter of practicality. Participation in civic affairs necessitated English literacy. Most state laws, government documents, and government affairs were conducted in English. This fact required a speaking and reading knowledge of English. Also, in business and industry, non-English speakers were seriously in danger at the workplace. Unable to read the safety procedures written in English, or unable to understand warnings shouted in English, the non-English-speaking workers were often injured on the job. Consequently, knowing how to speak, read, and write in English became necessary for civic participation, upward mobility, and economic success. Events between 1890 and 1920 added a new dimension to the importance of English literacy. Knowledge of English evolved into a national imperative: it became proof that one was a loyal American (Cubberly, 1909).

The national origins of European immigrants to the United States had changed substantially by 1896. Before 1812 most European immigrants to the United States came from Northern and Western Europe, primarily from Britain, Germany, France, Sweden, Norway, the Netherlands, and Switzerland. Between 1890 and 1920 the overwhelming majority came from Southern and Eastern Europe, primarily from the Balkan countries, Italy, Russia, and Poland (Handlin, 1959). These immigrants were viewed with distrust by many old immigrant citizens. The new immigrants were predominantly Jewish or Catholic; they represented diverse political traditions—monarchies, dictatorships, and democracies. The reaction to the demographic shift was xenophobia (Handlin, 1959). The fear arose that these new immigrants would not melt into the melting pot and would not be loyal to the traditional ways of the old immigrants.

The xenophobia was founded on the labor unrest during this time when the United States was industrializing. Labor leaders were often portrayed as agitators or anarchists bent on the overthrow of democratic traditions and the free enterprise system. The xenophobia was exacerbated by racist perceptions about the new immigrants. Europeans from Southern and Eastern Europe were considered genetically and culturally inferior to the older immigrants. The xenophobic flame was later fueled as war with Germany seemed imminent and relations with Japan and China worsened. Xenophobia reached its peak immediately following World War I, when German-American language and cultural activities (including parochial schools, magazines, and lodge meetings) and Chinese and Japanese immigration were curtailed.

Attempts to quell the xenophobia culminated in bills requiring immigrants to learn English as a condition for citizenship (Liebowitz, 1976). At this time, American English became the country's unofficial national language. The Nationality Act of 1906 required immigrants to speak English as a prerequisite for naturalization. The English requirement remained in force in the Nationality Act of 1940. In the Internal Security Act of 1950 the law was extended to include English reading and writing.

The public schools of the middle 1800s tolerated, at times even nurtured, the immigrant student's native language and culture. In states such as Wisconsin, many communities conducted all instruction in students' native languages, especially in private schools. As xenophobia increased the desire to forge a national identity based on the English language and Anglo-Saxon culture, the public schools shifted toward the Americanization and assimilation of non-English-speaking immigrants. The transformation started with state laws stipulating that certain school subjects be taught in English. The Bennett Law, passed in 1889 in Wisconsin, stipulated an English-only requirement in certain subjects (Jorgenson, 1956). The law's major intents were to control child labor and to provide compulsory school attendance. But the law's English-only requirement meant that the German parochial schools would have to change their medium of instruction from German to English. Also, the local public school officials resented the loss of local control—they would be under greater scrutiny by the state. The Bennett Act was summarily repealed in 1891 due to the strong reactions against it. Nonetheless, the stage was set for the English-only laws.

The intent of the English-only laws was to ensure English literacy for the multilingual, immigrant populations as part of the Americanization process. Often the laws were applied to the private and parochial schools. The English-only laws were directed toward the German-American schools, which consisted of a wide network of bilingual (elementary) and second language (secondary) programs in parochial, private, and public schools. For example, in 1914, at least one-third of the elementary students in the Milwaukee, Cincinnati, Cleveland, and Dayton public school districts were in bilingual (German/English) classrooms (Zeydel, 1964). Between 1917 and 1919, however, when the United States was at war with Germany, the German/English bilingual programs, along with many of the secondary-level German programs, were drastically reduced; practically speaking, the bilingual programs were eliminated. The English-only laws also stopped bilingual instruction in other languages, including Swedish, Norwegian, Danish, Dutch, Polish, French, Czech, and Spanish (Ovando & Collier, 1985).

The laws often prohibited the teaching of a foreign language (Geffert et al., 1975). The anti-foreign-language part of Nebraska's English-only law was challenged at the state level—where the law was left intact—and then at the U.S. Supreme Court in *Meyer* v. *Nebraska*. The Meyer decision ruled that the Nebraska statutory prohibition against teaching a foreign language in grades lower than ninth grade in religious schools limited the student's right to learn and the parents' right to control what their children would study. The intent of the statute was (Reutter & Hamilton, 1970, p. 110) "to promote civic development by inhibiting training of the immature in foreign tongues and ideas before they could learn English and acquire American ideals." The Nebraska law's intent was to use the schools as an agent for Americanization and assimilation. The *Meyer* decision left intact former court rulings that the state could require English-only instruction in publicly funded schools.

The English-only laws remained in effect until the civil rights movement of the 1960s. Before the civil rights movment, the English-only laws were enforced to promote the assimilation of linguistic minorities in the Southwestern states (U.S. Commission on Civil Rights, 1970), where large populations of linguistic minorities resided, as well as in Indian boarding schools operated by the Bureau of Indian Affairs (Prucha, 1975).

Although the anti-foreign-language laws of the 1920s were deemed unconstitutional, the laws precipitated a tradition of excluding foreign languages from the elementary public school curriculum. During the middle 1950s foreign language programs were included in the elementary grades. By the 1959–1960 school year, approximately 8,000 elementary schools offered FLES (Foreign Languages for Elementary Students) programs (Zeydel, 1964). The FLES programs relied heavily on federal funds provided by the National Defense Education Act (NDEA). When federal funding ended, the public schools tried to continue the FLES programs. Primarily for financial reasons the programs did not maintain their initial thrusts, and by slow degrees they were discontinued. Few, if any, existed in the 1970s.

During the late 1980s, in response to the geopolitical climate and the recognized need to teach students the languages and cultures of other countries, foreign langauge education programs emerged in some elementary schools. At least 35 cities in the United States offered elementary foreign language education programs during the 1992–1993 school year. Cities included Culver City and San Diego, California; Forth Worth; Baton Rouge; Tulsa; Milwaukee; Washington, D.C.; and Eugene, Oregon (Harvard University Press, 1985; Rhodes & Schreibstein, 1983).

During the 1980s two language political interest group formed, U.S. English, and English Plus. The U.S. English group advocated English as the nation's official language based on a philosophy that English is the nation's common language and should be the primary language of government. The group lobbied for federal and state laws that would eliminate the use of any languages other than English in all public and private sectors. The Arizona law it promoted, for example, would have prohibited the use of any language other than English by government workers at all times, even during their lunch hours. The law was declared unconstitutional by a federal court as a violation of First Amendment rights.

By March 1993 15 states had either amended their constitutions or enacted statutes making English their official language. Georgia enacted an English-only resolution that has the effect of law. Hawaii's law makes Native Hawaiian coequal to English as its official languages. Table 14.1 lists the states for which English is the official language (Joint Committee for Languages, 1992).

The U.S. English group also lobbied for a joint resolution in the U.S. Congress that would have made English the nation's official language. The SJ Resolution #20 proposed that the Constitution to be amended to read:

1. The English language shall be the official language of the United States;
2. The Congress shall have the power to enforce this article by appropriate legislation. (U.S. Government Printing Office, 1985, p. E2046–E2047)

By March 1993, the resolution languished in Congressional subcommittees and had not been acted on by either house.

TABLE 14.1   States in Which English Is the Offical Language

State	Year	Legislation
Alabama	1990	CA
Arkansas	1987	ST
California	1986	CA
Colorado	1988	CA
Florida	1988	CA
Georgia	1986	RE
Hawaii	1978	CA
Illinois	1969	ST
Indiana	1984	ST
Kentucky	1984	ST
Mississippi	1987	ST
Nebraska	1923	CA
N. Carolina	1987	ST
N. Dakota	1987	ST
S. Carolina	1987	ST
Tennessee	1984	ST
Virginia	1981	ST

*Code: CA = Constitutional Amendment
    RE = Resolution
    ST = Statute

Based on information in "1990 English Only Legislation." In *EPIC Events.* Vol. 3, No. 1 (March/April, 1990), p. 4. Newsletter of the English Plus Information Clearinghouse. Used with permission.

The English Plus group (National Council for Languages and International Studies, 1992. p. 1) advocated linguistic pluralism:

We hold that all persons in our culturally rich and linguistically diverse nation should be provided the opportunity and be encouraged to become proficient in more than one language.

The group advocated laws to foster educational programs that offer opportunities to learn a second language and develop cultural sensitivity. The Joint National Committee for Languages (JNCL) provided the group a forum for discussion and cooperation with language professionals. JNCL consists of 36 language associations that encompass most areas of the language profession, including the major and less commonly taught languages as well as English, English as a Second Language, bilingual education, and the classics. JNCL's political arm, the National Council for Languages and International Studies, lobbies Congress and state legislatures in an effort to facilitate laws that will provide funds for second-language education programs.

As opponents of the English-only laws, the English Plus group argues that bilingualism, especially when used in educational programs, emergency services, and ballots, greatly helps non-English speakers make the transititon from their native language to English. Further, the group argues, bilingualism is necessary in educational and other social service agencies to help with assimilation; otherwise, non-English speaking citizens and residents would be alienated from participation in public affairs, thereby posing a threat to national solidarity (Shumway, 1986).

As proponents of English-only laws, the U.S. English group argues that bilingualism is inimical to national solidarity. Using Canada as an example, the group argues that bilingualism fosters English illiteracy among immigrants and native non-English speakers, thereby making assimilation difficult for the non-English speakers (Torres, 1986).

Our language policies and practices are now at a crossroads. The two advocacy groups, U.S. English and English Plus, exemplify the second-language ambivalence held by people in the United States as the legacies of linguistic pluralism and English language ethnocentrism battle for political support of their causes. Given the perspective of more than 200 years of U.S. history, it is easy to understand English language ethnocentrism. During the eighteenth and nineteenth centuries the United States was in search of a clear self-identity and national cohesion, separate from the powerful European empires of England, Spain, and France. By embracing American English as its language, the country could develop its self-identity and provide national cohesion for the affairs of business, industry, government, and education.

Now, during the last decade of the twentieth century, the nation has matured. It has survived a Civil War, two World Wars, numerous political actions (undeclared wars), a major economic depression, and many recessions. The nation's self-identity has emerged clearly, operating on the principles of democratic institutions and free-market economies with a culturally and linguisitically diverse population in which the overwhelming majority of its citizens consider English the nation's lingua franca. A national policy of English language ethnocentrism is no longer justifiable and is inimical to the nation's future status as a participant in the global community. We are being nudged toward a policy of linguistic pluralism.

Equal Educational Opportunity and Language Programs

The federal government has formulated equal educational opportunity policies that focus on language education programs. Particularly the Bilingual Education Act and the U.S. District Court decisions, *Lau* v. *Nichols* and *School Children* v. *Ann Arbor School Board*, explicitly established policies that impact public school language instruction.

In 1968, Public Law 90–247, The Bilingual Education Act, was enacted. The Bilingual Education Act, the seventh amendment to the Elementary and Secondary Education Act of 1965 (Title VII), declared that it was (Geffert et al., 1975, pp. 121–123) *to be the policy of the United States to provide financial assistance to local education agencies to develop and carry out new and imaginative elementary and secondary school programs designed to meet the special education needs . . . [of] children who come from environments where the dominant language is other than English.*

The act stipulated it would be the policy of the U.S. government to assist financially in the development and implementation of bilingual education programs in U.S. public schools and trust territories.

In 1973, the act was changed to the Comprehensive Bilingual Education Amendment Act of 1973. The act was extended for training bilingual teachers and bilingual teacher trainers. The act's policy recognized that (1) large numbers of children have limited English-speaking ability, (2) many of these children have a cultural heritage that differs from that of English-speaking people, and (3) a primary means by which a child learns is through using language and cultural heritage. The act provided financial assistance for extending and improving existing bilingual-bicultural programs in public schools, for improving resource and dissemination centers, and for developing and publishing bilingual-bicultural curriculum materials. Assistance was also provided for stipends and fellowships so that teachers and teacher-educators could be trained in bilingual-bicultural methodology.

A major catalyst for bilingual instruction was the Supreme Court ruling of *Lau* v. *Nichols* that provisions for the same teachers, programs, and textbooks in the same language for all students in the San Francisco school district did not provide equal educational opportunity when the native language of a sizable number of the student body was not English. In part, the ruling held (*Lau v. Nichols*, 1974, p. 563).

There is no equality of treatment merely by providing students with the same facilities, textbooks, teachers, and curriculum; for students who do not understand English are effectively foreclosed from any meaningful education. . . . Where inability to speak and understand the English language excludes national origin-minority group children from effective participation in the education program offered by a school district, the district must take affirmative steps to rectify the language deficiency in order to open its instructional program to these students.

The ruling did not mandate bilingual instruction for non-English-speaking students, but it did stipulate that special educational programs were necessary if schools were to provide equal educational opportunity for such students.

Equal educational opportunity policy regarding speakers of Black English has been formulated. The policy was precipitated by the District Court ruling in *Martin Luther King Jr. Elementary School* v. *Ann Arbor School District* in 1979. A case was made for students who speak Black English, Black vernacular, or Black dialect as a home and community language. The plaintiffs argued that language differences impeded the equal participation of the African American students in the school's instructional program because the instructional program was conducted entirely in the standard school English dialect. Using linguistic and educational research evidence, the lawyers for the students established (Martin Luther King, Jr., 1979, p. 71861)

> *that unless those instructing in reading recognize (1) the existence of a home language used by the children in their own community for much of their non-school communications, and (2) that this home language may be a cause of the superficial difficulties in speaking standard English, great harm will be done. The child may withdraw or may act out frustrations and may not learn to read. A language barrier develops when teachers, in helping the child to switch from the home ("Black English") language to standard English, refuse to admit the existence of a language that is the acceptable way of talking in his local community.*

Therefore, the court ruled to require the defendant board to take steps to help its teachers recognize the home language of the students and to use that knowledge in their attempts to teach reading skills in standard English.

Language and Dialect

As children grow they develop a dialect spoken by their parents and immediate family. A dialect is a variation of an idealized language model; that is, a dialect is a valid communication medium that contains its own rules of logic and grammar (Labov, 1970). In the United States, most people speak a dialect of standard American English, which is the idealized version of the English language within the United States. (Of course, for some people in the United States, English is not the first dialect.) Standard American English is perceived to be the language's grammatical rules taught in the U.S. public schools and the usage used by journalists, television newscasters, and the educated populace. However, even though teachers and journalists write in standard American English, they nonetheless speak in a dialect of English.

The point is that language and dialect are not the same. A language is an idealized model for communication; dialect is a real speech and grammatical system a group uses for communication. Swiss linguist Ferdinand Saussure called the former *langue* (language) and the latter *parole* (dialect).

American English

The *langue* of United States society is the so-called standard English; its *parole* consists of at least four distinctively different dialects: Black English, Eastern

English, general American, and Southern English. The dialects are mutually intelligible, but they do differ in intonations and vocabulary. The latter three dialects are diverse; Eastern English is divided into three subdialects, as is the Southern dialect; the general American dialect is a conglomeration of all remaining United States English dialects spoken in the Midwest, Southwest, Far West, and Northwest. The three dialects differ primarily in vocabulary, intonation, and idioms; they are mutually intelligible, and their grammatical systems do not differ significantly (Edwards, 1976; Marckwardt, 1974).

Black English dialect, when compared to the other dialects, does differ grammatically. One theory about the origin of Black English is that it is a Creole or pidgin English dialect that evolved during slavery in the South (Stoller, 1975). With emancipation and the gradual emigration of African Americans, the dialect spread to other parts of the nation, in particular to large industrial cities in the Northeast and the Ohio Valley. Currently, it is still used in African American communities. Some of the dialect's characteristics, which distinguish it from other dialects, are (Baratz & Shuy, 1969; Fasold & Shuy, 1970; Wolfram, 1969):

1. The use of the third-person singular verbs without adding the "s" or "z" sound; e.g., "The man walk" instead of "The man walks."
2. Nonuse of "s" to indicate possessives; e.g., "The girl hat" instead of "The girl's hat."
3. The use of the "f" sound for the "th" sound at the end or middle of a word; e.g., "nufn" instead of "nothing."
4. Elimination of "l" or "r" sounds in words; e.g., "Tomorrow I bring the book" instead of "Tomorrow I'll bring the book;" and, "It is you book" instead of "It is your book."
5. The use of the verb "be" to indicate future time; e.g., "He be here in a few hours."
6. The use of "it" instead of "there"; e.g., "It's a boy in my room named Bill" instead of "There's a boy in my room named Bill."

Some Southern Whites (even those with enough status to escape the label of being nonstandard speakers) show characteristics that place their dialect close to Black English. Also, not all African Americans speak Black English.

We occasionally hear the criticism from language purists that American English is being adulterated by its many dialects and the many foreign languages spoken in the country. The notion that American English was once pure and now faces adulteration by other languages and dialects flies in the face of the fact that American English is very diverse. From its inception, the language has proved to be a sponge that borrows words from other languages and cultures (Simpson, 1986). Table 14.2 shows some commonly used American English words borrowed from various cultures.

These common words were taken from five different cultural groups. The words, which are not exotic or exceptional, are drawn from different U.S. groups and reflect the pluralism in the United States.

TABLE 14.2   English Words Borrowed from Other Nations

Dutch	French	German	Native American	Spanish
boss	depot	dunk	hickory	coyote
cookie	cab	noodle	pecan	corral
waffle	gopher	ouch	moose	ranch

Linking Ethnicity and Language

The fundamental role of a language or a dialect is group communication. Even though people are not restricted to language for communication, language is of overarching importance because it is the fundamental medium through which ethnicity is transmitted and shared. A language system in general, and a dialect in particular, serve as tools to categorize, interpret, and share experiences. Ethnicity and language thus intertwine, language being the medium and ethnicity the message.

Youngsters learn the content of their ethnic cultures through their parent's dialect. The dialect is used to convey ethnic meaning to the youngsters; later, as the youngsters master the dialect, they use it to convey ethnic content. The dialect serves the youngsters in the formation of their perceptions, attitudes, and values about their physical and social environments. Anthropologists Sapir (1958) and Whorf (1956) reported in their studies of language and perceptions that a person's dialect influences and informs his or her view and perception of reality. For example, in American English there exist only several conceptions of snow (e.g., powder snow or wet snow.) Within the Eskimo language, however, there exist many conceptions of snow. The reason for the difference is that snow is of greater economic and social importance to the Eskimo than it is to most English-speaking peoples. The vocabulary of a group's language reflects distinctions and categories important to the group. Conversely, relatively unimportant categories are reflected minimally, or the category may be nonexistent within the group's vocabulary.

The grammatical system of a group's language reflects the group's attitude toward its physical environment. For example, the Navajo language emphasizes the reporting of events in motion. For example, when describing a large mountain, a Navajo may say "the mountain is busy being big and blue." The Navajo describes the physical environment as fluid. In U.S. English, the mountain's description, "the mountain is big and blue," is of a static physical environment. Thus, the Navajo and English descriptions reflect differing ethnic interpretations of the natural environment (Hoijer, 1951).

These comments should not be interpreted to mean that language determines ethnicity. Rather, language serves as a mirror of ethnicity, reflecting a person's values, beliefs, and attitudes. Note what is being said regarding property in the following scenarios (based on personal observations):

Scenario I:
Ruth: Mom, where's my Barbie doll?

Mother: I lent it to Sue.

Ruth: Why'd you do that?

Mother: She wanted to play with it.

Ruth: But, it's my doll and . . .

Mother: Okay! Okay! Go tell her I said she's to give it to you.

Scenario II:
Rita: Mom, where's my Barbie doll?

Mother: I let your sister use it.

Rita: But I want to use it.

Mother: You can use one of your other dolls.

Rita: But Mom!

Mother: Maybe your sister would trade it for one of the other dolls.

Rita: Well, okay.

In scenario I is an implicit assumption that the doll is Ruth's exclusive property. The mother violated Ruth's property rights by lending the doll without talking to Ruth. The mother acted outside the bounds of her role. In this scenario, the mother's role is to enforce property rights. In scenario II is an implicit assumption that the dolls are the family's collective property. The mother acted within the bounds of her role as property rights coordinator. The language used in both scenarios serves as a microscopic reflection of the attitudes toward property ownership and the mother's role governing ownership.

Ethnicity impacts language, in particular its vocabulary items, in significant ways. Consequently, ethnicity—as a broadly based emotion and sense of group identity—is reflected in an ethnic group's dialect and lexicon. Because an ethnic group uses a dialect to embody and transmit its ethnic content, knowledge about the ethnic group presupposes knowledge of its dialect. To know an ethnic group one must know its dialect.

Language Acquisition of Native Bilinguals

Much confusion persists regarding bilingual persons (Williams & Snipper, 1990). The ideal bilingual person can speak, read, write, and think in two languages with nativelike control of both languages. Few persons ever reach the ideal. Rather, many bilinguals tend to favor one language over the other. Native bilinguals have used two languages since their preschool and primary years in school. Some have acquired both languages in their natural social settings by using them within the speech community of each language where the language is used for practical, communicative functions. Others have acquired their first language in natural setting—the home and community—but have learned their second language in the formal setting of school, where language is used both to communicate and conduct abstract thinking, which is decontextualized or removed from the practical, day-to-day affairs of most people.

Most people follow the same pattern when they acquire their first language. People have the innate ability to learn the sounds, rules, and patterns of any language. Through interaction with other people, infants experiment with speech and attempt to communicate. Their babble may be serious attempts to communicate, but until they use speech, "me hungry," they do not communicate meaningfully with adults. Eventually, infants discover simple sentences ("I am hungry"), more complex sentences, and finally full discourse. Adults provide a rich helping environment and rarely correct grammar or pronunciation. Incrementally, infants independently reconstruct the language spoken by adults and eventually communicate with it.

A long-held belief about language readiness is now under serious question. The belief is that language acquisition follows a linear progression by which children first learn to listen; when ready, they speak, read, and then write in successive stages. Transitions between each stage would occur when a child was ready to make the shift. Contemporary research on emergent literacy (Teale & Sulzby, 1989) or the early stages of reading, writing, and speaking among 2- to 4-year-old children, suggests that language acquisition is a holistic, cognitive process linked to the experiences of children. As a child's experiences expand so do his or her thinking and language proficiencies. Theoretically, reading, writing, and speaking emerge simultaneously since they may be the manifestation of the same cognitive capacity.

First- and second-language acquisition follows a similar basic pattern. Dulay and Burt (1974) recorded the English speech patterns of 145 children, ages 5 and 8, whose first language was Spanish and who were learning English as a second language. The researchers analyzed the speech samples for developmental and interference errors. Developmental errors are mistakes that most infants make when they are learning English as a first language. Interference errors are mistakes or habits that bilingual persons transfer from their first language to utterances in the second, such as the foreign accent of some bilinguals. Eighty-five percent of the errors were developmental; 10 percent were interference; the remainder were attributed to individual differences. The children were acquiring English much like children who acquire English as a first language.

The fundamental goal of language acquisition is communicative competence. Communicative competence refers to the ability of people to speak meaningfully so that native speakers of the language can understand the messages being sent and can respond with a meaningful message, that is, a person has communicative competence when speaking and can be understood by native speakers of the language. Competence refers to understanding and speaking a language; daily, thousands of people fill their basic needs without reading or writing because they accomplish their business affairs through speaking. Yet, some tasks require reading and writing abilities. The ideal goal of language acquisition is literacy, which refers to the ability to use the full range of the language arts, listening, comprehension, speaking, reading, and writing.

With bilingual students, the competency/literacy distinction is critically important. A bilingual's level of competence can have one of three effects on academic achievement: (1) additive bilingualism, which enhances academic achievement; (2) dominant bilingualism, which neither enhances nor retards academic achievement; or (3) subtractive bilingualism, which retards achievement. Additive bilinguals are equally competent and literate in two languages. They benefit from the linguistic and semantic flexibility that the two languages provide.

The additive bilingual has what Cummins (1979) calls Common Underlying Proficiency (CUP), which refers to the interdependence of the two languages. Once a concept is learned in one language it need not be learned in the second language. Dominant bilinguals are fully literate in their first language and are somewhat competent or literate in their second language. They are not affected in a positive or negative direction regarding academic achievement in their first language.

Subtractive bilingual, unlike their additive peers, have not developed full literacy in their first language although they may have developed communicative competence in their two languages. They are able to function interpersonally in two languages (they are conversationally competent); they have not developed the higher level thinking skills necessary for full literacy. Because they have not developed higher levels of thinking skills in their first language, they do not have these skills to transfer to the second language. Consequently, subtractive bilinguals should develop full communicative competence and rudimentary literacy in their first language before being formally introduced to their second language.

Research Bases of Bilingual Instruction

The educational purpose of bilingual instruction is supposed to increase academic achievement by using the student's home language as the main communication medium. Bilingual instruction involves the use of two languages for instruction for part or all of the activities within the classroom. One language is English; the other language is the student's home language, that is, the language spoken in the home. English is taught as a second language. Many times the student's first significant introduction to English is when he or she enters school. In other instances, the student may begin school with minimum English language skills.

Two methods of teaching the non-English-speaking students are Maintenance: Native Language (MNL) and Transitional: English as a Second Language (TESL). The maintenance native language methods uses the student's home language in all subject areas. After mastery in listening, speaking, reading, and writing, the student is introduced to English. The method's supposition is that native language literacy should be achieved before the student is introduced to the English language arts. Having achieved native language literacy, the student should have no difficulty transferring to English.

The second method, Transitional English as a Second Language is sometimes called the direct method. TESL teaches the student immediate English language skills. The TESL pull-out system takes the student out of the classroom daily for instruction in the English language arts. The student returns to the regular class for instruction in other subjects. The TESL intensive system immerses the student in the English language arts for extended time periods. When the student learns to speak the language, then reading in English is introduced. When the student reads English, he or she is returned to the monolingual English classroom.

The bilingual education debate of the 1980s and early 1990s centered on this question: Which method (MNL or TESL) best teaches English to the non-English speaker? The MNL camp reasoned that the method is effective because it builds a solid linguistic foundation in the student's native language before it attempts to teach the second language. This foundation provides a solid base from which the second language can be learned. However, the MNL methods take longer than does the TESL method. The MNL method requires the student to develop almost full literacy in the first language before attempting to learn the second language.

The TESL supporters identified the time factor as the critical flaw with the MNL method. Given the highly mobile nature of U.S. society, and given the possibility that linguistic minority students change school quite often, the TESL camp argued that the MNL method was not a practical way of teaching English to highly mobile populations. Rather, the more direct TESL method is preferable, because it provides the student with an immediate introduction to English, thereby ensuring an opportunity to learn English.

The weight of the research evidence tips the scale in favor of the MNL method because long-range academic achievement and educational development are its demonstrable outcomes (Moll, 1981; Swain & Lapkin, 1981). In terms of learning English—speaking, reading, writing—as well as learning other subjects, such as mathematics and the social sciences, the MNL method has demonstrated its efficacy. Willig's (1985) meta-analysis of 23 studies on the effectiveness of MNL conducted between 1968 and 1980 rendered the following results (p. 270):

> *Participation in bilingual education programs consistently produced small to moderate differences favoring bilingual education for tests of reading, language skills, mathematics, and total achievement when the tests were in English, and for reading, language, mathematics, writing, social studies, listening comprehension, and attitudes toward school or self when tests were in other languages.*

On a short-range basis, the TESL method more quickly teaches students to speak, read, and write English at a functional level. Yet, the TESL method only provides students a minimum of lower-level literacy skills in speaking, reading, and writing. For the sake of efficiency or expediency, the TESL method does not attend to deep structure cognitive abilities, such as some skills required for critical thinking—hypothesizing, predicting, and inferring.

The results of both the MNL and TESL methods are predictable given their respective operating assumption. The TESL method assumes its purposes to be compensatory; that is, the student's ability to use English is viewed as a deficiency that must be compensated for through a submersion into English-only instruction. Another assumption is that the student's first language is a liability that interferes with the development of the second language, or English, in the United States. Therefore, according to this assumption, the student's first language must be ignored, if not extinguished. By diminishing the value of the student's first language, and by ignoring or attempting to extinguish it, teachers using the TESL method create in their students a kind of subtractive bilingualism, that is, the students are not given the chance to develop fully in their first language. The short-range effect of the TESL method does produce English speakers who have superficial control of English and of their first language primarily because they have not developed the deep structure cognitive abilities attributed to full language literacy within a language.

The MNL method assumes its purpose to be enrichment. The student's inability to use English is viewed as a temporary condition, which can be ameliorated by fostering the enrichment and development of the student's first language. A corollary assumption is that the student's first language is worthy of development. What happens is that the MNL method, by valuing and developing full literacy in the first language, provides student's deep structure cognitive abilities that transfer to the second language, that is, additive bilingualism.

Global Stakes of Language Education

Now that the Cold War is over, we face an old challenge with a new twist—how to win the peace. We should think of peace as a condition sustained by deliberate, ongoing measures that eradicate the causes of war. To make and sustain peace, we must begin to think in new ways about language education. Language education has often been used as a weapon for cultural imperialism. It has been used to promote the best interests of sundry elite groups; religions, social classes, multinational corporations, and nations have all used language education to promote their self-interests. We must think of language education as a means to achieve cultural understanding. Once we can talk with each other, once we can understand each other's cultures, we can begin the arduous task of winning the peace by eradicating the causes of war.

The new way of thinking does not require national legislation, Consitutional amendment, or Supreme Court decisions. Teachers and schools have the power to implement courses and curricula dedicated to the eradication of ignorance and

ethnocentrism through language education based on a policy of linguistic pluralism. This policy would foster the knowledge of second languages and cultures; it
would foster respect for the languages and dialects spoken by other people within
the United States and throughout the world.

We should not teach young people that learning a language will give a
competitive advantage for getting into college or for doing a job. We should teach
them that learning another language and respecting the cultures of other people
are fundamental civic responsibilities within the human community. A policy of
linguistic pluralism should provide parameters so that teachers can accommodate
linguistic differences and teach about linguistic diversity. The policy should contain two dimensions (See Figure 14.1).

The two dimensions could be tied to a broader policy of ethnic pluralism (i.e.,
a policy setting parameters for accommodating ethnic differences and teaching
about ethnic diversity in the United States) (see Figure 14.2). To form and implement a pluralistic policy the following four benchmarks are suggested.

Benchmark 1: A Concise Statement Supportive of Linguistic Pluralism Should Be Made

School English ethnocentrism—the attitude that school English is superior to
other dialects and languages—is the nexus of the problem. The policy statement
would stand for linguistic pluralism and against school English ethnocentrism.
The statement would have two major dimensions: (1) accommodating linguistic
differences, and (2) teaching about linguistic diversity, both fostering a climate of
respect for linguistic differences.

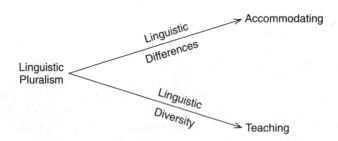

FIGURE 14.1 Educational Dimensions for Linguistic Pluralism

Linguistic pluralism operates within the dimensions of linguistic
differences and linguistic diversity. Teachers are encouraged to
accommodate their student's linguistic differences and also to
teach about linguistic diversity in the United States.

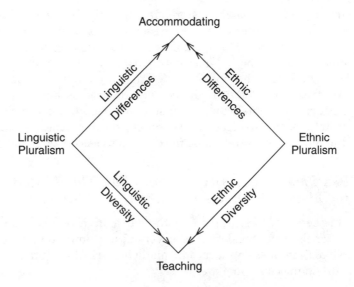

FIGURE 14.2   Dimensions of Linguistic and Ethnic Pluralism

Linguistic pluralism should be linked to ethnic pluralism, which operates within the dimensions of ethnic differences and ethnic diversity. Teachers are encouraged to accommodate their students' ethnic differences and also to teach about ethnic diversity in the United States.

Benchmark 2: Teachers Should Be Cognizant of Their Linguistic Biases against the Dialects or Languages of Linguistically Different Students

Again, linguistic ethnocentrism lies at the nexus of the problem. Primarily, respect for the student's home dialect should be fostered. Rather than viewing the home dialect as defective, teachers should view the dialect as a source of strength.

Students do not enter school speaking a substandard dialect; they may enter school speaking non-school-standard English or a different language. The position that youngsters speak a substandard version of English is an imposition of school English as the only English dialect capable of use for learning.

Benchmark 3: Instructional Strategies Should Accommodate Linguistically Different Students

Linguistically different students should not be placed in special language programs that segregate them from the regular classroom. In fact, positive intercultural experiences can be fostered in linguistically diverse classrooms. When there are a large number of non-English speakers of the same language, a bilingual teacher is feasible. However, if possible, monolingual English-speaking students should be incorporated into this otherwise linguistically segregated arrangement. With students who speak Black English, or other nonschool English dialects, standard school-English should be taught as an alternate dialect necessary for broader social interactions. All students need to learn to understand, read, and write in standard English. Therefore, the linguistic resources of linguistically different students should be maximized to teach basic English literacy.

Benchmark 4: Curriculum Materials Should Reflect the Linguistic Diversity in the United States

This benchmark requires that the curriculum be permeated with multilingual materials. Teachers should use every opportunity to incorporate nonschool English dialects and languages into all their curriculum materials. Examples I've seen work in the classroom are:

1. Learning to count in Spanish, French, German, or some other language
2. Learning that people call their neighborhoods by different names, *ghetto* (Italian origin), *barrio* (Spanish for neighborhood)
3. Learning to read the Chinese calendar.

The list is endless and the approach feasible. Incorporating linguistic diversity into curriculum materials adds variety to otherwise routine learning activities.

Benchmark 5: Schools Should Implement Second-Language Programs for All Students

On high school graduation, students should be fully literate in American English and in one or more second languages. For too long we have coddled the minds of our young people, wasting their time with elementary school language arts programs that have muted rather than empowered them to achieve full literacy in American English and in other languages. Yet, millions of children throughout the world have acquired second-language proficiencies often without the benefits of educational programs. Now that the English language arts are being integrated into the teaching of other subjects, such as the sciences and social studies, there is room in the elementary school curriculum to incorporate second-language learning and literature.

Summary

The emerging belief is that learning is a holistic phenomenon in which language and cognitive development dynamically interact. Literacy, that is, the ability to think speak, read, and write language, is viewed as a holistic manifestation of learning. Consequently, the methods used for teaching first- or second-language literacy should reflect the holistic nature of learning rather than attempt to inculcate literacy as separate, discrete skills. Methodologies should also approach language learning within the context in which it is to be used.

Each country has a formal or informal language policy that fosters a national language standard. The policy of the United States is assimilation. English as spoken and written in the United States is well established as the nation's language. Even though English is not designated as the nation's official language, it has a much more powerful designation that ensures its status as the nation's unofficial official language—the designation granted by more than 200 years of tradition and domination. Just because the nation's language policy has always favored assimilation does not mean that it always will. We are being nudged toward a policy of linguistic pluralism by the forces of global interdependence. The growth of the multinational corporations and the demise of the Cold War are forging new alliances among people, causing us to speak other languages and understand other cultures.

A workable policy of linguistic pluralism involves teaching within two dimensions: (1) linguistic differences and (2) linguistic diversity. The first dimension provides linguistic minority and bidialectal students an equal opportunity to learn school subjects. The second dimension provides all students with a broad, nonethnocentric understanding of multilingual diversity and an opporunity to learn a second language.

References

Baratz, J., & Shuy, R. (1969). *Teaching Black Children to Read*. Washington, DC: Center for Applied Linguistics.

Center for Applied Linguistics. (1981). *The Peoples and Cultures of Cambodia, Laos, and Vietnam*. Washington, DC: Author.

Cubberly, E. (1909). *Changing Conceptions of Education*. Boston: Houghton Mifflin.

Cummins, J. (1979). Linguistic Interdependence and the Educational Development of Bilingual Children. *Review of Educational Research, 49*, 222–251.

Dulay, H. C., & Burt, M. K. (1974). A New Perspective on Creative Construction Processes in Child Second Language Acquisition. *Language Learning, 24*, 253–278.

Edwards, A. D. (1976). *Language in Culture and Class*. London: Heinemann Educational Books.

Fasold, R. W., & Shuy, R. (1970). *Teaching Standard English in the Inner City*. Washington, DC: Center for Applied Linguistics.

Ferguson, C., & Heath, S. B. (Eds.). (1981). *Language in the USA*. New York: Cambridge University Press.

Fishman, J. (1966). *Language Loyalty in the United States*. London: Mouton Press.

Geffert, H., Harper, R., Sarmiento, S., & Schember, D. (1975). *Current Status of US Bilingual Legislation*. Arlington, VA: Center for Applied Linguistics.

Handlin, O. (1959). *Immigration as a Factor in American History*. Englewood Cliffs, NJ: Prentice-Hall.

Harvard University Press. (1985). Foreign Language in the Elementary School. In *Education Letter*. Cambridge: Author.

Heath, S. B. (1981). English in Our Language Heritage. In C. Ferguson & S. B. Heath (Eds.), *Language in the USA* (pp. 6–20). New York: Cambridge University Press.

Hoijer, H. (1951). Cultural Implications of Some Navajo Linguistic Categories. *Language, 27*, 111–120.

Joint Committee for Languages. (1992). *Official Language States.* Pamphlet. Washington, DC: Author.

Jorgenson, L. (1956). *The Founding of Public Education in Wisconsin.* Madison: Wisconsin Historical Society.

Labov, W. (1970). The Logic of Nonstandard English. In F. Williams (Ed.), *Language and Poverty* (pp. 153–189). Chicago: Markham.

Laird, C. (1970). *Language in America.* New York: The World Publishing.

Lau v. Nichols. 1974. 414 U.S. 563, 1974.

Liebowitz, A. H. (1976). Language and the Law: The Exercise of Power through Official Designation of Language. In U. M. O'Barr & J. F. O'Barr (Eds.), *Language and Politics* (pp. 449–466). The Hague: Mouton.

Marckwardt, A. H. (1974). Regional and Social Variations. In R. B. Glenn (Ed.), *Language and Culture* (pp. 181–193). Marquette: Northern Michigan Press.

Martin Luther King, Jr., Elementary School Children, et al. v. Ann Arbor School District Board, United States District Court, East District, Michigan. 1979 Civil Action No. 7–71861.

Moll, L. C. (1981). The Microethnographic Study of Bilingual Schooling. In *Ethnoperspectives in Bilingual Education Research* (pp. 430–446). Ypsilanti: Eastern Michigan University Press.

National Council for Languages and International Studies. (1992). *Language Competence and Cultural Awareness in the United States.* Pamphlet. Washington, DC: Author.

Ovando, C., & Collier, P. (1985). *Bilingual and ESL Classrooms.* New York: McGraw-Hill.

Prucha, P. (1975). *Documents of United States Indian Policy.* Lincoln: University of Nebraska Press.

Reutter, E. E., & Hamilton, R. R. (1970). *The Law of Public Education.* Mineola, NY: The Foundation Press.

Rhodes, N. C., & Schreibstein, A. R. (1983). *Foreign Languages in the Elementary School.* Wash-

ington, DC: Center for Applied Linguistics. ERIC ED 209 940.

Sapir, E. (1958). *Culture, Language, and Personality.* Berkeley: University of California Press.

Simpson, D. (1986). *The Politics of American English, 1776–1850.* New York: Oxford University Press.

Shumway, N. (1986). Should English Be Made Official? Yes. As recorded in the *Congressional Record,* pp. E2046–E2047.

Stoller, P. (1975). *Black American English.* New York: Dell Publishing Company.

Swain, M., & Lapkin, S. (1981). *Bilingual Education in Ontario: A Decade of Research.* Toronto: Ontario Institute for Studies in Education.

Teale, W. H., & Sulzby, E. (1989). *Emergent Literacy.* Norwood, NJ: Ablex.

Torres, A. (1986). Should English Be Made Official? No. As recorded in the *Congressional Record,* pp. E2046–E2047.

U.S. Commission on Civil Rights. (1970). *Mexican American Education Study.* Washington, DC: U.S. Government Printing Office.

U.S. Government Printing Office. (1985) *Congressional Record Senate.* Washington, DC: Author.

Whitemore, J. K. (1979). *An Introduction to Indochinese History, Culture, Language, and Life.* Ann Arbor, MI: Center for South and Southeast Asian Studies.

Whorf, B. L. (1956). *Language, Thought and Reality.* New York: Wiley.

Williams, J. D., & Snipper, G. (1990). *Literacy and Bilingualism.* New York: Longman.

Willig, A. (1985). A Meta-Analysis of Selected Studies on the Effectiveness of Bilingual Education. *Review of Educational Research, 55,* 269–317.

Wolfram, W. (1969). *A Sociolinguistic Description of Negro Speech.* Washington, DC: Center for Applied Linguistics.

Zeydel, E. (1964). *Reports of Surveys and Studies in the Teaching of Modern Foreign Languages.* New York: Modern Language Association.

Chapter 15

Curriculum Guidelines for Multicultural Education

Part One: A Rationale for Ethnic Pluralism and Multicultural Education

Three major factors make multicultural education a necessity: (1) ethnic pluralism is a growing societal reality that influences the lives of young people; (2) in one way or another, individuals acquire knowledge or beliefs, sometimes invalid, about ethnic and cultural groups; and (3) beliefs and knowledge about ethnic and cultural groups limit the perspectives of many and make a difference, often a negative difference, in the opportunities and options available to members of ethnic and cultural groups. Because ethnicity, race, and class are important in the lives of many citizens of the United States, it is essential that all members of our society develop multicultural literacy, that is, a solidly based understanding of racial, ethnic, and cultural groups and their significance in U.S. society and throughout the world. Schools cannot afford to ignore their responsibility to contribute to the development of multicultural literacy and understanding. Only a well-conceived, sensitive, thorough, and continuous program of multicultural education can create the broadly based multicultural literacy so necessary for the future of our nation and world.

In the United States, ethnic diversity has remained visible despite the acculturation process that takes place in any society made up of many ethnic groups. Although ethnic affiliations are weak for many U.S. citizens, a large number still have some attachments to their ethnic cultures and to the symbols of their ancestral traditions. The values and behavior of many U.S. citizens are heavily influenced by their ethnicity. Ethnic identification is often increased by the discrimination experienced by many because of their racial characteristics, language, or culture. Ethnic identification is also increased when significant numbers of new immigrants from the homeland arrive in the United States. Thousands of immigrants from Asia and Latin America made the United States their home during the 1980s. About 85 percent of the documented immigrants that settled in the United States between 1981 and 1989 came from Asia (47 percent) and Latin America (38 percent) (Banks, 1991a, p. 4).

During the 1980s and 1990s, a significant increase in the population of people of color in the United States and the expression of new forms of racism stimulated a vigorous and contentious debate among educators about the extent to which the curriculum should be revised to reflect ethnic and cultural diversity. At least three major groups that participated in this debate can be identified—the Western traditionalists, the Afrocentrists, and the multiculturalists. The Western traditionalists argue that content about Europe and Western civilization should be at the center of the curriculum in the nation's schools, colleges, and universities because of the extent to which Western ideas and values have influenced the development of U.S. culture and civilization (Howe, 1991; Ravitch, 1990; Schlesinger, 1991). The Afrocentrists maintain that it is essential that an African perspective be incorporated into the curriculum (Asante, 1991). The multiculturalists believe that concepts and events should be viewed from diverse ethnic and cultural perspectives (Banks, 1991a; Sleeter & Grant, 1987; Tetreault 1989). The multiculturalists also argue that the conception of Western civilization taught in schools should be reconceptualized to acknowledge the debt the West owes to Asian and African civilizations (Bernal, 1991). The multiculturalists also believe that the conflict inherent in the West's commitment to democratic ideals and the racism and sexism still practiced in Western societies should be made explicit in the curriculum.

The bitter debate about the extent to which issues related to race and ethnicity should be reflected in the curriculum of the nation's schools indicates that race and ethnicity are cogent forces in contemporary U.S. society. The debate over the curriculum canon is an appropriate one for a pluralistic democratic society. It reflects the extent to which various interest groups are trying to shape the national identity and culture in the United States in ways that are consistent with their views of the nation's past, present, and future.

The concept of cultural diversity embraced in these guidelines is most consistent with the position of the multiculturalists—a position that incorporates important elements of both the Western traditionalist and the Afrocentrist approaches. The multiculturalists' position contributes best to the building of a society that incorporates diversity within a cohesive and unified nation-state. Multicultural education supports and enhances the notion of *e pluribus unum*— out of many, one. To build a successful and inclusive nation-state, the hopes, dreams, and experiences of the many groups within it must be reflected in the structure and institutions of society. This is the only viable way to create a nation-state in which all groups will feel included, loyal, and patriotic.

The guidelines presented in this document are predicated on a democratic ideology in which ethnic and cultural diversity is viewed as a positive, integral ingredient. A democratic society protects and provides opportunities for ethnic and cultural diversity at the same time having overarching values—such as equality, justice, and human dignity—that all groups accept and respect. Ethnic and cultural diversity is based on the following four premises:

1. Ethnic and cultural diversity should be recognized and respected at individual, group, and societal levels.
2. Ethnic and cultural diversity provides a basis for societal enrichment, cohesiveness, and survival.
3. Equality of opportunity should be afforded to members of all ethnic and cultural groups.
4. Ethnic and cultural identification should be optional for individuals.

Characteristics of an Ethnic Group

Because this document focuses on ethnic pluralism and its implications for school reform, it is essential that we establish a working definition of *ethnic group* that reflects social science theory and research and facilitates school reform. No one definition of the term is accepted by all social scientists or is adequate for the purpose of this document. Consequently, the working definition used herein reflects a composite of existing definitions and the results of task force discussions.

An ethnic group is distinguished from other kinds of cultural groups in the definition for this document. An ethnic group is a specific kind of cultural group having all the following characteristics:

a. Its origins precede the creation of a nation-state or are external to the nation-state. In the case of the United States, ethnic groups have distinct pre–United States or extro–United States territorial bases, e.g., immigrant groups and Native Americans.
b. It is an involuntary group, although individual identification with the group may be optional.
c. It has an ancestral tradition and its members share a sense of peoplehood and an interdependence of fate.
d. It has distinguishing value orientations, behavioral patterns, and interests.
e. Its existence has an influence, in many cases a substantial influence, on the lives of its members.
f. Membership in the group is influenced both by how members define themselves and by how they are defined by others.

The definition of *ethnic group* stated above includes some groups that are distinguished primarily on the basis of race, such as African Americans and Japanese Americans, some that are distinguished primarily on the basis of unique sets of cultural and religious attributes, such as Jewish Americans, and some that are distinguished on the basis of national origin, such as Polish Americans. The criteria for characterization, of course, frequently overlap; Japanese Americans, for example, constitute an ethnic group characterized by national, cultural, and racial origins. The definition does not include cultural or regional groups of United States origin, such as those from the Appalachian region. This exclusion does not imply that such groups do not have unique cultural experiences that have teaching implications. Although they are not the primary focus of this document, many of the guidelines are applicable to the study of regional and other kinds of cultural groups. Factors such as region, race, gender, social class, and religion are variables that cut across ethnic groups. Students must examine these factors to gain a valid understanding of the nature of racial, ethnic, and cultural diversity in U.S. society.

Characteristics of a Cultural Group

A cultural group shares behavioral patterns, symbols, values, beliefs, and other human-constructed characteristics that distinguish it from other groups. Kroeber and Kluckhohn, (1952, p. 161), after surveying definitions of culture, concluded that "culture consists of patterns, explicit and implicit, of and for behavior acquired and transmitted by symbols, constituting the distinctive achievements of human groups, including their embodiments in artifacts; the essential core of culture consists of traditional . . . ideas and especially their attached values."

Like most social scientists today, Kroeber and Kluckhohn emphasize the intangible, symbolic, and ideational aspects of culture. Ideas, ways of thinking, values, symbols, and other intangible aspects of human life—and not tangible objects such as tools, clothing, or foods—distinguish one cultural group from another in modernized societies. Two cultural groups might eat the same foods but have different meanings and interpretations for them. It is their values, perspectives, and ways of viewing reality that distinguish cultural groups from one another in the United States, not their clothing, foods, or other tangible aspects of group life.

Principles of Ethnic and Cultural Diversity

1. *Ethnic and cultural diversity should be recognized and respected at the individual, group, and societal levels.*

Ethnic and cultural diversity is a social reality all too frequently ignored by educational institutions, yet it deserves open recognition. Members of ethnic and cultural groups often have worldviews, values, traditions, and practices that differ from those of the mainstream society and from those of other ethnic groups.

Even in the midst of a marked degree of assimilation and acculturation, and in spite of efforts to ignore, belittle, or eliminate some ethnic differences, many U.S. citizens have strong feelings of ethnic identity (Alba, 1990). Since the civil rights movement of the 1960s and 1970s, some ethnic groups have heightened their visibility and increased their demands for equal opportunity (Alba, 1990). Ethnic and cultural diversity continues to permeate life in the United States. Its persistence and our nation's changing demographics suggest that it will characterize the future (Hodgkinson, 1985).

Nearly half (46 percent) of school-age youths in the United States will be people of color by 2020 (Pallas, Natriello, & McDill, 1989). People of color, women, and immigrants will make up more than 83 percent of the new additions to the U.S. work force between now and the turn of the century. White men born in the United States will make up only 15 percent of the new additions to the labor force during this period (Johnson & Packer, 1987).

Simply recognizing ethnic and cultural diversity is not enough. Understanding and respect for diverse values, traditions, and behaviors are essential if we are to actualize fully our nation's democratic ideals. The call for understanding and respect is based on a belief that the existence and expression of differences can improve the quality of life for individuals, for ethnic and cultural groups, and for society as a whole.

For individuals, group identity can provide a foundation for self-definition. Ethnic and cultural group membership can provide a sense of belonging, of shared traditions, of interdependence of fate—especially for members of groups who have all too often had restricted access to institutions in the larger society. When society views ethnic and cultural differences with respect, individuals can define themselves ethnically without conflict or shame.

The psychological cost of assimilation has been and continues to be high for many U.S. citizens. It too often demands self-denial, self-hatred, and rejection of family and ethnic ties. Social demands for conformity, which have harmful human consequences, are neither democratic nor humane. Such practices deny dignity by refusing to accept individuals as persons in themselves and by limiting the realization of human potential. Such demands run counter to the democratic values of freedom of association and equality of opportunity.

A society that respects ethnic group differences aims to protect its citizens from discriminatory practices and prejudicial attitudes. Such respect supports the survival of these groups and augments their opportunities to shape their lives in ways they choose. For society as a whole, ethnic groups can serve as sources of innovation. By respecting differences, society is provided a wider base of ideas, values, and behaviors that increase its capacity for creative change.

Coping with change is fundamental to the survival of culture. Adapting to new conditions is critical. Without constructive reaction to change, cultures may weaken and deteriorate. In the face of rapidly changing conditions, the United States, as a nation, has to be concerned with ensuring mechanisms for coping with change. One way cultures change is through the process of innovation: a person (or persons) introduces new ways of thinking or behaving which are accepted by society or challenge cultural views. By respecting the plurality of ethnic and cultural life-styles, and by permitting them to flourish, our national culture may expand the base of alternatives from which it can draw in responding to new conditions and new problems.

Conversely, to the extent that a culture is homogeneous, its capability for creative change is limited. When the range of tolerated differences in values and behaviors is minimal, rigidity inhibits innovation. Too much conformity and convergence is characteristic of mass culture. On the other hand, too little acceptance of common cultural values and practices can produce social disorganization. The balance is a delicate one in a culture that must face up to the challenge of changing conditions; a dynamic and pluralistic nation cannot be left without access to competing, unique, and creative ideas. Recognition and respect for ethnic and cultural differences enable society to enhance the potential of individuals and the integrity and contributions of ethnic and cultural groups, and so to invigorate the culture.

   2. *Ethnic and cultural diversity provides a basis for societal enrichment, cohesiveness, and survival.*

   The principles on which these guidelines are based seek not only to recognize and respect ethnic and cultural diversity but to establish across racial, ethnic, and cultural lines intercultural bonds that will contribute to the strength and vitality of society.

   This position maintains the right of ethnic groups to socialize their young into their cultural patterns as long as such practices are consistent with human dignity and democratic ideals. Therefore, an individual's primary group associations—family relations, friendship groups, religious affiliations—may be heavily influenced by ethnic traditions. At the same time, members of ethnic groups have both the right and the responsibility to accept U.S. democratic values and to help shape the significant institutions of the larger society. Legal and educational institutions must have a strong commitment to affecting the conditions that will permit members of ethnic groups to become fully participating members of the larger society. Ethnic groups must feel that they have a stake in this society; to the extent that ethnic group members feel a sense of ownership in societal institutions, their cultural practices will reflect the inherent values of society as a whole. What is needed is a cohesive society, characterized by ethnic pluralism, wherein the self-identities of individuals allow them to say: "I am an African American (or a Polish American, or a Mexican American)—and I am an American."

   Respect for ethnic differences should promote, not destroy, societal cohesion. Although separatism is not the desire of most members of ethnic groups, they strongly demand that their histories and cultures become integral parts of the school curriculum and the larger society (Asante, 1987, 1991). To the extent that society creates an environment in which all ethnic groups can flourish, and in which such groups can contribute constructively to the shaping of public institutions, hostilities will be defused and the society will benefit from its rich base of ethnic traditions and cultures. In effect, unity thrives in an atmosphere where varieties of human potential are neither socially censored nor ignored, but valued.

   3. *Equality of opportunity must be afforded to all members of ethnic and cultural groups.*

   Recognition and respect for ethnic and cultural groups require legal enforcement of equal economic, political, and educational opportunity. Anything less relegates ethnic groups and their members to the inferior status that has too often limited the quality of their lives.

   Ethnic and cultural groups themselves continue to demand equal participation in society as a whole. If society is to benefit from ethnic and cultural differences, it must provide for significant interactions within social institutions. To reach this goal, ethnic and cultural groups must have access to the full range of occupational, educational, economic, and political opportunities. Society will benefit from structural integration and the mutual involvement of all sorts of people in political, educational, and economic life.

   4. *Ethnic and cultural identification for individuals should be optional in a democracy.*
   Although the assimilationist ideology has dominated our national thought for two centuries, ethnicity has proved to be a resilient factor in U.S. life and culture. The centrality of Anglo-American tradition notwithstanding, many individuals continue to derive their primary identity from their ethnic group membership. At the same time, it must be recognized that widespread cultural assimilation and acculturation have taken place in U.S. society. Many individuals of White ethnic origin are no longer identified ethnically with their original or primordial ethnic group. Although a large number of these individuals have intermarried and much cultural exchange among White ethnic groups has taken place, a new collective ethnic identity has emerged among White Americans that most of them share. Alba (1990) calls this new ethnic identity and group *European Americans.*

   The degree of individuals' ethnic attachments and affiliations vary greatly. The beliefs and behaviors of some individuals are heavily influenced by their ethnic culture or cultures; others maintain only some ethnic beliefs and behavioral characteristics; still others try to reject or lose, or are simply unaware of, their ethnic origins. There are also individuals of mixed ethnic origin who identify with more than one group or for whom ethnic identification may be difficult or impossible.

   For many persons, then, ethnic criteria may be irrelevant for purposes of self-identification. Their identities stem primarily from, for example, gender, social class, occupation, political affiliation, or religion. Moreover, ethnic origins ought not to be romanticized. Many, though not all, who left their original homelands did so because opportunities were closed to them there. However good "the good old days" were, they are gone. The "old countries" too have been changing. Ethnicity should not be maintained artificially.

   It is inconsistent with a democratic ideology to mandate ethnic affiliation. In an idealized democratic society, individuals are free to choose their group allegiances. Association should be voluntary—a matter of personal choice. In our society, however, members of some ethnic groups have this option while others do not. Society should maximize the opportunity for individuals to choose their group identifications and affiliations.

   Although a democratic society can and should protect the right to ethnic identification, it cannot insist upon it. To do so would violate individual freedom of choice. To confine individuals to any given form of affiliation violates the principles of liberty guaranteed by the basic documents upon which this nation was founded.

The Role of the School

The societal goals stated in this document are future oriented. In effect, they present a vision of our society that recognizes and respects ethnic and cultural diversity as compatible with national and societal unity rather than one that seeks to reduce ethnic and cultural differences. Further progress in that direction is consistent with the democratic ideals—freedom, equality, justice, and human dignity—embodied in our basic national documents. By respecting ethnic and cultural differences, we can help to close the gap between our democratic ideals and societal practices. Such practices are too often discriminatory toward members of ethnic and cultural groups.

It follows, therefore, that schools need to assume a new responsibility. Their socialization practices should incorporate the ethnic diversity that is an integral part of the democratic commitment to human dignity. At the same time, however, schools must help socialize youth in ways that will foster basic democratic ideals that serve as overarching goals for all U.S. citizens. The schools' goal should be to help attain a delicate balance of diversity and unity—one nation that respects the cultural rights and freedoms of its many peoples. As schools embark on educational programs that reflect multiculturalism, they must demonstrate a commitment to:

a. recognize and respect ethnic and cultural diversity;
b. promote societal cohesiveness based on the shared participation of ethnically and culturally diverse peoples;
c. Maximize equality of opportunity for all individuals and groups; and
d. facilitate constructive societal change that enhances human dignity and democratic ideals.

The study of ethnic heritage should not consist of a narrow promotion of ethnocentrism or nationalism. Personal ethnic identity and knowledge of others' ethnic identities is essential to the sense of understanding and the feeling of personal well-being that promote intergroup and international understanding. Multicultural education should stress the process of self-identification as an essential aspect of the understanding that underlies commitment to the dignity of humankind throughout the world community.

The Nature of the Learner

Research indicates that individual learning styles vary, that all people do not learn in the same way. Of particular interest to multicultural education is research suggesting that learning styles may be related to ethnicity in some ways (Hale-Benson, 1982; Shade, 1989). On the basis of this research, schools can reject the notion that all students learn in precisely the same way. For too long, educational practices have reflected such universal views of learning and have expected all students to conform to them. Schools should recognize that they cannot treat all students alike or they run the risk of denying equal educational opportunity to all persons. Educators should be aware of behavior that is normative and acceptable in various ethnic and cultural groups. The practices of multicultural schools must be both responsive and adaptive to ethnic differences.

Goals for School Reform

Two major goals for school reform follow. Both are based on what has preceded: the principles of ethnic and cultural diversity, the role of the school, and cultural differences among individual learners.

1. Schools should create total school environments that are consistent with democratic ideals and cultural diversity.

Schools reflect their values not only in their curricula and materials, but in policies, hiring practices, governance procedures, and climate—sometimes referred to as the informal, or "hidden," curricula. It can be argued that students often learn as much about the society from nonformal areas of schooling as from the planned curriculum. Education for multiculturalism, therefore, requires more than a change in curricula and textbooks. It requires systemwide changes that permeate all aspects of school life.

2. Schools should define and implement curricular policies that are consistent with democratic ideals and cultural diversity.

Schools should not promote the ideologies and political goals of any specific group, including those of dominant groups, but should promote a democratic ideology. Too often, school curricula have promoted the interests of dominant groups and, therefore, have been detrimental to the interests of some ethnic groups. Promoting the interests of any group over those of others increases the possibility of ethnic and racial tension and conflict.

In recent years, a contentious debate has taken place about whose culture or cultures should be reflected and represented in the school and university curriculum. The debate has centered on which social science, philosophical, and literary works should constitute the canonical knowledge taught in the nation's schools, colleges, and universities.

The Western traditionalists are concerned that more content about women and people of color will result in insufficient attention to the Western roots of American civilization (Howe, 1991; Ravitch, 1990). Multiculturalists have pointed out that the voices, experiences, and perspectives of people of color and women are often left out or muted in many school and university courses about Western civilization and U.S. society (Lerner, 1979; Sleeter & Grant, 1987; Tetreault, 1989). Other advocates have called for an Afrocentric curriculum for predominantly African American schools (Asante, 1987, 1990, 1991).

Curriculum transformation is necessary for the nation's schools, colleges, and universities to describe accurately the Western roots of American civilization and to depict the diversity that characterizes the West. The debt that Western civilization owes to Africa, Asia, and indigenous America should also be described in the curriculum (Bernal, 1991; Diop, 1974; Sertima, 1988; Weatherford, 1988).

The conception of Western civilization most often taught in schools, colleges, and universities should be broadened. Too often, the West is conceptualized in a narrow way to include primarily the heritage of Western European upper-class males. Yet the ideas and writings of women and people of color in the United States are also Western. Zora Neale Hurston, Maxine Hong Kingston, Rudolfo A. Anaya, W. E. B. DuBois, Carlos Bulosan, and N. Scott Momaday—like Milton, Shakespeare, Virgil, and Locke—are Western writers. The West should also be described in ways that accurately describe the gap between its democratic ideals and realities. Western civilization is characterized by ideals such as democracy and freedom but also by struggle, conflict, and deferred and shattered dreams.

The curriculum in the nation's schools, colleges, and universities should reflect all of its citizens. When particular groups feel excluded or victimized by schools and other institutions, conflicts, tensions, and power struggles ensue. The pluralist dilemma related to the curriculum canon debate can only be resolved when all groups involved—the Western traditionalists, the Afrocentrists, and the multiculturalists—share power and engage in genuine dialogue and discussion. Power sharing is a requisite to genuine debate and conflict resolution. When groups and individuals feel victimized by the school and the larger society because of ethnicity, conflict and tension result, and struggles to gain rights occur.

Part Two: Curriculum Guidelines for Multicultural Education

1.0 Ethnic and cultural diversity should permeate the total school environment.

Effective teaching about U.S. ethnic and cultural groups can best take place within an educational setting that accepts, encourages, and respects the expression of ethnic and cultural diversity. To attain this kind of educational atmosphere, the total school environment—not merely courses and programs—must be reformed. Schools' informal or "hidden" curricula are as important as their formalized courses of study.

Teaching about various ethnic or cultural groups in a few specialized courses is not enough. Content about a variety of ethnic groups should be incorporated into many subject areas, preschool through 12th grade and beyond. Some dimensions of multicultural education, however, have higher priority in some subject areas than in others. We can identify several dimensions of multicultural education, including *content integration,* the *knowledge construction process,* and an *equity pedagogy* (Banks, 1991b). In social studies, the humanities, and the language arts, content integration is often the first and most important concern. In physics, however, developing pedagogies that will help students of color and female students to excel academically might be of greater concern than content integration (Belenky et al., 1986). Students can examine how knowledge is constructed in each discipline.

Multicultural education clearly means different things in different disciplines and areas of study. To interpret or attempt to implement multicultural education the same way in each discipline or area of study will create frustration among teachers and build resistance to the concept. Nevertheless, teachers in each discipline can analyze their teaching procedures and styles to determine the extent to which they reflect multicultural issues and concerns. An equity pedagogy exists when teachers modify their instruction in ways that facilitate the academic achievement of students from diverse racial, cultural, gender, and social-class groups. This includes using a variety of teaching styles and approaches that are consistent with the wide range of learning styles found in various cultural, ethnic, and gender groups.

To permeate the total school environment with ethnic and cultural diversity, students must have readily available resource materials that provide accurate information on the diverse aspects of the histories and cultures of various racial, ethnic, and cultural groups. Learning centers, libraries, and resource centers should include a variety of resources on the history, literature, music, folklore, views of life, and art of different ethnic and cultural groups.

Ethnic and cultural diversity in a school's informal programs should be reflected in assembly programs, classrooms, hallway and entrance decorations, cafeteria menus, counseling interactions, and extracurricular programs. School-sponsored dances that consistently provide only one kind of ethnic music, for example, are as contrary to the spirit and principles of multicultural education as are curricula that teach only about mainstream U.S. ideals, values, and contributions.

Participation in activities—such as cheerleading, booster clubs, honor societies, and athletic teams—should be open to all students; in fact, the participation of students from various racial, ethnic, and cultural backgrounds should be solicited. Such activities can provide invaluable opportunities not only for the development of self-esteem, but for students from different ethnic and cultural backgrounds to learn to work and play together, and to recognize that all individuals, whatever their ethnic identities, have worth and are capable of achieving.

2.0 School policies and procedures should foster positive multicultural interactions and understandings among students, teachers, and the support staff.

School governance should protect the individual's right to (1) retain esteem for his or her home environment, (2) develop a positive self-concept, (3) develop empathy and insight into and respect for the ethnicity of others, and (4) receive an equal educational opportunity.

Each institution needs rules and regulations to guide behavior so as to attain institutional goals and objectives. School rules and regulations should enhance cross-cultural harmony and understanding among students, staff, and teachers. In the past, school harmony was often sought through efforts to "treat everyone the same"; experience in multiethnic settings, however, indicates that the same treatment for everyone is unfair to many students. Instead of insisting on one ideal model of behavior that is unfair to many students, school policies should recognize and accommodate individual and ethnic group differences. This does not mean that some students should obey school rules and others should not; it means that ethnic groups' behaviors should be honored as long as they are not inconsistent with major school and societal goals. It also means that school policies may have to make allowances for ethnic traditions. For example, customs that affect Jewish students' food preferences and school attendance on certain religious days should be respected.

Equal educational opportunity should be increased by rules that protect students from procedures and practices that relegate them to low-ability or special education classes simply because of their low scores on standardized English reading and achievement tests.

It is especially important for educators to consider equity issues related to testing because many groups and individuals are pushing for the establishment of a national test or tests. Unless significant changes are made within schools and society that will enable low-income students and students of color to perform well on national tests, these students will become double victims—victims of both a poor educational system and national tests that relegate them to inferior jobs and deny them opportunities for further education (Mercer, 1989). If developed, these national tests should be constructed and used in ways that are consistent with the principles of ethnic pluralism and multicultural education described in these guidelines.

Guidance and other student services personnel should not view students stereotypically regarding their academic abilities and occupational aspirations, and students must be protected from responses based on such views. Counselors should be cautioned to counsel students on the basis of their individual potentials and interests as well as their ethnic needs and concerns. Counselors will need to be particularly aware of their own biases when counseling students whose ethnicity differs from theirs.

Schools should recognize the holidays and festivities of major importance to various ethnic groups. Provisions should be made to ensure that traditional holidays and festivities reflect multicultural modes of celebration. For example, the ways in which some American Indian tribes celebrate Thanksgiving, Orthodox Greeks celebrate Easter, and Jews celebrate Hanukkah can be appropriately included in school programs.

3.0 A school's staff should reflect the ethnic and cultural diversity within the United States.

Members of various ethnic and cultural groups must be part of a school's instructional, administrative, policymaking, and support staffs if the school is truly multiethnic and multicultural. School personnel—teachers, principals, cooks, custodians, secretaries, students, and counselors—make contributions to multicultural environments as important as do courses of study and instructional materials. Students learn important lessons about ethnic and cultural diversity by observing interactions among racial, ethnic, cultural, and gender groups in their school, observing and experiencing the verbal behavior of the professional and support staffs, and observing the extent to which the staff is ethnically and racially mixed. Therefore, school policies should be established and aggressively implemented to recruit and maintain a multiethnic school staff, sensitive to the needs of a pluralistic democratic society.

In addition, students can benefit from positive and cooperative interactions with students from various racial, ethnic, and cultural groups (Slavin, 1983; Cohen, 1986). When plans are made to mix students from diverse groups— whether through school desegregation, exchange programs and visits, or program assignment—extreme care must be taken to ensure that the environment in which the students interact is a positive and enhancing one (Banks, 1991c). When students from different ethnic and racial groups interact within a hostile environment, their racial antipathies are likely to increase (Stephan, 1985).

4.0 Schools should have systematic, comprehensive, mandatory, and continuing staff development programs.

A teacher is an important variable in a student's formal learning environment. Attention should be devoted to the training and retraining of teachers and other members of the professional and support staff to create the kind of multicultural school environment recommended in these guidelines. Sound materials and other instructional program components are ineffective in the hands of teachers who lack the skills, attitudes, perceptions, and content background essential for a positive multicultural school environment. An effective staff development program must involve administrators, librarians, counselors, and members of the support staff such as cooks, secretaries, and bus drivers. This is necessary because any well-trained and sensitive teacher must work within a supportive institutional environment to succeed. Key administrators, such as principals, must set by example the school norms for ethnic and cultural differences. The need to involve administrators, especially building principals, in comprehensive and systematic staff development programs cannot be overemphasized.

Effective professional staff development should begin at the preservice level, continue when educators are employed by schools, and focus on helping the staff members: (a) clarify and analyze their feelings, attitudes, and perceptions toward their own and other racial, ethnic, and cultural groups; (b) acquire knowledge about and understanding of the historical experiences and sociological characteristics of ethnic and cultural groups in the United States; (c) increase their instructional skills within multicultural school environments; (d) improve their intercultural communications skills; (e) improve their skill in curriculum development as it relates to ethnic and cultural diversity; and (f) improve their skill in creating, selecting, evaluating, and revising instructional materials.

Staff development for effective multicultural schools is best undertaken jointly by school districts, local colleges and universities, and local community agencies. Each bears a responsibility for training school personnel, at both the preservice and in-service levels, to function successfully within multicultural instructional settings.

Effective staff development programs must be carefully conceptualized and implemented. Short workshops, selected courses, and other short-term experiences may be essential components of such programs, but these alone cannot constitute an entire staff development program. Rather, sound staff development programs should consist of a wide variety of program components including needs assessments, curriculum development, peer teaching, and materials selection and evaluation. Lectures alone are insufficient. Ongoing changes should be made to make staff development programs more responsive to the needs of practicing professionals.

5.0 The curriculum should reflect the cultural learning styles and characteristics of the students within the school community.

Students in a school responsive to ethnic and cultural diversity cannot be treated identically and still be afforded equal educational opportunities. Some students have unique cultural and ethnic characteristics to which the school should respond deliberately and sensitively. Research indicates that the academic achievement of African American and Hispanic students increases when cooperative teaching techniques such as the jigsaw are used (Aronson & Gonzalez, 1988). Moreover, *all* students develop more positive racial and ethnic attitudes when teachers use cooperative, rather than competitive, learning activities (Aronson & Gonzalez, 1988).

Research indicates that many students of color, especially those from low-income families, often have value orientations, behaviors, cognitive styles, language characteristics, and other cultural components that differ from those of the school's culture (Delpit, 1988; Deyhle, 1986; Fordham, 1991; Fordham & Ogbu, 1986; Gay, 1991; Heath, 1983; Hale-Benson, 1982; Shade, 1989). These components often lead to conflict between students and teachers. By comparison, most middle-class mainstream youths find the school culture consistent with their home cultures and are, therefore, much more comfortable in school. Many students, though, regardless of their racial, ethnic, or cultural identity, find the school culture alien, hostile, and self-defeating.

A school's culture and instructional programs should be restructured and made to reflect the cultures and learning styles of students from diverse ethnic and social-class groups (Banks & Banks, 1989). Research indicates that the instructional strategies and learning styles most often favored in the nation's schools are inconsistent with the cognitive styles, cultural orientations, and cultural characteristics of some groups of students of color (Aronson & Gonzalez, 1988; Fordham, 1991). This research provides important guidelines and principles that educators can use to change schools to make them more responsive to students from diverse cultural groups. Educators should not ignore racial and ethnic differences when planning instruction; nor should they dismiss the question of racial and ethnic differences with the all-too-easy cliché, "I don't see racial differences in students and I treat them all alike." Research on cognitive styles and language and communication characteristics of ethnic groups suggests that if all students are treated alike, their distinctive needs are not being met and they are probably being denied access to equal educational opportunities (Cummins, 1986; Heath, 1983; Kochman, 1981; Philips, 1983).

Although differences among students are accepted in an effective multicultural school, teaching students to function effectively in mainstream society and in social settings different from the ones in which they were socialized, and helping them learn new cognitive styles and learning patterns, must also be major goals. The successful multicultural school helps students become aware of and able to acquire cultural and cognitive alternatives, thus enabling them to function successfully within cultural environments other than their own.

6.0 The multicultural curriculum should provide students with continuous opportunities to develop a better sense of self.

The multicultural curriculum should help students to develop a better sense of self. This development should be an ongoing process, beginning when the student first enters school and continuing throughout the student's school career. This development should include at least three areas:

1. Students should be helped to develop accurate self-identities. Students must ask questions such as who am I? and what am I? in order to come to grips with their own identities.

2. The multicultural curriculum should help students develop improved self-concepts. Beyond considering such questions as who they are and what they are, students should learn to feel positively about their identities, particularly their ethnic identities. Positive self-concepts may be expressed in several ways. The multicultural curriculum, for example, should recognize the varying talents of students and capitalize on them in the academic curriculum. All students need to feel that academic success is possible. The multicultural curriculum should also help students develop a high regard for their original languages and cultures.

3. The multicultural curriculum should help students develop greater self-understanding. Students should develop more sophisticated understandings of why they are the way they are, why their ethnic and cultural groups are the way they are, and what ethnicity and culture mean in their daily lives. Such self-understanding will help students to handle more effectively situations in which ethnicity and culture may play a part.

Students cannot fully understand why they are the way they are and why certain things might occur in their future until they have a solid knowledge of the groups to which they belong and the effects of group membership on their lives. Multicultural education should enable students to come to grips with these individual and group relationships in general and the effects of ethnicity and culture on their lives in particular.

Looking at group membership should not undermine a student's individuality. Rather, it should add a dimension to the understanding of a student's unique individuality by learning the effects of belonging to groups. Neither are students to be assigned and locked into one group. Instead, students should be aware of the many groups to which they belong, both voluntarily and involuntarily, and recognize that at various moments one or more of these groups may be affecting their lives.

The multicultural curriculum should also help students understand and appreciate their personal backgrounds and family heritages. Family studies in the school can contribute to increased self-understanding and a personal sense of heritage, as contrasted with the generalized experiences presented in books. They can also contribute to family and personal pride. If parents and other relatives come to school to share their stories and experiences, students will become increasingly aware that ethnic groups are a meaningful part of our nation's heritage and merit study by all of us so that we can better understand the complexity of the nation's pluralistic experiences and traditions.

7.0 The curriculum should help students understand the totality of the experiences of ethnic and cultural groups in the United States.

The social problems that ethnic and cultural group members experience are often regarded as part of their cultural characteristics. Alcoholism, crime, and illiteracy, for example, are considered by many people cultural characteristics of particular racial or ethnic groups. Ethnicity is often assumed to mean something negative and divisive, and the study of ethnic groups and ethnicity often becomes the examination of problems such as prejudice, racism, discrimination, and exploitation. To concentrate exclusively on these problems when studying ethnicity creates serious distortions in perceptions of ethnic groups. Among other things, it stereotypes ethnic groups as essentially passive recipients of the dominant society's discrimination and exploitation. Although these are legitimate issues and should be included in a comprehensive, effective multicultural curriculum, they should not constitute the entire curriculum.

Although many ethnic group members face staggering sociopolitical problems, these problems do not constitute the whole of their lives. Nor are all ethnic groups affected to the same degree or in the same way by these problems. Moreover, many ethnic groups have developed and maintained viable life-styles and have made notable contributions to U.S. culture. The experiences of each ethnic group are part of a composite of human activities. Although it is true that each ethnic group has significant unifying historical experiences and cultural traits, no ethnic group has a single, homogeneous, historical-cultural pattern. Members of an ethnic group do not conform to a single cultural norm or mode of behavior, nor are ethnic cultures uniform and static.

Consequently, the many dimensions of ethnic experiences and cultures should be studied. The curriculum should help students understand the significant historical experiences and basic cultural patterns of ethnic groups, the critical contemporary issues and social problems confronting each of them, and the dynamic diversity of the experiences, cultures, and individuals within each ethnic group.

A consistently multifaceted approach to teaching benefits students in several major ways. It helps them to become aware of the commonalities within and among ethnic groups. At the same time, it helps counteract stereotyping by making students aware of the rich diversity within each ethnic group in the United States. It also helps students develop more comprehensive and realistic understandings of the broad range of ethnic group heritages and experiences.

8.0 The multicultural curriculum should help students understand that a conflict between ideals and realities always exists in human societies.

Traditionally, students in U.S. common schools have been taught a great deal about the ideals of our society. Conflicts between ideals, however, are often glossed over. Often values, such as freedom in the U.S. democracy, are treated as attainable ideals, and the realities of U.S. society have been distorted to make it appear that they have, indeed, been achieved. Courses in U.S. history and citizenship especially have been characterized by this kind of unquestioning approach to the socialization of youth. This form of citizenship education, "passing down the myths and legends of our national heritage," tends to inculcate parochial national attitudes, promote serious misconceptions about the nature of U.S. society and culture, and develop cynicism in youth who are aware of the gaps between the ideal and the real.

When ethnic studies emerged from the civil rights movement of the 1960s, there was a strong and negative reaction to the traditional approach to citizenship education. A widely expressed goal of many curriculum reformers was to "tell it like it is and was" in the classroom. In many of the reformed courses, however, U.S. history and society were taught and viewed primarily from the viewpoints of specific ethnic groups. Little attention was given to basic U.S. values, except to highlight gross discrepancies between ideals and practices of U.S. society. Emphasis was often on how ethnic groups of color had been oppressed by Anglo-Americans.

Both the unquestioning approach and the tell-it-like-it-is approach result in distortions. In a sound multicultural curriculum, emphasis should be neither on the ways in which the United States has "fulfilled its noble ideals" nor on the "sins committed by the Anglo-Americans" (or any other group of Americans). Rather, students should be encouraged to examine the democratic values that emerged in the United States, why they emerged, how they were defined in various periods, and to whom they referred in various eras. Students should also examine the extent to which these values have or have not been fulfilled, and the continuing conflict between values such as freedom and equality and between ideals in other societies.

Students should also be encouraged to examine alternative interpretations of the discrepancies between ideals and realities in the life and history of the United States. From the perspectives of some individuals and groups, there has been a continuing expansion of human rights in the United States. Others see a continuing process of weighing rights against rights as the optimum mix of values, none of which can be fully realized as ideals. Many argue that basic human rights are still limited to U.S. citizens who have certain class, racial, ethnic, gender, and cultural characteristics. Students should consider why these various interpretations arose and why there are different views regarding conflicts between the ideals and between the ideals and realities of U.S. society.

9.0 The multicultural curriculum should explore and clarify ethnic and cultural alternatives and options in the United States.

Educational questions regarding students' ethnic and cultural alternatives and options are complex and difficult. Some individuals, for a variety of complex reasons, are uncomfortable with their ethnic and cultural identities and wish to deny them. Some individuals are uncomfortable when their own ethnic groups are discussed in the classroom. Teachers need to handle these topics sensitively; they must not ignore them.

The degree of a class's resistance when studying ethnic or cultural groups is influenced by the teacher's approach to the study of diversity. Students can sense when the teacher or other students in the class are intolerant of their particular group or some of its characteristics. Students often receive such messages from nonverbal responses. The teacher can minimize students' resistance to studying their own heritage by creating a classroom atmosphere that reflects acceptance and respect for ethnic and cultural differences. Most importantly, teachers need to model their own acceptance of and respect for ethnic, racial, and cultural diversity.

Teachers should help students understand the options related to their own ethnic and cultural identity and the nature of ethnic and cultural identity and the nature of ethnic and cultural alternatives and options within the United States. Students should be helped to understand that, ideally, all individuals should have the right to select the manner and degree of identifying or not identifying with their ethnic and cultural groups. They should learn, however, that some individuals, such as members of many White ethnic groups, have this privilege while others, such as most African Americans, have more limited options. Most persons of European ancestry can become structurally assimilated into the mainstream U.S. society. When they become highly assimilated, they can usually participate completely in most U.S. economic, social, and political institutions. On the other hand, no matter how culturally assimilated or acculturated members of some ethnic groups become, they are still perceived and stigmatized by the larger society on the basis of their physical characteristics.

Students should also be helped to understand that although individualism is strong in the United States, in reality many Americans, such as American Indians and Chinese Americans, are often judged not as individuals but on the basis of the racial or ethnic group to which they belong. While teachers may give American Indian or Chinese American students the option of examining or not examining their ethnic heritage and identity, such students need to be helped to understand how they are perceived and identified by the larger society. Educators must respect the individual rights of students, at the same time, however, they have a professional responsibility to help students learn basic facts and generalizations about the nature of race and ethnicity in the United States.

10.0 The multicultural curriculum should promote values, attitudes, and behaviors that support ethnic pluralism and cultural diversity as well as build and support the nation-state and the nation's shared national culture. E pluribus unum *should be the goal of the schools and the nation.*

Ethnicity and cultural identity are salient factors in the lives of many U.S. citizens. They help individuals answer the question, Who am I? by providing a sense of peoplehood, identity, and cultural and spiritual roots. They provide a filter through which events, life-styles, norms, and values are processed and screened. They provide a means through which identity is affirmed, heritages are validated, and preferred associates are selected. Therefore, ethnicity and cultural identity serve necessary functions in many people's lives. Ethnicity and cultural identity are neither always positive and reinforcing, nor always negative and debilitating, although they have the potential for both. An effective multicultural curriculum examines all of these dimensions of ethnicity and cultural identity.

The curriculum should help students understand that diversity is an integral part of life in the United States. Ethnic and cultural diversity permeate U.S. history and society. Demographic projections indicate that the United States will become increasingly multiethnic and multicultural in the future. Consequently, schools should teach about ethnic and cultural diversity to help students acquire more accurate assessments of history and culture in the United States. Major goals of multicultural education include improving respect for human dignity, maximizing cultural options, understanding what makes people alike and different, and accepting diversity as inevitable and valuable to human life.

Students should learn that difference does not necessarily imply inferiority or superiority, and that the study of ethnic and cultural group differences need not lead to polarization. They should also learn that although conflict is unavoidable in ethnically or racially pluralistic societies, such conflict does not necessarily have to be destructive or divisive. Conflict is an intrinsic part of the human condition, especially so in a pluralistic society. Conflict is often a catalyst for social progress. Multicultural education programs that explore diversity in positive, realistic ways will present ethnic conflict in its proper perspective. They will help students understand that there is strength in diversity, and that cooperation among ethnic groups does not necessarily require identical beliefs, behaviors, and values.

The multicultural curriculum should help students understand and respect ethnic diversity and broaden their cultural options. Too many people in the United States learn only the values, behavioral patterns, and beliefs of either mainstream society or their own ethnic groups, cultural groups, or communities. Socialization is, in effect, encapsulating, providing few opportunities for most individuals to acquire more than stereotypes about ethnic and cultural groups other than their own. Therefore, many people tend to view other ethnic groups and life-styles as "abnormal" or "deviant." The multicultural curriculum can help students correct these misconceptions by teaching them that other ways of living are as valid and viable as their own.

The multicultural curriculum should also promote the basic values expressed in our major historical documents. Each ethnic group should have the right to practice its own religious, social, and cultural beliefs, albeit within the limits of due regard for the rights of others. There is, after all, a set of overarching values that all groups within a society or nation must endorse to maintain societal cohesion. In our nation, these core values stem from our commitment to human dignity, and include justice, equality, freedom, and due process of law. Although the school should value and reflect ethnic and cultural diversity, it should not promote the practices and beliefs of any ethnic or cultural group that contradict the core democratic values of the United States. Rather, the school should foster ethnic and cultural differences that maximize opportunities for democratic living. Pluralism must take place within the context of national unity. *E pluribus unum*— out of many, one—should be our goal.

Although ethnic and cultural group membership should not restrict an individual's opportunity and ability to achieve and to participate, it is sometimes used by groups in power to the detriment of less powerful groups. Individuals who do not understand the role of ethnicity often find it a troublesome reality, one extremely difficult to handle. Multicultural curricula should help students examine the dilemmas surrounding ethnicity as a step toward realizing its full potential as an enabling force in the lives of individuals, groups, and the nation.

11.0 The multicultural curriculum should help students develop their decision-making abilities, social participation skills, and sense of political efficacy as necessary bases for effective citizenship in a pluralistic democratic nation.

The demands upon people to make reflective decisions on issues related to race, ethnicity, and culture are increasing as the nation's ethnic texture deepens. When people are unable to process the masses of conflicting information—including facts, opinions, interpretations, and theories about ethnic groups—they are often overwhelmed.

The multicultural curriculum must enable students to gain knowledge and apply it. Students need a rich foundation of sound knowledge. Facts, concepts, generalizations, and theories differ in their capability for organizing particulars and in predictive capacity; concepts and generalizations have more usefulness than mere collections of miscellaneous facts. Young people need practice in the steps of scholarly methods for arriving at knowledge—identifying problems, formulating hypotheses, locating and evaluating source materials, organizing information as evidence, analyzing, interpreting, and reworking what they find, and making conclusions. Students also need ample opportunities to learn to use knowledge in making sense out of the situations they encounter.

When curricular programs are inappropriate, teaching is inept, or expectations are low for students of some ethnic groups, and especially for those who are low-income, the emphasis in class is likely to be on discrete facts, memorization of empty generalizations, and low-level skills. Even if the names, dates, and exercises in using an index are drawn from ethnic content, such an emphasis is still discriminatory and inconsistent with the basic purpose of multicultural education. All young people need opportunities to develop powerful concepts, generalizations, and intellectual abilities when studying content related to ethnic and cultural diversity.

Students must also learn to identify values and relate them to knowledge. Young people should be taught methods for clarifying their own values relating to ethnic and cultural diversity. Such processes should include identifying value problems (their own and others'), describing evaluative behaviors, recognizing value conflicts in themselves and in social situations, recognizing and proposing alternatives based on values, and making choices between values in light of their consequences.

Determining the basic ideas, discovering and verifying facts, and valuing are interrelated aspects of decision making. Ample opportunity for practice in real-life situations is necessary; such practice frequently requires interdisciplinary as well as multicultural perspectives. Decision-making skills help people assess social situations objectively and perceptively, identify feasible courses of action and project their consequences, decide thoughtfully, and then act.

The multicultural curriculum must also help students develop effective social and civic action skills because many students from ethnic groups are over-whelmed by a sense of a lack of control of their destinies. These feelings often stem from their belief that, as in the past, they and other people of color have little influence on political policies and institutions (Ogbu, 1990). The multicultural curriculum should help students develop a sense of political efficacy and become active and effective in the civic life of their communities and the nation. With a basis in strong commitments to such democratic values as justice, freedom, and equality, students can learn to exercise political and social influence responsibly to influence societal decisions related to race, ethnicity, and cultural freedom in ways consistent with human dignity.

The school, in many ways, is a microcosm of society, reflecting the changing dynamics of ethnic group situations. The school can provide many opportunities for students to practice social participation skills and to test their political efficacy as they address themselves to resolving some of the school's racial and ethnic problems. Issues such as the participation of ethnic individuals in school government, the uneven application of discriminatory disciplinary rules, and preferential treatment of certain students because of their racial, ethnic, cultural, and social-class backgrounds are examples of problems that students can help to resolve. Applying social action skills effectively, students can combine knowledge, valuing, and thought gained from multicultural perspectives and experiences to resolve problems affecting racial, ethnic, and cultural groups.

By providing students with opportunities to use decision-making abilities and social action skills in the resolution of problems affecting ethnic, racial, and cultural groups, schools can contribute to more effective education for democratic citizenship.

12.0 The multicultural curriculum should help students develop the skills necessary for effective interpersonal, interethnic, and intercultural group interactions.

Effective interpersonal interaction across ethnic group lines is often difficult to achieve. The problem is complicated by the fact that individuals bring to cross-ethnic interaction situations attitudes, values, and expectations that influence their own behavior, including their responses to the behavior of others. These expectations are sometimes formed on the basis of what their own groups deem appropriate behavior and what each individual believes he or she knows about other ethnic groups. Much knowledge about ethnic groups is stereotyped, distorted, and based on distant observations, scattered and superficial contacts, inadequate or imbalanced media treatment, and incomplete factual information. Attempts at cross-ethnic interpersonal interactions, therefore, are often stymied by ethnocentrism.

The problems created by ethnocentrism can be at least partially resolved by helping students recognize the forces operating in interpersonal interactions, and how these forces affect behavior. Students should develop skills and concepts to overcome factors that prevent successful interactions including identifying ethnic and cultural stereotypes, examining media treatment of ethnic groups, clarifying ethnic and cultural attitudes and values, developing cross-cultural communication skills, recognizing how attitudes and values are projected in verbal and nonverbal behaviors, and viewing the dynamics of interpersonal interactions from others' perspectives.

One of the goals of multicultural education should be to help individuals function easily and effectively with members of both their own and other racial, ethnic, and cultural groups. The multicultural curriculum should provide opportunities for students to explore lines of cross-cultural communication and to experiment with cross-ethnic and cross-cultural functioning. Actual experiences can be effective teaching devices, allowing students to test stereotypes and idealized behavioral constructs against real-life situations, and make the necessary adjustments in their frames of reference and behaviors. In the process, they should learn that ethnic group members, in the final analysis, are individuals, with all of the variations that characterize all individuals, and that ethnicity is only one of many variables that shape their personalities. Students will be forced to confront their values and make moral choices when their experiences in cross-ethnic and cross-cultural interactions produce information contrary to previously held notions. Thus, students should broaden their ethnic and cultural options, increase their frames of reference, develop greater appreciation for individual and ethnic differences, and deepen their own capacities as human beings.

13.0 The multicultural curriculum should be comprehensive in scope and sequence, should present holistic views of ethnic and cultural groups, and should be an integral part of the total school curriculum.

Students learn best from well-planned, comprehensive, continuous, and interrelated experiences. In an effective multicultural school, the study of ethnic and cultural content is integrated into the curriculum from preschool through 12th grade and beyond. This study should be carefully planned to encourage the development of progressively more complex concepts and generalizations. It should also involve students in the study of a variety of ethnic and cultural groups.

A comprehensive multicultural curriculum should also include a broad range of experiences within the study of any group: present culture, historical experiences, sociopolitical realities, contributions to the nation's development, problems faced in everyday living, and conditions of existence in society.

Students should be introduced to the experiences of persons from widely varying backgrounds. Although the study of ethnic and cultural success stories can help students of an ethnic group develop pride in their own group, the curriculum should include study of ethnic peoples in general, not just heroes and success stories. In addition, those outside of an ethnic group can develop greater respect for that group by learning about these heroes and successes. Moreover, in establishing heroes and labeling people as successes, teachers should move beyond the standards of the dominant society and consider the values of each ethnic group and the worth of each individual life. An active contributor to an ethnic neighborhood may be more of a hero to the local community than a famous athlete; a good parent may be more of a "success" than a famous politician.

For optimum effectiveness, the study of ethnic and cultural group experiences must be interwoven into the total curriculum. It should not be reserved for special occasions, units, or courses, nor should it be considered supplementary to the existing curriculum. Such observances as African American History or Brotherhood Week, Hanukkah, Cinco de Mayo, St. Patrick's Day, and Martin Luther King, Jr.'s, birthday are important and necessary, but insufficient in themselves. To rely entirely on these kinds of occasions and events, or to relegate ethnic content to a marginal position in the curriculum, is to guarantee a minimal influence of ethnic studies.

The basic premises and organizational structures of schools should be reformed to reflect the nation's multicultural realities. The curriculum should be reorganized so that ethnic and cultural diversity is an integral, natural, and normal component of educational experiences for *all* students, with ethnic and cultural content accepted and used in everyday instruction, and with various ethnic and cultural perspectives introduced. Multicultural content is as appropriate and important in teaching such fundamental skills and abilities as reading, thinking, and decision making as it is in teaching about social issues raised by racism, dehumanization, racial conflict, and alternative ethnic and cultural life-styles.

14.0 The multicultural curriculum should include the continuous study of the cultures, historical experiences, social realities, and existential conditions of ethnic and cultural groups, including a variety of racial compositions.

The multicultural curriculum should involve students in the continuous study of ethnic groups of different racial compositions. A curriculum that concentrates on one ethnic or cultural group is not multicultural. Nor is a curriculum multicultural if it focuses exclusively on European ethnics or exclusively on ethnic groups of color. Every ethnic group cannot be included in the curriculum of a particular school or school district—the number is too large to be manageable. The inclusion of groups of different racial compositions, however, is a necessary characteristic of effective multicultural education.

Moreover, the multicultural curriculum should include the consistent examination of significant aspects of ethnic experiences influenced by or related to race. These include such concepts as racism, racial prejudice, racial discrimination, and exploitation based on race. The sensitive and continuous development of such concepts should help students develop an understanding of racial factors in the past and present of our nation.

15.0 Interdisciplinary and multidisciplinary approaches should be used in designing and implementing the multicultural curriculum.

No single discipline can adequately explain all components of the life-styles, cultural experiences, and social problems of ethnic groups. Knowledge from any one discipline is insufficient to help individuals make adequate decisions on the complex issues raised by racism, sexism, structural exclusion, poverty, and powerlessness. Concepts such as racism, anti-Semitism, and language discrimination have multiple dimensions. To delineate these requires the concepts and perspectives of the social sciences, history, literature, music, art, and philosophy.

Single-discipline or mono-perspective analyses of complex ethnic and cultural issues can produce skewed, distorted interpretations and evaluations. A promising way to avoid these pitfalls is to employ consistently multidisciplinary approaches in studying experiences and events related to ethnic and cultural groups. For example, ethnic protest is not simply a political, economic, artistic, or sociological activity; it is all four of these. Therefore, a curriculum that purports to be multicultural and is realistic in its treatment of ethnic protest must focus on its broader ramifications. Such study must address the scientific, political, artistic, and sociological dimensions of protest.

The accomplishments of the United States are due neither to the ingenuity and creativity of a single ethnic or cultural group, nor to accomplishments in a single area, but rather to the efforts and contributions of many ethnic groups and individuals in many areas. African American, Latino, American Indian, Asian American, and European immigrant group members have all contributed to the fields of science and industry, politics, literature, economics, and the arts. Multidisciplinary analyses will best help students to understand them.

16.0 The multicultural curriculum should use comparative approaches in the study of ethnic and cultural groups.

The study of ethnic and cultural group experiences should not be a process of competition. It should not promote the idea that any one ethnic or cultural group has a monopoly on talent and worth, or incapacity and weakness, but, instead, the idea that each individual and each ethnic group has worth and dignity. Students should be taught that persons from all ethnic groups have common characteristics and needs, although they are affected differently by certain social situations and may use different means to respond to their needs and to achieve their objectives. Furthermore, school personnel should remember that realistic comparative approaches to the study of different ethnic and cultural group experiences are descriptive and analytical, not normative or judgmental. Teachers should also be aware of their own biases and prejudices as they help students to use comparative approaches.

Social situations and events included in the curriculum should be analyzed from the perspectives of several ethnic and cultural groups instead of using a mono-perspective analysis. This approach allows students to see the subtle ways in which the lives of different ethnic group members are similar and interrelated, to study the concept of universality as it relates to ethnic groups, and to see how all ethnic groups are active participants in all aspects of society. Studying such issues as power and politics, ethnicity, and culture from comparative, multicultural perspectives will help students to develop more realistic, accurate understandings of how these issues affect everyone, and how the effects are both alike and different.

17.0 The multicultural curriculum should help students to view and interpret events, situations, and conflict from diverse ethnic and cultural perspectives and points of view.

Historically, students have been taught to view events, situations, and our national history primarily from the perspectives of mainstream historians and social scientists sympathetic to the dominant groups within our society. The perspectives of other groups have been largely omitted in the school curriculum. The World War II Japanese American internment and the Indian Removal Act of 1830, for example, are rarely studied from the points of view of interned Japanese Americans or the American Indians forced to leave their homes and move west.

To gain a more complete understanding of both our past and our present, students should look at events and situations from the perspectives of the mainstream and from the perspectives of marginalized groups. This approach to teaching is more likely to make our students less ethnocentric and more able to understand that almost any event or situation can be legitimately looked at from many perspectives. When using this approach in the classroom, the teacher should avoid, as much as possible, labeling any perspective "right" or "wrong." Rather, the teacher should try to help students understand how each group may view a situation differently and why. The emphasis should be on understanding and explanation and not on simplistic moralizing. For example, the perceptions many Jewish Americans have of political events in the United States have been shaped by memories of the Holocaust and anti-Semitism in the United States.

Ethnicity and cultural diversity have strongly influenced the nature of intergroup relations in U.S. society. The way that individuals perceive events and situations occurring in the United States is often influenced by their ethnic and cultural experiences, especially when the events and situations are directly related to ethnic conflict and discrimination or to issues such as affirmative action and busing for school desegregation. When students view a historical or contemporary situation from the perspectives of one ethnic or cultural group only—whether majority or minority—they can acquire, at best, an incomplete understanding.

18.0 The multicultural curriculum should conceptualize and describe the development of the United States as a multidirectional society.

A basic structural concept in the study and teaching of U.S. society is the view that the United States has developed mainly from east to west. According to this concept, the United States is the product of the spread of civilization from Western Europe across the Atlantic Ocean to the east coast of what is today the United States and then west to the Pacific. Within this approach, ethnic groups appear almost always in two forms: as obstacles to the advancement of westward-moving Anglo civilization or as problems that must be corrected or, at least, kept under control.

The underlying rationale for this frame of reference is that the study of U.S. history is for the most part an account of processes within the national boundaries of the United States. In applying this frame of reference, however, educators have been inconsistent, including as part of the study of the United States such themes as pre–United States geography, the pre–United States British colonies, the Texas revolution, and the Lone Star Republic. In short, the study of the United States has traditionally included phenomena outside the boundaries of the political United States.

Yet, while including some non–United States themes as part of the traditional study of the United States, school programs have not adequately included study of the Native American, Hispanic, and Mexican societies that developed on land that ultimately became part of the United States. Nor has sufficient attention been devoted to the northwesterly flow of cultures from Africa to the United States, the northerly flow of cultures from Mexico, Latin America, and the Caribbean, the easterly flow of cultures from Asia, and the westerly flow of latter-day immigrants from Eastern, Central, and Southern Europe.

Multicultural education, from the early years of school onward, must redress these intellectually invalid and distorting imbalances by illuminating the variety of cultural experiences that compose the total U.S. experience. Multicultural education must consistently address the development of the entire geocultural United States—that area which, in time, was to become the United States and the peoples encompassed by that area. Moreover, the flow of cultures into the United States must be viewed multidirectionally.

19.0 Schools should provide opportunities for students to participate in the aesthetic experiences of various ethnic and cultural groups.

The study of ethnic and cultural groups should be based on more than the social sciences. Although incorporating statistical and analytical social science methodologies and concepts into the study of ethnic and cultural groups is valuable, an overreliance on these methods lacks an important part of the multicultural experience—participation in the experiences of ethnic and cultural groups.

A number of teaching materials can be used. Students should read and hear past and contemporary writings of members of various ethnic and cultural groups. Poetry, short stories, folklore, essays, plays, and novels should be used. Ethnic autobiographies offer special insight into what it means to be ethnic in the United States.

Ethnic music, art, architecture, and dance—past and contemporary—provide other avenues for experiential participation, interpreting the emotions and feelings of ethnic groups. The arts and humanities can serve as excellent vehicles for studying group experiences by focusing on these questions: What aspects of the experience of a particular ethnic group helped create these kinds of musical and artistic expressions? What do they reveal about these groups?

Studying multiethnic literature and arts, students should become acquainted with what has been created in local ethnic communities. In addition, members of local ethnic communities can provide dramatic "living autobiographies" for students; invite them to discuss their viewpoints and experiences with students. Students should also have opportunities for developing their own artistic, musical, and literary abilities, even to make them available to the local community.

Role playing of various ethnic and cultural experiences should be interspersed throughout the curriculum to encourage understanding of what it means to belong to various ethnic groups. The immersion of students in multiethnic experiences is an effective means for developing understanding of both self and others.

20.0 The multicultural curriculum should provide opportunities for students to study ethnic group languages as legitimate communication systems and help them develop full literacy in at least two languages.

A multicultural curriculum recognizes language diversity and promotes the attitude that all languages and dialects are valid communicating systems for some groups and for some purposes. The program requires a multidisciplinary focus on language and dialect.

Concepts about language and dialect derived from disciplines such as anthropology, sociology, and political science expand students' perceptions of language and dialect as something more than correct grammar. For example, the nature and intent of language policies and laws in the United States can be compared to those in bilingual nations. Students can also be taught sociolinguistic concepts that provide a framework for understanding the verbal and nonverbal behavior of others and themselves. Critical listening, speaking, and reading habits should be nurtured with special attention to the uses of language.

Research indicates that a school's rejection of a student's home language affects the student's self-esteem, academic achievement, and social and occupational mobility. Conversely, a school's acceptance and use of a student's home language improves the student's self-esteem, academic achievement, and relationships among students in a school (U.S. Commission on Civil Rights, 1975). In a multicultural curriculum, students are provided opportunities to study their own and others' dialects. They become increasingly receptive to the languages and dialects of their peers. Such an approach helps students develop concepts in their own vernaculars whenever necessary at the same time promoting appreciation of home language environments.

Literacy in U.S. English is a time-honored goal of schools and should be maintained. Another important goal of the multicultural curriculum, however, is to help all students acquire literacy in a second language. Second-language literacy requires students to understand, speak, read, and write well enough to communicate effectively with native speakers of the second language. Equally important, students should study the cultures of the people who use the second language. Ultimately, effective communication in the second language requires an understanding of its people and their culture.

Some students come to school speaking two languages. These students should be provided the opportunity to develop full literacy in their native language. In turn, these students and their parents can be used as resources for helping other students acquire a second language proficiency.

Second-language literacy complements other areas of the multicultural curriculum. For example, approaches for studying the culture of other people are described in several of the above guidelines. As students are learning a second language, they can learn skills in interpersonal and intercultural communications. Further, because these guidelines encourage multidisciplinary approaches, second language literacy can be achieved while other areas of the language arts and the social studies are taught.

21.0 The multicultural curriculum should make maximum use of experiential learning, especially local community resources.

An effective multicultural curriculum includes a study of ethnic and cultural groups not only nationally, but locally as well. An effective multicultural curriculum must expand beyond classroom walls. Teachers should use the local community as a "laboratory" in which students can develop and use intellectual, social, and political action skills. Planned field trips and individual or group research projects are helpful. Continuous investigation of the local community can provide insights into the dynamics of ethnic and cultural groups. It can create greater respect for what has been accomplished. It can promote awareness of and commitment to what still needs to be done to improve the lives and opportunities of all local residents.

Every member of the local community, including students' family members, is a valuable source of knowledge. There are no class, educational, or linguistic qualifications for participating in the U.S. experience, for having culture or society, for having family or neighborhood traditions, for perceiving the surrounding community, or for relating experiences. Teachers should invite local residents of various ethnic backgrounds to the classroom to share their experiences and views with students, relate their oral traditions, answer questions, offer new outlooks on society and history, and open doors of investigation for students. Special efforts should be made to involve senior citizens in school multicultural programs both to help them develop a higher sense of self-worth and to benefit the students and the school community.

It is important that students develop a sensitivity to ethnic differences and a conceptual framework for viewing ethnic differences before interacting with ethnic classroom guests or studying the local ethnic communities. Otherwise, these promising opportunities may reinforce, rather than reduce, ethnic stereotypes and prejudices.

In study projects, students can consider such topics as local population distribution, housing, school assignments, political representation, and ethnic community activities. Older students can take advantage of accessible public documents, such as city council and school board minutes, minutes of local organizations, and church records for insight into the community. To separate the local community from the school is to ignore the everyday world in which students live.

22.0 The assessment procedures used with students should reflect their ethnic and cultural experiences.

To make the school a truly multicultural institution, major changes must be made in the ways in which we test and ascertain student abilities. Most of the intelligence tests administered in the public schools are based upon a mainstream conformity, mono-ethnic model. Because many students socialized within other ethnic and cultural groups find the tests and other aspects of the school alien and intimidating, they perform poorly and are placed in low academic tracks, special education classes, or low-ability reading groups (Oakes, 1985). Research indicates that teachers in these kinds of situations tend to have low expectations for their students and often fail to create the kinds of learning environments that promote proficiency in the skills and abilities necessary to function effectively in society (Oakes, 1985).

In the final analysis, standardized intelligence testing frequently serves to deny some youths equal educational opportunities. The results of these tests are often used to justify the noneducation of students of color and low-income students and to relieve teachers and other school personnel from accountability (Deyhle, 1986; Mercer, 1989). Novel assessment devices that reflect the cultures of ethnic youths need to be developed and used. Moreover, teacher-generated tests and other routine classroom assessment techniques should reflect the cultures of ethnic youths. It will, however, do little good for educators to create improved assessment procedures for ethnic youths unless they also implement multicultural curricular and instructional practices.

23.0 Schools should conduct ongoing, systematic evaluations of the goals, methods, and instructional materials used in teaching about ethnic and cultural diversity.

Schools should formulate attainable goals and objectives for multicultural education. To evaluate the extent to which these goals and objectives are accomplished, school personnel must judge—with evidence—what occurs in their schools in three broad areas: (1) school policies and governance procedures; (2) everyday practices of staff and teachers; and (3) curricular programs and offerings, academic and nonacademic, preschool through 12th grade. These guidelines and the checklist in [the Appendix] will help schools' evaluation programs.

Many sources of evidence should be used. Teachers, administrators, support staff, parents, students, and others in the school community ought to participate in providing and evaluating evidence.

Evaluation should be construed as a means by which a school, its staff, and students can improve multiethnic and multicultural relations, experiences, and understandings. Evaluation should be oriented toward analyzing and improving, not castigating or applauding, multicultural programs.

References

Alba, R. D. (1990). *Ethnic Identity: The Transformation of White America.* New Haven, CT: Yale University Press.

Aronson, E., & Gonzalez, A. (1988). Desegregation, Jigsaw, and the Mexican-American Experience. In P. A. Katz and D. A. Taylor (Eds.), *Eliminating Racism: Profiles in Controversy* (pp. 301–314). New York: Plenum Press.

Asante, M. K. (1987). *The Afrocentric Idea.* Philadelphia: Temple University Press.

Asante, M. K. (1990). *Kemet, Afrocentricity, and Knowledge.* Trenton, NJ: African World Press.

Asante, M. K. (1991). The Afrocentric Idea in Education. *The Journal of Negro Education, 60,* 170–80.

Banks, J. A. (1991a). *Teaching Strategies for Ethnic Studies* (5th ed.). Boston: Allyn and Bacon.

Banks, J. A. (1991b). The Dimensions of Multicultural Education. *Multicultural Leader, 4,* 3–4.

Banks, J. A. (1991c). Multicultural Education: Its Effects on Students' Racial and Gender Role Attitudes. In J. P. Shaver (Ed.), *Handbook of Research on Social Studies Teaching and Learning* (pp. 459–469). New York: Macmillan.

Banks, J. A., & Banks, C. A. M. (Eds.). (1989). *Multicultural Education: Issues and Perspectives.* Boston: Allyn and Bacon.

Belenky, M. F., Clinchy, B. M., Goldberger, N. R., & Tarule, J. M. (1986). *Women's Ways of Knowing: The Development of Self, Voice and Mind.* New York: Basic Books.

Bernal, M. (1991). *Black Athena: The Afroasiatic Roots of Classical Civilization.* Vol. 2, *The Archaeological and Documentary Evidence.* New Brunswick, NJ: Rutgers University Press.

Cohen, E. G. (1986). *Designing Groupwork: Strategies for the Heterogeneous Classroom.* New York: Teachers College Press.

Cummins, J. (1986). Empowering Minority Students: A Framework for Intervention. *Harvard Educational Review, 56,* 18–36.

Delpit, L. D. (1988). The Silenced Dialogue: Power and Pedagogy in Educating Other People's Children. *Harvard Educational Review, 58,* 280–298.

Deyhle, D. (1986). Success and Failure: A Micro-Ethnographic Comparison of Navajo and Anglo Students' Perceptions of Testing. *Curriculum Inquiry, 16,* 365–389.

Diop, C. A. (1974). *The African Origins of Civilization: Myth or Reality?* New York: Lawrence Hill and Co.

Fordham, S. (1991). Racelessness in Private Schools: Should We Deconstruct the Racial and Cultural Identity of African-American Adolescents? *Teachers College Record, 92,* 470–484.

Fordham, S. & Ogbu, J. U. (1986). Black Students' School Success: Coping with the Burden of 'Acting White.' *The Urban Review, 18,* 176–206.

Gay, G. (1991). Culturally Diverse Students and Social Studies. In J. P. Shaver (Ed.), *Handbook of Research on Social Studies Teaching and Learning* (pp. 144–156). New York: Macmillan.

Hale-Benson, J. E. (1982). *Black Children: Their Roots, Culture and Learning Styles.* Baltimore: The Johns Hopkins University Press.

Heath, S. H. (1983). *Ways with Words: Language, Life and Work in Communities and Classrooms.* New York: Cambridge University Press.

Hodgkinson, H. L. (1985). *All One System: Demographics of Education, Kindergarten through Graduate School.* Washington, DC: The Institute for Educational Leadership.

Howe, I. (1992). The Value of the Canon. *The New Republic, 204,* 40–47.

Johnson, W. B., & Packer, A. E. (1987). *Workforce 2000: Work and Workers for the 21st Century.* Washington, DC: U.S. Government Printing Office.

Kochman, T. (1981). *Black and White: Styles in Conflict.* Chicago: University of Chicago Press.

Kroeber, A., & Kluckhohn, C. (1952). *Culture: A Critical Review of Concepts and Definitions.* New York: Vintage.

Lerner, G. (1979). *The Majority Finds Its Past: Placing Women in History.* New York: Oxford University Press.

Mercer, J. R. (1989). Alternate Paradigms for Assessment in a Pluralistic Society. In J. A. Banks & C. A. M. Banks (Eds.), *Multicultural Education: Issues and Perspectives* (pp. 289–304). Boston: Allyn and Bacon.

Oakes, J. (1985). *Keeping Track: How Schools Structure Inequality.* New Haven, CT: Yale University Press.

Ogbu, J. U. (1990). Overcoming Racial Barriers to Equal Access. In J. I. Goodlad & P. Keating (Eds.), *Access to Knowledge: An Agenda for Our Nation's Schools* (pp. 59–89). New York: The College Board.

Pallas, A. M., Natriello, G., & McDill, E. L. (1989). The Changing Nature of the Disadvantaged Population: Current Dimensions and Future Trends. *Educational Researcher, 18,* 16–22.

Philips, S. U. (1983). *The Invisible Culture: Communication in Classroom and Community on the Warm Springs Indian Reservation.* New York: Longman.

Ravitch, D. (1990). Multiculturalism E Pluribus Plures. *The American Scholar, 54,* 337–354.

Schlesinger, A. M., Jr. (1991). *The Disuniting of America: Reflections on a Multicultural Society.* Knoxville, TN: Whittle Direct Books.

Sertima, I. V. (Ed.). (1988). *Great Black Leaders: Ancient and Modern.* New Brunswick, NJ: Africana Studies Department, Rutgers University.

Shade, B. J. R. (Ed.). (1989). *Culture, Style and the Educative Press.* Springfield, IL: Charles C Thomas.

Slavin, R. E. (1983). *Cooperative Learning.* New York: Longman.

Sleeter, C. E., & Grant, C. A. (1987). An Analysis of Multicultural Education in the United States. *Harvard Educational Review, 57,* 421–444.

Stephan, W. G. (1985). Intergroup Relations. In G. Lindzey & E. Aronson (Eds.), *The Handbook of Social Psychology,* Vol. 2 (3d ed.) (pp. 599–658). New York: Random House.

Tetreault, M. K. T. (1989). Integrating Content about Women and Gender into the Curriculum. In J. A. Banks & C. A. M. Banks (Eds.), *Multicultural Education: Issues and Perspectives* (pp. 124–144). Boston: Allyn and Bacon.

United States Commission on Civil Rights. (1975). *A Better Chance to Learn: Bilingual-Bicultural Education.* Washington, DC: Author.

Weatherford, J. (1988). *Indian Givers: How the Indians of the Americas Transformed the World.* New York: Fawcett Columbine.

Multicultural Education Program Evaluation Checklist

Rating				Guidelines
Strongly ←——→ Hardly at all				

				1.0 Does ethnic and cultural diversity permeate the total school environment?
				1.1 Are ethnic content and perspectives incorporated into all aspects of the curriculum, preschool through 12th grade and beyond?
				1.2 Do instructional materials treat racial and ethnic differences and groups honestly, realistically, and sensitively?
				1.3 Do school libraries and resource centers offer a variety of materials on the histories, experiences, and cultures of many racial, ethnic, and cultural groups?
				1.4 Do school assemblies, decorations, speakers, holidays, and heroes reflect racial, ethnic, and cultural group differences?
				1.5 Are extracurricular activities multiethnic and multicultural?
				2.0 Do school policies and procedures foster positive interactions among the various racial, ethnic, and cultural group members of the school?
				2.1 Do school policies accommodate the behavioral patterns, learning styles, and orientations of those ethnic and cultural group members actually in the school?
				2.2 Does the school provide a variety of instruments and techniques for teaching and counseling students of various ethnic and cultural groups?
				2.3 Do school policies recognize the holidays and festivities of various ethnic groups?
				2.4 Do school policies avoid instructional and guidance practices based on stereotyped and ethnocentric perceptions?

Rating Strongly ←——→ Hardly at all				Guidelines
				2.5 Do school policies respect the dignity and worth of students as individuals *and* as members of racial, ethnic, and cultural groups?
				3.0 Is the school staff (administrators, instructors, counselors, and support staff) multiethnic and multiracial? 3.1 Has the school established and enforced policies for recruiting and maintaining a staff made up of individuals from various racial and ethnic groups?

				4.0 Does the school have systematic, comprehensive, mandatory, and continuing multicultural staff development programs?
				  4.1 Are teachers, librarians, counselors, administrators, and support staff included in the staff development programs?
				  4.2 Do the staff development programs include a variety of experiences (such as lectures, field experiences, and curriculum projects)?
				  4.3 Do the staff development programs provide opportunities to gain knowledge and understanding about various racial, ethnic, and cultural groups?
				  4.4 Do the staff development programs provide opportunities for participants to explore their attitudes and feelings about their own ethnicity and others'?
				  4.5 Do the staff development programs examine the verbal and nonverbal patterns of interethnic group interactions?
				  4.6 Do the staff development programs provide opportunities for learning how to create and select multiethnic instructional materials and how to incorporate multicultural content into curriculum materials?

				5.0 Does the curriculum reflect the ethnic learning styles of students within the school?
				  5.1 Is the curriculum designed to help students learn how to function effectively in various cultural environments and learn more than one cognitive style?
				  5.2 Do the objectives, instructional strategies, and learning materials reflect the cultures and cognitive styles of the various ethnic and cultural groups within the school?

				6.0 Does the curriculum provide continuous opportunities for students to develop a better sense of self?
				  6.1 Does the curriculum help students strengthen their self-identities?
				  6.2 Is the curriculum designed to help students develop greater self-understanding?
				  6.3 Does the curriculum help students improve their self-concepts?
				  6.4 Does the curriculum help students to better understand themselves in light of their ethnic and cultural heritages?

				7.0 Does the curriculum help students understand the wholeness of the experiences of ethnic and cultural groups?

Rating Strongly ←——→ Hardly at all					Guidelines
					7.1 Does the curriculum include the study of societal problems some ethnic and cultural group members experience, such as racism, prejudice, discrimination, and exploitation? 7.2 Does the curriculum include the study of historical experiences, cultural patterns, and social problems of various ethnic and cultural groups? 7.3 Does the curriculum include both positive and negative aspects of ethnic and cultural group experiences? 7.4 Does the curriculum present people of color both as active participants in society and as subjects of oppression and exploitation? 7.5 Does the curriculum examine the diversity within each group's experience? 7.6 Does the curriculum present group experiences as dynamic and continuously changing? 7.7 Does the curriculum examine the total experiences of groups instead of focusing exclusively on the "heroes"?
					8.0 Does the curriculum help students identify and understand the ever-present conflict between ideals and realities in human societies? 8.1 Does the curriculum help students identify and understand the value conflicts inherent in a multicultural society? 8.2 Does the curriculum examine differing views of ideals and realities among ethnic and cultural groups?
					9.0 Does the curriculum explore and clarify ethnic alternatives and options within U.S. society? 9.1 Does the teacher create a classroom atmosphere reflecting an acceptance of and respect for ethnic and cultural differences? 9.2 Does the teacher create a classroom atmosphere allowing realistic consideration of alternatives and options for members of ethnic and cultural groups?
					10.0 Does the curriculum promote values, attitudes, and behaviors that support ethnic and cultural diversity? 10.1 Does the curriculum help students examine differences within and among ethnic and cultural groups? 10.2 Does the curriculum foster attitudes supportive of cultural democracy and other unifying democratic ideals and values? 10.3 Does the curriculum reflect ethnic and cultural diversity? 10.4 Does the curriculum present diversity as a vital societal force that encompasses both potential strength and potential conflict?
					11.0 Does the curriculum help students develop decision-making abilities, social participation skills, and a sense of political efficacy necessary for effective citizenship?

Rating Strongly ←——→ Hardly at all					Guidelines
					11.1 Does the curriculum help students develop the ability to distinguish facts from interpretations and opinions?
					11.2 Does the curriculum help students develop skills in finding and processing information?
					11.3 Does the curriculum help students develop sound knowledge, concepts, generalizations, and theories about issues related to ethnicity and cultural identity?
					11.4 Does the curriculum help students develop sound methods of thinking about issues related to ethnic and cultural groups?
					11.5 Does the curriculum help students develop skills in clarifying and reconsidering their values and relating them to their understanding of ethnicity and cultural identity?
					11.6 Does the curriculum include opportunities to use knowledge, valuing, and thinking in decision making on issues related to race, ethnicity, and culture?
					11.7 Does the curriculum provide opportunities for students to take action on social problems affecting racial, ethnic, and cultural groups?
					11.8 Does the curriculum help students develop a sense of efficacy?
					12.0 Does the curriculum help students develop skills necessary for effective interpersonal and intercultural group interactions?
					12.1 Does the curriculum help students understand ethnic and cultural reference points that influence communication?
					12.2 Does the curriculum help students participate in cross-ethnic and cross-cultural experiences and reflect upon them?
					13.0 Is the multicultural curriculum comprehensive in scope and sequence, presenting holistic views of ethnic and cultural groups, and an integral part of the total school curriculum?
					13.1 Does the curriculum introduce students to the experiences of persons of widely varying backgrounds in the study of each ethnic and cultural group?
					13.2 Does the curriculum discuss the successes and contributions of group members within the context of that group's values?
					13.3 Does the curriculum include the role of ethnicity and culture in the local community as well as in the nation?
					13.4 Does content related to ethnic and cultural groups extend beyond special units, courses, occasions, and holidays?
					13.5 Are materials written by and about ethnic and cultural groups used in teaching fundamental skills?
					13.6 Does the curriculum provide for the development of progressively more complex concepts, abilities, and values?

Strongly ←⎯⎯→ Hardly at all				Guidelines
Rating				

Strongly ← → Hardly at all				Guidelines
				13.7 Is the study of ethnicity and culture incorporated into instructional plans rather than being supplementary or additive?
				14.0 Does the curriculum include the continuous study of the cultures, historical experiences, social realities, and existential conditions of ethnic groups with a variety of racial compositions?
				14.1 Does the curriculum include study of several ethnic and cultural groups?
				14.2 Does the curriculum include studies of both White ethnic groups and ethnic groups of color?
				14.3 Does the curriculum provide for continuity in the examination of aspects of experience affected by race?
				15.0 Are interdisciplinary and multidisciplinary approaches used in designing and implementing the curriculum?
				15.1 Are interdisciplinary and multidisciplinary perspectives used in the study of ethnic and cultural groups and related issues?
				15.2 Are approaches used authentic and comprehensive explanations of ethnic and cultural issues, events, and problems?
				16.0 Does the curriculum use comparative approaches in the study of racial, ethnic, and cultural groups?
				16.1 Does the curriculum focus on the similarities and differences among and between ethnic and cultural groups?
				16.2 Are matters examined from comparative perspectives with fairness to all?
				17.0 Does the curriculum help students view and interpret events, situations, and conflict from diverse ethnic and cultural perspectives and points of view?
				17.1 Are the perspectives of various ethnic and cultural groups represented in the instructional program?
				17.2 Are students taught why different ethnic and cultural groups often perceive the same historical event or contemporary situation differently?
				17.3 Are the perspectives of each ethnic and cultural group presented as valid ways to perceive the past and the present?
				18.0 Does the curriculum conceptualize and describe the development of the United States as a multidirectional society?
				18.1 Does the curriculum view the territorial and cultural growth of the United States as flowing from several directions?
				18.2 Does the curriculum include a parallel study of the various societies that developed in the geocultural United States?

Rating Strongly ◄──► Hardly at all				Guidelines
				19.0 Does the school provide opportunities for students to participate in the aesthetic experiences of various ethnic and cultural groups?
				19.1 Are multiethnic literature and art used to promote empathy and understanding of people from various ethnic and cultural groups?
				19.2 Are multiethnic literature and art used to promote self-examination and self-understanding?
				19.3 Do students read and hear the poetry, short stories, novels, folklore, plays, essays, and autobiographies of a variety of ethnic and cultural groups?
				19.4 Do students examine the music, art, architecture, and dance of a variety of ethnic and cultural groups?
				19.5 Do students have available the artistic, musical, and literary expression of the local ethnic and cultural communities?
				19.6 Are opportunities provided for students to develop their own artistic, literary, and musical expression?
				20.0 Does the curriculum provide opportunities for students to develop full literacy in at least two languages?
				20.1 Are students taught to communicate (speaking, reading, and writing) in a second language?
				20.2 Are students taught about the culture of the people who use the second language?
				20.3 Are second-language speakers provided opportunities to develop full literacy in their native language?
				20.4 Are students for whom English is a second language taught in their native languages as needed?
				21.0 Does the curriculum make maximum use of local community resources?
				21.1 Are students involved in the continuous study of the local community?
				21.2 Are members of the local ethnic and cultural communities continually used as classroom resources?
				21.3 Are field trips to the various local ethnic and cultural communities provided for students?
				22.0 Do the assessment procedures used with students reflect their ethnic and community cultures?
				22.1 Do teachers use a variety of assessment procedures that reflect the ethnic and cultural diversity of students?
				22.2 Do teachers' day-to-day assessment techniques take into account the ethnic and cultural diversity of their students?
				23.0 Does the school conduct ongoing, systematic evaluations of the goals, methods, and instructional materials used in teaching about ethnicity and culture?
				23.1 Do assessment procedures draw on many sources of evidence from many sorts of people?

Rating Strongly ←——→ Hardly at all				Guidelines
				23.2 Does the evaluation program examine school policies and procedures? 23.3 Does the evaluation program examine the everyday climate of the school? 23.4 Does the evaluation program examine the effectiveness of curricular programs, both academic and nonacademic? 23.5 Are the results of evaluation used to improve the school program?

Index